The Book of Bread

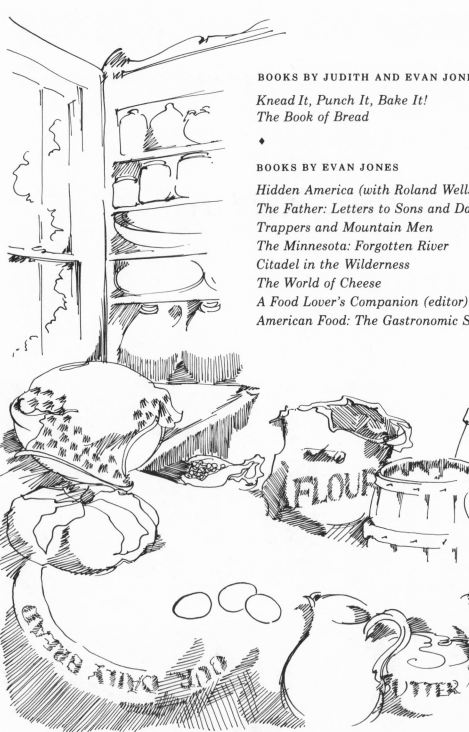

BOOKS BY JUDITH AND EVAN JONES

Knead It, Punch It, Bake It!
The Book of Bread

◆

BOOKS BY EVAN JONES

Hidden America (with Roland Wells Robbins)
The Father: Letters to Sons and Daughters
Trappers and Mountain Men
The Minnesota: Forgotten River
Citadel in the Wilderness
The World of Cheese
A Food Lover's Companion (editor)
American Food: The Gastronomic Story

The Book of Bread

JUDITH & EVAN JONES

Drawings by Lauren Jarrett

HARPER & ROW, PUBLISHERS ◆ NEW YORK
CAMBRIDGE, PHILADELPHIA, SAN FRANCISCO, LONDON
MEXICO CITY, SÃO PAULO, SYDNEY

A portion of this work originally appeared in *Family Circle*.

The recipes for Scandinavian rye bread, *hapanleipa,* and *vorterkaker* by Beatrice O. Ojakangas, which originally appeared in *Gourmet* magazine in February 1976, are reprinted by permission of *Gourmet*.

Several of the embellished bread recipes first appeared in *Gourmet* in October 1979.

The recipes for cream of wheat *idlis* and hoppers originally appeared in *Madhur Jaffrey's World-of-the-East Vegetarian Cooking,* copyright © 1981 by Madhur Jaffrey. Reprinted by permission of Alfred A. Knopf, Inc.

The recipe for Chinese steamed meat buns first appeared in *The Key to Chinese Cooking* by Irene Kuo, copyright © 1977 by Irene Kuo. Reprinted by permission of Alfred A. Knopf, Inc.

The recipe for cheese bread from *The World of Cheese,* copyright © 1976 by Evan Jones and Judith Jones, is reprinted by permission of Alfred A. Knopf, Inc.

Designer: Helene Berinsky

Library of Congress Cataloging in Publication Data

Jones, Judith.
  The book of bread.

  Includes index.
  1. Bread. I. Jones, Evan.   II. Title.
TX769.J647 1982   641.8′15   82–47527
ISBN 0-06-181434-2   AACR2

82 83 84 85 86 10 9 8 7 6 5 4 3 2

For
James A. Beard,
an inspiration

Contents

Preface 9

1. The Beginnings 12
2. How to Make Bread 20
3. Basic White Breads 52
4. Whole Wheat and Grain Breads 74
5. Rye Breads 108
6. Embellished Yeast Breads 122
7. Yeast Rolls 152
8. Sweet Breakfast and Tea Breads, Rolls, and Buns 176
9. Baking Powder and Soda Breads 208
10. Muffins, Corn Sticks, Popovers, and Biscuits 226
11. Fried Breads 248
12. Steamed and Poached Breads 264
13. Skillet and Stone-Baked Breads 276
14. Flat Breads 298
15. Shaped Breads 312
16. Bread as Casings 328
17. Sabbath and Holiday Breads 342

Helpful Equipment 363
Mail Order Sources 367
Index 369

Preface

♦ Why another bread book? There have been books exclusively devoted to the subject since *The Nature of Bread,* by James Manning, was published in London in 1757. Since Mary Randolph's *The Virginia Housewife* appeared in 1824 Americans have been able to consult their kitchen libraries for specific New World methods of forming and baking loaves of various grains. ("Do not constantly make bread in the same shapes," housewives were admonished in another book before the Civil War; "each morning try to have some variation. . . . loaves, twists, turnovers, light biscuits make pleasant and appetizing variety.")

If another bread book is in order, then, it is because anything as versatile and creative and satisfying as making bread is open to endless interpretation. Each person finds a singular way of pursuing the goal. The fact that most of us eat bread every day at almost every meal in one form or other is reason enough to want to vary any bread repertoire.

Once you start to meet this challenge—to bake for yourself—chances are you'll be hooked, and never again want to buy another commercial loaf. And why should you, when making bread at home is so satisfying—replete with the guarantees of absolute freshness, of no preservatives, of the best of ingredients, as well as so much more variety than can ever be found at the supermarket or even the bakery.

All of us like diversity in our daily menus. Why not on the bread plate? Have buttery avocado rolls with a peppery Mexican chicken dish for dinner. Serve hearty rye twists to guests with a luncheon soup. Or at breakfast greet the day with warm slices of bread made with prunes steeped in spiced tea and accented by black walnuts. Have quince bread to celebrate the orchard you wish you had, tofu-spinach muffins for the vegetarians coming for the weekend—the possibilities are myriad. There are constantly new ingredients that cry out to be tried in the breads you make for yourself—Jerusalem artichoke flour, sunflower seed meal, the new grain called triticale, all the soy products from flour to bean curd and sprouts (sprouted grains with neither leaven nor liquid make for moist texture and invigorating flavor when slowly baked in a free-form, remarkably sliceable loaf sometimes called Essene bread). The garden harvest that must be eaten quickly is the source for zucchini bread and inspires—it did us anyway—the creation of bread based on a carrot-beet purée, or the combination of green tomatoes and maple syrup, or rhubarb and oatmeal muffins, or onion-studded crescents.

Tempting in another direction is the lore of bread. There are seemingly inexhaustible versions of the origin of hot cross buns, the making of black bread before the discovery of either coffee or chocolate. Some time ago, gathering material for the gastronomic story of American food, we tripped on intriguing accounts of ryaninjun bread, of black cooks who baked the first sweet-potato breads, of tacos made by Hopi tribeswomen, the saga of the Reverend Sylvester Graham, who warred with commercial bakeries and gave his name to a whole wheat flour that helped to make American bread better and produced the graham cracker as a by-product.

We've been baking bread since one of our daughters, much interested in sculpture in her teen-age years, made a discovery. Her hands worked as carefully and with as much unconscious affinity when they kneaded as they did when she was forming clay. Soon each of us had reasons for finding fun in turning out homemade bread. Like a lot of men and women in this country recently, we found breadmaking a way to unwind from the day's work. Kneading helps to work out some of the outside frustrations, and baking helps one to express creative urges. When that sculpting daughter grew up, her children joined our unofficial bakers' guild. When the grandchildren's hands were too small to knead effectively, they tossed the balls of dough from one to another and accomplished much the same thing. In a Vermont hill country farmhouse we've even taught our eighty-six-year-old mother to make her own loaves—it's never too late to learn to produce your own bread.

A magazine editor heard about these goings-on and sent a photographer to the farmhouse. There a still life of breads was arranged on a time-smoothed trencher table and a picture was taken that aroused the interest—when it was published with a piece we wrote—of another editor who asked us to do a book on bread for children.

Somehow the pleasures of a lifetime couldn't be contained in that small volume, so we've been tempted again to share our experience, our travels of exploration and talks with other bakers, our ways of making bread, and our fascination with its history, in a book that goes beyond the culinary world of twelve-year-olds.

We start with the history. Some glimpses may be familiar, but the story of bread is such an integral part of making it (indeed so much a part of everyone's ethnic memories) that this book wouldn't seem complete without a look at the beginnings.

The Book of Bread

1 · The Beginnings

"Bread," says the adage, "is older than man." In fact, there is evidence that primitive bread was baked on hot stones in open fires early in the Neolithic Age. From the first circular cakes that were thin, flat, and brittle, to the great variety of shapes known today, bread in simple terms is a mixture of grains and liquid that has been cooked—by heat that comes from fire or even from the sun.

We are most apt today to think of bread as airy loaves that have achieved their light, crusty texture through the use of yeast or another leavening agent like baking powder. But bread that is soft yet resilient enough to be cut in slices is a comparatively recent development in western Europe and America. In other regions the basic breads may be flat and tough like India's chapatis, or made of corn flour like tortillas. Some bread in Scandinavia may be baked with rye flour into large, round, very chewy cakes that have a hole in the center and are no thicker than a man's thumb. Scottish bakers produce flat bread the size of a dinner plate by using oat flour, and the Welsh still serve *haidd,* a shallow chewy round made of barley flour.

Barley, indeed, may be the most ancient of cultivated grains, and was the chief bread plant in the ancient world, as well as for hundreds of years in Europe. Certainly it was one of the earliest grains to be harvested by man and to be stewed in boiling water to make a crude porridge; it may be a safe assumption that from this earliest of recipes there evolved another, resulting in the transformation of grains crushed by stones into portable cakes, after the mixture was baked. Stone Age cooks discovered the nutritional value of bread perhaps without real recognition of the fact. And long before the phrase was coined they knew it to be "the staff of life." Experience proved that no other food was so convenient a source of energy.

Paleontologists working in the Nile Valley have unearthed mortars and pestles used for grinding grain and other evidence suggesting the production of primitive bread as early as seventeen thousand years ago. The wild grain these Stone Age people harvested seems to have been barley and a basic form of wheat. At least nine thousand years ago, in the fertile valleys of Mesopotamia,

Sumerian farmers began harvesting wheat they themselves had planted, and because they had learned to make beer it is clear they had some idea of the fermentation caused by the wild yeasts that developed naturally when they mixed crudely fragmented grains with liquid. The dough they made soured slightly and was baked into heavy, coarse-textured loaves. Such partially leavened breads—some with the consistency of sponges, like Iran's *sang-gak*, and some as thin as muslin, like the Bedouin *shrak*—are still reproduced daily in the Middle East. These forms evolved naturally, governed somewhat by the contours of stones on which they were baked by the Sumerians.

Later, the Nile Valley Egyptians invented the oven, and the process of leavening (deliberately leaving dough to ferment) was perfected.* Records show that Egyptian home cooks and commercial bakers produced thirty kinds of bread. And bread became so important a symbol of life that it was invariably prepared to accompany deceased persons on their journey after death. (In a royal tomb opened by archaeologists in 1936 there were found several loaves that were thirty-five centuries old.) At the height of the Roman Empire bread was so basic to every diet that the word was used as a synonym for all food; Roman bakers were trained by the government, and at least sixty-two kinds of bread were regularly produced.

Like people, breads have national characteristics, evident in the form they take and the grains on which they are based. Before the invention of baskets, clay pots, and metal pans, all of which were used as molds, most bakers made round loaves because it was natural to form dough into a ball. Before there were ovens, it was equally natural to flatten balls of dough as much as possible, for the thinner the shape the easier it was to cook the bread through on heated stones.

Round loaves have been common in every period of history, no matter what improvements have been made in ovens. The Sardinian housewife still makes crackling rounds so thin they are called *fogli di musica* (sheets of music). Another round Italian bread is known as *focaccia*, a name derived from *focus*, the Latin word for the hearth on which it was originally cooked. Indeed, throughout southern Italy, the country bread on the family table is much like the loaves excavated at Pompeii that were baked on August 24, A.D. 79, the day Mount Vesuvius erupted. These were mounds of dough made from wheat and barley flour and were scored across the surface so they divided easily into wedge-shaped pieces. Today in France there are at least twenty-eight loaves of varying shapes—some whimsical and some as *serieuse* as the long thin bread that almost literally represents "the staff of life." The crisp rod-shaped baguette is about two feet long and is stretched out in this fashion so it may be

---

* It may be noted that at the Oxford Symposium on National and Regional Styles of Cookery, in 1981, Naria Johnson discussed on-going archaeological digs in the Balkans at which several clay models of bread ovens have been discovered; the assertion was made that these finds constitute "the oldest bread oven models that we have evidence of anywhere in the world."

cut at an angle into many slices, each of which will have maximum crust and ample interior. Across the English Channel, the old-fashioned round loaves called Coburgs are slashed around the crown just before going into the oven. And most characteristic and distinctive of all English breads is the topknotted cottage loaf: two round shapes of dough baked one on top of the other, the top always being smaller. "The cottage loaf was possibly improvised," according to Elizabeth David, "to economize baking space in a small oven."

Regardless of shape, the most popular breads (which does not mean the best) everywhere are white and are made from specially produced wheat flour. This appetite for white bread was not established in the beginning, but evolved over centuries as machinery for grinding grain improved. When the seeds of plants were ground by hand between two stones it was difficult to keep foreign particles out of the meal that resulted. The same difficulty remained even after the invention of windmills and gristmills powered by water. Flour was still contaminated by various kinds of dirt, and similar adulteration of bread dough occurred in kitchens and bakeries. The color of whole grain flour was naturally dark enough to obscure the presence of much foreign matter. Thus, when white flour was available from millers who made a point of sanitation, it was reserved for the rich and powerful, and white bread for religious use was given priority.

If a loaf of bread seemed to be plain white, it was believed to be natural and free of dirt from the millwheel or from the floor. Dark breads, especially those produced from barley and rye flours, were suspected of being impure and were therefore unacceptable to those who had a choice; but dark breads were good enough for peasant farmers or the urban poor. "To know the color of one's bread" was a Roman phrase that meant knowing one's place in the social caste system—the lowlier the class the darker the bread. Ironically, perhaps, this didn't necessarily mean purity for the privileged. Affluent Romans so admired whiteness in bread that they unwittingly accepted loaves which had been adulterated with chalk to enhance the appearance.

Basically, breadmaking has changed little since the ancient Egyptians found that fermentation, or the leavening process, would make a lighter, more open-textured loaf. The grain is ground; the dough is mixed with liquid and a leavening agent like yeast or baking powder (causing fermentation that brings air into the mass) and is allowed to rise, increasing its bulk. Then, more often than not, it is baked. But whether a loaf contains flour made from barley, oats, rye, or wheat, it may also be cooked by poaching (dumplings, for example), by frying in deep fat, or by steaming as in Boston brown bread or the Chinese steamed buns called *man-t'ou.*

During the early days of imperial Rome the citizens who did know the color of their bread required an estimated fourteen million bushels of grain a year which bakers turned into loaves of many kinds—honey-and-oil bread, suet bread, cheese bread, square loaves called dice seasoned with cheese and anise,

mushroom shapes sprinkled with poppy seeds, wafer bread, and rolls baked on
a spit by mess sergeants for soldiers' rations. Rome had proprietary rights on
all wheat produced in Egypt and North Africa, and was never short of barley,
apparently.

Today barley is widely grown in Europe, America, and Australia, and rye has
always thrived in eastern and central Europe because it grows in soil poorer
than that required for other cereals. Thus rye bread is popular in the Soviet
Union, Poland, Germany, and throughout Scandinavia. It is unsifted rye dough,
allowed to rise for twenty-four hours, then to bake very slowly for another
twenty-four hours, that produces the traditional coarse, almost black pumpernickel bread that originated in Westphalia. In Russian Ukraine one of the most
popular rye loaves is called *chernyi klib,* the black bread of poor farmers that is
now considered chic by many Americans. (Not to mention the fact it tastes so
good.) A traditional Scandinavian loaf is made by seasoning rye dough with
fennel and anise and grated orange rind to produce *limpa* bread. Many countries now use corn meal, but the epitome of corn breads is that simple loaf
called johnnycake, still produced in much the way it was made by American
Indian cooks from the grain that was native to North America.

Just as the American Indian believed that corn was the gift of the Great
Spirit, mankind through time has given homage to bread. Many early cultures
assumed the origin of wheat to be supernatural. The Chinese also were convinced that wheat and rice were direct gifts from heaven. In Britain early Saxon
yeomen baked loaves of bread from the first harvest and offered them to God.
Swedes used to mold dough in the shape of a female figure in gratitude for the
earth's fertility, and Norwegians made gingerbread men at the grain harvest
festival. In France Norman soldiers demanded white bread to give them cour-
age. Elsewhere farmers believed wheat should not be cut in the light of the
moon or the bread would be dark.

In much of the world bread has been used as a synonym for life, and is held
to be sacred by many families. The peoples of some Middle Eastern countries,
Claudia Roden has written, consider bread a direct gift from God—"a hungry
man will kiss a piece of bread given him as alms. An invocation to God is
murmured before kneading the dough, another before placing it in the oven. A
piece of bread found lying on the floor is immediately picked up and respectful-
ly placed on the table." Children in Europe learn an almost identical ritual.
According to George Lang's *The Cuisine of Hungary,* bread is more revered
than any food. "As a child," Lang wrote, "if I dropped a slice of bread, I had to
kiss it before eating it." Bread has had symbolic Christian meaning since Jesus
said to his disciples, "I am the bread of life." At the Last Supper, he took bread
and broke it, saying: "This is my body which is given for you: do this in remem-
brance of me," and Christians ever since have celebrated his words in the Eu-
charist.

The Jews eat matzoh, or bread without yeast, to mark the eviction by the pharaohs. "They baked matzoh of the unleavened dough which they had brought out of Egypt, for it had not leavened because they were thrust out of Egypt and could not linger, nor had they prepared any food for the journey" (Exodus 12:39). Leaven thus became for them the symbol of evil and selfishness*—fermentation being seen as a corruption of the dough, which could not be offered to an incorruptible God—and matzoh is a reminder of freedom.

With or without leavening, bread symbolizes various things in various cultures. Since the seventeenth century, and even earlier, the word "bread" has been used as a reference to money; for more than a century family providers have been known as "breadwinners." The intrinsic value of bread in the survival of mankind makes it easy to understand the use of "bread" in the jargon of jazz musicians as a synonym for ready cash. Small wonder parents need no explanation today when a young person, having spent the allowance, announces, "I need bread."

The word may have added layers of richness as a part of the language, yet bread as one of our most fundamental foods has been through some hard times. It might be said that the most productive period in the history of American government was during the Civil War, when the Capitol was turned into a bakery—ovens were set up in the Senate wing, and sixteen thousand loaves of bread were baked there daily for Union soldiers. Washington, D.C., however, exercised no influence over the usual commercial baking, although there had been protests from consumers for years. Bakers in England who were caught adulterating flour might be pilloried "with the offending loaf tied around their necks," but in the nineteenth century, during a so-called Bakers' Riot in Boston, the local government refused to protect demonstrators who accused the city's bread factories of whitening their dough with lime.

In the twentieth century, U.S. mills have increased the whiteness of flour not by adding but by extracting 28 to 30 percent of the wheat kernel's bulk, including the wheat germ and bran. This, too, roused protests and brought about a 1941 law that requires the addition of thiamine, niacin, riboflavin, and iron, to make up for the deficiency. But crusaders for "natural foods" have underscored the fact that "enriched bread" has only a fraction of the nutrients removed from whole grain flour. One result has been a surprising increase in the baking of bread at home. In a parochial poll in the 1970s, 30 percent declared the bread their families ate was created in their own kitchens.

No other sensory experience is quite like working flour into dough, shaping the live, risen sponge into loaves, filling the kitchen with tantalizing, yeasty

---

*St. Paul, who had been raised in the Judaic tradition, wrote in his letter to the Corinthians: "Let us keep the feast not with the old leaven, neither with the leaven of malice and wickedness, but with the unleavened bread of sincerity and truth."

aroma, then—at last—slicing through the crust of newly baked bread. The whiff of a hot loaf fresh from the oven used to be part of the birthright of almost every child in the American hinterland. Now, with active dry yeast easily available and whole grain flour (stone ground in the traditional way) packed in five-pound bags on supermarket shelves across the country, fragrant home-made bread is again a triumphant accomplishment for cooks of all ages—and a reward that every home baker's family and friends will devour with delight.

2 · How to
Make Bread

I n making bread regularly in the confines of a city apartment we prove to ourselves once more that kneading resilient dough is a soothing experience. In the gentle labor of breadmaking we've found means to express creative urges—seldom do we make the same kind of bread twice in a row.

It relates us to times past, when many an American housewife making her own loaves believed baking to be the most rewarding of all she did to feed her family. It was as much a part of the rhythm of her life as washing her face. She used no directions that were written down and rarely measured except by eye. Bread baking was never boring because there was, particularly in those gone days, something unpredictable about it. Even today, with easy, reliable leaveners to depend upon, there is still something mysterious, almost suspenseful about creating a loaf of bread, no matter how many times you have done it.

Yeast as a Leavener

Beautifully risen loaves not only are by far the most fun to make but in a way that is difficult to explain they give one the most satisfaction. Perhaps the secret is in the yeast—one never ceases to wonder at how this uninteresting, dead-looking granulated substance can bring life to a mixture of flour and water. Yeast's capacity to create alcohol in the making of dough is, of course, the same kind of fermentation that takes place in producing wine, beer, and other liquors. In fact, the definition of the term "yeast" derives from the Old English word meaning "to seethe, to froth"—then as now bakers depended on brewers for their yeast.

As scientists define yeast, it is a culture of microscopic fungi or mushroom-like plants far too small to be seen by the human eye. These tiny plant bodies feed primarily on natural sugars—carbohydrates—and they give off carbon dioxide and alcohol; in turn, these help to make the lightness and the satisfying taste of bread as they feed, grow, reproduce, and expire in the expanding dough. The enzymes contained in flour cause its starch content to be transformed into carbohydrates, thus providing sustenance to keep yeast cells alive.

Yeast lives in this way all around us. It lives in the air, on leaves of trees, in the bark, in the skin of fruit, and in the soil—wherever carbohydrates are found. It is carried by insects and birds. These facts, however, remained unknown until Dr. Louis Pasteur, discoverer of the process which bears his name, found the source of fermentation in winemaking. He established that powdery growth on the skin of grapes, not the juice within, makes wine ferment. Pasteur's experiments also proved that yeast is a minuscule living plant and that only its living cells can cause fermentation.

More than four thousand years ago, without arriving at scientific understanding, those ancient Egyptian bakers had found that a mixture of wheat and water began to ferment when left in a warm place. The bread it made was lighter than the usual hard cakes—it was honeycombed with tiny air pockets and it had more flavor. It must have been easy enough to recognize then that small quantities of leftover dough could be saved and used as "starters" for new batches of bread because they contained the mysterious quality later identified as active yeast. Just as simple was the use of "barm," the foam that forms on the top of beer or ale when it is fermenting, which was stirred into flour to serve as the leavening agent. In later centuries, when barm was not available, women in farm kitchens, with no brewers as neighbors, commonly produced homemade yeast by boiling potatoes with the leaves of hops (a standard ingredient in beermaking). The liquid that resulted could be mixed with flour to help the fermentation process.

It's not hard to produce this simple leavener, but neither are there guarantees of success. Still, if you would like to try a century-old way to make your own homemade yeast, here's a formula to try, granting you find about a cup of hop leaves. Gently stew the hops in an equal amount of water for about an hour and a half, then strain the liquid and let it cool. Add to it four tablespoons of flour and one tablespoon of unrefined brown sugar, mix it well, and pour into three pint bottles. Cork them, and tie down the corks with string. The next two or three days shake the bottles three times every day. When the fermentation is done, the bottles will open with a loud pop and some foaming.

Not until the nineteenth century did breweries develop packaging for the yeast they produced as a by-product. Now American yeast, sold in firm blocks like butter, in hermetically sealed containers or dated airtight foil envelopes, is manufactured in mammoth quantities, and the formula has greatly improved in recent years; active dry yeast with its consistency of fine granules is easy to dissolve, permitting the use of higher temperatures in the mixing liquid. If you do a lot of baking, you will find it more convenient and economical to buy your yeast in larger quantity than the half-ounce envelopes. Health food stores and mail order places specializing in baking supplies sell yeast in larger packages and often in bulk; sometimes supermarkets have four-ounce jars. When you store a sizable amount of yeast in the refrigerator, you'll find it will keep a long time.

The yeast available in compressed form, shaped as a small moist cake, must be kept at low temperature to preserve it; it may also be frozen. Some cooks who are bound by tradition believe fervently that these yeast cakes make better bread; they do have a nostalgic old-fashioned fragrance and they seem wonderfully creamy in texture. But again and again we have tried producing the same loaf, first with dry yeast and then with cake yeast, and when both loaves were sampled no difference in taste or texture could be detected. So in our recipes we call for dry yeast simply because it is easier to buy and to keep. If you want to substitute, use an equal amount of fresh yeast—that is, ½ ounce—to 1 tablespoon of dry yeast.

(Confusing though it seems, in addition to active yeast packaged in cake form and in granules, there is a bottled powder called brewer's yeast that has no leavening properties; when this is mixed into bread dough the purpose is solely to provide added nutrition.)

If you have any doubt about the freshness of active yeast, it may be tested, or proofed, to be sure it's still alive. Stir it into three or four times as much warm water, add a little sugar, and set it aside until the mixture swells slightly—it should take less than five minutes; if it shows no sign of swelling in that time, the yeast is past its prime, so throw it out. Manufacturers say that because their products are so thoroughly pasteurized today's yeast no longer bubbles as it once did. Only when flour is added to the yeast and the mixture allowed to rest do bubbles appear.

In England "aerated" white bread became famous more than a century ago when Dr. John Dauglish set out to deal with the belief of some consumers who saw fermentation as decay and wanted no part of bread made with yeast. Dauglish devised a method for putting bread dough in tight vessels and pumping carbonated water into it before baking. His bread was full of air, no doubt, and it developed a following that still lingers on, but "A.B.C. bread," as it is called, is devoid of the taste that a good loaf has naturally.

Sourdough Starter

People who love sourdough bread swear by its pungent, earthy taste. The aroma stirs various feelings: sometimes the picture of California miners called forty-niners who made the Gold Rush of the mid-nineteenth century famous, sometimes of Alaska pioneers who turned Klondike mining camps into make-or-break festivals and often slept with their pots of sourdough starter, as the surest way of keeping it warm and lively enough to help turn out a batch of biscuits or flapjacks. The way this worked for one westerner was to add milk in the morning to the sourdough pot, then, to stiffen it, he said: "You add flour, and thoroughly work it till you get a good thick batter. Then you set it behind the stove where it will keep warm for five or six hours . . . let it raise and sour. When you are ready to make your biscuits, you add salt and soda and some fresh flour, pinch off your big fat biscuits, roll them in melted lard, and let them set fifteen or twenty minutes to make their chemical change, then put them in the hot oven to bake. There's no biscuit worth bothering about when you've been used to sour dough."

But the same kind of sourdough starter has been around virtually as long as bread itself, of course. Far from being left to frontier bachelors, sourdough was carried in most of the covered wagons taking families west. Pioneer women became so expert at keeping starters at the peak of liveliness that they had bread ready to eat soon after the wagon trains stopped each night for meals.

Salt-Rising Bread

Salt-rising bread is leavened by the fermentation of milk and flour, and though it causes a foul odor in the process, it is the nostril-twitching smell that ensures the sweetness of the loaves. It begins with a starter to be made with corn meal, water, and salt. Salt-rising bread requires warmth while fermenting, as well as a longer baking time. We've tried making it often and found it delicious (see page 69 for details).

Baking Soda and Baking Powder as Leaveners

In passing Great Salt Lake in Utah, pioneers who took that route discovered large natural deposits of saleratus, the mineral now better known as baking soda. The covered wagon women gathered it up in its pure state and wrote home that "it makes splendid bread." But soda by itself does need something sour to unleash its rising power, so no doubt these women used sour milk or cream in their dough to have made the discovery of its rising power.

However, baking powder, which was discovered just before the Civil War and marketed as a substitute for yeast, is a more sophisticated agent containing its own souring potential so that we don't have to add one in the dough or batter. For half a century before, any cook trying to bake without yeast had been dependent on the use of pearlash or potassium carbonate that was produced by burning wood (and incidentally led to wholesale destruction of much American forest land). In turn, pearlash produced carbon dioxide in baking bread, causing it to rise slightly; the effect was comparable to that induced by saleratus. The first improvement in the ingredients available for making nonyeast breads was a baking powder first manufactured in the 1850s by Preston & Merrill of Boston. It was a combination of bicarbonate of soda and tartaric acid in one of several forms, but the compound—commercial variations were numerous—was too suspect because of questionable purity to persuade cookbook authors to recommend anything other than plain soda and cream of tartar in stipulated portions. Finally, toward the end of the nineteenth century, manufacturers began to guarantee unadulterated baking powders that would create a spongy texture during baking and result in good bread and cake. Today manufacturers' formulas may call for three parts soda to two parts cream of tartar (potassium bitartrate), with another three composed of cornstarch, rice flour, potato flour, or arrowroot to prevent precipitous chemical action and to keep the compound dry. The so-called self-rising flours called for in cake recipes and frequently for bread are packaged formulas containing baking powder.

Recipes for breads generally known as quick breads, because they don't have to be kneaded and require no time for rising, use baking powder as the sole leaven—or sometimes baking powder in combination with baking soda, or sometimes even baking soda alone, when there is a sour agent in the recipe. Today we are apt to use buttermilk or yogurt in recipes that call for soda, or sometimes milk that has been soured with a little lemon juice; sometimes an acid fruit will do the job, or even molasses.

Baking soda is the component that gives character to the internationally re-nowned Irish soda bread, a very good loaf when it is baked by an experienced cook with Gaelic blood coursing her veins. One such, the Irish writer Maura Laverty, has slight misgivings, however. "Unpatriotic though it may seem," she wrote in *Feasting Galore*, "pride of place must be given to yeast bread—for the very good reason that yeast bread is better for us. When we add bicarbonate of soda to foods, we reduce their content of Vitamin B_1—the all-important vita-min necessary for muscular energy, steady nerves, healthy skin, good appetite, sound digestion. (Because it is especially important to expectant mothers it is known as 'the women's vitamin.')"

Flours for Bread—Milling

Flour for bread produced in any number of ways has been refined from virtual-ly every grain known to man. But the flour that instantly comes to mind when the word is said is the white powdery stuff made from wheat. Mankind has eaten loaves composed of wheat flour as long as there has been real bread.

Wheat, barley, rye, corn, and rice are the chief grains to be finely ground and reduced to flour or meal, and wheat remains most important because the bread it makes is lighter.

More than 90 percent of the flour available today is milled in huge factories, instead of in the small gristmills of which there once were perhaps as many as fifty thousand scattered across the land. Romans invented the watermill before the Christian era, and the windmill first appeared in A.D. 634 in a part of Persia where the wind blows three-quarters of the year. Among the earliest watermills in this country, the Old Wye Mill on Maryland's Eastern Shore still grinds grain just as it has since the middle of the seventeenth century. Flumes guide water from the mill pond as it pours over the giant bucketed wheel that turns circular stones. Grooves and furrows engraved in the grinding stone crush the grain to a fineness that depends upon the miller's setting, and it is this ancient process that produces flour or corn meal of quality more natural than that manufactured by modern technology. Some people think the heat generated by steel rollers destroys the nutrients in the grains.

Fortunately, there is an increasing awareness of the need to preserve and restore the imposing water wheels around which many American towns grew up, as well as other mills dependent upon wind for power. You can visit grist-mills that have gone back to producing stone-ground flour in the Midwest and in the old colonial states, particularly. The trip from Manhattan to the mill at

Philipsburg Manor, near Tarrytown, is an easy one, and we've watched the wheels turn at several sites in New England, as well as in Europe. At the Welsh Folk Museum outside Cardiff a small flour mill has been re-erected, and at Cwm Cou near Newcastle Emlyn in Dyfed, a mill almost four hundred years old is again supplying stone-ground whole wheat. On the Danish island of Bornholm we stopped at a windmill whose giant slatted wooden sails whipped the air about our ankles as we got out of the car. Climbing the ladderlike stairway four flights up, we watched sacks of grain being emptied down the chute and felt the power of the wind moving gigantic wooden gears, the joints and teeth wheezing and groaning as the kernels of wheat were pulverized by the horizontal grindstones. When we left, we were covered with a fine farinose coating.

Grinding flour in our own kitchen through the use of a small machine called Magic Mill II seems at first a little like grinding coffee beans; as with coffee, you can start with your own selection of grains. (We have made flour of oats, barley, corn, rice, chickpeas, soybeans, sunflower and other seeds, chestnuts, and dried blue corn from the Southwest.) The difference is that Magic Mill's process is an improvement on grinding, using its patented process of "Micronizing" or exploding each grain into minute particles. But whether you use this new method or the grinding attachment of a Kitchen Aid mixer, your own flour will make homemade bread even more rewarding to produce. One of our daughters swears by a Retsel home grinder that operates with two stone wheels on the same principle as old-fashioned water-powered gristmills. The stones are adjustable to refine any grain to any desired degree. Other kitchen mills include traditional grinders to be bolted to a sturdy surface and operated by hand; some of these have stones of a petrified carbon material to refine any dry grain, as well as easily interchangeable metal plates for such jobs as cracking wheat. More expensive are large electric mills which can grind as much as fifty pounds of flour per hour. Most may be ordered by mail from one of the sources listed on page 367.

Whatever the milling method—at home or on the banks of an old millstream—the wheat flour that makes white bread white may be sifted to remove the bran and germ, which provide color and texture in all whole grain flours. The term "bolting" on many wheat flour sacks means winnowing ground grains through cloth. At home the same result is obtained by using a fine sieve, but factory flours may look whiter because the yellow carotenoids are removed in the process of bleaching.

Common Types of Flours and Meals

There are different varieties of wheat, grown for different reasons. Therefore there are several kinds of wheat flour commercially available, each of which makes a difference in baking results:

ALL-PURPOSE FLOUR. A blend of hard and soft wheat (soft has less gluten) bleached flours to which nutrients have been added. The most readily available, and perfectly satisfactory for use in any of our recipes that call for white flour.

UNBLEACHED FLOUR. A blend of hard and soft flours that have not been exposed to any whitening process; more natural than all-purpose flour. We tend to favor unbleached for bread when we don't have plain hard wheat flour; however, you may find very little difference in the final loaf whether you use unbleached or all-purpose.

BREAD FLOUR. Hard wheat flour, referred to as bread flour in old recipe books, previously purchasable at small bakeries willing to accommodate consumers. A new mixture of flours labeled "bread flour" now appears on supermarket shelves. It has been described as "a combination of higher-gluten-and-protein content wheat flour and barley malt flour, to which has been added a dough conditioner known as potassium bromate." This new product tends to make a very airy loaf, tasting too much like the average factory bread. It rises too fast, something not desirable, because it is the quality of slow rising that develops flavor and good texture. We don't particularly recommend the commercial bread flour available to home bakers as of 1982.

HARD WHEAT FLOUR. Whole wheat or white flour, usually made from spring wheat; it is best for bread because it has a larger amount of gluten. ("Gluten is to wheat what lean is to meat," someone once said.) It is the flour most commercial bakers use and is not generally sold in supermarkets; look for it in health food stores or order by mail (see page 367). If you obtain it, use it in any recipe in this book in place of white flour, or whole wheat, as the case may be.

WHOLE WHEAT FLOUR. The term used after the wheat kernel has been ground; some whole wheat flour has the husk (bran) sifted out entirely, part of the husk is left in others, and most are ground to medium-fine texture.

GRAHAM FLOUR. As defined by Sylvester Graham, whose name it bears and who crusaded against commercial white bread in the nineteenth century, graham flour is produced by grinding the entire wheat berry or kernel; the term, however, is used loosely for whole wheat flours, sometimes more coarsely ground.

STONE-GROUND FLOUR. Grains pulverized between stone grinding wheels, or buhrstones, often turned by water wheels; when so identified, stone-ground (occasionally called water-ground) flour is considered more "natural" than flour refined by steel rollers in large factories.

RYE FLOUR. Milled in various grades, from pale, delicate color and flavor to whole grain rye that contains the entire kernel. Our recipes do not specify dark or light because it is usually difficult to purchase rye flour graded this way and in the final analysis, any rye flour can be used in a rye bread recipe; a dark rye will have a more pronounced flavor and deeper color.

RYE MEAL. Usual term for coarsely ground rye kernels.

PUMPERNICKEL FLOUR. Term used loosely for rye flours; properly denotes dark unsifted whole grain rye flour including husk.

SEMOLINA. The granular product that results from milling hard or durum wheat. When the bran or outer skins are removed from the wheat berry, and before it is ground into flour, the largest particles of the endosperm may be detached and are known as semolina; when pulverized, semolina is known as the finest wheat flour. It is essential to the production of good pasta, but is not often used in breadmaking in Europe and America.

WHEATBERRY. A kernel of wheat, commonly called grain, is the berry or dehydrated fruit of the plant, consisting of the endosperm, the starchy base of white flour, the germ or live part that contains enzymes, fat, and much vitamin E, and the outside shell known as bran.

TRITICALE. Combining the Latin terms *triticum* (wheat) and *secale* (rye), triticale is a new hybrid grain that makes deliberate what often happened accidentally in nature. From the beginning, farmers have known that fields of untended wheat soon became fields of wheat and rye that resulted in spontaneous crosses though no hybrid seeds were produced. When the wheat-rye harvests

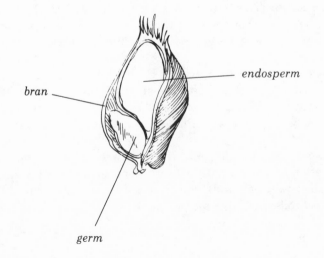

bran —

endosperm

germ

were milled into flour, bakers came to recognize it as superior pastry flour, with a higher protein content than either rye or wheat. After recent years of careful plant breeding, a marketable self-reproducing cross-bred grain labeled triticale by scientists was perfected, and it is being grown as an aid to feeding starving regions of the world. For bread, triticale requires gentler kneading to encourage development of gluten, and some cooks assert one rising is preferable. The flour is perishable and should be refrigerated or frozen. It is generally available at health food stores or by mail from a few mills.

GLUTEN FLOUR. Made from white flour from which almost all the starch has been washed away, gluten flour is used primarily for dietetic purposes. We sometimes add gluten flour in relatively small quantities (it is expensive) to very heavy doughs—that is, breads made up primarily of flours and grains that contain little or no gluten.

SOY FLOUR. Sometimes this term is strictly applied to flour made of raw soybeans, while *soya flour* sometimes is applied when soybeans have been toasted before grinding. (To give added flavor, our recipe suggests toasting soy flour at home.) When soya flour is used in bread baking the usual result is a dark crust; lower temperatures are therefore recommended. Flour from soybeans helps prevent all baked goods from becoming stale, and it is high in protein, increasing nutritive value.

Other Flours and Meals

Medium-ground flour is produced from *wheat bran, buckwheat* (which is really a species of herb), *barley, millet* (see below), *rice,* and various other seeds, as well as bananas, yams, potatoes, Jerusalem artichokes, cassava, chestnuts, and carob pods.

Oat groats are whole grain oats with only the hull removed. *Oat flour* consists of finely ground oats produced for making oatmeal bread, muffins, etc. Cooked *oatmeal cereal* is made with the steel-cut oats available in supermarkets, and *rolled oats* are flakes of the whole oat kernel compressed by heavy steel rollers.

Corn meal is equally simple to use whether white or yellow, and stone-ground corn meal contains the flavorful germ, much of which is eliminated in supermarket boxed varieties. *Cornstarch,* sometimes called corn flour, can be used as a sauce thickener, but does not have enough body to make bread by itself. It is, however, added to *cake flour* to cut down on the gluten proportion, and for that same reason we add a little cake flour to some doughs—see recipes for croissants and Danish pastry.

Wheat germ is the sprouting segment of the wheatberry and contains fat that is often sifted out of flour; wheat germ is sold separately and may be added to bread doughs, in either powdered or whole form. When *wheatberries* are sprouted (like alfalfa seeds or mung beans), they can be added to bread dough to give a nutty, chewy, sweet flavor (see page 36). The sprouts can also be dried to make a wheat malt, an excellent natural sweetener (see page 36).

Cracked wheat is not ground but cut—to be used as a cooked cereal, or to add crunchy texture to bread flours.

Millet is one of the most ancient grains and, although very bland in taste, is sometimes added to corn meal in making tamales, or to wheat flour in various breads.

Storing Flours and Meals

Commercial all-purpose flour, which contains preservatives, keeps indefinitely in a canister or flour bin just about anywhere in the kitchen. However, if you get unadulterated flours and grains, you should store them in a cool, dry place in airtight containers. We like to use large glass jars or a big Italian *biscotti* box with a glass window so we can keep track of quantity and watch for the possible appearance of tiny mites. The minute you see them, strain the flour through a fine sieve, wash the container thoroughly, and put the strained flour in the refrigerator (it is quite all right to use it). In summer, at least in a humid city kitchen, we try to put all unadulterated flours in the refrigerator; in the country, we store large sacks on a cellar shelf, keeping enough for our immediate needs in canisters in the kitchen.

Liquids for Bread Doughs

All bread requires liquid, for it is necessary to stimulate the elasticity in gluten and essential in causing yeast to bring about fermentation. The kind of liquid is immaterial; it may be water, milk, yogurt, beer, juice of fruits or vegetables, or purées. Dough prepared with too little liquid is dry and brittle when baked. One of the ways we have of achieving good consistency is by using warm water mixed with nonfat dry milk—it is equally nourishing and flavorful as milk from the dairy, and it's easier to work with because the liquid doesn't have to be heated.

Fats for Bread Doughs

Fats are used to enrich the flavor and character of dough, resulting in bread that is tender, flakier, and likelier to keep longer than when it is prepared with only a liquid to bind the flour. Any form of shortening gives bread the quality of breaking and crushing easily, producing a soft, velvety, easily sliceable crumb. (The familiar phrase "to break bread" comes from the dim past when loaves were made with so little fat they literally had to be broken by force.) These are the fats most commonly used in bread baking:

BUTTER. If used in quantity, butter adds flavor. Used in small proportions—2 tablespoons to a pound (3½ cups) of flour—it is really hard to detect a butter flavor, and therefore if for any reason you prefer another fat, substitute a vegetable oil or shortening in the same amount. By the same token, it makes little difference whether the butter is salted or unsalted. In certain recipes, where a large proportion of butter is called for and it really counts, we will specify sweet butter. Be sure, then, that the butter is fresh with a clean, sweet flavor; in supermarkets in which there is little call for it, unsalted butter is sometimes frozen—a safe way of preserving it; at other times it may not always be impeccably fresh and it would be better, in that case, to use a lightly salted butter. Taste is your only guide.

OILS. Any kind of vegetable oil—corn, peanut, palm, safflower, soy, sunflower—can be used. Sometimes we call for an unsaturated safflower oil in a particularly healthful bread, but another vegetable oil will do equally well. We know a professional cook who has proved to her own satisfaction that breads made with peanut oil keep longer. Olive oil adds a good flavor and helps to tenderize pizza dough; walnut oil is delicious in a walnut bread. Experiment and decide for yourself.

LARD. Because most of the lard you buy today is not fresh, unadulterated pork fat—which does lend a good flavor (see Italian Pork Bread)—we seldom call for it. But if you do have some on hand, feel free to substitute.

MARGARINE. This is acceptable as a substitute for butter or other fats, but there is more and more evidence that it's not particularly good for you.

VEGETABLE SHORTENING. The solid, white, tasteless canned shortening (such as Crisco or Spry) is just fine in breads, giving a slightly more crisp texture than other fats.

In mixing any dough, the proportion of fat to flour and liquid varies with the recipe and the type of bread. A sweet breakfast bread, for instance, may use twice or more the amount of butter called for in a basic white loaf. In making flaky danishes or croissants, the dough consists of hundreds of paper-thin layers which are prevented from sticking together by fat (somewhat like the mortar between bricks). The butter used in this way is folded into the dough in thin layers. When this dough is baked, steam caught between the layers of dough forces them to rise, and as the baking continues, with the steam evaporating, the fat is absorbed into the dough. The result is delicate and flaky, unlike an average loaf of bread.

Creative home bakers continue to use this flaky dough to form many classic shapes—like croissants. Interestingly, the unpretentious design of croissants is so naturally aesthetic it has been used for the door handles of the French Museum of Bread in Paris. Is it too much to think that the making of real crescents of flaky dough helps to open the mind to the wonders of baking? In another museum of the baker's arts, in Ulm, Germany, are four terra cotta figures from sixth-century Greece that show every step of breadmaking, the grinding of grain, dough mixing, the firing of ovens, and the offering of bread for sale.

Tofu

Only recently considered part of the English language, tofu is a Japanese word for cakes made of soybean curd that are traditionally used in Oriental cooking. Extremely low in its fat content as well as high in protein, tofu is good in soups, sauces, and salads and, in the current vogue, is gaining American popularity as the base of ice cream in various flavors. To produce it, soybeans are washed, soaked, then finely ground and boiled; the "milk" thus made is strained to remove fiber and is heated with a coagulant to make the curds that are pressed into blocks or formed somewhat like cushions. Tofu was first made by Chinese experimenters about 164 B.C. The firm, medium-texture tofu (called Chinese style) is the most commonly available and what we use in breadmaking, but the softer, wetter Japanese type also serves well in the recipes in this book. Whatever the manufacturing process, tofu is still known in this country as bean curd cakes.

Salt in Bread Doughs

Then and now the use of so-called table salt has been common in bread baking, but in our kitchen we are persuaded that noniodized, non-dehydrator-treated coarse salt, often packaged as kosher salt, or pure sea salt crystals, gives better flavor and generally improves the quality of most breads. Italy's *focaccia cole sale* requires coarse salt in proportions of about 30 percent to the amount of flour. This traditional family bread derives from primitive loaves cooked under a blanket of ashes. Traditional Tuscan bread, on the other hand, is made without any salt.

In most parts of the world, however, the simplest leavened bread is made with salt, flour, yeast, and water, for salt is helpful in governing the action of yeast and in strengthening the gluten, in addition to imparting flavor to each loaf. If you use table salt, figure on one-half to one-third the amount of coarse salt. As the proportion of salt added to the dough is increased the required fermentation time is increased; we find that about one-half ounce or a level tablespoon of kosher or sea salt to a pound of flour will give desired results. Breads with assertive flavor need less salt, and a sweet bread requires only a small accent. Salt prevents dough from becoming too sticky and is one of the factors needed to achieve a crisp crust.

For people on a restricted diet we have made bread eliminating the salt. Such saltless bread does have a bland flavor that may seem hard to get used to, but the loaves are certainly edible as well as perfectly presentable. Our best advice when it comes to challenges of this sort is to choose a bread recipe that offers a lot of flavor—herbs, dried fruits, root vegetables—to modify the lack of salt.

Sweeteners in Bread Doughs

Sweetness in bread is a matter of taste, and sometimes health. We find that impatient bakers, particularly those in commercial plants in this country, use too much sweetening to hurry along the natural fermentation. Not only is there no need for that, but breadmaking should be allowed to take its own natural time. In general terms, our own taste dictates that breads served with dinner shouldn't be sweet; we use a piece of bread to prevent a meat sauce from being wasted, or as the impeccable accompaniment for the cheese course; and for such things a sweet taste is more often than not a clashing note. The exception may be a somewhat sweet dinner roll which is so much a part of the American tradition that there may be a place for it, especially with a roast turkey dinner or with creamed chicken served for lunch.

There are no hard rules. As we see it, certain whole grain breads are often enhanced by the addition of some sugar. Similar results come when honey, molasses, brown sugar, or syrups produced from maple sap, corn, or cane are used. Such sweeteners are often employed to give bread a particular flavor. White sugar has no nutritive factors other than calories, but molasses (especially blackstrap) contributes B vitamins and minerals, in addition to strong taste. Honey adds fragrance as well as flavor. So do fruits and vegetables. It was not a surprise to us to find some of our Vermont neighbors using maple syrup in bread dough, for they could make use of sap not good enough to produce Grade A Fancy syrup.

Making Caramel

Caramel is also used as a sweetener, but its prime purpose is to add color to a bread. Here's how to make it:

Dissolve ½ cup sugar in 2 tablespoons water over moderate heat in a small heavy saucepan. Stir down the crystals as they form, using a wooden spoon. Let boil heartily about 3 minutes. Then the caramel will darken; you can see how quickly and deeply it suddenly turns dark beneath the bubbles, so continue to stir with your wooden spoon. As it turns from café au lait to molasses color, quickly remove from the heat (it will be smoking, so handle carefully). Let cool slightly, then pour in 1 tablespoon of boiling water. Store in a jar when completely cool.

Barley or Wheat Malt

The malt produced from whole barley kernels makes an excellent sugar substitute and has long been used by European and Scandinavian breadmakers. In addition to providing sweetness, the malt helps the yeast to do its work.

We find that the barley malt available commercially, usually sold in health food stores, is much more concentrated than what we make at home. One teaspoon of the commercial preparations, liquid or powdered, is enough for one pound of flour, whereas with our malt 2 tablespoons is about the right proportion for one pound of flour. And it seems to taste more pleasing. Anyway why buy something you can make so easily and cheaply yourself?

It is a problem, however, to get hold of barley kernels with the husk left on (don't be deceived by the packaged supermarket barley labeled "unhulled" that looks as though it were unhusked; it isn't, and you'll have to find either a farmer growing barley or urge one of the sources on page 367 to get it for you). The alternative is to make the malt with wheat kernels, which are more easily available and almost as good. Start the process three days ahead.

In a 2-quart jar or a bean-sprouter cover ½ cup whole barley or wheat kernels with warm water up to the rim. Make a cheesecloth covering for the jar, fastened around the neck with an elastic band. Let stand overnight in a dark place. The next morning pour the water off through the cheesecloth, shake gently to extract as much water as you can, then lay the jar on its side in a dark place until evening. Pour warm water into the jar again, swish it around, and pour off. Do this twice a day for two more days, always storing the jar in the dark.

By the end of three days you will have well-sprouted kernels. Drain them and spread them out on a cookie sheet. Dry in a 200° oven overnight. The next morning pulverize the dried sweet kernels in a coffee or spice mill or a blender and store in a tightly lidded jar. The malt will keep indefinitely.

Making Yeast Dough—Mixing

For any bread that rises with yeast instead of baking powder, the simplest way to start is to dissolve active dry yeast in warm liquid—usually water at a temperature of no more than 110°, because higher heat will kill the yeast cells. You don't have to play nurse and take the liquid's temperature every time; just stick your finger in and be sure you can hold it there comfortably, or splash a little on your wrist. It should feel like a properly warmed baby's formula. You can be sure the yeast is active when it begins to swell. You could add some sweetening to cause the swelling to happen more quickly but, as we've said, it isn't necessary. You may find also that some books call for mixing dry granular yeast directly into flours and grains, then adding very warm liquid; that makes it impossible to be sure your yeast is active before you proceed, and you don't have the reward of that first step—seeing the yeast change character as it comes alive.

We almost always dissolve the yeast in a large 5-quart bowl that is the right size for mixing dough that will use about 2 pounds of flour (about 2 quarts). It saves one thing to wash, and you don't lose the yeast that clings when you have to pour it from a small container. For smaller loaves, a medium-size bowl of about 8 cups will do.

Once the yeast is swelling in the bottom of the big bowl, we stir in any required warm liquids with fat, salt, sweeteners; and any other desired flavorings. Then we stir in flours and grains, cup by cup. We've found that it helps to hold back on the flour as the dough becomes harder to stir. Remember that different flours contain different degrees of moisture, varying with the manufacturer. In addition, weather can greatly affect how much liquid a flour will absorb—a rainy day, even a torpid one, will require adjustments of specified amounts, just as an extra dry day will. That's why we always call for a variable amount of flour in these recipes. If you dump in the maximum amount listed in the ingredients for most recipes, often you'll find yourself struggling to amalgamate a resisting mass. But if you have held back on the flour while mixing, reserving some to be incorporated as you knead the dough, you can control the final texture.

Once the dough is thoroughly mixed it is scraped out onto a floured working surface and left to rest for a few minutes while you clean and grease the bowl. You can use butter, oil, vegetable shortening, lard—whatever you like—to grease the bowl; it makes little difference. We tend to use whatever fat we've used in the recipe and therefore often describe the process as "buttering" or "oiling" the bowl, perhaps out of resistance to the unattractive term "greasing," which sounds like something you do to an automobile. When the bowl is ready—and incidentally there are some recipes that call for *no* greasing of the bowl, while others specify a warm bowl—then you start kneading. That kneading process—turning the dough over and over—is the way to activate the gluten in the flour.

Electric Mixer with Dough Hook Method

If you have a large standing electric mixer with a dough hook attachment, it will do the job of mixing and kneading for you quickly and efficiently. You may miss the satisfying pleasure that comes from slapping the dough around and kneading it, but there are times when you'll more than welcome the help that a modern appliance can give. Simply use the bowl of the mixer to dissolve the yeast in, then add the other ingredients, holding back some of the flour. Turn the switch to set the dough hook in motion and let it do the work. In less than a minute everything will be blended and the dough hook will make the sticky dough turn over and fold under—a kneading motion that moves far faster than hands can manage (with the hook, dough is kneaded in one-quarter of the traditional time). At that point the dough will have come clean from the mixing bowl. If it hasn't, your dough must be too liquid and you will have to add flour, making a funnel with a sheet of waxed paper so you can slide it in while the hook is still in motion. It is helpful to use a plastic collar known as a shield over the bowl, one of the extra attachments for the Kitchen Aid Mixer; it keeps the flour from flying all over the counter and you won't have to improvise a funnel when adding more flour to the dough as it is being kneaded. When the dough seems right (no longer sticky), we always turn it out and knead it a couple of turns just to make sure it has the same texture and consistency—the same silky, resilient feeling—as hand-kneaded dough.

Mixing and Kneading in a Food Processor

Yeast bread dough can be successfully mixed and kneaded in a food processor, if you have a machine with a sufficiently strong motor. If you don't, the motor

will overheat and slow down; as soon as that happens, turn it off, remove the
dough, and finish it by hand. The drawback for making bread in the standard-
size food processor is that it can only handle dough that uses about 3 cups of
flour. The large models will handle a dough of 8 cups of flour. Any dough could,
of course, be divided into two or more pieces, each of which can then be separately kneaded in the processor, but you have to first do a careful mixing job by
hand before you feed pieces into the machine.

As of this writing, one manufacturer—Robot-Coupe C—has introduced a
dome top that fits both its standard and large models. This increases the capacity of the container so that the standard size can knead dough containing 5
cups of flour—the larger model, 10 cups. The plastic blade with foreshortened
ends kneads more efficiently than the standard blade, making the dough turn
up and over.

The manufacturer of the Dough Kit recommends mixing the dough by aerat-
ing the flour and other dry ingredients first—giving them a quick spin—then
adding, while the motor is going, the dissolved yeast and other liquid ingredients in a steady stream through the opening in the top. We find this method
good in that it eliminates the chances of having a little of the dough stick in the
corners of the container, but when we are using some kind of purée as the base
of a dough, we just toss whatever we're puréeing in first, make the purée, add
the yeast and other liquid, then dump flour on top, mix, knead—and it works
beautifully. The joy is that the food processor is so efficient at performing all
these tasks and you have only one thing to clean.

We've made a note on recipes where we feel the food processor is particularly
effective. But if you have a good machine and it's a help to you, there's no
reason why it shouldn't be used for any of the yeast breads in this book; just
remember to break up the dough for larger recipes, as we've suggested.

Hand Kneading

We recommend a clean counter top or a slab of marble or a smooth board as a
working surface; if using the latter, it needn't be any larger than 14 square
inches unless you are making a dough that requires a large surface—for instance, Danish pastry. For best results the counter should be at about the same
height as your waist. You want to be able to put your body into the motion of
kneading, from the shoulders down. It is not just an exercise for hands—the
thrust of kneading uses the force and weight of shoulders and upper torso.

After you've let the dough rest a couple of minutes and have cleaned and
greased the bowl, you'll start the kneading process. Pull the far sides of the
dough up and over toward you and then press into it with the heels of your
hands, pushing away from you. After each push, give the dough a quarter turn
and repeat. Don't tear the dough; as it becomes more pliable, you'll feel it de-

veloping an elastic cloak and you don't want to break that—just stretch it. It usually takes about 8 to 10 minutes of kneading before the dough is really smooth and resilient and no longer at all sticky to your hands, but that, too, can vary—with experience, with the size of your hands, with the amount of weight you put into each thrust. Moreover, doughs containing whole wheat and rye flour and other meals low in gluten are more sticky than one of all white flour and they will absorb more flour as you knead before they lose their tackiness.

To test whether the dough is sufficiently kneaded, plunge a couple of fingers into it and remove them quickly; if the dough springs back at you, that's a sign

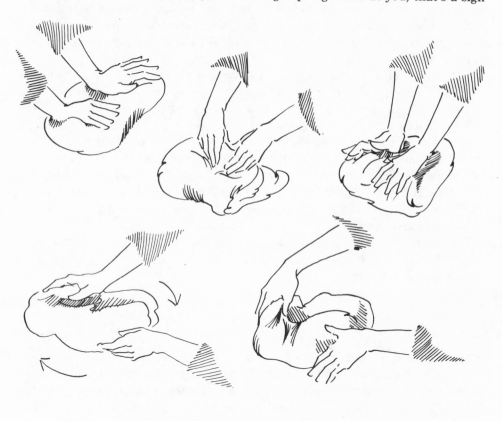

that it has been kneaded enough (although overkneading never hurt a dough). But even more important is the feel: a well-kneaded dough should be bouncy and alive, as though it had a life of its own.

Now put the dough in the bowl and cover it securely with plastic wrap, which is by far the best covering for the first rising because it seals in the moisture. Leave the bowl in a draft-free place to rise until it is double in bulk. For more detail on timing and the amount of warmth needed for rising, see the remarks below.

In anywhere from about fifty minutes to two to three hours, the dough will have doubled in bulk. At this point it will look swollen and rounded on top, and it will be very light and springy to the touch, perhaps having a few air blisters on the surface. If it is in a glass bowl, you can see the masses of bubbles that push the dough up.

The Sponge Method

In another method used in some of our recipes, we make a sponge first. A sponge is really a light dough consisting of the yeast, some of the liquid, and, if you're using it, a sweetener, plus some of the flour, all beaten well to help activate the gluten. Instead of incorporating all of the required flour, the sponge is set aside, covered, long enough to foam and bubble up—for thirty minutes or as long as eight hours; longer than that, the yeast will begin wearing itself out and more yeast will have to be added for the final rising. The advantage of beginning with a sponge, some claim, is that the first frothy rising before the salt goes in adds to the flavor and texture of the final loaf when baked. In our own findings, the sponge does make for a slightly denser loaf, desirable for sandwiches, for instance; and since the timing of the sponge is flexible, it doesn't seem an added burden.

Rising Time

Nothing is more important to remember than *not* to hurry the process if you want the best bread you can make. As we have suggested, that's why commercial breads today taste so cottony; the conditioner that has been added to hurry them up ruins the natural texture and minimizes the development of flavor. When you are the baker, however, this doesn't mean you have to hover over the dough nervously. If you suddenly want to go off to a movie, simply slow down the rising process by putting the bowl of dough in the refrigerator, covered with floured plastic wrap with a heavy plate on top so the dough doesn't ooze over the brim. When you return, carry on where you left off. The final rising will take a little longer if the dough is cold, but you can warm it up in your hands as you shape it. Just be patient.

As we've already indicated, rising time is affected by the conditions in your kitchen. In a way that may seem similar, the amount of wild yeast in the air can vary, too. We've become convinced that yeast spores accumulate in kitchens where bread baking is a regular activity. Years ago when we first made French bread, it would take six or seven hours—as it's supposed to—to develop a dough with real French flavor and good crumb. But today we have to hold the dough back by putting it in a cold window, sometimes even refrigerating it, because it rises so quickly. In our country kitchen, however—a relatively new kitchen where so far we haven't had as much opportunity to bake bread regularly—that same dough will take almost three times as long to rise. Perhaps it's a little like old-fashioned cheesemaking in dairy rooms where the natural bacteria thrive in the walls and rafters.

Most instructions say "a warm place" is necessary for dough to rise happily. We find that not to be true for the average loaf. Most kitchens are usually plenty warm—between 68° and 75° or more. But when you are faced with a very cold day and no cooking has been done to warm up your kitchen, for the first rising the dough can be put in an oven heated only by its pilot light (or an oven can be heated to warm and then turned off). Putting the dough near a radiator, or in a patch of sunshine, or on a shelf above the stove, will also help to get it started. Some doughs that have a lot of butter and eggs really do require a warm place, and in those instances we have made specific suggestions in the recipes.

With working days often lasting until six o'clock, we sometimes find it convenient to start the dough the night before, leave it on a cold windowsill or

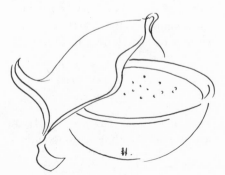

refrigerate it, and shape the loaves and bake them at breakfast time; or we'll do the kneading in the morning before work, let the dough rest in the refrigerator during the day, then shape a small loaf or some rolls to let rise and bake in time for dinner; larger loaves can rise and bake during the evening. Usually the dough seems to mature and improve during its chilly rest. So the lesson seems to be proved: in breadmaking you can do things at your own convenience.

Some breads require another rising in addition to that of allowing the dough to expand in loaf pans after it has been shaped. This added step helps to develop more flavor and is essential, we find, in such simple, classic breads as the French and Italian loaves that consist of only yeast, flour, water, and salt.

Shaping the Loaves

The way dough is firmed and finished says much about the ethnic background of various loaves. The commonest breads in France today retain traditional shapes—the extended ovals that are known as baguettes and the sticklike form of the *flute* and the *ficelle*. The length makes it easy to cut the loaves diagonally so that there is more surface to spread with butter or as a base for pâté de campagne, and it also helps to give more crust than soft crumb, a factor applauded by almost all habitual bread eaters. Some Russian breads are thin curved loaves that take their shape from the contours of the jarlike ovens in which they are cooked, and others are fancifully braided so that the heat of baking can penetrate more evenly. Scandinavians make many thin, crisp, and sometimes chewy breads that are designed to last for months. British bakers devised a pan loaf called Church and Chapel that rises over the rim in a sort of cathedral-like fashion. And the traditional Coburg bread that sometimes looks like a royal British crown is said to have been named to honor Prince Albert, who hailed from the German state of Saxe-Coburg-Gotha.

No matter what shape is aimed at, and no matter how quirky the dough, bread loaves seem to want to respond to the whims of fanciful bakers. But you should remember the importance of gently stretching and easing the dough into the shape you want so that its invisible elastic skin, which can be felt only through gentle touching, is not broken.

To make the ordinary bread-pan loaf simply pat the dough into an oval approximately the pan's length, then ease and tuck the long sides under, plump-

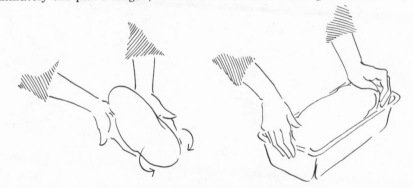

ing the loaf as you do so. Pinch the seams together on the bottom side and place in a greased pan, filling it two-thirds to three-quarters full.

Here are some other shapes to play with:

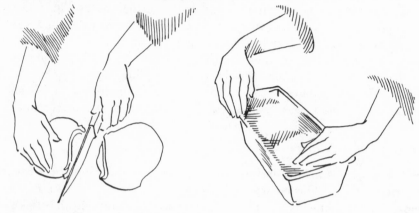

DOUBLE LOAF. Instead of forming a single loaf for whatever bread pan you are going to use, divide the same amount of dough in half and form two loaves, placing them side by side. This way a little more of the surface acquires a crust, and the two mounds, which knit together in the middle, seem to swell higher.

TWISTED OR BRAIDED LOAF. Twisting and braiding need not be reserved for free-form loaves only. A stubby twist or braid placed in a bread pan gives the loaf an elegant finish, and if it is one you plan to glaze and sprinkle with seeds or nuts, your topping will stick better on the uneven surface of a braid. See page 358 for a braided loaf recipe.

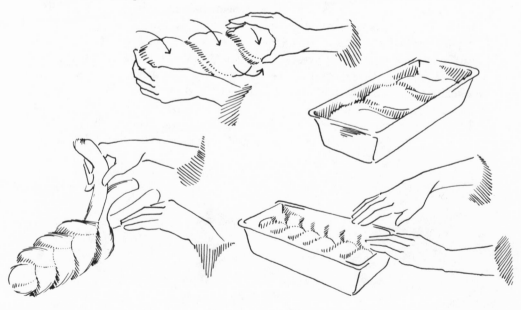

PULLMAN. A loaf that is baked in a pan with a lid, thus producing a flat top and a dense loaf with four even sides—an advantage if you're making sandwiches or fancy canapés or a smorgasbord. There are special pullman loaf pans with covers that slide into grooves, but you can also improvise by using an ordinary bread pan and putting a cookie sheet over it with a weight on top. In either case, be sure not to fill the pan more than two-thirds full, and grease the underside of the pan's cover.

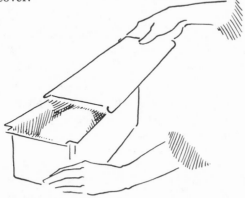

RINGS. Make rings in a free-form shape, in which case be sure to widen the center of the dough because it tends to close up when it rises and bakes, or you can purchase ring molds designed for breadmaking. Ring baking is particularly nice for doughs with a vegetable or fruit purée, as they pick up an attractive crust.

COBURG. Shaped like a crown, particularly good for a predominantly whole wheat bread baked in an improvised clay oven; see page 80.

COTTAGE LOAF. A double-decker round loaf with a hole hollowed out through the center, giving extra crust and a very handsome look.

LONG FRENCH LOAVES OR BAGUETTES. These can be created free form (but carefully shaped; see page 62) or made in special French loaf pans, which can be improvised out of stovepipe, if you like (see page 60). A nice touch is to give your French loaf an ear-of-wheat shape, which exposes even more surface to crust in the hot oven, as described on page 64.

ROUNDS AND OVALS. Usually free form, so the dough should have body. In other words, don't try to make these with a soft dough, and ideally the loaves should be slipped onto a hot oven surface such as tiles or a baking stone; the hot floor thus created will make the loaves plump up immediately and hold their shapes. Their tops should be slashed before baking to let steam escape.

LOAVES BAKED IN LA CLOCHE. See page 365. Almost any loaf using 7 cups of flour or less can be baked in this clay oven. After a slow first rising, the dough should be punched down and formed into a round loaf, coaxing and tucking the sides under to make it plump, and then allowed to rise on the well-greased clay bottom covered by the dome. When doubled in volume, plump the loaf again and slash the top. Let settle 15 to 30 minutes, then bake in a hot (usually 425° oven) for almost an hour.

The Final Rising—Glazing and Slashing

The final rising should never be too long, or the loaf will puff too high and, when exposed to the oven's heat, sink. The general rule in our recipes is to have the dough double in volume; sometimes an increase of only one-third or less is stipulated, particularly if the mixture contains different kinds of meal that tend to make a crumbly loaf.

Sometimes loaves are brushed with a glaze just before going into the oven. Plain water will give the bread a crustier surface on top; whole egg beaten with a little water makes for a shiny, golden crust; white of egg produces a very crisp, lightly colored crust; yolk, sometimes mixed with a little milk or cream, makes a deeper brown, glossy surface; and occasionally a solution using a little molasses or caramel is brushed on to give the loaf a mahogany crust. It is sometimes nice to dust a little flour over a loaf before baking, which makes a streaky contrast against a golden brown crust.

Slashing the top of the loaf just before baking gives certain breads a professional look characteristic of the particular type and place of origin; but, of course, there is a fundamental reason, for slashes also keep crusts from cracking like mud that has baked in the sun, and allow some moisture to escape which might otherwise burst through the side of the loaf. You must use a very sharp knife or a razor blade to score bread dough, and the cuts shouldn't go deep—

recipes will tell you when and how to slash. Sometimes one pricks a loaf all over on top so that it will remain rather flat and dense.

The standard sizes for bread loaf pans are: 8½ inches by 4½ by 2½; 9¾ by 5¾ by 2¾; and miniature sizes in variety. Pans may be made of cast iron, but usually are aluminum (with and without nonstick treatment), foil, ovenproof glass, or clay. We find that aluminum pans are reliable, and the nonstick kind makes extracting a loaf particularly easy. They are also quick to wash. All bread pans, incidentally, should simply be rinsed out, not scoured with detergents. Many bread bakers feel that the heavy black pans currently in vogue turn out a crustier loaf and it is true that you get a deeper brown, thicker crisp crust, but they are expensive and they don't come in standard sizes, so you have to make adjustments in all recipes.

Unless otherwise specified, dough for one loaf should fill a pan two-thirds to three-quarters full. But don't worry if you have to use a larger pan—the finished loaf simply won't be as high.

Baking the Loaves—and Creating Steam

Most pan breads are baked in a moderate oven for approximately 45 minutes, but some doughs require longer cooking and smaller loaves shorter cooking; some benefit from starting off in a hot oven, then lowering the heat, while to get a very crusty loaf you need consistently high heat and quick cooking. Then there is the cottage loaf that starts out in a cold oven. So there are no hard and fast rules.

It is not easy when you are new to bread baking to be certain when a loaf is done. The standard test is to tap the bottom: if it sounds hollow, the loaf is supposed to be done. But often it will sound hollow when the bread hasn't yet cooked through. It's better to press the sides and see if they still seem soft. Also, color is an indicator; if the sides and bottom are pale, more baking is usually in order. We sometimes just put the loaf back on the oven shelf and let it brown 5 to 10 minutes longer, free of its pan, particularly if a crusty loaf is desirable. But all of these recipes will call for a specified baking time which we have worked out carefully; use that as your best guide.

Free-form breads—that is, those shaped in rounds or ovals and not confined to pans—are usually baked on cookie sheets that are greased and/or sprinkled with corn meal. Certain long loaves (as well as round or oval) rise best and develop wonderful crusty bottoms when they are slid directly onto a hot flat surface in the oven in a fashion very like the technique of traditional bakers in the past; using a peel or wooden paddle they jiggled their ready-to-bake loaves onto the hot brick floor of the oven, jerking back the paddle and leaving the bread behind. To simulate that kind of baking in your own range, you can buy a Home Hearth, or baker's stone, made to fit the average oven. Or use flat squares of tile to line the rack of your oven, thus contriving a semblance of the fundamental element in old brick ovens.

One of the most recent products available to bakers interested in emulating ancient techniques and, better still, the high quality of bread made by age-old methods, is a bell-shaped clay oven or oven-within-an-oven. Called La Cloche, it consists of a large unglazed earthen circular platter on which a commodious "bell" of the same material fits snugly to make the oven within which bread can be baked. When it contains a round loaf of bread and is put in a contemporary kitchen oven it works very well, browning evenly and creating a crisp, pliable crust.*

In old European houses, especially, brick ovens were built next to the chimney on the outside wall, and thus they absorbed moisture from the elements when not in use. When they were heated, brick and clay emitted steam, and sometimes the oven floors were swabbed to encourage more steam. The damp floor of the oven and moisture in the dough itself create an atmosphere of mist that is necessary in the hot oven—it is the steam, of course, that encourages the hard crust so typical of all good European peasant breads. Today's commercial bakeries have a steam-producing device in their ovens, but, alas, we who bake at home have no such specially designed contrivance. There are ways of producing steam, though, and our suggestions are on page 64, following the recipe for French bread.

Alternatives to Oven Baking

Oven baking is not the only way to cook bread. In this country Basque sheepherders, who live for months at a time high up in the Rocky Mountains, use cast iron or cast aluminum pots (sometimes called Dutch ovens) which, when

---

*Before he discovered La Cloche, Chuck Williams was known among his California friends for the extraordinary round loaves he baked in his kitchen oven. His secret: inverting a pottery mixing bowl over a pottery pie dish, a simple idea worth trying on your own.

buried in a shallow pit under an outdoor fire, make wonderful dome-shaped loaves. You can bake a fair imitation of this Basque bread with the dough for any basic loaf by first lining your cast iron pot with greased aluminum foil. Put dough in the pot, cover it, and leave it in a warm place until the dough pushes up the cover about half an inch. Instead of going outside, you can bake this loaf in the covered pot in a 375° oven for about twelve minutes, then uncovered for about thirty-five minutes. In rural Ireland, where peat is still burned in indoor fireplaces, the soda bread made for teatime serving is a biscuitlike loaf cooked over coals in a suspended iron pot.

For hikers and others who cook outdoors, there are simple productions often called skillet breads. They can be made with various flours and are usually leavened by a sourdough starter, or with baking powder. You may choose to make biscuits that nestle together in a skillet, or pour in the dough to cover the bottom of a greased skillet and bake under a tight-fitting lid over a bed of glowing ashes.

With young neighborhood cronies, we used to make campfire bread of biscuit dough by rolling it out in a thick rope; we would cut some green saplings and peel them, then wind the "snake" of flour-dusted dough around the greased stick, which we propped in the ground over the edge of a campfire that had burned down to coals. If our hikes took us through a berry patch, we would sometimes pick berries to work into the dough.

Fishing trips in the South are said to have been responsible for naming the small breads of corn meal called hush puppies. Blacks who liked to fry freshly caught fish in boiling lard were also partial to fried bread. They made a stiff mixture of corn meal to sizzle crisply alongside the fish, and quieted their dogs who wailed at the smell of food by tossing them any extra fried bread. "Hush, puppies!" they cried, and the words became the accepted term for an American regional classic.

Fried bread brings doughnuts to our minds, first of all, but frying—never as common as baking, of course—has been a popular way of cooking various kinds of breads in many countries where oil or lard is abundant. Closest to home is the *sopaipillas,* or fried bread, of the American Southwest. A specialty we have discovered and feel almost proprietary about is made of a batter laced with Minnesota wild rice that serves as a fine breakfast bread when accompanied by sausages and eggs. In this vein there are several kinds of yeast-risen fritters, including "chicken bread," a sort of corn meal biscuit cooked in the same fat as southern fried chicken, corn dodgers, and "corn oysters."

We may tend to forget how often cooks have had to get along without ovens because there simply weren't any; they therefore made bread that could be cooked in oil or fat—or in steam. In many parts of the old South, and in Oklahoma where it is called "steamed Indian bread," a soda-risen dough of corn meal, corn kernels, white flour, and unsulfured molasses is sealed in cans or other greased containers and steamed. So is the Boston brown bread developed by early Yankees before ovens were common in most houses. But the oldest form of steamed bread may well be *man-t'ou,* the buns made of wheat dough that for centuries have been cooked in steam by Chinese housewives (recipe, page 273).

Storing Bread

No matter how bread is cooked, when it is made without preservatives—as are all those in this book—care must be taken to keep it fresh as long as possible. The wonder of mid-twentieth-century plastic wrap, which seals the moisture in, has made it possible to store bread successfully in the refrigerator for up to a week (the less fat content the faster bread dries out, so a French loaf, for instance, shouldn't be held more than a day or so). In fact, this new and better method of storage has eliminated need for a breadbox, which seems to encourage mold when a plastic-wrapped loaf is placed in one.

So today you can make bread in quantities as large as you like. Any of our recipes can be doubled without adding extra work. To preserve the loaves, always let them cool off, then wrap them tightly in good plastic wrap, pushing out the air; seal them securely with tape or by tying the open end of a bag. We find that with French loaves particularly, an additional layer of foil squeezed tightly around each loaf helps to keep the crust from breaking away from the bread, which sometimes happens when it is reheated. Refrigerate the bread you'll be eating within the week; freeze the remaining loaves, or cut a loaf in half and freeze the half you don't expect to use immediately.* To unfreeze, remove bread to room temperature for three to four hours before serving. If you are in more of a hurry wrap the ordinary loaf in foil and put it in a 400° oven for ten to fifteen minutes. However, a crusty frozen loaf is better left unwrapped.

Today it's easy to bake at your own convenience, to use a modern kitchen appliance when you're too pressed for time to enjoy the relaxation of kneading by hand, and to make bread in quantity so that you'll always have a fragrant, tempting loaf in the freezer ready to be brought to room temperature in time for the next meal.

Reflections and Observations

There are so many slight variables in bread baking that you'll soon learn to be your own judge about a finished loaf. Make a note if it seems too dry (you've probably added too much flour in the final stage) or if it is still tacky (your dough was too moist) or undercooked (next time put it back, freestanding, in the oven for five or ten minutes more baking).

If a loaf, when baking, bursts through its elastic skin on one side, it's proba-

---

*As a matter of fact, you can freeze dough after its first rising. Punch the dough down, place in a floured plastic bag, and seal tightly. Unfreeze as you would a finished loaf.

bly because the oven floor was too hot when it went in or the loaf should have
been slashed to let steam escape. But a slightly lopsided loaf is not something
to apologize for—it happens to the best of bakers.

The thing to remember is that there is nothing easier or more natural to a
fledgling cook than making bread. Enjoy it and be relaxed. Yeast doughs are
very accommodating and easy to work with—far less intimidating, it seems to
us, than other kinds of baking. The dough manages to let you know when it
feels right (unlike a cake). And the labor involved in breadmaking is so mini-
mal. Although it may take three hours or more from start to finish to bake
bread, the actual working time is probably no more than fifteen minutes—less
if you let a machine do the kneading while you are preparing supper.

Here are some observations and remedies that we have jotted down over the
years of breadmaking, which may be helpful to you:

• If your finished loaf doesn't have a good crumb, it usually means that you
haven't kneaded long enough or that you didn't break down the dough sufficiently after the first rising; it really needs to be punched all over. Sometimes
the dough has risen too quickly because your kitchen is very warm and steamy.
If you see that happening, put the bowl of dough in a cooler place—even in the
refrigerator for a while—to slow it down.

• If a loaf seems crumbly, it's a good idea to slice it from the side. Always use
a long, sharp, serrated bread knife. Still you'll find that certain loaves will not
slice as successfully as others, usually because they have a higher proportion of
meal or cereal that has no gluten or of other embellishments. We have tried to
forewarn in these recipes when we've found a loaf particularly crumbly—but
still so good it belongs among the favorites—and have suggested baking in a
small-size loaf pan.

• Never hurry a dough by adding extra yeast or forcing a rising. Only doughs
that have a high proportion of butter and eggs and sugar need to be put in a
particularly warm place, sometimes over hot water.

• If you want a loaf that is fairly dense so that it holds together well in a
sandwich, don't let the dough rise too long in the pan before baking; put it in
the oven when it's only a third of its original volume—just to the top of the
pan. And remember, if you let it rise too long at this stage, it is bound to sink
again when it bakes. It's better, if you've forgotten about it or stayed too long
on the telephone, to remove the loaf, punch it down again, re-form the loaf, and
let it rise the proper amount of time.

We hope our own relaxed approach will encourage you and help you feel
confident. For those who are already seasoned bakers (but like us are greedy for
new ideas) we trust that what follows will quell that hunger and inspire new
accomplishments.

3 · Basic White Breads

Basic White Bread I
  (yeast, salt, water, and flour)
Basic White Bread II
  (yeast, salt, milk, sugar, and flour)
Basic White Bread III
  (yeast, salt, milk, sugar, eggs,
  sweetener)
Buttermilk, Yogurt, or Sour Cream Bread
French Bread
French or Italian Round Loaves
Basic Sourdough Starter
Sourdough Bread
Salt-Rising Bread
Potato Bread
Saffron Bread
Tofu Bread
No-Knead Batter Bread

To be young, in Paris, and living on the Rue du Cherche-Midi was to know that down the street was the Poilane bakery where Left Bank housewives, morning after morning, queued up to buy *du vrai pain,* real bread. The round loaves made by Lionel Poilane, his brothers, and their helpers weigh about five pounds and are baked down a steep flight of stairs in the ovens of a cellar that once was a monastery. The dusty brick walls and the heat from wood fires in which the famous Poilane bread is baked are reminders of the ancient traditions to which this Paris firm adheres. Modern yeast isn't used, the proprietors will tell you, because it is manufactured in a laboratory. Poilane bread begins with sourdough—"It's natural"—and the minimum time for fermentation of the dough is six hours. The flour is stone-ground. "Wholesome bread that tastes like something" is a phrase Lionel Poilane once used to describe his bread. When we used to pass this *boulangerie* long ago, the aroma alone was enough to tell us what those words meant. Now the bakery's reputation is such that jet set customers have their orders flown to New York at as much as forty dollars a loaf.

We (like an increasing number of Americans) would rather bake French bread than pay such prices. Any fear we once had of the hours it might take to turn out a good French loaf has vanished in mastering the tricks of arranging breadmaking time to fit with other activities. It can be true for you as well, once you get your hands into the dough. To break yourself in gradually, we think it's a good idea to begin with one or another of more familiar loaves.

Here are the basic white breads. The first loaf has no sugar in it, no milk—only water—and no fat. As a result the bread has a wonderfully chewy texture and is a little more dense than the breads with sweeteners, although a good loaf should have almost a lacy pattern, revealing the little pockets of air that the yeast has created. This basic formula is the same as the one used for French, Italian, and other crusty white table breads, and because there is no fat, the bread will dry out faster. However, if it goes stale before you're able to eat it all up, this particular bread makes wonderful bread crumbs (just lop off the crusts, tear in rough pieces, and spin in a blender or food processor or crumble with your hands). Bread crumbs can be frozen wrapped tightly in a plastic bag, as, of course, can any of these loaves (see page 50).

Basic White Bread I

Makes two 8-inch loaves

1 tablespoon active dry yeast
3 cups warm water
1½ tablespoons coarse salt or 1 tablespoon table salt
6½–7½ cups white flour, preferably unbleached

Put the yeast in a large bowl and pour ¼ cup of the warm water over it. Stir gently and let sit a few minutes until it is thoroughly dissolved and looks creamy.

Pour the rest of the warm water into the bowl along with the salt, stirring to dissolve. Now add the flour, cup by cup, stirring well after each. After the sixth cup or so, the dough should be getting hard to stir. Scrape it out of the bowl onto a well-floured working surface and let it rest while you wash out the bowl and butter or oil it.

Start kneading the dough, scraping it up from the working surface and slapping it around a bit to activate the gluten. Knead the dough for 8–10 minutes, adding more flour as necessary to keep it from sticking. When it is smooth and elastic, return it to the buttered bowl, cover with plastic wrap, and let rise until double in volume. Because this dough has no sugar in it, it will take longer than the next recipe—anywhere from 1½ hours to perhaps 3, depending on the warmth of your kitchen.

Turn the risen dough out again onto a lightly floured surface, punch it down, and divide it in half. Form each half into an 8-inch long loaf and place in two buttered or oiled bread pans. Cover lightly with a kitchen towel and let rise until the dough swells over the tops of the pans or until almost double in volume—anywhere from 45 minutes to well over an hour. Don't let it rise too high, however, or it will sink when it is baked.

Bake in a preheated 350° oven for 40 minutes. Remove the loaves from their pans and let them cool on racks.

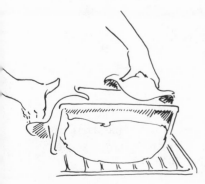

Basic White Bread II

This bread uses milk, a sweetener, and butter or shortening. The bread will be lighter than the first basic white loaf as well as being somewhat sweet, and it is what we think of as a typical American loaf. If you like a slightly more compact bread that will hold together well for sandwiches, we'd recommend either making the preceding basic white or using the alternate method for this bread—that is, making a sponge first (see page 41). It will take longer, but the loaf seems to develop more flavor and will be less airy.

Makes two 8-inch loaves

1 tablespoon active dry
  yeast
¼ cup warm water
2½ cups milk or ½
  cup nonfat dry milk
  mixed with 2 cups
  warm water
4 tablespoons butter or
  vegetable shortening
4 tablespoons sugar or
  honey
1 tablespoon coarse
  salt or 2 teaspoons
  table salt
6½–7½ cups white
  flour, preferably
  unbleached

1. Follow the first paragraph of Basic White Bread above.

2. Heat the milk and dissolve the butter or shortening, sugar or honey, and salt in it. Let cool to 110° or until you can hold your finger comfortably in the milk. Or if using dry milk, simply beat everything together. Add to the yeast and stir in 6 cups of the flour.

3. Follow the directions for kneading, rising, and baking as described in Basic Bread I.

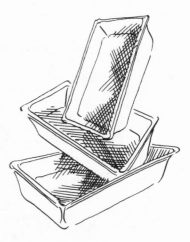

Basic White Bread III

This last Basic White Bread is the same as II except for the addition of eggs. The eggs add color and a touch of flavor, as well as a little more density than you get in the airy number II bread.

Makes two 8-inch loaves

1 tablespoon active dry
  yeast
¼ cup warm water
2 cups milk or ⅓ cup
  nonfat dry milk
  mixed with 1¾ cups
  warm water
4 tablespoons butter or
  vegetable shortening
  or oil
4 tablespoons honey or
  light brown sugar
2 teaspoons coarse salt
  or 1 teaspoon table
  salt
2 eggs
6½–7½ cups white
  flour, preferably
  unbleached

1. Follow the first paragraph of Basic White Bread I.

2. Heat half the milk just enough to dissolve the butter, shortening, or oil, honey or sugar, and salt in it. Add the rest of the milk, then the eggs, and beat until they are thoroughly broken up and well blended. Or if using dry milk simply beat everything together. Add to the yeast and stir in 6 cups of the flour.

3. Follow the directions for kneading, rising, and baking as described in Basic White Bread I.

◆ ALTERNATE SPONGE METHOD FOR WHITE BREAD

This method can be used in making any of the above breads. The first rising, before the addition of salt, tends to develop a little more flavor in the loaf, but we have found the most important advantage is that this method produces a more compact loaf, good for easy slicing to make sandwiches. It's all a matter of personal taste. To make the sponge: dissolve the yeast, add ½ the total amount of liquid you are using, and stir in 2 cups of the flour. Beat about 100 strokes or 30 seconds in an electric mixer, 10 seconds in a food processor. Cover the bowl with plastic wrap and let rise anywhere from half an hour to 8 hours— whatever is convenient. Then add the rest of the ingredients and proceed as above. You will find that the sponge method uses less flour; therefore, hold back on the last cup when you are mixing it in so that you don't let the dough become too dry; it should have the same texture as the other basic white doughs for its second and final rises.

Buttermilk, Yogurt, or Sour Cream Bread

Scientists continue to experiment with the old notion that fermented mixtures may contribute to longevity in people whose diets include yogurt, buttermilk, and sour cream. In this recipe there aren't any promises you'll live as long as some yogurt eaters of the Caucasus Mountains, but breads seem to rise faster when made with such a sour agent as buttermilk, yogurt, or sour cream. The latter particularly makes a creamy, compact loaf, and yogurt, especially if it is very tart, gives a slight but appetizing sourness, a bit like sourdough.

Makes two 8-inch loaves

1 tablespoon active dry
  yeast
½ cup warm water
¼ cup light brown
  sugar
2 cups buttermilk,
  yogurt, or sour
  cream*
6–6½ cups unbleached
  or hard wheat white
  flour
1 tablespoon coarse
  salt or 2 teaspoons
  table salt
4 tablespoons (½
  stick) butter

Make a sponge by dissolving the yeast in the warm water in a large bowl. Mix in the brown sugar. Heat the buttermilk, yogurt, or sour cream to lukewarm and add 1 cup of it. Stir in 3 cups of the flour, cover the bowl with plastic wrap, and leave it in a warm place for 30–40 minutes until it swells and bubbles on the top.

Meanwhile dissolve the salt and melt the butter, cut up in small pieces, in the remaining warm buttermilk, yogurt, or sour cream, heating it up again if necessary. Let cool to lukewarm, and when the sponge is ready add this to it along with all but ½ cup of the remaining flour. Mix well until it becomes hard to stir, then turn out on a floured working surface and knead, adding more flour as necessary until the dough is smooth and resilient—about 8–10 minutes.

Clean out the bowl, oil or butter it, and return the dough, turning to coat with grease. Cover with plastic and leave to rise until double in bulk, an hour or a little more.

Turn the dough out, punch down, then form into two loaves. Place in greased bread pans, cover lightly with a towel, and let rise again until double, about 45 minutes. Bake in a preheated 425° oven 10 minutes, then lower the heat to 350° and continue to bake 30 minutes. Cool on racks.

*Note: You may need to thin the yogurt or sour cream with a few tablespoons of milk or water to make it the consistency of buttermilk.

◆ YOUR OWN CULTURED BUTTERMILK

Mix 2 tablespoons sugar with 1 tablespoon of
active dry yeast. Gradually add 1 pint of tepid
milk mixed with 1 pint of tepid water. Cover and
leave at room temperature until "milk" smells and
tastes like buttermilk. Strain through a colander
lined with two layers of cheesecloth or a
Handiwipe. Then gently pour over the residue in
the colander 1 cup tepid water to rinse off all sour
milk. To start a new lot of "buttermilk" scrape the
"plant" from the cheesecloth, place in a scalded
vessel, and add 1 quart tepid milk-and-water (half
and half). Cover and leave as before in warm place
to increase and multiply. The first ounce of yeast
will go on growing, producing buttermilk. But it
must be given a certain amount of care: it must be
strained at least every 5 days; and the milk-and-
water mixture must never be more than tepid.
(Strong heat kills yeast.) Cleanliness is very
important. The careful rinsing after straining and
the scalding of the container are necessary if
buttermilk production is to continue.

◆ WINTER BUTTERMILK

¼ cup flake oatmeal
6 cups water
2 mashed potatoes
2 raw potatoes, grated

Mix oatmeal to paste with 1 cup water; put in
large jug or crock. Add potatoes and remaining 5
cups water. Cover and leave in warm place 2 days,
stirring occasionally. When baking, carefully pour
off as much liquid as needed, without disturbing
sediment. Add fresh water to make up the amount
used. Stir, cover, and leave in warm place until
next baking. Every 2 weeks make fresh supply.

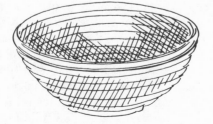

French Bread

Good French bread depends on slow rising to develop its honest flavor and chewy texture, and these skinny loaves need a hot oven and a great whoosh of steam to acquire the deep, golden, crunchy crust. So take your time once you start; the dough can always be left to rise in the refrigerator, or overnight on a cool windowsill, if that works best for you.

The simplest way to bake these long loaves called baguettes is to use forms that are designed for the purpose. These are neither cheap nor readily available; so, if you want forms to help the loaves hold their shape, we suggest you do what we did. We bought in a Vermont hardware store an 18-inch section of stovepipe that was 3 inches in diameter and we devised our own French-loaf pans with it. We opened the pipe lengthwise and enlisted a local garage man to help us score it down the middle and then bend it into the shape of two semi-circular troughs that were joined together. When we shaped the dough into long soft bars (baguette is a French word for rod), we lifted them into the troughs for their final rising, then slid them into the oven. (The more authentic way is to let the long loaves rise for the last time on a canvas sheet, then flip them over onto a baker's peel and slip them directly onto the hot oven floor.)

Some years ago Paul and Julia Child spent months perfecting a method to create in American home ovens the true characteristics of crusty French loaves, and the recipe we give here is based on their invaluable findings, along with some touches we've worked out in our own kitchen as we've baked this bread almost weekly over the years. The use of just a little roughly ground wheat flour, while perhaps not authentic in this classic white flour loaf, adds a little texture that we like.

Makes 5 free-form loaves, 3–4 in pans

1 tablespoon active dry yeast

2¾ cups warm water

2 tablespoons coarse salt or 4 teaspoons table salt

5–6 tablespoons whole wheat flour

5½–6 cups white flour, preferably unbleached

Corn meal

Put the yeast in a large bowl with 1 cup of the warm water. When dissolved, stir in the remaining water, salt, whole wheat flour, and about 5½ cups of the white flour—enough to make a dough that holds together. Turn out on a floured work surface and let rest while you clean the bowl.

Scrape the dough up—it will be quite soft and very sticky—and slap it down hard against the counter. Repeat several times and then start kneading, adding more flour as necessary. Knead for about 10 minutes until the dough is smooth, no longer sticky, and full of bounce. Return the dough

to the clean, ungreased bowl, cover with plastic
wrap, and let stand at no more than 68° for at
least 3 hours, until triple in volume. We've found
that it is even better to leave the dough overnight
on a cold windowsill, or if the weather is warm to
let it rise for about 1 hour at room temperature,
then refrigerate overnight (or all day if you've
mixed the dough in the morning); weight down
with a heavy plate.

After the first rising, turn the dough out, punch
it thoroughly all over, return it to the bowl, cover
again with plastic wrap, and let rise at room
temperature until double in volume—probably
1½–2½ hours depending on how cold the dough
was.

Punch the dough down and turn out on a lightly
floured work surface. Divide into 5 equal parts,
covering the others with a piece of floured plastic
wrap as you work with one. To form each loaf, pat
the dough into an oval, then fold lengthwise in
thirds. Now, with the side of your hand, firmly
punch a trough down the center lengthwise and
fold over, pinching the seams together securely.

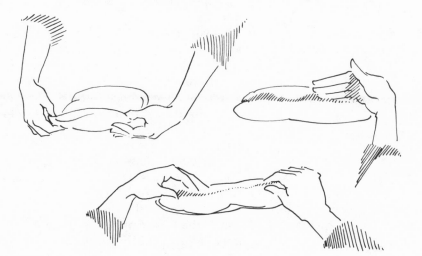

Flour a large area to work on and roll the dough, starting from the center and working outward until you have a long loaf of about 18 inches. Pick it up and place on the edge of a well-floured kitchen towel. Pleat the edge up on the long side to separate this loaf from the next one you'll make and put alongside it; continue with the rest of the loaves, overlapping a second floured towel when the space on the first one has been used up. To prevent the loaves from spreading out, prop the ends with something that is the length of the loaves; the back of your counter can serve as one prop, some loaf pans as the other. Cover loosely with a towel and let rise until double—about 45 minutes.

(If you have French bread pans, grease them and simply place the formed loaves in, cover with a kitchen towel, and let rise. This amount of dough would probably fill three or four forms, two-thirds full, depending on the size of the pans.)

Meanwhile set in motion whatever device you're using for creating steam (see notes at end of recipe) and preheat the oven to 450° about 30 minutes in advance. When loaves have doubled, remove them one by one with a baking sheet or stiff cardboard sprinkled with corn meal, leveling out the pleat so the sheet can be inserted between two of the loaves and using the towel to flip the bread over. If the dough sticks to the towel, as sometimes happens in humid weather, just ease it gently away. Even though the bread seems to collapse, it will recover and swell up splendidly when it hits the hot oven floor. Slash each loaf diagonally three times and slip quickly onto the hot oven tiles or baking stone, shutting the door between times; try to work as quickly as you can until all five loaves are in.

(If you are using French bread pans, eliminate this step; just place them in the oven.)

Bake 20–25 minutes or until the loaves are crusty and golden. After 15 minutes remove your steaming device so the loaves will finish baking in a dry oven. You may want to shift the loaves around if they seem to be baking unevenly. Remove the loaves and let cool on racks or propped up so that the air circulates; listen for the wonderful mysterious sound the loaves make when you put your ear to them! Eat the same day if possible.

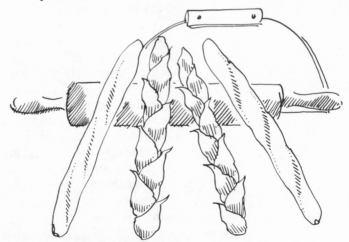

What isn't consumed, freeze as soon as the loaves are thoroughly cooled, wrapping plastic wrap around as snugly as possible to seal out the air and tying or taping the ends together. To restore frozen loaves, put unwrapped in a cold oven, set it to 400°, and in 15–20 minutes the bread will be warm through and crisp again. Even if you are serving fresh loaves, warm them again if they have cooled off completely.

TO MAKE EAR-OF-WHEAT SHAPES: Let the loaves have their final rising placed 6 inches apart on corn-meal-sprinkled baking sheets. Then, instead of slashing the tops, with scissors make deep V-shaped cuts 2–3 inches apart down the length of each loaf. Immediately pull one V-shape all the way over to the left so that the point rests on the baking sheet, then pull the next one to the right, repeating, alternating left and right, to resemble an ear of wheat. Bake as above.

♦ TO MAKE A BAKER'S OVEN

If you are baking the loaves the traditional French way, you will need to concoct something that resembles the hot brick floor of the baker's oven. One way is to line a rack of your oven with tiles; another is to get a large baking stone (see page 365). Preheat the oven 30 minutes before baking to get the tiles or stone good and hot.

To create steam: the best way is to heat some object like a brick or large stone or piece of cast iron, such as an old-fashioned iron, which is what we use; get it really hot by setting it on top of the stove over your highest heat for 30 minutes. Then after you have placed the last loaf in the oven, lift the red-hot element with heavy tongs and place it in a pan of water on the oven floor. Shut the door immediately to lock in the steam.

If this method seems too hazardous, try, instead, spraying the loaves with cold water (a plant atomizer is very useful) just before they go in and then repeat two or three times during the first 10 minutes of baking. Also, set a pan of boiling water

on the oven floor when you preheat it, but because
you will be losing steam as you put each loaf in
the oven, toss a trayful of ice cubes in the pan just
before you finally shut the door. However, the first
method is the most effective for an immediate and
steady whoosh of steam.

If you are using French bread forms, set a pan
of boiling water on the oven floor when you
preheat and brush the loaves with cold water just
before they go in (because they all go in at the
same time, you don't risk losing the steam).

♦ FRENCH OR ITALIAN ROUND LOAVES

Prepare the preceding French Bread dough.

After the second rising divide the dough in half
and form two round loaves. First pat each half
into a round cake about 7 inches in diameter.
Then, using the palms of your hands, lightly
floured, coax the sides of the dough down and
under all the way around, at the same time
plumping up the loaf. You will feel an invisible
elastic cloak of gluten; just stretch it, don't break
it. Pick up the round and pinch together the
seams on the bottom. Place, seam side down,
either on a corn-meal-sprinkled paddle, if you are
going to bake the loaves directly on hot tiles or a
baking stone, or on a greased baking sheet
sprinkled with corn meal. Let rise, covered lightly
with a kitchen towel, until double in size—about
45 minutes.

Half an hour before baking set in motion your
device for creating steam (see opposite page) and
preheat the oven to 450°. Just before putting the
loaves in, slash them with either three long, curved
slashes or slashes going both ways in a tic-tac-toe
pattern. Brush with water. Slip the loaves onto
your hot surface, pulling away the paddle with a
firm jerk, or place the baking sheets in the oven.

Bake 15 minutes at 450°, then lower the heat to
375° and continue baking another 20 minutes or
until the loaves are nicely browned, crusty, and
hollow-sounding when tapped on the bottom. Cool
on racks.

To make small round loaves: High, puffy round loaves—roughly the size of a bowling ball—are popular today among U.S. commercial bakers (it's not a classic French shape), and they look attractive on the table. To emulate this crusty round loaf with a slashed top, you must have a hot oven floor so that the round immediately puffs up and the slash spreads open, as well as a steaming device. This is one instance when we would recommend using commercial bread flour because of the extra lift it will give the loaf; simply substitute for the whole wheat and white flour in the master recipe an equal amount of bread flour. Proceed the same way in the mixing, kneading, and first two rises. Then shape rounds a little bigger than a billiard ball. Let rise, covered, on a corn meal-sprinkled paddle or baking sheet until double in volume. Just before baking make a ¾-inch-deep slash all the way across the tops, plump the loaves up again, and quickly slide onto hot tiles or baking stone. Bake 25 minutes at 450°.

Sourdough

San Francisco sourdough is said to derive from a wild yeast spore peculiar to that area. Once a good starter is obtained, it is perpetuated by tearing off a hunk of the mixed dough—what the French call the *levain*—to be incorporated in the next day's bread dough.

It is not easy—perhaps because of the preservatives in most commercial flours or perhaps because there is not as much wild yeast floating around in the average kitchen—to get a successful starter going using only flour and water. More often it will spoil, separating and turning a pinkish color with a very bad odor, before it turns sour; and once it has spoiled, its leavening power is gone.

We have tried to capture yeast, using only flour and water, in our kitchen, where we bake bread often, and we have managed after 4 or 5 days, leaving it in a warm place, to obtain a pretty good starter with genuine, though not strong, sour flavor. But, in truth, when we incorporate this into a batch of dough, we do include some active dry yeast to make sure we get a well-leavened loaf.

A more foolproof method is to make your own starter with yeast and flour and water. The yeast gets the fermentation going and there seems to be less chance this way of the starter spoiling before it gets a chance to sour.

But neither method produces the pronounced tang of the genuine San Francisco sourdough. Some bread bakers add vinegar to simulate that sourness, but it's not the real thing. We'd rather settle for a less sour but at least an authentic flavor. Incidentally, the packages of dried sourdough starter sold on the West Coast don't produce anything better than you can make yourself at home.

◆ OUR SOURDOUGH STARTER

2 cups unbleached
* flour**
2 cups warm water

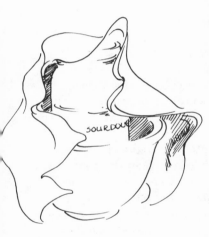

Mix 1 cup flour and 1 cup warm water together in a 1½- to 2-quart jar. Place it in a bowl of warm water and cover with cheesecloth. You want to keep the waterbath at a warm, even temperature but it should not go into an oven with a pilot light. We put our bowl in a warm spot on top of the stove, kept hot by the pilot light below, then we wrap a towel around—but not over the cheesecloth—to keep the warmth in. If you don't have this kind of range, you might try putting the bowl on an electric heating pad.

After 24 hours the mixture should be foamy. Leave another day, at which point the foam will have subsided. Stir in the remaining flour and water and leave, as before, for another 2 to 3 days.

This kind of starter is best used immediately when it is ready. It does not seem to maintain much life refrigerated, as does the yeast starter that follows.

* If you can get unbleached flour with no preservatives directly from a mill, so much the better.

◆ FOOLPROOF SOURDOUGH STARTER

1 tablespoon active dry
* yeast*
2½ cups warm water
2½ cups white flour,
* preferably*
* unbleached*

Let yeast dissolve in ½ cup warm water in a pottery or glass bowl, then stir in flour and 2 cups warm water; mix well. Pour into plastic, glass, or crockery container, cover, and let stand 3–5 days in a warm place—near but not directly over the stove pilot light is a good choice.

When the mixture is ready to use, it may be stabilized by being kept in the refrigerator. When the liquid rises to the top, mix gently with a fork to blend before using.

Feed the starter every 5 days by mixing in ⅓ cup flour and ⅓ cup warm water.

Each time the starter is used, reserve at least 1 cup, replacing the amount you have taken out with equal amounts of flour and water.

Sourdough Bread

Makes 1 large round loaf

1 tablespoon active dry
    yeast
¾ cup warm water
2 cups Foolproof
    Sourdough Starter
    (preceding recipe),
    at room temperature
1 tablespoon coarse
    salt or 2 teaspoons
    table salt
2½–3 cups white flour,
    preferably
    unbleached
Corn meal

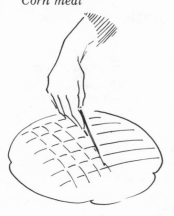

In a large bowl dissolve the yeast in the warm water. Then mix in the sourdough starter, the salt, and about 2 or 2½ cups of flour, a cup at a time, until the dough becomes hard to stir.

Turn the dough out onto a floured working surface and let it rest while you clean the bowl.

Scrape up the dough, slap it around a few times, and then knead it, adding more flour as necessary, until it is smooth and elastic—about 10 minutes. Return the dough to the clean ungreased bowl, cover with plastic wrap, and let rise until triple in bulk— 2–2½ hours.

Turn the dough out onto a floured surface, punch it down, and form into a large round loaf by molding it with your hands, stretching and tucking under, then pinching together the seams on the bottom to close them. Place on a baking sheet that you've sprinkled with corn meal, cover with a kitchen towel, and let rise until double—about 1 hour.

With a sharp knife make 6 slashes going one way and then the other in a tic-tac-toe pattern across the top of the loaf, then brush with water. Bake in a preheated 450° oven for 15 minutes, then reduce the heat to 350° and bake 25 minutes more. Cool on a rack.

Salt-Rising Bread

Until recent years leaveners have always been a challenge to home bread bakers; however, memories of a nineteenth-century salt-rising formula often cause contemporary Americans to wax nostalgic. Salt-rising bread is always tricky, and it may be more difficult if you live in an air-polluted area, but the rewarding result is worth several tries—and it reminds us of this quote from *Housekeeping in Old Virginia*: "Resolve that you *will* have good bread," Mable Cabell Tyree wrote in 1877, "and never cease striving after this result till you have effected it. If persons without brains can accomplish this, why can't you?"

Makes 1 8-inch loaf

1 cup milk, scalded
1 tablespoon sugar
2 teaspoons coarse salt
    or 1 teaspoon table
    salt
¼ cup corn meal

Remove scalded milk from heat and stir in sugar, salt and corn meal. Turn into a 2-quart jar or pitcher and set in pan of hot water (110°–115°). Let stand uncovered in a warm place 20 to 24 hours, until it ferments.* When gas escapes freely, proceed with the next step:

½ cup lukewarm water
½ cup lukewarm milk
1 tablespoon sugar
2 tablespoons
    shortening
About 3¼ cups white
    flour, preferably
    unbleached
Melted butter

Beat the water, milk, sugar, shortening, and 2¼ cups of the flour into the mixture in the jar. Put the jar or pitcher of "risin' " in a pan of hot water (115°) and let rise until the sponge is very light and full of bubbles.

Empty the sponge into a thoroughly greased warm bowl and gradually blend in the remaining cup of flour to make a stiff dough. Turn the dough out onto a floured working surface and let rest while you clean and grease the bowl again. Knead the dough until smooth. Return the dough to the bowl and let rise until double in volume—2 hours or more.

Shape into a loaf and put in well-greased loaf pan. Brush with melted butter, cover, and put in a warm place to rise. It should gain two and a half times its original bulk. Bake at 375° for 10 minutes; turn heat to 350°, and continue baking about 25 minutes.

* Mrs. Nelle Key Belle, writing to Craig Claiborne on the subject, recommended the pan of water be set on a heating pad turned on low.

Potato Bread

The French scientist Antoine-Auguste Parmentier once gave a dinner—with Benjamin Franklin among the guests—that included no dish in which potatoes were left out of the ingredients. Who made the first potato bread may not be known, but Englishmen who love toast have long preferred bread containing potatoes because it is lighter and (according to a London M.D. early in the nineteenth century) "will imbibe the butter with more freedom." Potatoes keep bread beautifully moist, producing a kind of rough-hewn loaf with subtle flavor.

Be sure to save the potato water when you boil the potatoes for mashing.

Makes two 9-inch loaves

2 tablespoons active
    dry yeast
½ cup warm water
2½ cups warm potato
    water
2 cups mashed
    potatoes
4 tablespoons (½
    stick) soft butter
2 tablespoons coarse
    salt or 4 teaspoons
    table salt
¾ cup whole wheat
    flour
8–9 cups white flour,
    preferably
    unbleached
2 teaspoons caraway
    seeds (optional)
Softened butter

In a large bowl let the yeast dissolve in the warm water.

Stir the potato water into the yeast. Whip the potatoes with the butter and the salt and beat into yeast. Stir in the whole wheat flour and 6 cups of the white flour. Beat 100 strokes. Cover with plastic wrap and refrigerate overnight.

Turn the dough out onto a very well-floured working surface. Punch down, then scrape up and knead, liberally flouring your hands and the surface as necessary. The dough will be very sticky and will absorb 2–3 cups more flour as you knead it. Add caraway seeds, if desired. When bouncy and relatively smooth— after about 10 minutes of kneading—divide in half and form 2 large loaves. Place in greased 9-inch bread pans, cover lightly with a towel, and let rise until the dough swells slightly over the tops of the pans.

Bake in a preheated 350° oven for 1 hour and 10 minutes. Rub the tops of the loaves with butter while still warm. Turn out onto racks to cool.

Saffron Bread

Saffron, the stigma of the crocus flower, has been used for hundreds of years in England's West Country to enhance bread. Some say saffron was brought to Cornwall and Devon by the Phoenicians when they arrived to operate tin mines. Whatever the facts of origin, it takes upwards of 85,000 flowers to make a pound of saffron, and cost is not surprisingly almost as out of sight as that of caviar. Fortunately, it takes only a few of the red gold threads to turn a basic white bread like this one into something that seems exotic. Each loaf you make will be infused with color and pungent flavor—the tiny red threads at the center of the deep yellow stains in the dough are sure signs of the real thing, not a substitute in powdered form that bears the saffron label.

Makes one 9-inch loaf

½ teaspoon saffron
  threads
¼ cup boiling water
1 tablespoon active dry
  yeast
1½ tablespoons sugar
⅓ cup warm water
1¼ cups buttermilk
1 tablespoon butter
2 teaspoons coarse salt
  or 1 teaspoon table
  salt
3–3½ cups white flour,
  preferably
  unbleached
Softened butter

Steep the saffron in the boiling water and set aside to cool. In a medium-size bowl dissolve yeast and sugar in the warm water, and let stand until yeast starts to swell.

Warm half of the buttermilk with the butter and salt to dissolve; stir in the remaining buttermilk and the saffron and its marigold-colored liquid. Combine with yeast, mix well, and beat in 3 cups or more of flour until mixture is hard to stir. Turn out on floured surface and knead, adding a little more flour as necessary, until smooth and resilient.

Clean the mixing bowl and butter it. Put the dough in, turning to coat. Cover with plastic wrap and let rise slowly in a cool place (even the refrigerator) until more than double in bulk—2 hours or more (4 if refrigerated).

Punch down and form a loaf. Place in a buttered 9-inch loaf pan and let rise, covered loosely, at room temperature until double in volume. Bake in preheated 425° oven for 10 minutes, reduce heat to 350°, and bake 25 minutes more. Remove to a rack, and brush the top with soft butter.

Tofu Bread

Increasing numbers of Americans seem to be discovering that they are allergic to milk products, our niece Sally among them. She urged us to develop a recipe for a bread more nourishing than one using just water as the liquid, and after many experiments we arrived at this loaf which is made with highly nutritious tofu or bean curd cakes (see page 34 for more about tofu).

Makes one 8-inch loaf

2 cakes (about 12 ounces) tofu or bean curd

1 tablespoon active dry yeast

½ cup warm water

1 tablespoon coarse salt or 2 teaspoons table salt

2 tablespoons brown sugar or homemade barley malt (see page 36)

2 tablespoons vegetable oil

1 cup whole wheat flour

2½–3 cups white flour, preferably unbleached

Bring tofu to room temperature if it is cold, and mash it either with a fork or by spinning it in a food processor.

In a medium-size bowl dissolve the yeast in the warm water. Stir in the salt, brown sugar or barley malt, oil, mashed tofu, whole wheat flour, and as much of the white flour as can easily be incorporated.

Turn the dough out onto a floured work surface and let rest while you clean the bowl and oil it. Knead the dough, adding more flour as necessary, for 8–10 minutes until it is smooth and elastic. Return it to the bowl, cover with plastic wrap, and let rise until double in volume (this dough rises more slowly than usual and may take 2 hours).

Turn the dough out, punch it down, and form into an 8-inch loaf. Oil an 8-inch bread pan, tuck the loaf in, cover loosely with a kitchen towel, and let rise until double again in size.

Bake in a preheated 350° oven for 45 minutes. Turn out of the pan and cool on a rack.

No-knead Batter Bread

The chief distinction of loaves that are formed of dough mixed by beating instead of kneading—hence the name batter breads— goes back to ancient times; in fact, the English term may have first been used in the Middle Ages. Batters that contain eggs make richer breads, and the addition of yeast produces soft, feathery loaves. We prefer baking this bread in small loaf pans, and it is so quickly made that very often you can start the bread as you prepare a meal and have a warm loaf ready to eat with it. This batter bread is also delicious toasted.

Makes four 5½-inch loaves

1 tablespoon active dry
  yeast
½ cup warm water
1 cup milk
3 tablespoons butter
2 tablespoons cottage
  cheese
2 eggs, beaten
3 tablespoons honey
2 teaspoons coarse salt
  or 1½ teaspoons
  table salt
4 cups white flour,
  preferably
  unbleached

Put the yeast in a large bowl and pour the warm water over it.

Heat the milk with the butter just long enough to melt the butter. Stir in the cottage cheese, beaten eggs, honey, and salt. Pour this over the dissolved yeast and stir in the flour; the consistency will be a little thicker than thick cake batter. Beat at least 100 strokes by hand or for 1 minute with an electric beater at medium speed. Cover with plastic wrap and let stand in a warm place for 1 hour, when the batter will almost have tripled in volume.

Stir the batter down and spread it evenly into 4 small greased loaf pans (if you don't have enough 5½-inch loaf pans, use casserole dishes 3–4 inches across). The batter will be very gummy and you will have to cut the dough off and into the pans. Let rise until it just swells to the tops of the pans—about 20–25 minutes.

Bake in a preheated 350° oven for 35 minutes. Cool on racks, although this bread may be eaten while still warm.

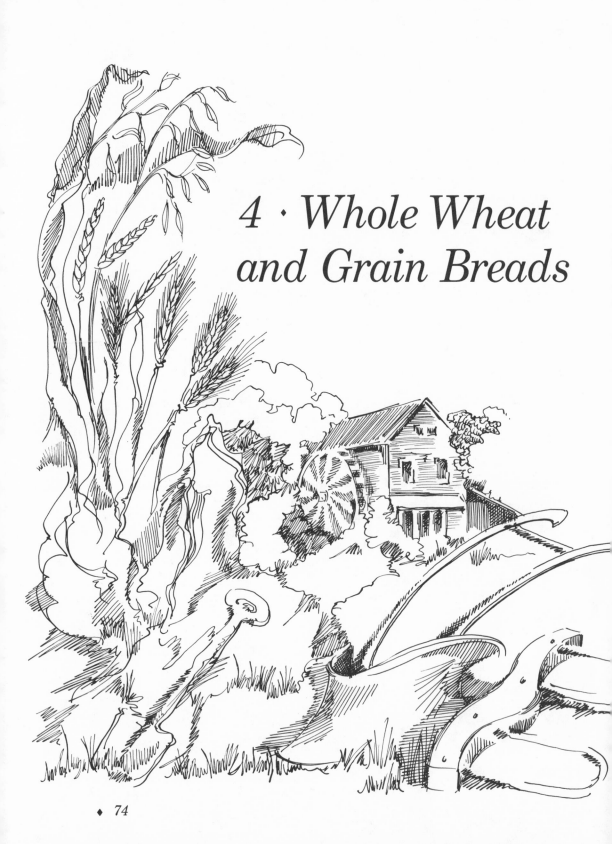

4 · Whole Wheat and Grain Breads

Whole Wheat Bread
100 Percent Whole Wheat Bread
Herb Wheat Bread
Coburg Loaf
Oatmeal Cottage Loaves
Wheat Flake and
    Maple Whole Wheat Bread
Mixed Grains Bread
Anadama Bread
Caspian Pond Sunday Corn Bread
Oatmeal-Corn Meal Bread
Broa—Portuguese Corn Bread
Walden Wheat Corn Bread
Toasted Cracked Wheat
    and Honey Bread
Buckwheat Groats or
    Kasha Bread
Bran Buckwheat Bread
Sunflower Wheat Bread
Sprouted Wheatberry Bread

Philpy
Toasted Brown Rice Flour Bread
Brown Rice Bread
Wild Rice Flour Bread
Millet Bread
Semolina Bread
Moroccan or Tunisian Bread
Barley Bread with
    Malt Syrup
Welsh Barley Bread
Barley Bread with
    Pearl Barley
Oat Flour and
    Maple Syrup Bread
Pure Triticale Bread
Starch-free Jerusalem
    Artichoke Flour Bread
Shredded Wheat Bread
Lumberjack Mush Bread

A few years back there was news from antiquity. An archaeologist who had found a small number of grains in a burial site that was four thousand years old exposed them to sunlight and watched with surprise when those grains, so long kept sealed in an ancient container, began to sprout. It is not certain what kind of grains they were, but specialists compared them with millet, one of the oldest of the seeds that have fed mankind.

Today few people may worship grain as a god—as was true in many primitive cultures. But the new awareness of whole grains and fiber content in healthful diets has helped many of us to rediscover the goodness of bread made from whole grains as well as the enjoyment of the natural flavor of flour that hasn't been overrefined. Another thing: there is almost no end to the various combinations that can be tried in baking loaves that are based on whole grain flours. In fact, this chapter is composed of several dozen recipes resulting from our kitchen experiments. Try them, and then take off on your own.

Whole Wheat Bread

Bread that is characterized as whole wheat naturally enough must be produced from whole wheat flour, but when refined whole wheat kernels and white flour are combined as they are in this recipe, the resulting bread has more gluten. Because of the gluten in the white flour the dough will rise more actively and the loaves will be airier and lighter and slice more easily than if the bread were 100 percent whole wheat (as in the following recipe).

Makes two 8-inch loaves

1 ½ tablespoons active
   dry yeast
½ cup warm water
2 cups milk
4 tablespoons butter
¼ cup honey,
   molasses, brown
   sugar, or
   combination
1 tablespoon coarse
   salt or 2 teaspoons
   table salt
2–3 cups white flour,
   preferably
   unbleached
3 cups stone-ground
   whole wheat flour
½ cup wheat germ

In a large bowl dissolve yeast in warm water. Warm half the milk and stir in the butter, sweetener, and salt. Add remaining milk and when cool to the touch combine with the dissolved yeast. Add 2 cups of the white flour, the whole wheat flour, and the wheat germ; blend thoroughly.

Turn out on a floured surface; let rest while you clean and grease the bowl. Knead the dough about 10 minutes, adding as much white flour as necessary to keep dough from sticking. When it is smooth and elastic, return the dough to the greased bowl. Let rise in a draft-free place, covered with plastic wrap, until doubled in bulk—about 1½ hours.

Punch the dough down, knead 1 minute, then shape into 2 loaves and put in greased 8-inch bread pans. Cover with a towel and let rise about 45 minutes, until dough just swells over top of pans.

Bake in preheated 425° oven 10 minutes, turn heat to 350°, and bake 25 minutes longer, until loaf sounds hollow when tapped on the bottom. Cool on racks.

100 Percent Whole Wheat Bread

Although a pure whole wheat bread may not rise as high as one that includes some white flour, it has an attractive lacy texture and it tastes deliciously wheaty. We like to make it with wheat kernels that retain their warmth from the mill after we've ground them.

Makes two 8-inch loaves

1 tablespoon active dry yeast
2½ cups warm water
2 tablespoons molasses
2 tablespoons honey
1 tablespoon coarse salt or 2 teaspoons table salt
¼ cup melted butter or safflower oil
4 cups wheat kernels* ground, or 6 cups whole wheat flour

In a large bowl dissolve the yeast in ½ cup of the warm water. Stir in the molasses, honey, salt, butter or oil, the remaining water and the flour, cup by cup, until the dough becomes hard to stir.

Turn the dough out, using the same flour to dust your work surface. Let rest while you clean out and grease your bowl. Knead the dough, adding more of the same flour as required, until it becomes smooth and loses most of its tackiness— about 8–10 minutes. Return it to the greased bowl and cover with plastic wrap. Let rise until almost double its volume—about 2 hours or more.

Punch the dough down, then shape it into two 8-inch loaves and place in greased bread pans. Cover lightly with a towel and let rise until the dough almost reaches the tops of the pans—about 1 hour or so.

Bake in a preheated 350° oven for 45 minutes. Remove the loaves and cool on racks.

* 4 cups wheat kernels ground will make 6 cups flour.

Herb Wheat Bread

When a cook remembers that in ancient Persia it was the custom for women to eat herbs with bread and cheese at the end of a meal to help them keep their husbands from submitting to temptation, it's easy enough to think of them sprinkling unbaked dough with minced herbs to add flavor as well as to protect their marital interests. This American loaf is accented by easily available garden or window-box herbs, plus a combination of dried oregano and thyme.

Makes 1 large or 2 small round loaves

1 tablespoon active dry
  yeast
1 cup warm water
1 cup warm milk
2 tablespoons sugar
1 tablespoon coarse
  salt or 2 teaspoons
  table salt
3 tablespoons chopped
  fresh parsley
2 tablespoons chopped
  fresh basil or 1
  tablespoon dried
1 tablespoon chopped
  fresh chives
1 teaspoon dried
  oregano
½ teaspoon dried
  thyme leaves
3½–4 cups white flour,
  preferably
  unbleached
1 cup stone-ground
  whole wheat flour

Put the yeast and warm water in a large bowl and
leave until yeast swells. Stir in the warm milk, the
sugar, salt, all of the herbs, 3 cups of the white
flour, and all of the whole wheat flour. Mix well
and beat with a wooden spoon for about 1 minute.
Turn the dough out on a floured surface and let
rest while you clean and grease the bowl. Knead
the dough, working in as much of the remaining
white flour as necessary until the dough is smooth
and shiny. Return the dough to the bowl, turning
to coat all over. Cover with plastic wrap and let
rise until doubled in bulk—about 1–1½ hours.

Turn dough out and knead about 1 minute.
Grease a shallow 1½-quart casserole to make 1
large loaf (use 2 small casseroles to make 2 loaves).
Shape the dough into a large round (or 2 small)
and put in the casserole(s). Let rise, covered with
a towel, for 45 minutes, until the dough swells
enough to make a rounded dome.

Brush or spray the top of the bread with cold
water and put the casserole in a preheated 375°
oven. Brush or spray top twice more in the first 10
minutes. Bake 1 hour if using large casserole, 50
minutes if using small casseroles. Remove from the
oven and let cool in the casserole if you want a
soft crust; if not, ease out of the dish and cool on a
rack.

Coburg Loaf

This is the loaf that is shaped like England's crown (see page 43). The dough should be made up of at least 7 parts whole wheat flour to one part white, and you will want to use a coarsely ground, preferably stone-ground, whole wheat flour or meal, as it is sometimes called when the whole kernel is coarsely milled. It needs a slow, cool rising to develop flavor and stability, and if you have La Cloche (see page 365), the clay oven will ensure a proper crust for this handsome crown; if you don't have one, try baking the loaf directly on tiles or a stone and cover it with a large earthenware bowl.

Makes 1 crown

1 tablespoon active dry
    yeast
3 cups warm water
1 cup white flour,
    preferably
    unbleached
7–7½ cups coarsely
    ground whole wheat
    flour
1½ tablespoons coarse
    salt or 1 tablespoon
    table salt
1 tablespoon olive oil

Make a sponge by dissolving the yeast in 1 cup of the warm water, then stirring in the white flour and 1 cup of the whole wheat flour. Beat thoroughly, then cover with plastic wrap and let stand from 1 to 4 hours.

In a large bowl mix the sponge with the remaining water, salt, and as much of the remaining whole wheat flour as you can manage to stir in. Turn the dough out on a floured working surface and let rest while you clean the bowl. Knead the dough, adding more flour as necessary, for 8–10 minutes until it is smooth and no longer tacky; it will be quite solid but with a certain elasticity. Return the dough to the ungreased bowl, rub the surface with olive oil, cover with plastic wrap, and leave in a cool place either overnight or all day if you have started in the morning.

Turn the dough out and punch it down thoroughly. Divide it in half and form two rather flat rounds 8–9 inches in diameter. Place one on

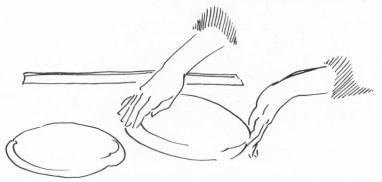

the well-greased base of La Cloche (or on a baking
sheet sprinkled with corn meal if you will be
baking on tiles or a stone instead). Brush lightly
with cold water and sprinkle just a little white
flour over the top to help make the second round,
which you will now place on top, stick. At intervals
of about 1½ inches cut with scissors deep, even
gashes all around the circumference of the top tier.
Place the dome top on and let stand 20 minutes.

Just before baking plump up the loaf again to
heighten it a bit. Bake, covered with the dome top,
in a preheated 450° oven for 10 minutes, then
lower the heat to 400° and bake another 55
minutes. If you are baking on tiles, slip the loaf
directly onto the hot surface, cover with an
earthenware bowl, and bake at 400° for 10
minutes, then lower the heat to 350° and bake
another 40 minutes. Cool on a rack.

Oatmeal Cottage Loaves

This is made in the form of an English cottage loaf—a sort of "double decker" made up of a small round loaf on top of a larger round loaf. Some cooks think it originated when ovens were too narrow to accommodate two large loaves side by side. You can also use the same recipe to make two ordinary loaves.

Makes 2 cottage loaves or 9-inch loaves

2 cups rolled oats
3 cups boiling water
4 tablespoons butter or
  vegetable shortening
¼ cup nonfat dry milk
¼ cup molasses or
  maple syrup
1 tablespoon coarse
  salt or 2 teaspoons
  table salt
2 tablespoons active
  dry yeast
½ cup warm water
2 cups whole wheat
  flour
3–4 cups white flour,
  preferably
  unbleached
⅔ cup raisins

Put the oats in a large mixing bowl and pour boiling water over them. Stir in the butter or shortening, dry milk, molasses or syrup, and salt. Let stand until cool. Be sure mixture is really cool—the only way to tell is to stir up the mixture, then stick a finger deep into it; you should be able to hold it there comfortably.

Dissolve the yeast in the warm water and add this to the oatmeal mixture. Stir in the whole wheat flour and about 3 cups of the white flour until it becomes difficult to stir.

Turn the dough out onto a floured working surface and let rest while you clean out and grease your bowl. Then start kneading, adding more white flour as necessary. It will be a very sticky dough and you'll have to keep adding more flour in order to knead, but 10 minutes and 1 additional cup of the white flour will be enough. Sprinkle the raisins over the dough and knead them in. Place the dough in the greased bowl, turning to coat. Let rise, covered with plastic wrap, until double in bulk—about 1½ hours.

Turn the dough out and divide in half.* To make cottage loaves break up each half into two pieces—one piece for the topknot, which should be a third of the total. Separate these pieces and cover with plastic wrap, leaving them simply on your work area, for 45 minutes.

Now take one of the larger pieces and pat it out into a flat 7-inch circle. With a sharp knife, make

* If you want to make regular baking pan loaves, simply form into the usual loaf shapes and place in 2 greased 9-inch bread pans. Cover and let rise 45 minutes, then bake in a 375° preheated oven for 45 minutes.

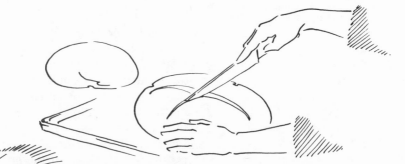

a cross about 1½ inches across. Shape one of the smaller pieces into a ball and place it on top of the circle. Now making a cone of your thumb and fingers, thrust them through the center of the topknot straight down through into the circle base of the dough to form a hole. Repeat the same procedure with the other two pieces. With a spatula transfer the loaves onto greased baking sheets. Let rest 10 minutes.

Place the baking sheets on the lowest shelf of an *unlit* oven and set the temperature at 450°. As the oven heats up the loaves will expand, which is fun to watch if your oven has a glass door and a light inside. After 25 minutes, check to see if the loaves are getting too brown on top; if so, cover them with foil. They'll need a total of 40 minutes baking. Then remove the loaves and cool on racks.

Wheat Flake and Maple Whole Wheat Bread

Tender, crunchy, chewy, light—these are words for the wheat flakes we found one day in a natural food store in Vermont's Northeast Kingdom. Processed by modern machinery but untainted by sugar or chemical additives, they are golden brown scales a little like thin shavings of butternut that are wonderful to munch as they come, and their unusual taste and texture inspired this recipe, which proves also that it's not necessary to use the most expensive "fancy" grade of maple syrup in cooking—Grade B does equally well. It's also worth noting here that maple syrup has an advantage over honey as a natural sweetener because honey loses its nutritional value when overheated while maple syrup is unaffected.

Makes one 9- or 10-inch loaf

1 tablespoon active dry
   yeast
½ cup warm water
2 cups buttermilk
3 tablespoons butter
2 teaspoons coarse salt
   or 1 teaspoon table
   salt
⅓ cup maple syrup
1½ cups wheat flakes
1½ cups whole wheat
   flour
2–2½ cups white flour,
   preferably
   unbleached

In a large bowl dissolve the yeast in the warm water. Heat the buttermilk and butter just long enough to melt the butter, cool to lukewarm, then stir into the yeast along with the salt and maple syrup. Stir in the wheat flakes, whole wheat flour, and enough of the white flour until the dough starts to leave the sides of the bowl.

Turn the dough out onto a floured working surface and let rest while you clean out and grease the bowl. Knead the dough, adding more white flour as necessary, until it is smooth and resilient—about 5–8 minutes. Return the dough to the bowl, turning to coat with grease, and cover with plastic wrap. Let rise until double in volume—about 1 hour.

Turn the dough out, punch it down, then shape into loaf that will fit into an 9- or 10-inch greased bread pan. Cover with a towel and let rise about 40 minutes.

Bake in a preheated 350° oven for 50 minutes. Turn the loaf out and let it cool on a rack.

Mixed Grains Bread

You don't have to be a health food buff to recognize the inherent life-giving force of six different grains—wheat-soy grits (now conveniently packaged), rolled oats, stone-ground corn meal, wheat flour, bran flakes—in a single bread. The texture itself is graphic evidence of nutritive value. We think of it as an entire breakfast in a slice (toasted, preferably), yet the white flour keeps it from being obnoxiously heavy.

Makes three 8-inch loaves

2 cups boiling water
1 cup stone-ground
   corn meal

In a large bowl pour the boiling water over corn meal, wheat-soy grits, and rolled oats, and set aside to cool.

1 cup wheat-soy grits
  (85 percent bulgar
  wheat plus 15
  percent soy grits)*
1 cup rolled oats
2 tablespoons active
  dry yeast
⅓ cup warm water
3½ cups white flour,
  preferably
  unbleached
1½ cups whole wheat
  flour
1 cup bran flakes
1 cup plain yogurt
1 cup milk
⅓ cup firmly packed
  dark brown sugar
¼ cup peanut oil
2 tablespoons coarse
  salt or 4 teaspoons
  table salt

In a small bowl dissolve the yeast in the warm water.

Stir white and whole wheat flour into wheat-soy grits mixture and stir in the yeast; add bran flakes, yogurt, milk, sugar, oil, and salt, and continue stirring until thoroughly blended, and the dough is stiff.

Turn dough out on a floured surface and let rest while you clean the bowl and grease it with peanut oil. Knead the dough, adding more white flour as necessary, for 10 minutes. When the dough is smooth, form it into a ball and put it in the greased bowl; turn it so it becomes coated all over. Cover with plastic wrap and let rise until double in bulk—about 2 hours.

Punch the dough down, and divide in thirds. Form into 3 loaves, and put them in 3 oiled 8-inch loaf pans. Let loaves rise, covered by a towel, for 1 hour, until doubled. Bake in preheated 375° oven 50 minutes. Turn out onto rack to cool.

*If you can't find wheat-soy grits, use instead a combination of cracked wheat and grits or additional cornmeal.

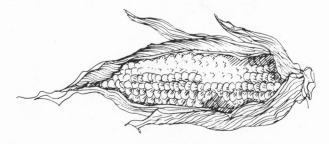

Anadama Bread

For generations this bread was a New England secret. They used to tell a story at Rockport, Massachusetts, about a Yankee whose wife was so lazy and uncaring that one day she left him in the midst of preparing the corn meal mush that, with a pitcher of molasses, was all she had planned for supper. Angrily the husband tossed the mush and molasses together, added flour and yeast, and muttered over and over, "Anna, damn 'er!" As the bread he thus contrived became better known, polite society memorialized the incident by naming the delicious but accidental bread Anadama.

ANADAMA BREAD, CONTINUED

Makes two 8-inch loaves

*1 tablespoon active dry
yeast*
½ cup warm water
*2 tablespoons butter or
other shortening*
½ cup molasses
2¼ cups hot water
*4–5 cups white flour,
preferably
unbleached*
*2 teaspoons coarse salt
or 1 teaspoon table
salt*
1½ cups corn meal

In a large bowl dissolve the yeast in the warm water. Melt the butter or shortening and molasses in hot water, then cool to lukewarm and stir into the yeast mixture. Mix 4 cups of flour with salt and corn meal and—1 cup at a time—blend this into yeast-molasses mixture; continue to add flour until you have a stiff dough.

Turn out onto a floured board and let rest while you clean and grease your bowl. Knead the dough for 10 minutes, adding flour as necessary to achieve smooth and elastic consistency. When the dough springs back from the pressure of your finger, put it in the greased bowl and turn to coat all over. Cover with plastic wrap and let rise until it doubles in bulk—about 1 hour.

Punch down, knead again for a minute or two, then shape into 2 loaves. Place in greased 8-inch bread pans. Cover with a towel and let rise again in a warm place until dough has risen over tops of pans by about ½ inch—about 40 minutes.

Bake in preheated 400° oven for 15 minutes, then reduce heat to 350°; continue baking 35–40 minutes longer. Remove and cool on racks.

Caspian Pond Sunday Corn Bread

In parts of the South, and among purists in Rhode Island, only white corn meal is considered acceptable for good bread. Water-ground white flint corn "is silkier and sweeter by far than most varieties," an old Yankee once said. "Down East yellow meal is something you feed to chickens or to swine." Nevertheless, kiln-dried stone-ground meal gives flavor and character to this family favorite.

Makes 2 round loaves 8 inches in diameter

*1½ tablespoons active
dry yeast*

In a small bowl dissolve the yeast and honey in the warm water. Put the fat in a large bowl, add

2 tablespoons honey
½ cup warm water
3 tablespoons chicken
  or goose fat
1 cup hot water
1 teaspoon salt or ½
  teaspoon table salt
3–3½ cups white flour,
  preferably
  unbleached
1 cup yellow corn meal

hot water and salt, set aside to cool, then stir in the dissolved yeast and enough flour to make a moist dough. Turn out on floured working surface and work in the corn meal, kneading about 10 minutes.

Clean the bowl, grease it, and return the dough to it, turning to coat. Cover with plastic wrap and let rise until it doubles in bulk—about 1 hour.

Punch the dough down, knead a little, divide, and form into 2 round loaves. Place in 8-inch buttered pie tins, cover with towel, and let rise, once more doubling in bulk—about 40 minutes.

Bake in a preheated 350° oven 45 minutes. Remove from the tins and cool on racks.

Oatmeal Corn Meal Bread

This combination of oatmeal and corn meal gives you an oatmeal-flavored bread with a little crunch. Don't let it rise too much in the pans—the bread will slice more easily if it's not too airy.

Makes two 8-inch loaves

2 cups oatmeal or
  rolled oats
⅔ cup corn meal
2 cups boiling water
1 cup cold milk
¼ cup molasses
2 tablespoons active
  dry yeast
⅓ cup vegetable oil
1½ tablespoons coarse
  salt or 2 teaspoons
  table salt
1 cup whole wheat
  flour, preferably
  stone-ground
4–4½ cups white flour,
  preferably
  unbleached

In a large bowl mix the oatmeal and corn meal together and pour boiling water over. Let stand about 10 minutes.

Add the milk and molasses to the oatmeal mixture and stir. When cool enough—test by sticking your finger deep into the warm mixture and be sure you can hold it there comfortably for a minute—sprinkle on the yeast. Then stir to mix along with the oil, salt, whole wheat flour, and enough of the white flour until the dough becomes hard to stir.

Turn the dough out onto a floured working surface and let rest while you wash out and oil your bowl. Knead the dough, adding more white flour as necessary—it will be sticky and eat up a lot. After 8–10 minutes the dough should have lost its tackiness and be smooth and resilient. Return it to the bowl, cover with plastic wrap, and let rise until double in volume.

When it has doubled, punch it down, and let it rise again until double. This step is not absolutely necessary, but the bread develops more flavor, we find, with the additional rising.

Turn the dough out, punch it down, and form into two 8-inch loaves. Place in oiled bread pans—they will be quite full—and let rise only a third again as much until the loaves swell slightly over the pans.

Bake in a preheated 375° oven for 10 minutes, then lower the heat to 350° and bake another 45 minutes. Turn out and cool on racks.

Broa—Portuguese Corn Bread

In the rugged north country of Portugal, where the cooking is outstanding, this airy corn bread is served with the kale, bean, and sausage soup known as *caldo verde*. On Martha's Vineyard the wives of Portuguese fishermen, who originated in the Azores, also make *broa*, preferring the white meal that comes from flint corn. It is excellent with almost any hearty soup, with a good tossed salad, or at breakfast when cut into wedges and generously buttered.

Makes 4 to 6 servings

1 tablespoon active dry
  yeast
1 teaspoon sugar
¼ cup lukewarm water
1 cup boiling water
1½ cups white or
  yellow corn meal
1½ teaspoons coarse
  salt or 1 teaspoon
  table salt
1½ tablespoons olive
  oil
2 cups white flour,
  preferably
  unbleached

In a small bowl mix yeast and sugar with warm water and let stand until dissolved.

Pour the boiling water over the corn meal and the salt in a large bowl and beat until smooth. Add the olive oil and let cool. When the corn meal mixture has cooled to lukewarm (stick a finger deep into it to make sure), mix in the yeast and, stirring constantly, gradually add the flour. Cover with plastic wrap and leave for about 30 minutes, or until it doubles in volume. Coat the bottom and sides of a 9-inch pie pan with olive oil.

Turn the dough out on a lightly floured surface and punch it down. Knead for about 5 minutes, adding more flour as necessary—no more than 1 cup—until the dough has lost most of its stickiness and is firm. Shape it into a round flat loaf and place it in the oiled pan. Cover the loaf lightly with a towel and set it aside for about 30 minutes, until it doubles again.

Bake in a preheated 350° oven for about 40 minutes. Cool on a rack and serve from the pan.

Walden Wheat Corn Bread

Baking bread "before my fire outdoors on a shingle," and finding dough consisting of "a mixture of rye and Indian meal most convenient and agreeable," as he says in *Walden,* Henry David Thoreau produced loaves not unlike those that result from this recipe. (The name, however, comes from the coincidental fact that our country kitchen is in the township of Walden, named for a Vermont soldier.) "Indian meal," or corn meal, is now easily found in supermarkets, but the best quality is still the kind ground by buhrstones often powered by water wheels. The pleasure of this particular bread lies in its crustiness—with a soft interior that is moist and not too sweet. It makes a hit with a crowd when served from a skillet.

Makes one 12-inch round

1 tablespoon active dry
  yeast
½ cup warm water
2 tablespoons honey or
  brown sugar
1 teaspoon coarse salt
  or ½ teaspoon table
  salt
¾ cup corn oil
2 eggs
1½ cups milk
1½ cups yellow corn
  meal
½ cup wheat germ
½ cup whole wheat
  flour
1½–2 cups white flour,
  preferably
  unbleached
2 tablespoons butter

In a large bowl let the yeast dissolve in the warm water along with the honey or brown sugar. Beat in the salt, oil, eggs, and milk. Then add the corn meal, wheat germ, whole wheat flour, and about 1½ cups of the white flour to make a very soft dough. Cover with plastic wrap and set the bowl in a warm place for 45–60 minutes until it has swollen to about twice its volume.

Stir down the mixture and add a little more white flour if needed—you want a soft but not a runny dough. Melt the butter in a 12-inch iron skillet and when sizzling turn the dough into the pan, spreading it to even it out. Bake immediately in a preheated 425° oven for 20 minutes. Serve warm from the skillet.

Toasted Cracked Wheat and Honey Bread

Cracked wheat, or bulgur, is common in many Middle Eastern cuisines and is cooked in many ways. It probably was first used unconsciously long ago, when larger fragments of wheat kernels were not strained out of hand-ground flour. When toasted, in any event, the bits of wheat kernels add surprising flavor as well as texture to loaves like this one, in which we've also used dark honey to point up what seems to be all the richness of a grain field harvest.

Makes two 8-inch loaves

1½ cups fine cracked
  wheat
2 tablespoons active
  dry yeast
2½ cups warm water
¼ cup nonfat dry milk
¼ cup dark honey,
  such as buckwheat
  or avocado
1 egg
1 tablespoon coarse
  salt or 2 teaspoons
  table salt
3 tablespoons soft
  butter
1½ cups whole wheat
  flour
3½–4 cups white flour,
  preferably
  unbleached
Milk

Put the cracked wheat into a medium-size iron skillet and toast, stirring a little at first, then constantly, for about 5 minutes until the kernels begin to darken a little and you can smell the wheat cooking; don't let it get dark brown. Remove from the heat and cool.

In a large bowl dissolve the yeast in ½ cup of the warm water. Stir in the dry milk, honey, and remaining water. Beat in the egg and the salt and soft butter. Add the whole wheat flour, stirring, and then, cup by cup, the white flour until the dough begins to get stiff.

Turn the dough out onto a floured working surface and let rest while you clean out the bowl and butter it. Knead the dough, adding more flour as necessary, for 7–8 minutes until it loses its tackiness and feels resilient and relatively smooth. Place it in the buttered bowl, cover with plastic wrap, and let rise until double in volume—about 1½ hours. If you want, put it in the refrigerator overnight; this is a dough that develops even more flavor with a slow, cool rising.

Turn the dough out, punch it down, and form into two 8-inch loaves. Place in buttered loaf pans, cover lightly with a towel, and let rise again until almost double in volume—45 minutes to over an hour depending on how cold the dough is.

Bake in a preheated 375° oven for 45 minutes. Halfway through the baking, brush the tops with milk. Let the loaves cool on racks.

Buckwheat Groats or
Kasha Bread

Pancakes made of buckwheat are famous in Brittany and Russia as well as the United States, but because buckwheat is not a cereal—it belongs to the same botanical family as rhubarb—and has almost no gluten content it is not used often in breadmaking. In Russia and eastern Europe buckwheat kasha is cooked like bulgur (cracked wheat) and served as a vegetable, and this is one of the forms in which buckwheat contributes to give bread unusual flavor. A recipe for molasses-flavored nut and buckwheat biscuits can be found on page 245.

Makes two 9-inch loaves

*1 cup buckwheat
   groats (kasha)*
1 egg, lightly beaten
2 cups hot water
*2 tablespoons active
   dry yeast*
½ cup warm water
*4 cups white flour,
   preferably
   unbleached*
*1½ cups lukewarm
   milk*
½ cup rye flour
*¼ cup firmly packed
   dark brown sugar*
*1 tablespoon coarse
   salt or 2 teaspoons
   table salt*
Vegetable oil

In a saucepan combine buckwheat groats and the egg, and cook, stirring, over medium heat until grains separate. Add the hot water, bring to a boil, cover, and simmer about 20 minutes, until the groats are fluffy and tender; use a fork to stir air into the mixture.

In a large bowl dissolve the yeast in the warm water until it starts to swell. Stir in the white flour, buckwheat groats, milk, rye flour, sugar, and salt. When the mixture is well blended it will form a stiff dough. Turn it out on a floured surface and let rest while you clean and grease the bowl.
Knead 10 minutes, adding white flour as necessary to make the dough smooth. Form it into a ball and put in the greased bowl, turning it to coat all over. Cover with plastic wrap and let rise 1½–2 hours, until doubled.

Punch the dough down, cover with a towel, and let it rise 1 hour longer, until it doubles again.

Turn the dough out, divide it, and form each half in loaves. Put in 2 oiled 9-inch loaf pans. Cover with a towel and let rise about 45 minutes, until the loaves double in size.

Bake in a preheated 350° oven 1 hour. Turn loaves onto a rack to cool.

Bran Buckwheat Bread

Buckwheat flour, as called for below, may be ordered by mail or purchased in health food stores, or you can grind your own from groats. A quick buckwheat biscuit (page 245) may be made with baking powder and a little molasses, but the recipe here is unusual in calling for bran flakes as well as whole wheat flour. It's a healthy, fibrous, earthy bread.

Makes two 8-inch loaves

2 tablespoons active
  dry yeast
3 cups warm water
1 cup bran flakes
1 cup buckwheat flour
⅓ cup brown sugar
¼ cup safflower oil
1 tablespoon coarse
  salt or 2 teaspoons
  table salt
2½–3 cups whole
  wheat flour
2½–3 cups white flour,
  preferably
  unbleached

In a large bowl dissolve the yeast in the warm water. Stir in the bran flakes, buckwheat flour, brown sugar, oil, salt, and about 2 cups each of the whole wheat and white flour. At this point the dough should be quite stiff and hard to stir.

Turn the dough out onto a floured working surface to rest while you clean and grease your bowl. Knead the dough, adding more of the whole wheat and white flour as necessary; this will be quite a tacky dough and will absorb a lot more flour as you knead, but 10 minutes of kneading should be enough. Put the dough in the greased bowl, turning to coat. Cover with plastic wrap and let rise until double in bulk—about 1½ hours, maybe 2 hours.

Turn the dough out, punch it down, and form it into 2 loaves. Place in greased 8-inch bread pans—they will be quite full. Don't let it rise too long this time or the bread will be crumbly—about 35 minutes, uncovered.

Bake in a preheated 350° oven for 50 minutes. Turn out onto a rack to cool.

Sunflower Wheat Bread

To make your own sunflower meal, all you need do is buy the hulled seeds at a natural foods store, then spin them in a blender, about ⅓ cup at a time, until they are pulverized, or put through a flour mill, if you have one. If there are small bits left that aren't as finely ground, we've found that only adds a certain pleasant texture to the bread. This is a loaf that's not only nutritious and tantalizing in flavor, but makes one want to go out and plant millions of sunflowers to provide more of this source of protein to stretch the waning wheat of the world.

Makes one 10-inch loaf or two 8-inch loaves

1 tablespoon active dry
  yeast
½ cup warm water
1½ cups boiling water
3 tablespoons honey
2 teaspoons coarse salt
  or 1 teaspoon table
  salt
2 tablespoons butter
¼ cup nonfat dry milk
1¾ cups sunflower
  meal (see note
  above)
1½–1¾ cups white
  flour, preferably
  unbleached
1⅓–1¾ cups whole
  wheat flour

Place the yeast in a large bowl and pour the warm water over it. Let stand until it is dissolved and starts to swell.

Meanwhile mix the boiling water, honey, salt, butter, and dry milk together until everything is dissolved and well blended, then let cool to lukewarm. Add to the yeast and mix well. Add all of the sunflower meal and about 3 cups of the white and whole wheat flours combined, mixing until the dough becomes hard to stir. Turn out onto a floured working surface and let rest 3–4 minutes while you clean and grease your bowl liberally. Then knead for 10 minutes, adding more flour as necessary, until the dough is smooth and resilient; it will probably still be a bit sticky because a dough of this kind of meal seems to want to keep on absorbing flour the more you knead. Put the dough in the greased bowl, turning to coat. Let rise, covered with plastic wrap, until double in bulk—about 2 hours.

Turn the dough out, punch it down, and form into 1 large or 2 small loaves. Place in greased 10-inch pan or two 8-inch pans; cover lightly with a towel. Let rise until double in bulk, about 1 hour.

Bake in a preheated 425° oven for 10 minutes, then lower the heat to 350° and bake another 50 minutes for the large loaf, 40 for the smaller. Turn out and cool thoroughly on racks. This bread is better not sliced for 6–8 hours.

Sprouted Wheatberry Bread

Wheat sprouts are among the most nutritious, with good protein, C and E vitamins, and vitamin B complex, and those who know best say that hard wheat kernels sprout better than soft. You'll have to start sprouting the wheat berries three days before you make this bread.

Makes two 8-inch loaves

¼ *cup wheatberries or*
  kernels
1 *tablespoon active dry*
  yeast
2¼ *cups wheatberry*
  sprouting liquid
2 *tablespoons dark*
  brown sugar
3 *tablespoons nonfat*
  dry milk
1 *tablespoon coarse*
  salt or 2 teaspoons
  table salt
2 *tablespoons butter or*
  shortening
2½ *cups graham flour*
2½–3 *cups white flour,*
  preferably
  unbleached

Three days ahead put the wheatberries in a 2-quart glass jar, and follow the directions for sprouting them on page 36. Be sure, however, to reserve 2¼ cups of the drained warm water from the last rinsing.

Now put the yeast in a large mixing bowl, pour ¼ cup of the berry sprout liquid over it, and mix in the brown sugar. Let stand until the yeast is dissolved and starts to swell.

Meanwhile mix the dry milk, salt, and butter or shortening with the remaining berry water, heating it a little if necessary to melt the butter. Cool to lukewarm, then pour onto the yeast and mix well. Add the graham flour, the sprouted berries, and all but ½ cup of the white flour; mix until you have a stiff dough. Turn out onto a floured work surface and let rest while you clean and grease your bowl. Knead the dough, adding more of the white flour as necessary until you have smooth resilient dough, about 8–10 minutes. Place the dough in the greased bowl, turning to coat. Cover with plastic wrap and let rise to double its volume—about 1½–2 hours.

Punch down the dough and leave to rise again—about 1 hour.

Turn the dough out, form 2 loaves, and place in greased 8-inch bread pans. Cover lightly with a towel and let rise until double in volume—about 45 minutes.

Bake in a preheated 425° oven for 10 minutes, then lower the heat to 350° and bake another 35 minutes. Turn out of the pans and cool on a rack.

Philpy

In antebellum days, many southern breads took the names of the plantations where their recipes were developed. In the same period, when rice was the most common grain raised in the Carolina Low Country and elsewhere, breads based on rice flour and/or cooked rice were highly appreciated. Philpy comes down to us with no clue to the derivation of its name, but its qualities have helped it survive in several regions, including the West Coast. It's dense, moist, almost puddinglike (note that there is no leavener), and should be served in wedges to be split and buttered liberally. Or you may simply break off pieces. Spread with jam, it's an old southern breakfast favorite.

Makes 1 round

2 eggs
2 cups cooked rice
1 cup milk
1 cup corn meal
1 tablespoon melted
    butter
1 teaspoon coarse salt
    or ½ teaspoon table
    salt

Beat the eggs lightly. Mix in the rice, milk, corn meal, butter, and salt. Beat thoroughly and pour into a round buttered shallow mold about 10 inches in diameter—a pie pan is fine.

Bake in a preheated 375° oven for about 35 minutes or until lightly browned. Serve warm from its pan.

Toasted Brown Rice Flour Bread

The way to bring out the flavor of the brown rice is by "toasting" the flour (see below). It will then give such an interesting, indefinable taste to this nourishing bread that everyone will be guessing about the nature of the secret ingredient.

Makes two 8-inch loaves

1½ tablespoons active
    dry yeast
1 cup warm water
¼ cup brown sugar
Approximately 3 cups
    whole wheat flour
2 cups brown rice flour
¼ cup safflower oil
⅓ cup wheat germ
2 teaspoons coarse salt
    or 1 teaspoon table
    salt
½ cup yogurt

Put the yeast in a large bowl and mix in the warm water and brown sugar. When thoroughly dissolved stir in 2 cups of the whole wheat flour. Cover with plastic wrap and let sit while it seethes and bubbles; this sponge can be left anywhere from 30 minutes to 2–5 hours, whatever works into your schedule.

Meanwhile heat a large, heavy skillet and toss the brown rice flour in. Brown the flour slowly over a medium-low fire, stirring constantly with a spatula and scraping the flour from the bottom as it toasts, turning the topside under; it will start to brown very quickly suddenly, so take care not to let it burn. When it's a deep café au lait color, remove from the heat and let cool.

Stir the rice flour, oil, wheat germ, and the salt dissolved in the yogurt into the sponge and add enough more whole wheat flour to make a fairly stiff dough. Turn out on a floured working surface and knead until smooth, adding more flour as necessary—about 8–10 minutes. Clean out the bowl, grease it, and return the dough to it to rise, covered, until double in bulk—about 1½ hours.

Turn the dough out and punch it down. Divide in half, form 2 loaves, and place in greased 8-inch bread pans. Cover with a towel and let rise again until almost double.

Bake in a preheated 425° oven for 10 minutes, then lower heat to 350° and bake another 30 minutes. Turn out of the pans and cool on racks.

Brown Rice Bread

This makes a wonderful chewy bread with a tantalizing flavor. The bread will slice more easily if it is baked in fairly small loaves in three pans.

Makes three 8-inch loaves

2 tablespoons active
    dry yeast
3 cups warm water
¼ cup maple syrup or
    brown sugar
⅓ cup nonfat dry milk
1 tablespoon coarse
    salt or 2 teaspoons
    table salt
2 cups cooked brown
    rice
1 cup whole wheat
    flour
6–7 cups white flour,
    preferably
    unbleached

In a large bowl let the yeast dissolve in ½ cup of the warm water. Stir the maple syrup or brown sugar, dry milk, and salt into the remaining water, then add to the yeast. Stir in the brown rice, whole wheat flour, and as much of the white flour as you can manage, then turn out onto a floured work surface while you clean out and grease the bowl.

Knead the dough, adding as much more white flour as necessary, until the dough loses its tackiness; it will be sticky and absorb a good deal of flour as you knead. Ten minutes should be enough to have a relatively smooth, resilient dough. Return it to the bowl, turning to coat with grease, cover with plastic wrap, and let rise until double in volume—about 1½ hours.

Turn the dough out, punch it down, and divide in thirds to make three 8-inch loaves. Place in greased pans and cover lightly with towels. Let rise for 45 minutes.

Bake the loaves in a preheated 375° oven for 50 minutes. Turn out onto racks to cool.

Wild Rice Flour Bread

Like wheat, wild rice is a member of the botanical family of grasses, growing on the shores of lakes instead of on prairies; the supply is very limited, and natural harvests are reserved for the Chippewas, who speak of themselves as the "wild rice" Indians. Broken kernels of wild rice are sometimes ground to make wild rice pancake mixtures, but the work of gathering wild rice is so arduous that the cost to the consumer is high, so most of it is used in whole grain dishes, as is the better-known white rice. Wild rice has more nutrients than white rice and is comparable in food value to wheat, corn, and oats, although it contains less fat. Some flour for baking is produced commercially, but it's a simple task to grind wild rice at home, either in a blender or in a flour mill if you have one.

Makes one 9-inch loaf

1 tablespoon active dry yeast
1¾ cups warm water
½ cup wild rice flour
2 teaspoons coarse salt or 1 teaspoon table salt
3 tablespoons safflower oil
3–3½ cups white flour, preferably unbleached
1 cup cooked wild rice

Put the yeast in a medium-size bowl, cover with the warm water, and let stand until dissolved. Stir in the wild rice flour, salt, oil, and enough white flour until the dough becomes hard to stir.

Turn out onto a floured work surface and let rest while you clean out and grease the bowl. Knead the dough lightly—this will be a soft dough—adding a little more flour as necessary to keep from sticking. When it starts to become smooth and elastic—after 2–3 minutes—spread out the dough, sprinkle the wild rice evenly over the surface, then roll up to distribute the rice evenly throughout. Return the dough to the greased bowl, turning to coat, cover with plastic wrap, and leave to rise until double in volume—about 1½ hours.

Turn the dough out onto a floured work surface, punch down, knead a couple of turns, then shape into a loaf and place in a greased 9-inch bread pan. Cover lightly and let rise 45 minutes.

Bake in a preheated 350° oven for 50 minutes. Turn out and let cool on a rack.

Millet Bread

A dense, beautifully textured bread with a golden wheat color, millet bread slices well, is therefore fine for sandwiches, and is also particularly good toasted. (Our recipe calls for buckwheat honey, which adds an enhancing flavor to the toast.) The bread dries out quickly, so be sure to wrap it tightly in a plastic bag and store in the refrigerator.

Makes two 9-inch loaves or three 8-inch loaves

1 tablespoon active dry yeast

3 cups warm water

1 cup nonfat dry milk

¼ cup honey, preferably buckwheat

5 cups white flour, preferably unbleached

4½–5 cups whole wheat flour

2 cups whole grain millet

1¼ tablespoons kosher salt or 2 teaspoons table salt

¼ cup vegetable oil, preferably safflower

½ cup wheat germ

1–1½ cups white flour

Put the yeast in a large bowl and pour a little warm water over it. Let it stand until dissolved. Add remaining warm water, the dry milk, the honey, and mix well. Add 3½ cups of the white flour and 3½ cups of whole wheat flour and beat about 50 strokes. Cover with plastic wrap, and let stand in a warm place for 1–3 hours.

Stir all the remaining ingredients into the sponge, holding back ½ cup of white flour.

Turn the dough out onto a floured surface, let rest a few minutes while you clean out the bowl and grease it, then knead 8–10 minutes, incorporating as much of the remaining flour as necessary until you have a smooth, elastic dough. Put the dough back in the greased bowl, turning to coat; cover with plastic wrap and let stand about 1–1½ hours, until double in bulk.

Punch down and let rise, covered, until double—about 45 minutes.

Form into 2 loaves and put in 2 greased 9-inch bread pans (or you can use three 8-inch pans). Cover lightly with a towel and let rise 30 minutes.

Bake 10 minutes in preheated 400° oven, then reduce heat to 350° and continue baking 35 minutes. Turn out of the pans and cool on racks.

Semolina Bread

One is generally told that semolina, the pure heart of the wheat kernel that is used to make pasta, is not good as a bread flour. But on a tip from James Beard, who never takes anything as gospel until he has tried it, we experimented with a loaf of pure semolina. It is excellent—the ice cream of breads, you might say. It has a lacy texture, a luscious creamy yellow color, and it tastes a little bit like a delicate corn pudding.

Makes one 8-inch loaf

1 tablespoon active dry yeast

1 ½ cups warm water

2 tablespoons soft butter

2 tablespoons nonfat dry milk

2 teaspoons coarse salt or 1 teaspoon table salt

3 cups semolina flour

In a medium-size bowl dissolve the yeast in ½ cup of the warm water. Mix the butter and the dry milk into the remaining cup of water and add to the yeast along with the salt. Stir in the semolina.

Turn the dough out onto a working surface dusted with a little more of the semolina flour and let rest while you clean out and grease your bowl. Knead the dough for 8–10 minutes until it is smooth and lively, then return it to the greased bowl. Cover with plastic wrap and let rise until double in volume—it will take about 1 ½ hours, maybe more.

Turn the dough out, punch down, then form into a loaf and place in a greased 8-inch bread pan. Cover with a towel and let rise until double—about 50 minutes.

Bake in a preheated 350° oven for 40 minutes. Turn the loaf out and let cool on a rack.

Moroccan or Tunisian Bread

French culture has impressed itself on both Morocco and Tunisia, but things as basic as Arab bread don't change in North Africa. Visiting the home of Fatima Azouz in Matmata, not far from Tunis, a bread-baking daughter of ours watched her hostess grinding grains that included semolina (seldom used for bread in this country), as well as whole wheat and rye. Although Mrs. Azouz sometimes made bread from semolina exclusively, it is at least as common in this region to mix grains, and our version of the bread called *khobz* uses semolina plus whole wheat flour and a little rye, along with the traditional accents of anise and sesame. We find it one of the most delicious breads we've ever made. The finished loaves are round and flattish with a shallow dome.

Makes 2 large rounds

*1 tablespoon active dry
  yeast*
2 cups warm water
*1 tablespoon coarse
  salt or 2 teaspoons
  table salt*
4 tablespoons olive oil
1 tablespoon aniseed
*1 teaspoon sesame
  seeds*
*1 cup whole wheat
  flour*
½ cup rye flour
*4–4½ cups semolina
  flour**

An Arab cook would mix together the flours, then make a well in the center and add the water with the yeast dissolved in it, but we find it easier to follow our usual method of dissolving the yeast in the warm water in a large bowl. Stir in the salt, olive oil, aniseed, sesame seeds, wheat and rye flour, and enough of the semolina until the dough becomes hard to stir.

Turn the dough out and let rest while you wash out the bowl. Knead the dough, adding more semolina—as much as it will incorporate; you want a stiffer-than-usual dough. When you have kneaded for about 10 minutes, divide the dough in half. Take one half in your hand and swirl it around the cleaned bowl until you have a cone shape, then plop the dough down on an oiled baking sheet or a round earthenware dish (such as the bottom of La Cloche). Repeat with remaining dough and let the loaves rise, uncovered, for 30 minutes.

Using the tines of a fork, prick the dough around the sides in four places (this helps to make the dough swell dome-shaped only in the center). Bake in a preheated 400° oven for 10 minutes, then reduce the heat to 325° and bake another 35 minutes. Remove and cool on racks.

*If semolina is not available, use white flour, preferably unbleached.

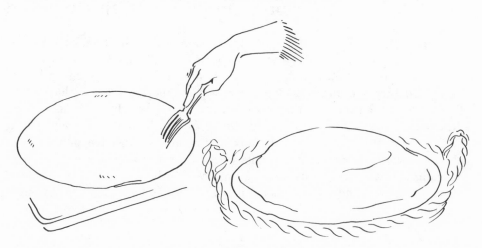

Barley Bread with Malt Syrup

Makes two 8-inch loaves

1 ½ tablespoons active
    dry yeast
2 teaspoons malt
    syrup*
3 cups warm water
¼ cup nonfat dry milk
1 tablespoon coarse
    salt or 2 teaspoons
    table salt
4 tablespoons
    vegetable shortening,
    melted
2 cups barley flour
5–6 cups white flour,
    preferably
    unbleached

In a large bowl let the yeast and malt syrup dissolve in 1 cup of the warm water. Stir in the remaining water, dry milk, salt, shortening, barley flour, and enough of the white flour to make a dough that starts to leave the sides of the bowl.

Turn the dough out on a floured surface to rest while you clean and grease the bowl. Start kneading, adding more white flour as necessary; this will be a thirsty dough that wants to consume quite a lot more flour. After about 6–8 minutes of kneading, when the dough ceases to be sticky and feels resilient, place it back in the bowl, cover with plastic wrap, and let rise until double in volume— about 1 hour.

Turn the dough out and punch it down thoroughly. Form into two 8-inch loaves and place in greased bread pans. Cover lightly with a towel and let rise until almost double again—about 40 minutes.

Bake in a preheated 400° oven for 10 minutes, then lower the heat to 350° and bake another 35 minutes. The loaves will still look quite pale, so we like to put them back in the oven, free of their pans, for another 10 minutes to get a good crust. Cool on racks.

* Or use instead 2 tablespoons homemade barley malt (see page 36) or brown sugar.

Welsh Barley Bread

There is a healthy confection called barley fudge that combines barley flakes, chopped dates, caramel syrup, cocoa, margarine, salt, and water and is steamed like brown bread, but the barley loaf the Welsh call *haidd* is a grainy dry-textured bread (note that there is no final rising) that has an earthy fragrance and is delicious when served right out of the oven with cold butter, or with honey. It's much like the barley bread made in Ireland, Scotland, and other parts of the world, including Egypt.

WELSH BARLEY BREAD,
CONTINUED

Makes one 8-inch round loaf.

1 tablespoon active dry
  yeast
1 teaspoon sugar
1½ cups warm water
3 cups barley flour
2 teaspoons coarse salt
  or 1 teaspoon table
  salt
Softened butter

In a large bowl mix the yeast, sugar, and a little of
the warm water. When yeast is swollen, add flour,
a little at a time, and salt, stirring in the
remaining water to make a well-mixed dough.
Cover with plastic wrap and let stand in a warm
place about 1½ hours; it will rise only a little.

Turn the dough out on floured surface and
knead for 2–3 minutes, then fit it into a buttered
8-inch round cake tin. Bake in preheated 400°
oven for 25 minutes. Spread softened butter over
top. Cut in wedges and eat with plenty of butter
and honey. A wedge of barley bread may be split
like an English muffin and toasted for breakfast.

Barley Bread with Pearl Barley

This is a good bread to make if you have some left-
over cooked pearl barley and have saved the water—which is what inspired us.
It makes a chewy, moist loaf, particularly good toasted. Having it for breakfast
is like having a creamy cereal and good slice of toast all in one.

Makes one 9-inch loaf

1 tablespoon active dry
  yeast
½ cup warm water
1 cup barley cooking
  water
1 cup cooked barley
2 teaspoons coarse salt
  or 1 teaspoon table
  salt

Dissolve the yeast in the warm water in a large
bowl. Add the barley water, cooked barley, salt,
barley flour, and as much of the white flour as the
dough will take before it becomes too hard to stir.

Turn the dough out onto a floured surface and
let rest while you clean and butter the bowl.
Knead the dough, adding more white flour as
necessary. It will be very sticky, but after a good 8
minutes of kneading, absorbing more flour along

WHOLE WHEAT AND GRAIN BREADS

1½ cups barley flour
2½–3 cups white flour,
    preferably
    unbleached

GLAZE

    1 egg beaten with 1
    teaspoon water

the way, it will have lost its tackiness. Return it then to the bowl, cover with plastic wrap, and let rise until double in volume, which will take at least 1½ hours.

Turn the dough out on a floured surface, punch it down, then shape it into 9-inch loaf. Place in a buttered pan, cover with a towel, and let rise until it just swells over the top of the pan—about 40 minutes.

Brush the top of the loaf with egg glaze and bake in a preheated 375° oven for 45 minutes. Turn out and cool on a rack.

Oat Flour and Maple Syrup Bread

Makes two 8-inch loaves

2 tablespoons active
    dry yeast
½ cup warm water
2 cups milk
4 tablespoons (½
    stick) butter, cut in
    bits
1 tablespoon coarse
    salt or 2 teaspoons
    table salt
3 cups whole wheat
    flour
1½ cups oat flour
1 cup gluten flour
½ cup maple syrup
1¼ cups white flour,
    preferably
    unbleached
⅓ cup dried currants

In a large bowl dissolve the yeast in the warm water.

In a saucepan combine milk, butter, and salt and heat slowly until butter melts and salt dissolves; cool mixture to lukewarm. Stir it into the yeast and add the whole wheat, oat, and gluten flours and maple syrup. Stir in enough of the white flour until it becomes hard to stir.

Turn the dough onto a floured surface and let rest while you clean out and grease your bowl. Knead, adding a little more white flour if the dough is sticky, for 10 minutes. When it is smooth, form the dough into a ball and put it in the greased bowl, rotating it to coat all over. Let it rise, covered with plastic wrap, about 1 hour, until it doubles in bulk.

Knead the currants into the dough, then divide it into halves and form each into a loaf; put loaves in 2 greased 8-inch pans. Cover them with a towel and let the loaves double in size.

Bake in preheated 375° oven 45 minutes. Put loaves on rack to cool.

Pure Triticale Bread

Triticale is a hybrid of wheat and rye whose name derives from Latin: *triticum* (wheat) and *secale* (rye), and its addition to the ingredients of packaged "high-nutrient" breads may be noted on some commercial labels. Actually, triticale has about the same nutritional characteristics as rye and the baking qualities of wheat, and it has been thought that a supplement of white flour was required to ensure good texture. In trying to produce a pure triticale loaf we arrived at the following method, with a final result that turns out to be most like those Scandinavian dense-texture pumpernickel breads so ideal for open-face sandwiches of cheese, herring, etc. If you want the flat top typical of a smorgasbord bread, bake it as a pullman loaf (see page 45). Turn to page 145 for a bread that uses half white flour with the triticale, along with honey and cheese—a very different loaf in texture and flavor.

Makes one 8-inch loaf

1 tablespoon active dry
  yeast
1¼ cups warm water
¼ cup nonfat dry milk
2 tablespoons brown
  sugar
1 tablespoon coarse
  salt or 2 teaspoons
  table salt
2 tablespoons safflower
  oil
¼ cup wheat germ
3–3½ cups triticale
  flour

In a medium-size bowl dissolve the yeast in ¼ cup of the warm water. Stir the dry milk, brown sugar, and salt into the rest of the water to dissolve, then add to the yeast along with the oil, wheat germ, and enough of the white flour until it becomes hard to stir. Turn the dough out onto a floured work surface while you clean out and grease the bowl.

Knead the dough, adding more flour as necessary, until it becomes smooth and loses almost all its tackiness. Return the dough to the greased bowl, cover with plastic wrap, and let sit until it almost doubles in volume. This will take a long time—maybe 4–5 hours—but don't let it rest longer than that.

Turn the dough out onto your work surface, knead a few turns, and form into a loaf. Place in a greased 8-inch loaf pan, cover lightly with a towel, and let rise slowly about 1½ hours. It will never swell up more than slightly.

Bake in a preheated 350° oven for 50 minutes. Let cool on a rack and let it rest several hours before slicing. Keep refrigerated tightly wrapped in plastic. Slice thin when serving.

Starch-free Jerusalem Artichoke Flour Bread

Toward the end of the eighteenth century, when the experiments of Antoine-Auguste Parmentier helped to make the potato popular, the Frenchman was also finding that Jerusalem artichokes (a tuber much used by American Indian cooks) are rich in carbohydrates as well as being starch-free. But it was not until 1925 that Anthony DeBole, a Long Islander interested in horticulture, developed the first Jerusalem artichoke flour to be used in baking and the production of pasta. Today DeBole's heirs grind flour that is sold in some specialty food stores. We've found in using it that the artichoke flavor is subtler in this bread than when the vegetable itself is used, and that the flour gives bread a soft beige mushroom color. It produces a dense loaf that slices well, and is especially recommended when spread with cream cheese.

Makes 1 double loaf in 9-inch pan

1 tablespoon active dry
  yeast
1½ cups warm water
2 tablespoons nonfat
  dry milk
2 tablespoons melted
  butter or vegetable
  oil
2 teaspoons coarse salt
  or 1 teaspoon table
  salt
1 cup Jerusalem
  artichoke flour
2½–3 cups white flour,
  preferably
  unbleached

GLAZE
1 tablespoon cream

In a large bowl dissolve the yeast in the warm water. Stir in the dry milk, butter or oil, salt, Jerusalem artichoke flour, and enough of the white flour until the dough starts to come away from the sides of the bowl.

Turn the dough out onto a floured working surface and let rest while you clean out the bowl and grease it. Knead the dough, adding more flour as necessary, until it is smooth and resilient— about 8–10 minutes. Return the dough to the greased bowl, turning to coat, and cover with plastic wrap. Let rise until double in volume; this is a slow-rising dough, and it may take 2 hours or more.

Turn the dough out, punch it down, and divide in half. Shape the pieces into loaves half the size of your 9-inch loaf pan, then place them side by side in the greased pan. Cover lightly with a towel and let rise until double in volume—at least an hour.

Bake in a preheated 350° oven for 50 minutes. Brush cream lightly over the entire exposed surface of the double loaf while still hot. Turn out and let cool on a rack.

Shredded Wheat Bread

This makes a dense moist loaf, easy to slice, and good for sandwiches because it holds together well.

Makes two 8-inch loaves

2 cups boiling water
2 shredded wheat
  biscuits
2 teaspoons coarse salt
  or 1 teaspoon table
  salt
¼ cup molasses
3 tablespoons butter or
  shortening
2 tablespoons active
  dry yeast
½ cup warm water
5–6 cups white flour,
  preferably
  unbleached

Pour the boiling water over the shredded wheat. Stir in the salt, molasses, and butter or shortening to melt. Let cool.

In a large bowl dissolve the yeast in the ½ cup of warm water. Add the shredded wheat mixture when cool and add enough flour, cup by cup, until it becomes hard to stir.

Turn the dough out onto a floured work surface and let it rest while you clean and grease the bowl. Knead the dough, adding more white flour as necessary, until you have a smooth, resilient dough—about 8–10 minutes. Return the dough to the greased bowl, cover with plastic wrap, and let rise until double in volume—about an hour or so.

Form the dough into 2 loaves and place in greased 8-inch bread pans. Cover with a towel and let rise until the dough swells to the top of the pans—about 30 minutes.

Bake in a preheated 325° oven for 50 minutes. Turn out and cool on racks.

Lumberjack Mush Bread

In the tradition of breads made with hasty pudding, or cooked grits, this loaf was devised by using as a base the packaged cereal we often purchase by mail from the Vermont Country Store at Weston. It has enough hearty flavor and natural vitamin content to fodder a platoon of Paul Bunyans.

Makes two 8-inch loaves

1 cup boiling water
2 cups Lumberjack
  Mush
2 tablespoons butter

In a large bowl pour boiling water over Lumberjack Mush; add butter, milk, and honey, mixing well. Dissolve the yeast in the warm water.

When the mush has cooled so that you can

1½ cups milk

¼ cup honey

1½ tablespoons active
dry yeast

¼ cup warm water

1 tablespoon coarse
salt or 2 teaspoons
table salt

1 cup whole wheat
flour

3–4½ cups white flour,
preferably
unbleached

½ cup gluten flour

comfortably hold your finger in it, add the dissolved yeast, the salt, whole wheat flour, about 3½ cups of the white flour, and the gluten flour. Turn this dough out on a floured surface and knead until smooth, about 8–10 minutes, adding up to ½ cup more white flour as necessary. Clean the bowl and butter it; return the dough to it and let it rise, covered, until doubled in bulk.

Turn the dough out, punch it down, shape it into 2 loaves, and fit into 2 buttered 8-inch bread pans. Let rise again loosely covered, until doubled in bulk. Bake in a 375° oven for 50 minutes. Turn out and cool on racks.

5 · Rye Breads

Beatrice's Scandinavian Rye Bread

Rye Beer Bread

*Pumpernickel Bread with
    Sourdough Starter*

Pumpernickel Bread

Limpa

Rye and Walnut Bread

Ryaninjun

Jewish Rolled Raisin Bread

American Black Bread

*Danish Wheat–Rye Bread
    with Wheat Kernels*

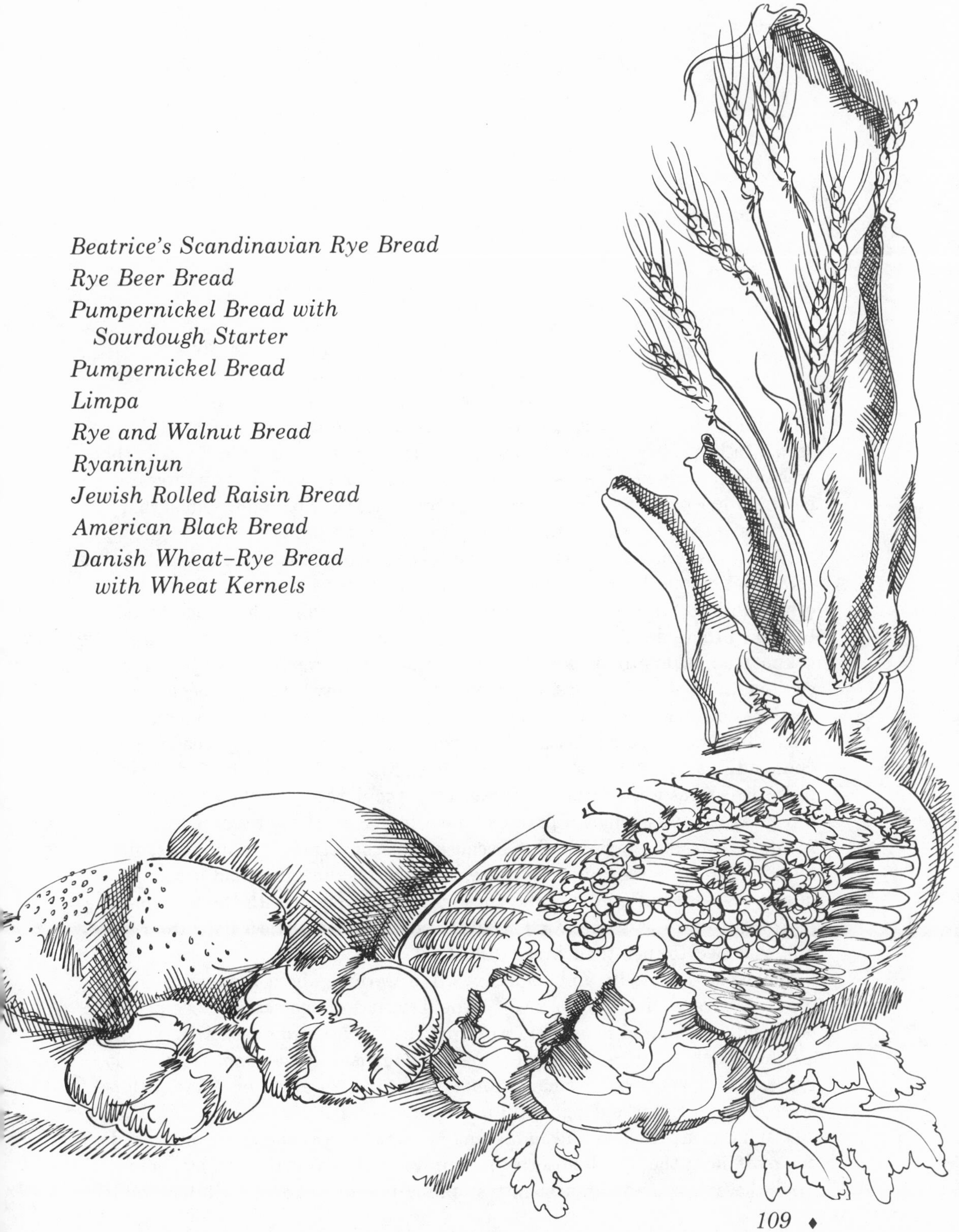

"Rye can stand alone with hardly any additional flavors," Beatrice Ojakangas once wrote, "or it can complement beautifully such flavors as molasses, orange peel, caraway, anise, and dill seed." In her memories of a Minnesota childhood she recalled the smells that greeted her on baking day when she got off the school bus. Wafting toward her from her mother's kitchen were the fragrances of "peasant breads that characterize the heartiness of the peoples they represent."

Here are a number of recipes for rye breads—some with independent flavor, some that emphasize the special rye qualities by using a sourdough starter, others with interesting accents. Among them is the type called black bread, for which there developed in the 1970s a nationwide enthusiasm that caused commercial bakers to use food coloring and other intrepid cooks to work out combinations of such things as strong coffee and unsweetened chocolate to produce soft loaves as dark as teakwood but certainly not much like any bread baked by a beleaguered peasant housewife. The primitive dark breads—dark enough to be thought of as black—resulted, first of all, from the fact that primitive grains were naturally darker than the darkest rye flour produced today. Also, it was common practice in earlier times to roast grains to facilitate threshing and grinding because heat converts starch into dextrin and, in turn, stimulates fermentation. Brewery residues that had leavening quality were also often dark, and these things combined with the fact that the poor had to deal with the worst quality and often the dirtiest flour from the miller helped to turn their bread "black."

Whatever the quality and color, a word of warning about rye flour is in order: it is very sticky to work with. You'll need a dough scraper (see page 363) and well-floured hands and working surface. A sturdy electric mixer with a dough hook is a great help kneading rye doughs in large quantity. A food processor is good, too, for smaller amounts, but be sure you have one with a strong motor, as these doughs will put a strain on it.

You'll be surprised to find in making rye breads that the more you knead, the more flour the dough absorbs; it simply insists on turning tacky again. You'll have to come to an arbitrary stopping point or else you will have added too much flour and the bread will be dry. So with these rye doughs, stop kneading when you have fulfilled the time called for in the recipe and have used up the stipulated amount of flour, even if your dough isn't smooth and satiny. It will never be like a white flour dough—but it will feel resilient and sluggishly alive.

◆

Beatrice's Scandinavian Rye Bread

An adaptation of a recipe by a talented Minnesota cook, this is similar to Sweden's classic *limpa* bread (see page 116) and is made wherever Scandinavians settle.

Makes 3 small round loaves

1 cup water
½ cup unsulfured
    molasses
Grated rind of 6
    oranges
2 tablespoons fennel
    seed, crushed
2 tablespoons caraway
    seeds, crushed
1 tablespoon butter
1 tablespoon coarse
    salt or 2 teaspoons
    table salt
2 cups buttermilk
½ teaspoon baking
    soda
2 tablespoons active
    dry yeast
¼ cup warm water
4 cups rye flour
3–4 cups white flour,
    preferably
    unbleached
GLAZE
1 tablespoon
    unsulfured molasses
    mixed with
1 tablespoon water

In a saucepan combine the water, molasses, grated orange rind, crushed fennel and caraway seeds, butter, and salt. Heat slowly until the butter melts; add the buttermilk and soda and stir. Set aside to cool.

Dissolve the yeast in warm water in a large mixing bowl. Stir in the cool molasses mixture. Add rye flour, then 3 cups of the white, a cup or so at a time, mixing thoroughly. Turn the dough out onto a floured surface, cover with plastic wrap, and let it rest 10 minutes. Clean and grease the bowl.

Knead the dough, adding more flour as required, until it is smooth and resilient—about 10 minutes. Return the dough to the greased bowl, turning to coat. Cover, and let rise about 1½ hours, until doubled in bulk.

Punch the dough down, and knead a few more turns. Divide it into 3 parts and shape each third

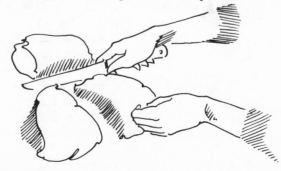

into a round loaf. Arrange on buttered baking
sheets. Use a razor blade or sharp knife to cut a
large cross about ⅓ inch deep in the center of each
loaf; the cross will open as the loaves rise under
a towel for about 1 hour, until double in bulk.

Bake in a preheated 375° oven about 35
minutes. Brush with the glaze, and bake 5 minutes
longer. Remove to racks and cool.

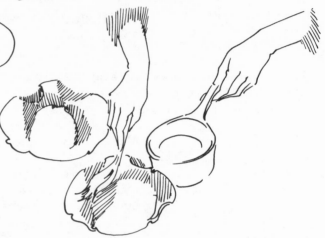

Rye Beer Bread

To make lighter bread, Celts of the Iron Age en-
couraged the fermentation of dough by adding beer barm and thus turned out
loaves much airier and more edible than those of the Romans and even earlier
bakers. In the seventeenth century Robert May, author of *The Accomplisht
Cook*, specified ale in his recipe for French bread, as indeed today do some
current French methods of making *bâtards*. The dark beer called for below
produces rich round loaves excellent for sandwiches.

Makes 2 round loaves

*1 ½ tablespoons active
    dry yeast*
½ cup warm water
*2 cups dark beer, at
    room temperature*
*2 tablespoons caramel
    (see page 35) or
    molasses*

In a large bowl dissolve the yeast in the warm
water. Stir in the beer, caramel or molasses, lard,
caraway seeds, salt, rye flour, and enough white
flour until the dough becomes difficult to stir.

Turn the dough out onto a floured working
surface and let rest while you clean out and grease
your bowl. Knead the dough, adding more white
flour as necessary; it will be very tacky, but up to

2 tablespoons lard or
vegetable fat, melted
2 tablespoons crushed
caraway seeds
1½ tablespoons coarse
salt or 1 tablespoon
table salt
3 cups rye flour
2½–3 cups white flour,
preferably
unbleached
Corn meal

3 cups of white flour in all and about 8–10 minutes of kneading should be enough. Return the dough to the greased bowl, cover with plastic wrap, and let rise until double in volume—about 2 hours.

Turn the dough out, punch it down, and form into 2 rounds. Place far apart on a greased baking sheet sprinkled with corn meal. Let rise covered with a towel until double—about 45 minutes. If you have tiles or a baking stone, heat the oven well ahead to 375° to warm them, and to get a good crust use one of the devices to create steam described on page 64.

If you don't want to bother with a steaming device, brush the loaves with cold water before they go in the oven and again two or three times during the first 10 minutes. If you have tiles or a baking stone, slip the loaves directly onto the hot surface; otherwise simply bake the loaves on the baking sheet. After 10 minutes reduce the heat to 350° and bake another 40 minutes. Cool on racks.

Pumpernickel Bread with Sourdough Starter

You have to make the starter for this bread at least a day in advance, and the bread itself requires long, slow risings to give it its deep, rich, tangy flavor. Molasses or caramel coloring will add color, and the inclusion of last week's toasted crumbs is undoubtedly a more authentic way of darkening the bread, used simply as an economical device by European peasants.

Makes two 9-inch or round loaves

THE SOURDOUGH
STARTER

1 tablespoon active dry
yeast
⅓ cup nonfat dry milk
1 cup warm water
¾ cup white flour
½ cup rye flour

Mix all the ingredients for the starter together in a medium-size bowl, beating into a smooth batter. Cover with plastic wrap and leave in a warm place, such as on top of the stove near a pilot light or close to a radiator. The starter will rise and bubble up, then sink back. It is ready to use after 24 hours.

To keep: put in a screwtop jar—1-quart size or larger, if you want to keep adding to it—and refrigerate. About every five days feed your starter ½ cup flour (3 parts white to 1 part rye) and ½ cup water mixed with 2 tablespoons dry milk. Leave, covered, in a warm place until it bubbles up again, then use what you want of it to make bread; return the rest—or all of it, if not using immediately—to the refrigerator.

Make a sponge first by mixing 1⅓ cups of the starter, the dry milk, 1½ cups warm water, 1 cup of the white flour, and 1 cup of the pumpernickel flour. Cover with plastic wrap and leave in a warm place 2–3 hours.

In a large bowl dissolve the yeast in the remaining cup of warm water. Stir in the sponge, salt, corn meal, malt or molasses or caramel, the bread crumbs or wheat germ, and the remaining flours, holding back about ¾ cup of the white flour. Turn the dough out on a floured working surface after it becomes too stiff to stir and let rest while you clean out the bowl. Knead the dough, adding more flour as necessary. The dough will be very sticky. After 10 minutes kneading, return the dough to the cleaned ungreased bowl, cover, and let rise until double in volume—about 2 hours.

Punch down the dough, knead briefly in the bowl, cover, and let rise again until double in volume—about 1½ hours.

Turn the dough out and divide in half. Either shape into 2 loaves to go into two greased 9-inch bread pans or make 2 round loaves and place far apart on a greased baking sheet sprinkled with corn meal. Let rise, covered with a kitchen towel, for about 1 hour.

Brush the loaves with glaze. Bake in a preheated 425° oven—if you have tiles or baking stone, slide the round loaves directly onto the hot surface. Bake 10 minutes, then lower heat to 350° and bake 35 minutes more. Remove and cool on racks.

THE BREAD DOUGH

*1⅓ cups of the above
     starter*
⅓ cup nonfat dry milk
2½ cups warm water
*3–3½ cups white flour,
     preferably
     unbleached*
*2–2¼ cups
     pumpernickel flour**
*1 tablespoon active dry
     yeast*
*1½ tablespoons coarse
     salt or 3 teaspoons
     table salt*
*¾ cup stone-ground
     corn meal*
*2 tablespoons
     homemade wheat or
     barley malt (page
     36) or 2 tablespoons
     molasses or caramel
     (page 35)*
*¾ cup toasted rye
     bread crumbs or
     wheat germ*
*Corn meal (for round
     loaves)*

GLAZE

*1 tablespoon molasses
     or caramel mixed
     with 1 teaspoon
     water*

---

*If you cannot get a coarse pumpernickel flour, usually available only in health food stores or mail order flour sources, use instead dark rye flour and bran in proportions of 2 to 1.

Pumpernickel Bread

Originally the coarsest of loaves, made with unbolted rye, pumpernickel is now stylishly popular, and a good dark loaf results from this recipe.

Makes 2 large round loaves

*1 tablespoon active dry
yeast
1 cup warm water
1 tablespoon carob
powder
2 cups yogurt, at room
temperature
1 ½ tablespoons coarse
salt or 3 teaspoons
table salt
4 tablespoons (¼ cup)
vegetable shortening,
melted
3 cups pumpernickel
flour or 1 cup bran
mixed with 2 cups
rye flour
2 cups whole wheat
flour
About 2 cups white
flour, preferably
unbleached
Corn meal*

GLAZE

*1 egg beaten with 1
teaspoon water
About ½ cup cracked
wheat or wheat germ*

In a large bowl dissolve the yeast in the warm water. Stir in the carob powder, yogurt, salt, and shortening (be sure it is not too hot—just warm). Mix well.

Stir in the pumpernickel or its bran-rye substitute and whole wheat flour, and almost 2 cups of the white flour until the dough gets too hard to stir. Then turn it out on a floured work surface and let rest while you clean out the bowl.

Scrape up the dough and start to knead, adding more white flour as necessary. This will be a sticky dough and will absorb flour as you knead—10 minutes will be enough even if it is still a little sticky.

Grease the cleaned bowl and return the dough to it, turning to coat. Cover with plastic wrap and let rise until double in bulk—about 2 hours.

Punch the dough down, turn it out onto a floured work surface, and divide in half. Shape each half into a large round, molding the sides down and under and pinching together the seams at the bottom.

Place the loaves on a greased baking sheet, sprinkled with corn meal, or paddles if you are using a baking stone or tiles, cover loosely with a kitchen towel, and let rise until double in bulk— about 45 minutes.

Paint the tops of the loaves all over with the egg glaze, then sprinkle either cracked wheat or wheat germ (or do one of each) generously over the surface. Put the baking sheet in a preheated 350° oven or slip the loaves on hot stone or tiles and bake for 1 hour. Remove to racks and let cool.

Limpa

Here's the classic Swedish rye loaf as we make it, after a boyhood in Minnesota.

Makes 2 round loaves

1 ½ tablespoons active
  dry yeast
3 cups warm water
¼ cup homemade
  barley or wheat malt
  (page 36)* or ½
  teaspoon commercial
1 tablespoon coarse
  salt or 2 teaspoons
  table salt
¼ cup soy oil
1 cup toasted soy flour
3 cups rye flour
1 tablespoon fennel
  seed
2 teaspoons aniseed
2 teaspoons cardamom,
  lightly crushed or
  ground
Roughly grated peel of
  4 oranges
3½–4 cups white flour,
  preferably
  unbleached

GLAZE

1 egg white beaten
  with 1 teaspoon
  water

Dissolve the yeast in the warm water in a large bowl. Stir in the malt, salt, oil, soy and rye flours, spices, and grated orange peel (be sure the oranges are roughly grated; use the coarse side of a grater or peel off the skins in strips with a zester and chop them roughly). Start adding the white flour a cup at a time, stirring well, until the dough becomes too stiff to handle.

Turn the dough out on a floured work surface and let rest while you clean out and oil the bowl. Knead the dough, adding more flour as necessary; it will absorb a lot. After 8–10 minutes it should have lost its tackiness and will be quite smooth and resilient, though not airy. Put the dough in the oiled bowl, cover with plastic wrap, and let rise until double in volume.

Turn the dough out, punch it down to flatten, and form into 2 rounds. Place these spaced well apart on an oiled baking sheet unless you have a baking stone or tiles in your oven and can bake directly on that hot surface, in which case place the loaves on a paddle or sheet sprinkled with corn meal. Prick the loaves in about a dozen places with a trussing or knitting needle going at least ½ inch deep. Cover lightly with a kitchen towel and let rest for 40 minutes.

Paint the tops of the loaves with the egg white glaze and bake in a preheated 350° oven for 50 minutes. Remove and cool on racks.

* If you don't want to bother with these malts, use ¼ cup brown sugar or honey instead.

Rye and Walnut Bread

Søren Gericke was chef-proprietor of an intimate dinner restaurant called Anatole's in Copenhagen, and for a season he was famous not so much for his elegantly served nouvelle cuisine but for the breads he baked himself, especially rolls contrived of dark rye flour and bits of walnut meats. After our meal that included breast of pigeon in a sauce flavored with August apples, the young chef took us into his kitchen and talked of how he had adapted the recipe for the dough that had turned out the crusty morsels we said we admired. His method works well in American kitchens.

Makes 3 round loaves or 20 rolls

2 tablespoons active
   dry yeast
1 cup warm water
2¼ cups whole wheat
   flour
1 cup milk
1¼ cups rye flour
⅓ cup walnut oil
2 teaspoons coarse salt
   or 1 teaspoon table
   salt
1½–2 cups white flour,
   preferably
   unbleached
⅔ cup coarsely
   chopped walnuts
Corn meal

In a large bowl dissolve yeast in the warm water until it is creamy and swells. Stir in all the whole wheat flour, a little at a time, and continue stirring as you add milk, rye flour, walnut oil, and salt. Add enough white flour until the dough becomes hard to stir.

Transfer the dough to a floured surface and let rest while you clean the bowl and grease it with a little more walnut oil. Knead the dough, incorporating more white flour if it is sticky; knead for 8–10 minutes, or until smooth. Form the dough into a ball, put it into the greased bowl, and turn it to coat all over with the oil. Let the dough rise, covered with plastic wrap, for about 1½ hours, or until double in bulk.

Punch down the dough, turn it out on a floured surface, and knead in chopped walnuts. Cut the dough in thirds and form each part into a round loaf (or into rolls). Put loaves several inches apart on a baking sheet sprinkled with corn meal. Let the loaves rise, uncovered, for 40 minutes, or until almost double in bulk.

Just before baking, cut three crescent-shaped slices on the top of each loaf (one slash for rolls) with a razor blade or a very sharp knife. Brush the tops with water and bake 5 minutes in an oven preheated to 400°. Brush again with water and bake 30 minutes longer (10 minutes for rolls). Transfer to a rack and let them cool.

Ryaninjun

Many New England houses still have brick ovens built into fireplace walls, and some of the ovens once more are used for baking the kind of bread that helped the colonists build a nation. "Ryaninjun" was an affectionate term for bread of rye flour and corn meal (Indian meal), the grains that grew best on hard and stony soil. "I can inform all," Harriet Beecher Stowe told her nineteenth-century readers, "that rye and Indian bread smoking hot, on a cold winter morning, together with savory sausages, pork, and beans, formed a breakfast fit for a king—if the king had earned it by getting up in a cold room, washing in ice-water, tumbling through snowdrifts, and foddering cattle." Before molasses was shipped into Boston from the West Indies, stewed pumpkin was used as a breadmaker's sweetener, and often a bed of oak leaves was spread on the oven bottom to give the loaves a special flavor.

Makes 2 dome-shaped loaves

2 cups yellow corn
    meal
About 1¼ cups boiling
    water
½ cup cold water
2 tablespoons active
    dry yeast
½ cup molasses
1 teaspoon coarse salt
    or ½ teaspoon table
    salt
¼ teaspoon baking
    soda
2 cups rye flour
1–1¼ cups white flour,
    preferably
    unbleached

Put the corn meal in a large mixing bowl and pour over it just enough boiling water to wet it; set aside for 10 minutes.

Stir cold water into the corn meal a little at a time until you have a soft batter. Stir in the yeast; in about 5 minutes add molasses, salt, baking soda, and the rye flour, beating until you have a sticky dough. Cover with plastic wrap, and leave in a warm place overnight.

In the morning, punch down the dough and turn it out on a well-floured surface. It will be very sticky, and although it must be kneaded only very briefly, you'll find that you will have to add about 1 cup white flour to work it successfully.

Divide the dough in two, and with well-floured hands shape each piece into a cylinder 6–8 inches long. Flouring your hands again, set each cylinder on its end, far apart, on a greased baking sheet

and let it sink slowly into a dome shape. Cover loosely with a kitchen towel and let rise until almost double—about 1 hour.

Sprinkle the tops of the domes with flour and bake 2 hours in a preheated slow oven, 325° Remove to rack and let cool.

Jewish Rolled Raisin Bread

A great favorite in New York Jewish delicatessens, particularly good with real cream cheese.

Makes 1 7-inch free-form loaf

1½ tablespoons active dry yeast
1½ cups warm water
2 teaspoons coarse salt or 1 teaspoon table salt
¼ cup homemade barley or wheat malt (page 36) or brown sugar
1½ tablespoons caramel (page 35)
1¾ cups rye flour
1¾–2 cups white flour, preferably unbleached
1½ cups raisins
Corn meal

In a medium-size bowl dissolve the yeast in the warm water. Stir in the salt, malt or brown sugar, 1 tablespoon of the caramel, the rye flour, and enough of the white flour until the dough becomes too thick to stir.

Turn the dough out onto a floured working surface and let rest while you wash out and oil the bowl. Knead the dough, adding more white flour as necessary, until it is no longer tacky and has become resilient—about 8–10 minutes. Return the dough to the bowl, cover with plastic wrap, and leave to rise until double in volume.

Punch the dough down in its bowl and let rise again until double its size.

Turn the dough out onto a slightly floured surface and roll out to a rectangle about 7 by 10–11 inches. Spread a carpet of raisins all over the dough, then roll it up tightly, starting at the narrow side. Pinch the seam together and place on a greased baking sheet sprinkled with corn meal, seam side down. Cover lightly with a towel and let rise until almost double its size again.

Dilute the remaining ½ tablespoon of caramel with an equal amount of water and brush the top and sides of the loaf with this mixture. Make 4 short slashes on top about 1½ inches apart. Slide the loaf onto hot tiles or a baking stone if you have them in the oven; otherwise bake the loaf on the baking sheet in a preheated 400° oven for 10 minutes, then lower the heat and bake another 35 minutes at 350°.

American Black Bread

Most examples of this kind of rye bread are called Russian, and it is certainly believable that many such loaves have been made in this country by immigrant cooks. Indeed, this recipe is an adaptation of one attributed to an aunt who came from Russia and mastered the use of stateside ingredients. As darkening agents some home bakers use toasted crumbs of dark breads, or whole bran cereal, or Postum (a noncaffeine beverage made from cereal), or instant coffee powder, or carob powder. In some recipes you'll find caramel among the ingredients, and others use beer as a souring liquid. This one results in a brownish black loaf that is rich in flavor.

Makes 1 large round loaf

1 tablespoon active dry yeast
1 cup strong black coffee, lukewarm
4–5 tablespoons dark molasses
4 tablespoons vinegar
4 tablespoons (½ stick) butter
1 square (1 ounce) unsweetened dark chocolate, cut up
3 cups rye flour
1 tablespoon coarse salt or 2 teaspoons table salt
2 tablespoons caraway seeds
½ teaspoon fennel seeds
¾–1 cup white flour, preferably unbleached

In a large bowl dissolve the yeast in the lukewarm coffee.

In a saucepan combine the molasses and vinegar and bring to a boil. Remove from the heat and stir in the butter and chocolate; when they have melted, set aside to cool to lukewarm.

Add the chocolate-butter mixture to the yeast and stir in the rye flour, salt, caraway, fennel, and as much of the white flour as can readily be absorbed. Turn the dough out on a floured surface to rest while you clean and grease the bowl.

Knead the dough, adding more white flour as it gets tacky, until it is smooth and resilient—about 10 minutes. Return the dough to the greased bowl, covering with plastic wrap. Let rise slowly 4–5 hours, until doubled in bulk.

Punch dough down and knead about 5 minutes, then shape into a round loaf. Arrange on greased baking sheet, cover with a towel, and let rise 1½–2 hours, until loaf doubles in size.

Bake the loaf in a preheated 375° oven about 45 minutes, until deeply browned on top. Remove to a rack and allow to cool.

Danish Wheat–Rye Bread with Wheat Kernels

In Denmark, smørrebrød means in literal transla-
tion butter/bread—and breads in great variety form the foundation of many
meals, whether snacks at the office, lunch at home, or party buffets. The bread
for smørrebrød must be firm and closely grained so it makes buttering easy; it
must also be thinly sliced. Most smørrebrød is made with different kinds of rye
bread, ranging from very dark to blond; one day we stopped to learn more
about this Danish penchant for specialty breads from Magnus Olsen, who is a
traditional baker on the island of Bornholm. Here is one of the whole grain
breads we tasted and, with Master Baker Olsen's tips, set out to duplicate.

Makes 2 free-form loaves or 8-inch loaves

½ cup wheat kernels
2 cups boiling water
1 tablespoon coarse
　salt or 2 teaspoons
　table salt
1 tablespoon active dry
　yeast
½ cup warm water
1 tablespoon brown
　sugar
2 cups dark rye flour
1 cup whole wheat
　flour
½ cup bran flakes
2½–3 cups white flour,
　preferably
　unbleached
Corn meal (for free-
　form loaves)

GLAZE

　1 egg white, lightly
　beaten

Put wheat kernels in a saucepan, cover with
boiling water, and boil 1 minute. Stir in the salt
and set aside to cool.

In a large bowl dissolve yeast in the warm water
along with the brown sugar.

Mix rye flour, whole wheat flour, and the bran
flakes, and place in a moderate oven until warm
through. Add this flour mixture and the wheat
kernels and their water to the dissolved yeast. Mix
well and blend in 2½ cups of the white flour.

Turn out on a floured surface and knead for 10
minutes, adding up to ½ cup more of white flour,
as needed. Clean the bowl, oil it lightly, and return
the dough to it. Cover and let rise until the dough
has doubled in volume—about 1½ hours.

Punch dough down and let rise again until
double—about 1 hour.

Turn the dough out, punch it down, and form
into loaves: make either 2 oval or round free-form
loaves and place well apart on a cookie sheet
sprinkled with corn meal, or divide dough and
place in two 8-inch greased loaf pans. Let rise
again, uncovered, until double—about 45 minutes.

Brush the tops with lightly beaten egg white and
bake 1 hour in a 375° oven. If you have tiles or
baking stones, preheat them in the oven, slide the
free-form loaves directly onto the heated surface,
and bake.

6 · Embellished Yeast Breads

Prune Bread

Pear or Quince Bread

Applesauce and Hazelnut Bread

Dill Casserole Bread

Carrot-Ginger Bread

Italian Pork Bread

Tomato Bread

Cheese Bread

Casserole of Yeast Bread with
Corn "Milk"

Dill-flavored Beet and Carrot
Bread

Toasted Soy and Graham Bread
with Alfalfa Sprouts

Sunflower Meal Bread with
Sunflower Seeds and
Yellow Raisins

Sun Choke with Sunflower Seeds
Bread

Rosemary and Black Walnut
Round Loaf

Chestnut Flour Bread with
Chestnuts

Sesame Sweet Potato Bread

Olive Bread with Mint and Onions

Triticale, Cheese, and Honey
Bread

Zucchini and Cottage Cheese
Graham Bread

Bara Brith or Welsh Raisin Bread

Whole Wheat with Cheese
and Ham

Fig Bread with Lemon Zest

Turmeric and Black Caraway
Seed Bread

Curry, Cilantro, and Scallion
Bread with Mustard Seeds

Among almost numberless ways of embellishing honest loaves without overpowering their natural good flavor are recipes combining various flours with fruits or vegetables, as well as with seeds to give texture and flavor, and herbs to add taste and sometimes color. "'Twas beautiful dough," writes Dorothy Hartley, quoting an English countrywoman, "like a milking breast it was." Home bakers are justly proud of the unadulterated quality of their loaves, and not the least of that kind of pride comes from being able to supply themselves with flour that is free of dirt or grease from the mill wheels. In times of famine, however, they might once have had to use any flour that came their way, and therefore to disguise its poor qualities by stirring herbs or spices into the dough. Out of such dire straits, as always not surprisingly, came bread that was improved by judicious embellishment—a practice that continues in thousands of kitchens where imagination is a lively part of developing innovative recipes. You'll find a few of our own playful and palatable and highly nourishing combinations among the following breads.

Prune Bread

This bread was inspired by a description in the wonderful cookbook by Alice B. Toklas, friend of the writer Gertrude Stein. In Paris at the time of their residence there was a boulangerie or bakery on practically every street, so people seldom baked at home. In that light, Miss Toklas suggests starting this bread with dough from the boulanger, then kneading some ripe prunes into it, shaping it into a loaf, and putting it in a crockery baking dish to return to the baker and the boulangerie ovens. Our version is based on making our own dough and using plump dried prunes, just fresh from their vacuum-sealed package so they aren't *too* dry; it turns out a lovely loaf.

Makes 1 round loaf

1 tablespoon active dry yeast
1¼ cups warm water
2 tablespoons honey
1½ teaspoons coarse salt or 1 teaspoon table salt
3¼–3½ cups white flour, preferably unbleached
Grated peel of 1 orange
1 cup roughly chopped pitted prunes
Powdered sugar

In a large bowl dissolve the yeast in ¼ cup of the warm water. Stir in the honey and when thoroughly dissolved add the rest of the warm water and the salt. Add 3 cups of the flour, stirring to mix until the dough becomes hard to stir, then turn out on a floured working surface and knead until smooth, adding more flour as necessary—about 5–6 minutes. Work in the grated orange peel.

Let the dough rest while you clean the bowl and grease it, then return the dough to it, turning to coat. Cover with plastic wrap and let rise until double in bulk—about 1 hour.

Sprinkle the chopped prunes with flour and knead into the dough. Shape into a round and place in an 8-inch earthenware casserole (or a pie plate will do). Cover lightly with a towel and let rise until double in bulk—about 45 minutes.

With a sharp knife or razor make 4 horizontal slashes across the top, then 4 vertical. Bake in a preheated 350° oven for 40 minutes. Turn out onto a rack and when cool to the touch sprinkle liberally with powdered sugar, using a shaker or a small strainer to distribute evenly.

Pear or Quince Bread

Birnbrot is a Swiss pear bread that distinguished a breakfast we once had in the home of a Swiss acquaintance in Bern—it was made with dried pears, Kirsch, and walnut halves. Using fresh fruit at home, we're more apt to make the regional bread that comes from central France, where luscious pears grow in abundance. There cooks accent the subtle flavor of the pears with freshly ground black pepper, and shape the loaves, unlike the small ovals of the Swiss, in a *couronne* or crown. It has become such a favorite of ours and all of our bread-baking friends that recently when we were blessed with an armful of fresh quinces, which are really first cousins to pears, we tried a variation on the pear bread. We've accented the quinces, which have a more astringent and dominant flavor, with a little ginger instead of the pepper. It's hard to decide which of the breads is more delectable.

Makes 2 rings or, if you prefer, 8-inch loaves

1 tablespoon active dry yeast

⅓ cup warm water

1 cup puréed uncooked pear or cooked quince*

¼ teaspoon black pepper or ground ginger

2 tablespoons honey

1 teaspoon coarse salt or ½ teaspoon table salt

2 large eggs

3½–4 cups white flour, preferably unbleached

In a medium mixing bowl dissolve the yeast in the water. Add the fruit purée, black pepper (if it is pear) or ginger (if it is quince), honey, salt, and eggs, and beat thoroughly. Add 2 cups of the flour and beat again for about 1 minute.

Stir in enough of the remaining flour until the mixture becomes hard to stir. Turn out on a floured working surface and knead for 5 minutes, adding more flour as necessary, until the dough is shiny and smooth.

Clean out the bowl, grease it, and return the dough to it. Let rise, covered with plastic wrap, until double in bulk, about 1½ hours.

Turn the dough out and divide in half. Pat each half into a round of about 7 inches. With a floured

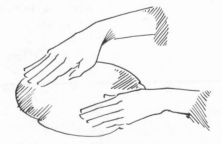

*For 1 cup quince purée, core but do not peel 3–4 quinces (about 1 pound), roughly chop, cover with 1 inch water, and mix in ½ cup sugar; boil gently, covered, for about 40 minutes, or until soft. Purée in a food processor or blender or put through a vegetable mill. Let cool.

GLAZE

*1 egg mixed with 1
teaspoon water*

finger punch a hole in each center, then twirl around to enlarge the hole to about 4 inches diameter.

Place the rings on each end of a greased baking sheet and put a well-greased small, empty can or cookie cutter in each of the holes—otherwise they will close up when baked. Cover lightly with a towel. Let rise until double in size—about 45 minutes.

Paint the tops of the loaves with the egg glaze and bake in a preheated 350° oven for 40 minutes—the aroma will be heavenly. Remove from baking sheet and cool on racks.

Applesauce and Hazelnut Bread

Here is a recipe that can easily be made in a food processor, which will chop the nuts as it spins the flour. We also like to bake it in La Cloche (see page 365), which gives it a particularly nice crust. But if you don't have these particular pieces of equipment handy, the loaf can be made in the conventional way; just follow the mixing and kneading procedure of Pear or Quince Bread (opposite page).

Makes 1 round loaf

1 tablespoon active dry
*   yeast*
¾ cup warm apple
*   cider*
¾ cup hazelnuts
3–3¼ cups white flour,
*   preferably*
*   unbleached*
2 tablespoons brown
*   sugar*
6–7 gratings fresh
*   nutmeg (¼*
*   teaspoon)*
¾ teaspoon cinnamon
½ teaspoon coarse salt
*   or ¼ teaspoon table*
*   salt*
1 egg
1 cup applesauce

In a cup with a spout dissolve the yeast in ½ cup of the cider.

Spin the hazelnuts and 3 cups of the flour together in a food processor until the nuts are roughly chopped. Add the brown sugar, spices, and salt. Pour the dissolved yeast in through the funnel with the motor running. Crack the egg and let it fall through to amalgamate with the flour. Add the applesauce, still spinning, and a little more cider if the dough seems dry, or a little more flour if the dough seems too wet and doesn't form a ball around the center shaft.

Turn the dough out onto a floured surface and knead a few turns. Place in a buttered bowl, covered with plastic wrap, to rise until double in volume—about 1 hour.

Punch the dough down thoroughly, form into a round loaf, and place on the greased base of La Cloche. Cover with its dome top and let rise until almost double—35–40 minutes.

Plump up the loaf again to give it height, as it will have spread, and bake, covered, in a preheated 425° oven for 50 minutes. Let cool on a rack.

Dill Casserole Bread

It's not uncommon to find dill used as a seasoning in rye breads, but the recipe below is for a white casserole loaf enlivened by both fresh dill and dill seeds, with some scallions to add zest to the flavor and accent the color. Relatively quick to make, it can be served still warm with creamed chicken, perhaps, or to accompany a soup supper or a salad lunch—good, too, the next day when spread with cream cheese.

Makes one 8-inch round

1 tablespoon active dry
*   yeast*
¼ cup warm water

In a medium-size mixing bowl dissolve yeast in the warm water.

1 cup milk
2 tablespoons sugar
2 teaspoons coarse salt
  or 1 teaspoon table
  salt
3 tablespoons butter
8 scallions, minced,
  using some of the
  green tops
1 tablespoon fresh
  minced dill
1 tablespoon dill seed
1 egg
3½–3¾ cups white
  flour, preferably
  unbleached
Softened butter

Heat the milk and add sugar, salt, and 2 tablespoons of the butter, stirring until dissolved. Add minced scallions, fresh dill, and dill seed, and beat in the egg; cool to lukewarm.

Blend the cooled milk mixture with the swollen yeast. Add 3 cups of the flour and stir until you have a thick dough. Turn out onto floured surface and knead about 10 minutes, until dough is smooth, adding more flour if necessary.

Clean the mixing bowl and butter it; put the dough in it, turning to coat. Cover with plastic wrap and let rise in a warm place. In about 30 minutes it will have doubled in bulk.

Punch down and let rest while you butter a shallow casserole 8 inches in circumference. Shape the dough into a round, rub the top gently with softened butter, and put in the casserole. Cover and let rise until double, about 25 minutes.

Bake in preheated 350° oven for 35 minutes. Remove to rack and immediately rub crust with butter.

Carrot–Ginger Bread

If, in the usual recipes, carrot loaves are leavened with baking powder and are sufficiently sweetened to be accepted as cakes, this may come as a mild surprise. It's a yeast loaf, with fine subtle texture, that slices well, makes wonderful toast and can be the basis of out-of-the-ordinary sandwiches. Famine times in England have caused country cooks to make bread by extending what flour they could get with ground dried legumes like peas and beans, but there aren't many loaves in old recipe collections that depend on root vegetables. In fact, in our research we've found only a couple of formulas for combining flour and grated carrots to produce an airy yeast bread. One recipe that has rather excessively sweet flavor is accented with raisins and poppy seeds. Our method, below, may be unique in combining the color and moisture of carrots with the tang of ginger, a subtle blend of taste sensations.

Makes two-8-inch loaves

1 tablespoon active dry
   yeast
½ cup warm water
1½ cups tea, steeped 5
   minutes and cooled
   to lukewarm
2 cups grated carrots
2 tablespoons chopped
   preserved ginger*
2 tablespoons
   preserved ginger
   syrup or honey
2 teaspoons coarse salt
   or 1 teaspoon table
   salt
Several gratings fresh
   nutmeg (about ¼
   teaspoon)
5½–6 cups white flour,
   preferably
   unbleached

In a medium-size bowl dissolve the yeast in the warm water. Stir in the tea, grated carrots, ginger, syrup or honey, salt, nutmeg, and enough of the flour to make a cohesive dough.

Turn the dough out onto a floured working surface and let it rest while you clean and butter the bowl. Knead, adding more flour as necessary, until it is smooth and bouncy—about 5–6 minutes. Return the dough to the bowl, cover with plastic wrap, and let rise until double in volume—about 1 hour.

Turn the dough out, punch it down, and form into 2 loaves. Place in buttered 8-inch loaf pans, cover with a kitchen towel, and let rise until double in volume—about 40 minutes.

Bake in a preheated 350° oven for 45 minutes. Remove to racks to cool.

* If you do not have preserved ginger, use the same amount of candied ginger or a tablespoon of minced fresh ginger plus an additional 2 teaspoons honey.

Italian Pork Bread

In nineteenth-century Britain, heartily embellished breads were known as drover's bread, or sometimes as traveler's bread, and they consisted most often of beefsteak cut in small fingers wrapped in the dough with salt, pepper, and a pinch of mustard. Sometimes bacon was substituted for the beef, and sometimes mutton and chopped mint. The cautionary note urged the dough be so sealed as to "keep in the gravy." Meat baked in bread is a part of many cultures—even in New York, where recently we spent a morning beside the century-old brick ovens at the Palermo bakery. There we observed the making of dough for round loaves invested with bits of pork butt, as Baker Prestamo had learned how to produce from his Sicilian grandfather.

Bread lovers come by subway and bus to take home the savory Palermo loaves that we have reproduced in our kitchen.

Makes 3 round loaves

1 tablespoon active dry
  yeast
3 tablespoons sugar
1¾ cups warm water
About 3½–4 cups
  white flour,
  preferably
  unbleached
1 tablespoon coarse
  salt or 2 teaspoons
  table salt
1 teaspoon freshly
  ground black pepper
½ pound well-cooked
  shredded pork and
  fat*

In a large bowl dissolve the yeast and sugar in 1 cup of warm water, then beat in 1 cup white flour. Beat for about 1 minute, then cover the bowl with plastic wrap and let sit for anywhere from 1 to 3 or 4 hours. (You could be letting the sponge sit while you cook the pork.)

Add the remaining ¾ cup warm water to the sponge, and stir in the salt, pepper, pork and fat, and as much of the remaining white flour as the dough will absorb easily. Because you want to have a soft dough, you should knead it with a dough hook or in a food processor; otherwise beat the dough a good 100 strokes with a wooden spoon, let it rest, and beat again. Cover the bowl with plastic wrap and let rise until double in volume.

Turn the dough out onto a floured work surface and divide into three equal pieces. Roll each piece out to about 12 inches, very lightly, using only your floured hands, then pick up the rope, twist it four or five times quickly, form a circle, pinching the ends together, and place on a greased baking sheet. Repeat with the other pieces. The dough

*You should have twice as much fat as pork, so use a very fatty piece of pork (or if you are taking off a piece from a roast, add additional pork fat); let it cook slowly in the fat for at least 2 hours in a slow oven, shred (may be done in a food processor), then cool.

should have a rough-hewn, uneven look, and you should widen the hole once the pieces are on the baking sheet so that it doesn't close up completely. Let rise, uncovered, for 20 minutes.

Bake in a preheated 400° oven for 40 minutes. Cool on racks, but serve the bread warm. To reheat wrap in foil.

Tomato Bread

A fine bread to make when you have an abundance of ripe tomatoes in the garden. Or it can be made with your own preserved tomatoes (or store-bought) to give you a memory of summer in the midst of winter. It's best to use fresh herbs; not only do the dried leaves tend to over-power the barely discernible tomato flavor but you won't get the nice flecks of green that fresh herbs will give. Fresh Italian parsley is good, and dill, but we've also found that just about whatever green herbs in our garden have flow-ered at the time the tomatoes are really ripe might be the right complement. Last time we made this bread we used fresh oregano—the milder variety—with a few of the dark pink flowers included. The color of the bread, incidentally, is pale tomato with a burnt-orange crust. Because the crust is so colorful we like to braid the loaf to make the most of it. And we usually reserve enough of the mixture to make about 10 small plump rolls.

Makes 10 rolls and one 8-inch loaf, or one 9-inch loaf

1 tablespoon active dry yeast
½ cup warm water
1½ cups skinned and chopped ripe tomatoes or canned plum tomatoes with some of their juice
2 tablespoons sugar

In a large bowl (or in the bowl of a food processor) dissolve the yeast in the warm water.

Purée the tomatoes by putting them through a food mill or spinning in the food processor (if using the food processor, simply add them to the dissolved yeast in the bowl). Blend the yeast, puréed tomatoes, sugar, oil, salt, and herbs together, then stir in as much of the white flour as can easily be absorbed. (If using the food

*2 tablespoons safflower
oil*
*2 teaspoons coarse salt
or 1 teaspoon table
salt*
*1 tablespoon chopped
fresh herbs (see
above suggestions)*
3½–4½ cups white
flour, preferably
unbleached*

GLAZE

*Melted butter or egg
glaze (1 egg mixed
with 1 teaspoon
water) for rolls*

processor, dump everything on top of the dissolved yeast along with 3½–4 cups of the flour; process, adding more flour if necessary, until the dough forms a mass and leaves the sides of the bowl clean.) If you are hand-kneading clean out the bowl and knead about 5–6 minutes, adding more flour as necessary until you have a smooth dough.

Put the dough into a greased bowl, cover with plastic wrap, and let rise until double in volume—about 1–1½ hours.

Punch the dough down, turn out onto a floured working surface, and tear off 10 pieces the size of golf balls. Form them into small rolls, pinching the seams at the bottom, and place 2 inches apart on a greased baking sheet.

Cut the remaining dough into three equal pieces, roll into fat rolls, and braid, pinching the ends together. Place in a greased 8-inch bread pan. (Or simply form all of the dough into a loaf and place in a 9-inch greased bread pan.)

Cover rolls and loaf lightly with a kitchen towel and let rise until double in volume—about 30–40 minutes in a warm kitchen.

Brush the rolls either with melted butter or egg glaze. Bake both bread and rolls in a preheated 400° oven for 15 minutes, then remove the rolls and continue baking the loaf at 350° for another 25 minutes (the 9-inch loaf should have 5 minutes more). Serve the rolls warm; cool bread on a rack.

*Fresh tomatoes will provide less liquid, thus less flour is needed.

Cheese Bread

What was said about this recipe in *The World of Cheese* may bear repeating: "This deliciously chewy and flavorful cheese bread can be baked either in a bread pan, making a loaf that is wonderful for canapés, sandwiches, toast, and croutons, or in a free-form French loaf, which is superb served warm for dinner."

Makes one 8-inch loaf plus 1 French-style baguette

1 tablespoon active dry yeast
1¾ cups warm water
2½ teaspoons coarse salt or 1½ teaspoons table salt
4–5 cups white flour, preferably unbleached
1 cup grated sharp Cheddar cheese
Corn meal

Dissolve yeast in a large bowl with ¼ cup of the warm water. Mix the salt with the remaining water and stir into the yeast. Add the flour, 1 cup at a time, mixing thoroughly. Stir the dough thoroughly until it becomes difficult to stir, then turn out on a floured surface. Let the dough rest while you clean and grease the bowl. Knead the dough about 10 minutes, adding a little flour as required.

Put dough in a large greased bowl, turn it around until it is coated, then cover with plastic wrap and let it rise slowly at average room temperature until it is triple in bulk.

Punch the dough down, and let rise until it is double in bulk.

Turn the dough out, add cheese, and knead just long enough to incorporate the cheese into the dough. Shape about two-thirds of the dough to fill a greased 8-inch bread pan. Roll the remaining dough into a French-style loaf about 10–12 inches long (see page 65) and put on a baking sheet sprinkled with corn meal. Let both loaves rise to double.

Bake the loaves in a preheated 450° oven (brush or spray the French loaf lightly with water as it goes into the oven and again in about 2 minutes). Remove the French loaf after 20 minutes; bake the pan loaf 5–10 minutes longer at 350°. Let both cool on racks.

Casserole of Yeast Bread with Corn "Milk"

When the corn harvest makes tassled green ears available in abundance this is a welcome recipe. If you have a corn scraper—an old-fashioned one or one of the newly devised gadgets—it will make the job of extracting the milk and flesh without the skin of the kernel much easier. Otherwise, you can run a sharp knife down the center of each row to split the kernels, then use the back of the knife to press out the interior.

Makes one 6-inch round loaf

1 tablespoon active dry yeast
1 tablespoon honey
½ cup warm water
1 cup scraped corn (about 5 ears)
1 teaspoon coarse salt or ½ teaspoon table salt
2 tablespoons melted butter
2¾–3¼ cups white flour, preferably unbleached
Corn meal

In a medium-size bowl dissolve the yeast and the honey in the warm water.

Mix the corn, salt, and melted butter in with the dissolved yeast and stir in enough of the white flour until it gets a bit difficult to stir. Turn the dough out onto a floured surface while you clean out and grease the bowl.

Knead this dough very lightly for only 2–3 minutes, flouring your hands and the work surface as necessary, because it will be very sticky. Don't push the dough down too hard, and use a dough scraper, if necessary, to clean off the board after each turn.

Return the dough to the greased bowl, cover with plastic wrap, and let rise until double in volume—about 1 hour.

Turn the dough out and form lightly into a ball. Grease a shallow casserole, preferably earthenware, about 6 inches in diameter, and place the dough in it. Cover lightly with a towel and let rise for about 30 minutes.

Sprinkle the top of the risen dough with a little corn meal and bake in a preheated 350° oven for 30 minutes, then raise the heat to 400° and bake another 5 minutes to toast the top. Let the bread rest a half hour or so, then serve it warm from its casserole. To reheat, wrap in aluminum foil.

Dill-flavored Beet and Carrot Bread

Like many kinds of good cooking, breads that are based on unusual ingredients developed out of necessity. Peas and potatoes have been common ways of adding bulk to bread doughs, and sixteenth-century records cite the use of parsnips and beetroot. The idea for this loaf derives from James Beard's most recent book, in which he heartily recommends the combination of beet and carrot purée as a vegetable course. When we served this dish and had some leftovers, we made it into a bread that proved especially winning when shaped in individual-size loaves for dinner.

Makes one 9-inch loaf, or one 8-inch plus 1 small 4-inch loaf, or 4 small 4-inch loaves

1½ tablespoons active
  dry yeast
¾ cup warm water
1 cup beet and carrot
  purée*, at room
  temperature
1 tablespoon coarse
  salt or 2 teaspoons
  table salt
2 eggs
2 tablespoons chopped
  fresh dill
4–4½ cups white flour,
  preferably
  unbleached

In a large bowl dissolve the yeast in the warm water. Beat in the purée, salt, and eggs until well blended. Stir in the dill and enough white flour until the dough becomes hard to stir.

Turn the dough out onto a floured work surface and let rest while you wash the bowl. Let it sit in hot water while you knead.

Knead the dough, adding more white flour as necessary, until it is smooth and elastic—about 6–8 minutes. Butter the dried warm bowl and return the dough to it. Cover with plastic wrap and let rise until double in volume.

Turn the dough out, punch it down, and shape it into the number and size of loaves you are planning to make (see suggestions above). Butter the bread pans and fill them two-thirds full. Cover lightly with a towel and let rise until almost double or until the dough swells over the sides of the pans.

Bake in a preheated 375° oven for 10 minutes, then lower the heat to 350° and continue to bake for another 35 minutes. For smaller loaves, bake 10 minutes at 375° and 15 minutes at 350°. Turn out and cool on racks.

*The purée is made of equal parts of cooked beets and carrots mashed or puréed in a food processor.

Toasted Soy and Graham Bread with Alfalfa Sprouts

As with wheatberries (page 36), alfalfa seeds may be sprouted in a wide-mouth jar covered with cheesecloth and after three or four days exposed to light to develop chlorophyll. Alfalfa sprouts have a mild grassy taste, and they give moisture and texture to a loaf. This one is especially healthful without being heavy.

Makes two 9-inch loaves

⅔ cup yellow raisins
½ cup orange juice
1 tablespoon active dry yeast
3 cups warm water
1 cup nonfat dry milk
⅓ cup honey
About 5½ cups white flour, preferably unbleached
1 cup toasted soy flour
2 teaspoons coarse salt or 1 teaspoon table salt
1 cup graham flour
⅓ cup safflower oil
1 cup alfalfa sprouts

Let the raisins sit in the orange juice to get plump. Prepare a sponge first by dissolving the yeast in 2 cups of the warm water and mixing in the dry milk, honey, and 2 cups of the white flour. Beat thoroughly—at least 50 strokes. Cover with plastic wrap and let seethe and bubble ½–2 hours, whatever is convenient.

Meanwhile toast the soy flour by heating in a skillet over a medium flame, stirring constantly and turning until the flour becomes light tan and begins to give off a pleasant toasted aroma.

When your sponge is ready, mix the salt with the remaining cup of warm water and stir this into the sponge along with the toasted soy, graham flour, oil, alfalfa sprouts, raisins, and enough of the remaining white flour to make the dough fairly stiff. Turn out on a floured work surface to rest while you clean out and grease your bowl. Then knead the dough, adding more white flour as necessary, until it is smooth and resilient—about 10 minutes. Put the dough back in the greased bowl, turning to coat. Cover with plastic wrap and let rise until double in volume—about 1–1½ hours.

Turn the dough out, divide in half, and form 2 loaves. Place in greased 9-inch bread pans and let rise again covered with a towel until almost double—about 30–40 minutes.

Bake in a preheated 425° oven for 10 minutes, then lower the heat to 350° and continue to bake 30 minutes. Turn the loaves out and cool on racks.

Sunflower Meal Bread with Sunflower Seeds and Raisins

Long before the sunflower plant was introduced to Europe, Hopi Indians in America's Southwest ate the seeds and ground them into flour, knowing intuitively perhaps that the seeds are 24 percent protein, about the same as beef. They're also rich in thiamine and niacin, and are ground into nourishingly digestible flours or meals (see recipe page 92). The loaf below has additional fiber quality through the use of chopped seeds in the dough.

Makes two 8-inch loaves, or one 8-inch loaf and one 10-inch roll

1 tablespoon active dry
  yeast
2 cups warm water
¼ cup honey
¼ cup nonfat dry milk
1 teaspoon coarse salt
  or ½ teaspoon table
  salt
1 cup sunflower meal
4½ cups plus 2
  tablespoons white
  flour, preferably
  unbleached
½ cup yellow raisins
1 cup roughly chopped
  sunflower seeds

GLAZE

  1 egg white, lightly
  beaten

In a large bowl dissolve the yeast in half the warm water. Stir the honey, dry milk, and salt into the remaining water to dissolve well, then add to the yeast. Stir in the sunflower meal and enough of the white flour until it becomes hard to stir.

Turn the dough out onto a floured work surface to rest while you clean out and grease the bowl. Knead the dough, adding more flour as necessary, until it is smooth and bouncy. Return the dough to the greased bowl, cover with plastic wrap, and let rise until double in volume—about 1 hour or so.

Toss the raisins and ¾ cup of the chopped sunflower seeds in 2 tablespoons flour. Turn the dough out on a floured surface, spread it out, then sprinkle the raisins and sunflower seeds evenly over the surface. Roll the dough up and cut in half. Place in two greased 8-inch bread pans seam side down, or if you want to make a long loaf out of one part, roll it out to a length of about 12 inches; either place in a well-greased long clay flowerpot trough, if you happen to have one as we did, or arrange on a greased baking sheet. Cover the loaves lightly with a kitchen towel and let rise until double in volume—about 40 minutes.

Brush the loaves with egg white, then sprinkle the remaining chopped sunflower seeds on top. Bake in a preheated 350° oven for 45 minutes—only 40 minutes for the long loaf. Turn out and cool on racks.

Sun Choke with Sunflower Seeds Bread

Jerusalem artichokes, discovered after Columbus made his landfall, got their name from the mispronunciation of the word *gira-sole* (turning with the sun) by Englishmen. The Jerusalem artichoke is really the root of a sunflower plant and, indeed, you'll find them often called sun chokes today. In our combination of the puréed vegetable and sunflower seeds, a wonderfully subtle and fragrant bread is made—it's different from any other we know.

Makes one 9-inch loaf

1 tablespoon active dry
   yeast
¾ cup warm water
1 tablespoon honey
2 teaspoons coarse salt
   or 1 teaspoon table
   salt
2 tablespoons soft
   butter
1¼ cups puréed
   Jerusalem
   artichokes*
3½–4 cups white flour,
   preferably
   unbleached
⅓ cup sunflower
   seeds, toasted

In a medium-size bowl dissolve the yeast in the warm water and stir in the honey. Add the salt and the butter to the puréed chokes and mix well, then stir into the yeast. Add 3½ cups of the flour and beat 100 strokes or beat with a hand-held electric mixer or, even better, use a dough hook for about a minute and a half; this dough is too sticky to knead by hand. Add more flour if necessary, until the dough comes away from the sides of the bowl, and stir in the sunflower seeds.

Turn dough out on a floured surface and rest it while you clean and grease the bowl. Return the dough to it, turning to coat, and let rise, covered, in a draft-free place, until double in bulk.

Turn out, punch down, form into a loaf, and place in a greased 9-inch bread pan. Let rise again, covered with a kitchen towel, for 40 minutes.

Bake in a preheated 350° oven for about 45 minutes until top is nicely browned. Cool on a rack.

*It takes about 1½ pounds of Jerusalem artichokes to make 1¼ cups purée. Boil or steam the chokes until tender. When cool enough to handle, peel off the skins, retaining as much of the inner flesh as you can. Purée them in a food processor or put through a vegetable mill.

Rosemary and Black Walnut Round Loaf

A medieval Welsh herbalist recommended a solution made by soaking rosemary leaves as a face wash to ensure perpetual youth. In bread dough it's the flavor and aroma of the herb that seem to work wonders; it makes a pungent loaf combined with the slightly fermented flavor of black walnuts—delicious with cold chicken and mild fresh cheeses.

Makes 1 round loaf

1 tablespoon active dry yeast
1½ cups warm water
2 tablespoons fresh rosemary or 2 teaspoons dried
2 scallions, chopped, including most of green tops
2 teaspoons coarse salt or 1 teaspoon table salt
Freshly ground black pepper
1 tablespoon olive oil
½ cup rye flour
About 3 cups white flour, preferably unbleached
¾–1 cup shelled black walnuts

In a large bowl dissolve the yeast in the warm water. Then stir in the rosemary, scallions, and salt. Add about 15 turns of the pepper grinder (about 1 teaspoon), preferably somewhat coarsely ground, the olive oil, rye flour, and enough of the white flour until it becomes hard to stir.

Turn the dough out onto a floured work surface and let rest while you wash the bowl and oil it. Knead the dough, adding more flour as necessary, until it is elastic. Return it to the bowl, cover with plastic wrap, and let rise until double in volume. Punch the dough down thoroughly, cover the bowl again, and let rise once more until double.

Turn the dough out and knead the black walnuts into it, distributing them through the dough as evenly as possible. Shape into a large round and place on a baking sheet or a paddle (if you have a baking stone or tiles) sprinkled with corn meal. Cover lightly with a towel and let rise until double. (Or let the formed loaf rise and then bake in La Cloche. For directions see page 128).

Slash the top of the loaf all over in a tic-tac-toe pattern, then brush with water. Bake on the baking sheet or slide onto a hot stone or tiles in a preheated 425° oven. After 20 minutes lower the heat to 350° and bake another 25 minutes. Cool on rack.

Chestnut Flour Bread
with Chestnuts

Tourists in Tuscany are apt to discover that the shallow cake called *castagnaccio* is genuine only when based on chestnut flour, just as is true of the sconelike breads of Emilia-Romagna. But our first encounter with chestnut flour was during research for a piece on Corsica and its Italo-Franco cuisine. Corsicans who are traditionalists still make their polenta with ground chestnuts, as well as their *pisticcini* (see page 207), the bread consisting only of chestnut flour, water, and salt that is baked on a bed of chestnut leaves. The recipe below which we devised is a yeast bread using some white flour; it is studded with braised chestnut halves to deepen the flavor and add texture. Because it is a little crumbly, we recommend baking it in small loaves to make it more sliceable. It also makes interesting rolls—their earthy, almost mushroomlike flavor offers a particularly good accompaniment to duck or pork.

Makes 4 small 5-inch loaves, or 3 small loaves and 8 rolls

1 cup peeled chestnuts*
1 tablespoon Madeira
2 tablespoons butter
1 tablespoon active dry yeast
1½ cups warm water
2 teaspoons honey
2 teaspoons coarse salt or 1 teaspoon table salt
1½ cups chestnut flour
About 2½ cups white flour, preferably unbleached
Soft butter (for rolls)

Put the chestnuts in one layer in a cooking pot. Pour enough water over them to cover; add the Madeira and butter. Cover and cook gently for 20–25 minutes until just tender but not at all mushy. Let cool. Remove the chestnuts and cut in half. Reserve the cooking liquid, pouring it into a cup measure; you'll need ½ cup, so if you don't have quite enough just add a little milk or water to bring it up to ½ cup.

In a medium-size bowl dissolve the yeast in the warm water along with the honey. Stir in the chestnut cooking liquid, salt, chestnut flour, and enough of the white flour to make a soft dough.

Turn the dough out onto a floured work surface while you wash out and butter the bowl. Start kneading, adding more flour as necessary, and when the dough starts to lose its stickiness and become pliant, spread it out, scatter the chestnuts over it, then roll up and knead gently—so as not to crush the chestnuts—until smooth (a total of 5–6 minutes kneading). Return the dough to the

---

* Now that one can get frozen chestnuts from Italy that come all peeled, it makes cooking with chestnuts a lot easier.

CHESTNUT FLOUR
BREAD, CONTINUED

bowl, cover with plastic wrap, and let rise until double in volume.

Turn the dough out, pat it down, and if you want to make rolls, tear off 8 pieces the size of golf balls and shape them into rolls. Place on a buttered baking sheet, 2 inches apart. With the remaining dough—or with all of it—make loaves to fit 3 or 4 buttered 5-inch bread pans. Place inside, then cover rolls and pans with kitchen towels and let rise until almost double—about 40 minutes.

Bake in a preheated 400° oven for 10 minutes, then turn the heat down to 350° and bake the rolls another 5–6 minutes until browned on top, and the loaves another 20 minutes. Remove and cool the bread on racks. Rub a little soft butter over the tops of the rolls and serve them fresh and warm. The bread will need a little time to settle down before slicing.

Sesame Sweet Potato Bread

Yams are dried and ground into flour in West Africa, but the soft glowing orange color of these sweet potato loaves comes from the fact that the vegetable itself is mashed and combined with white flour. In the old South black cooks were skilled in the use of both yams and sweet potatoes, and many of them brought sesame seeds to this country as a memento of their homeland, often using sesame as a subtle flavor in their baking. We discovered that that flavor is heightened by toasting the seeds and the bread is lighter than it otherwise might be because of the addition of gluten flour.

Makes three 8-inch loaves

2 large sweet potatoes
1 tablespoon active dry
  yeast
2 cups warm water
7 cups white flour,
  preferably
  unbleached
2 cups whole wheat
  flour
½ cup gluten flour
1 tablespoon coarse
  salt or 2 teaspoons
  table salt
¼ cup sesame seeds,
  preferably unhulled
Vegetable oil

GLAZE

  1 egg white, lightly
  beaten

Put sweet potatoes in a saucepan and cover with cold water; bring to a boil over moderately low heat, and cook, covered, about 45 minutes, until potatoes are tender. Remove potatoes and let them cool. When they can be handled, peel and put them in a bowl and mash them; you should have at least 1¼ cups. Cover mashed potatoes and set aside.

In a large bowl dissolve the yeast in ½ cup of warm water until it swells; stir in the reserved sweet potatoes while still warm and add the remaining warm water. Stir in, a little at a time, about 6½ cups of the white flour, the whole wheat flour, gluten flour, and salt. When the dough is well blended and stiff, transfer it to a floured surface and let rest while you clean out and grease your bowl. Knead the dough 8–10 minutes, incorporating more white flour as necessary. Toast the sesame seeds in a covered skillet over moderate heat for 2 minutes, shaking the skillet, until they have turned deep golden and, if unhulled, start to pop. Knead 3 tablespoons of toasted seeds into the dough and transfer it to the greased bowl, turning to coat all over. Cover with plastic wrap and let dough rise about 1½–2 hours, or until doubled in bulk.

Turn the dough out, punch down, and divide it into thirds. Shape into 3 loaves and put them in 3 greased 8-inch bread pans. Cover and let rise 1 hour or until loaves have doubled.

Brush with lightly beaten egg white and sprinkle tops with remaining sesame seeds. Bake in a preheated 375° oven for 50 minutes. Put the loaves on a rack to cool.

Olive Bread with
Mint and Onions

Olives are used in making bread wherever olive trees grow—in California and throughout the Mediterranean world. One of Cyprus's singular breads is this one combining olives, onions, and mint as accents—proving, as we learned in Athens from food historian Chrissa Paradissis, that Greek bread has been full of flavor since the pre-Christian period when "Theorion, a Greek from Sicily, perfected the process of its preparation." Called *eliopsomo,* the name of this bread conjures the memory of the plains below the Delphic ruins that are literally covered with olive trees.

Makes 1 large round loaf

1 tablespoon active dry
  yeast
½ teaspoon sugar
1½ cups warm water
½ cup whole wheat
  flour, preferably
  coarsely ground
3–3½ cups white flour,
  preferably
  unbleached
3 tablespoons olive oil
2 teaspoons coarse salt
  or 1 teaspoon table
  salt
1 small onion, chopped
2 teaspoons dried mint
12 black Greek olives,
  pitted and halved
Corn meal

Make a sponge by dissolving the yeast and sugar in the warm water and stirring in the whole wheat flour and 1½ cups of the white flour. Beat at least 50 strokes, then cover with plastic wrap and let stand anywhere from 1 to 6 hours.

Stir all but a teaspoon of the olive oil into the dough, as well as the salt, the chopped onion, dried mint, and olives. Then work in remaining white flour until it becomes hard to stir.

Turn the dough out onto a floured working surface and let rest while you clean out the bowl. Knead dough for about 8–10 minutes, adding more flour as necessary, until the dough is resilient. Lightly oil the bowl, return the dough to it, turning to coat, and cover with plastic wrap. Let rise until double in volume—about 1½ hours.

Turn the dough out, punch it down, and form into a large round loaf. Place on a baking sheet sprinkled with corn meal. Cover loosely with a towel and let rise again until double—about 45 minutes. (Or let rise and bake in La Cloche; for directions see page 128.)

If you have baking tiles in your oven, be sure they are good and hot by preheating the oven to 425° during the last 30 minutes of the final rising. Slip the loaf onto the tiles (if you're not using them, simply put the baking sheet in the preheated oven) and bake for 15 minutes, then lower the heat to 350° and bake another 35 minutes. Brush with the remaining olive oil and let cool on a rack.

Triticale, Cheese, and Honey Bread

With the nutritional characteristics of rye and the baking qualities of wheat, triticale flour requires the addition of white flour for good texture, but the virtue of this loaf is its attractive nutty flavor in combination with cheese.

Makes two 8-inch loaves

2 tablespoons active
  dry yeast
2¼ cups warm water
About 3¾ cups white
  flour, preferably
  unbleached
⅓ cup honey
2 teaspoons coarse salt
  or 1 teaspoon table
  salt
¼ cup unsweetened
  evaporated milk
3 cups triticale flour
1⅓ cups diced
  Monterey Jack or
  muenster cheese
Vegetable oil

In a large bowl dissolve the yeast in ½ cup of the warm water. Add 3 cups of the white flour, 1 cup at a time; add honey and beat thoroughly until you have a smooth dough. Cover it with plastic wrap and leave to rise in a warm place 30 minutes, until it doubles in bulk.

Punch down, and add the salt and evaporated milk, mixing thoroughly. Stir in 2½ cups of triticale flour ½ cup at a time, blending with 1¾ cups warm water and diced cheese. Turn the dough out on a surface floured with ½ cup triticale flour; let rest while you clean and grease your bowl. Knead 8–10 minutes while adding about ¾ cup white flour. Form the dough into a ball; put it into the greased bowl, turning it so it is greased all over. Cover with plastic wrap, and let the dough rise about 1 hour, until doubled.

Turn out on a floured surface and knead about 1 minute before dividing in halves and putting into 2 greased 8-inch loaf pans. Cover with a dish towel and leave the loaves to rise 45 minutes, until they have just risen over the edges of the pans.

Bake in a preheated 400° oven 10 minutes; reduce heat to 350° and continue baking 35 minutes longer. Remove the loaves from the pans and cool on racks.

Zucchini and Cottage Cheese Graham Bread

The enthusiasm for zucchini breads—there are many kinds of recipes—is a recent phenomenon based on sound ideas that have been around for generations. This one uses yeast and yogurt and is seasoned with chives or minced scallions. For a sweet version see page 215.

Makes 2 round loaves

2 tablespoons active
   dry yeast
½ cup warm water
2½–3 cups white flour,
   preferably
   unbleached
1 cup graham (or
   whole wheat) flour
1 cup grated zucchini
¾ cup cottage cheese
¾ cup plain yogurt
3 tablespoons minced
   scallion tops or
   chives
1 tablespoon coarse
   salt or 2 teaspoons
   table salt

In a large bowl dissolve the yeast in the warm water. Stir in 2½ cups white flour, 1 cup of graham flour, and the grated zucchini; add cottage cheese, yogurt, scallion tops or chives, and salt; blend thoroughly.

Turn the dough out onto a floured surface and let rest while you clean and grease your bowl. Knead 8 to 10 minutes until no longer sticky, incorporating more white flour as necessary. When it is smooth and elastic, form dough into a ball, put it in the greased bowl, and turn to coat. Cover with plastic wrap and let the dough rise about 1 hour, until doubled in bulk.

Halve the dough, form each half into a round loaf, and put them in two 8-inch cake pans. Cover with a kitchen towel and let rise 45 minutes, until doubled.

Brush loaves with water and bake in preheated 375° oven for 3 minutes; brush again with water and bake 45 minutes longer, until they sound hollow when you tap bottoms. Remove from oven, turn out on racks and let them cool completely.

Bara Brith or Welsh Raisin Bread

Welsh cooks, wherever they may have settled throughout the world, are famous for their "speckled bread" (as the words in their native tongue translate). In the Jones family we know best, the heirloom recipe from a Cardigan farm called for baking powder, but it is yeast that should be used when a light, firm loaf is desired, and the slices should be closely studded with raisins, currants, and candied peel. It's great for breakfast toast and, of course, standard fare as part of a proper British tea.

Makes two 8-inch loaves or one 1-quart melon mold and one 8-inch loaf

1 tablespoon active dry yeast
1½ cups warm milk
3 tablespoons brown sugar
¼ cup melted butter or shortening
1 teaspoon coarse salt or ½ teaspoon table salt
¾ teaspoon mixed spices: equal parts nutmeg, mace, cinnamon, and allspice, with a pinch of ground cloves
About 3½ cups white flour, preferably unbleached, warm
⅔ cup yellow raisins (or yellow and black mixed)
⅔ cup currants
½ cup chopped candied orange peel
2 cups strong hot tea

In a large bowl dissolve the yeast in the warm milk. Stir in the brown sugar, melted fat, salt, spices, and almost all of the white flour.

Turn the dough out and let rest while you clean out the bowl (keep it warm). Knead the dough, adding a little more white flour if necessary until it is smooth and elastic. Grease the warm bowl and put the dough into it. Cover with a towel and let rise in a warm place until double in volume—about 40 minutes.

Meanwhile steep the raisins, currants, and candied peel in the hot tea.

Turn the risen dough out onto a floured surface and spread it out. Drain the fruits thoroughly and then spread them over the dough. Roll it up, knead a few times (it will be hard and the fruits will tend to burst out), then put it back to rest in the bowl, sprinkling a little flour over it. After resting about 10 minutes it will be easier to knead a bit and incorporate the fruits. Divide in half and form into 2 loaves. Place in warmed greased 8-inch pans or a warmed melon mold if you are using one—and that must be very thoroughly greased. Cover with a towel and let rise until double in volume—about 30–40 minutes.

Bake in a preheated 350° oven for 1 hour. Let the loaves cool for a few minutes in the pans before turning out.

Whole Wheat with Cheese and Ham Bread

Here is a bread that can take the place of a sandwich, good with a soup or a green salad. It's best served warm; to reheat, wrap in foil.

Makes 1 round loaf

2 tablespoons active
  dry yeast
2 cups warm water
2½ cups or more white
  flour, preferably
  unbleached
2 cups whole wheat
  flour
1 cup bran flakes
1 tablespoon coarse
  salt or 2 teaspoons
  table salt
6 ounces mozzarella
  cheese
¼ pound prosciutto
  ham, trimmed, in
  ¼-inch dice
Corn meal

In a large bowl dissolve the yeast in ½ cup of the warm water. Stir in both kinds of flour, the remaining warm water, the bran flakes, and the salt. Blend ingredients thoroughly, adding more white flour if necessary to make a soft but not sticky dough.

Transfer the dough to a floured surface and let rest while you clean and grease your bowl. Knead, adding a little more white flour if dough seems sticky, for 8–10 minutes, or until it is smooth. Form into a ball and put it in the greased bowl, turning to cover dough all over. Cover bowl with plastic wrap and let the dough rise about 1½ hours until it is three times its original bulk.

Punch down, cover with a towel, and let rise again 1 hour, until double in bulk.

Cut mozzarella cheese into ¼-inch dice, and knead cheese and ham into the dough. Form dough into 1 large round loaf; put it on a baking sheet sprinkled with corn meal. Let the loaf rise uncovered for 1 hour, until double.

(Or let rise and bake in La Cloche; for directions see page 128.)

Brush the top of the loaf with water, sprinkle with corn meal, and place in a preheated 425° oven, into which you have set a pan of boiling water. Bake for 10 minutes, then reduce heat to 350° and bake 30 minutes longer, removing the pan of water during the last 15 minutes of baking. Transfer to rack to cool.

Fig Bread with Lemon Zest

Figs being among those things Plato listed as foods to ensure long life, we mentioned them in our talk with Toula Vresa one day in Thessalonika, and she told us that figs, like honey and bread, are used by Greek cooks today in much the way they were in the ancient past. In western Greece, where she grew up, bread is still baked in outdoor ovens—"right on the bricks of the oven floor after the fire has been pushed back," she said. She described the round loaves, sometimes made of only salt, water, dark flour, and yeast, sometimes accented by honey and fruit. This is a fig bread devised when we returned from Macedonia, and we found that we could use La Cloche (page 365) to get an effect very close to that brought about by traditional village ovens.

Makes 1 round loaf

1 cup boiling water
7 ounces dried figs (½ package of Greek style)
1 tablespoon active dry yeast
2 tablespoons honey
½ cup warm water
1 egg
1½ tablespoons chopped lemon peel
1 teaspoon coarse salt or ½ teaspoon table salt
About 4 cups white flour, preferably unbleached

Pour boiling water over the figs and let steep about 25 minutes. Remove the figs, reserving the water, and chop each fig into 5–6 pieces, discarding any hard stem.

In a large bowl dissolve the yeast and honey in the warm water. Whisk in the egg until well blended, then add the reserved fig water, lemon peel (which should be stripped from the lemons with a vegetable peeler or zester, then roughly chopped), salt, and enough of the white flour to make a firm dough.

Turn the dough out on a floured surface and let rest while you clean and butter the bowl. Then start kneading, adding more flour as necessary, until fairly pliant. Now spread the dough out and scatter the figs over it; roll up and knead again until smooth—a total kneading time of about 6–7 minutes. Return the dough to the bowl, cover with plastic wrap, and let rise until double in volume.

Turn the dough out, punch it down, and shape into a round. If you are using La Cloche, place the dough directly on its lightly buttered dish, and put the cloche top on to let rise for 45 minutes. Otherwise place on a buttered baking sheet and cover with a towel.

For La Cloche, bake in a preheated 400° oven, covered, for 50 minutes. Otherwise start the loaf at 400°; lower the heat after 10 minutes to 350°, and bake another 30 minutes. Remove and cool on a rack.

Turmeric and Black Caraway Seed Bread

Before European colonization, bread was unknown in most of black Africa, but resourceful indigenous cooks have since adapted native ingredients to create their own versions of corn bread, especially, along with loaves based on cassava, banana, plantain, rice, and yam flours—as well as wheat. They make yeast from bananas and frothy palm wine. Pursuing some leads that Edna Lewis gave us as a result of her research on West African cooking, we came up with this bread which contains turmeric and *black* caraway as well as rust red palm oil (African cooks often mix corn oil with paprika to get the same effect when palm oil is too dear, and you can do the same if it isn't readily available). The bread has a tawny color and an exotic flavor—reminiscent of curry without its sharpness. We like to serve it with a pilaf, but the truth is it's good with almost anything—with cream cheese, toasted with honey, or as the bread for a Western sandwich.

Makes one 8-inch loaf

1 tablespoon active dry
  yeast
1¼ cups warm water
1½ tablespoons honey
2 tablespoons red palm
  oil
2 teaspoons black
  caraway seeds
1 tablespoon turmeric
2 teaspoons coarse salt
  or 1 teaspoon table
  salt
3–3¼ cups white flour,
  preferably
  unbleached

In a medium-size bowl dissolve the yeast in the warm water along with the honey. Stir in the oil, caraway seeds, turmeric, salt, and enough of the flour until you have a dough that is hard to stir.

Turn the dough out on a floured working surface and let rest while you clean and oil the bowl. Knead the dough, adding more flour as necessary, until you have a smooth, resilient dough. Place in the bowl, turning to coat, cover with plastic wrap, and let rise until double in volume.

Turn the dough out, punch it down, and form an 8-inch loaf. Dust the loaf with flour and place in an 8-inch bread pan that you have greased, preferably with the red palm oil. Cover loosely with a towel and let rise until double in volume.

Bake in a preheated 350° oven for 45 minutes. Turn out and cool on a rack.

Curry, Cilantro, and Scallion Bread with Mustard Seeds

This bread is particularly delicious baked in a clay pot because the clay seals in the unusual aromatic flavors and gives the bread a grand crust. Use an oval-shaped Romertopf, shaping the bread into a small oval—the sides should not touch because you want the steam the clay creates to circulate—or double the recipe and form a round to bake in La Cloche (see page 128).

Makes 1 small oval loaf (or double the ingredients and make 1 large round)

3 tablespoons chopped scallions, including some green
1 tablespoon butter
2 teaspoons active dry yeast
½ cup warm water
1 egg
1 teaspoon coarse salt or ½ teaspoon table salt
½ teaspoon curry powder
3–4 tablespoons chopped cilantro (Chinese parsley)
About 2 cups white flour, preferably unbleached

GLAZE

1 egg white, beaten
2 teaspoons black mustard seeds

In a small skillet sauté the scallions in the butter 2–3 minutes until they just begin to turn limp.

Dissolve the yeast in the warm water in a medium-size bowl. Whisk in the egg, salt, curry, and cilantro. Stir in enough white flour until the dough gets a bit hard to stir.

Turn the dough out onto a floured surface and let rest while you clean out and butter the bowl. Knead the dough, adding more flour as necessary, for 5–6 minutes, until it is smooth and elastic. Return it to the bowl, turning to coat, and cover with plastic wrap. Let rise until double in volume.

Turn the dough out, punch it down, and form into an oval shape. Place it in the bottom of a lightly greased clay oval pot. Cover with the clay top and let rise until double in volume—about 45 minutes. Or if you have doubled the recipe, let rise in La Cloche.

Brush the loaf with egg white and sprinkle black mustard seeds on top. Bake, covered, in a preheated 450° oven for 40 minutes. (If you are doing a loaf twice this size, bake 55 minutes.) Cool on a rack. This bread is good served slightly warm.

7 · Yeast Rolls

Hard Rolls
Dinner Rolls—with Six Shapes
Icebox Rolls
Canadian Buttermilk Honey Rolls
Graham Bran Rolls
Potato Celeriac Rolls
Honeyed Wheat Hamburger Rolls
Parsnip (or Pumpkin or Squash) Rolls
Sweet Potato Ginger Rolls
Spiced Cranberry Rolls
Onion Rolls
Brazilian Beer Rolls
Papaya Bread Rolls
Earl Grey Tea Rolls
Avocado Rolls
Rye Twists
Khachapuri (Georgian Cheese Cushions)

H ot rolls with meals are not exclusively
     American—the Scots call the buns they
     eat with breakfast *baps,* and Swedish
hostesses serve soft, puffy *bergis* at dinner. But Parker House rolls, or
pocketbook rolls, are a Yankee classic that first appeared a century ago at
Harvey Parker's Boston hotel. And guests at tables in the South are still
admonished when bread fresh from the oven appears to "take two and butter
them while they're hot." Hearty eaters yearn for bread of any kind at
mealtime, and good cooks have been inventive in offering a great variety of
small breads to go with good food. This chapter includes quite a few that are
highly recommended.

Rolls should be made of relatively light bread doughs and can be crusty or
soft, depending on the consistency of the dough and the way it is shaped and
baked. Almost any of the white bread doughs in Chapter 3 could be formed
into rolls instead of loaves and then baked quickly; a soft batter bread would
need to be baked in muffin tins for the rolls to hold their shape. Most of the
whole grain and rye bread doughs in Chapters 4 and 5 would make too heavy
a dinner roll, but Chapter 6, "Embellished Breads," offers many kinds of
unusual doughs, particularly those with a base of puréed fruits or vegetables,
that could be fashioned into delicious small dinner rolls. Sometimes it is fun
to pinch off just a few pieces of a bread dough you may be making and
quickly bake a few rolls to have warm for dinner.

By the same token the recipes that follow for rolls could as easily be baked
in bread pans. A dough using about 3 to 3½ cups of flour would be right for
an 8-inch pan; if the amounts called for are smaller, use smaller pans, or
double the recipe. Here is a chance to improvise on your own.

Hard Rolls

To get a good hard roll, you'll need to create steam in your oven; see page 64 for suggestions. These rolls are also good made with some wheat flour; just substitute ½ cup whole wheat or graham flour for ½ cup of the white.

Makes 18 rolls

1 tablespoon active dry yeast
1½ cups warm water
1 tablespoon kosher salt or 2 teaspoons table salt
3½–3¾ cups white flour, preferably unbleached
Corn meal

GLAZE

1 egg white beaten with 2 teaspoons water
Poppy seeds or sesame seeds (optional)

In large bowl let the yeast dissolve with ½ cup of the warm water. Mix the salt with the rest of the water and add to the yeast. Stir in about 3 cups of the flour until it becomes hard to stir, then turn the dough out onto a floured work surface and knead for 8–10 minutes until smooth and resilient, adding more flour as needed.

Clean out the bowl and return the dough to it. Cover with plastic wrap and let rise; it will take longer than usual because there is no sugar in this dough—perhaps as much as 2 to 4 hours.

Turn out onto a floured surface and tear off pieces of dough one and a half times the size of a golf ball. Flatten slightly, then using your cupped hands, lightly floured, ease the edges of the dough under, at the same time plumping up the ball of dough, stretching its gluten cloak, not breaking it. Pinch the seams at the bottom and place, seam side down, 2 inches apart on baking sheets sprinkled with corn meal. Cover lightly with a towel and let rise until doubled in volume—about 50 minutes.

Brush the tops of the rolls with the egg glaze and, if you like, sprinkle poppy seeds or sesame seeds on top. Or for a classic French look, omit the egg glaze and, instead, dust lightly with flour, then make 3 slashes around the top—roughly the shape of a triangle with unjoined sides. Bake in a preheated 450° oven for 15 minutes.

Dinner Rolls

Here is a basic recipe for the soft dinner rolls that are a traditional accompaniment to American meats. We have made these rolls less sweet than most, and their character can be changed by the shape you give them, whether you nestle the rolls close together in a pan, which makes for softer rolls, or whether you set them apart on a baking sheet so that the surface becomes more crisp all around, whether you give them a glaze or just brush them with butter. Any of these rolls can be sprinkled with poppy, caraway, or sesame seeds just before going in the oven, in which case it's wise to use an egg glaze first so the seeds will adhere.

Makes 24–30 rolls

1 cup rich milk or
   half-and-half
2 tablespoons butter
1 tablespoon white or
   light brown sugar
1 teaspoon coarse salt
   or ½ teaspoon table
   salt
2 teaspoons active dry
   yeast
2 tablespoons warm
   water
2½–3 cups white flour,
   preferably
   unbleached

Heat the milk to the boiling point, add the butter, sugar, and salt, stir to dissolve, and then let cool.

In a medium-size bowl dissolve the yeast in the warm water, then add the lukewarm milk mixture. Stir in about 2½ cups of the flour until the dough resists stirring and starts to leave the sides of the bowl.

Turn out on a floured working surface and knead, adding more flour as necessary, for 8–10 minutes until smooth and springy. Clean out your bowl, butter it, and return the dough to it. Let rise, covered with plastic wrap, until doubled in bulk—about 1½ hours. Turn the dough out and form into any of the following shapes.

GLAZE

Melted butter, or milk, or 1 egg beaten with 1 teaspoon water

ROUND ROLLS: Pull off pieces of dough slightly larger than a golf ball. Flatten slightly, then using your cupped hands, lightly floured, ease the edges of the dough under, at the same time plumping up the ball of dough, taking care that you stretch the gluten cloak, not break it. Pinch together the ends of the dough where they meet on the bottom. For soft rolls, place side by side in 2 greased 8-inch cake tins or one larger baking pan that will just hold them and brush with butter. For crisper rolls, set 1 inch apart on greased baking sheets and brush with egg glaze.

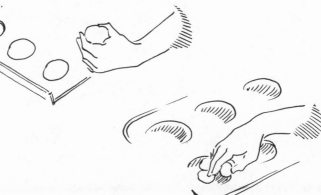

CLOVER-LEAF ROLLS: Make very small balls—one-third the size of a golf ball—and place 3 together in the greased cup of a muffin pan. Continue until all the dough is used up; this will probably make almost 2 dozen rolls, so if you don't have enough muffin pans, stagger the procedure and do it in two or three batches. You can also use custard cups. Brush the filled pans with butter.

DINNER ROLLS, CONTINUED

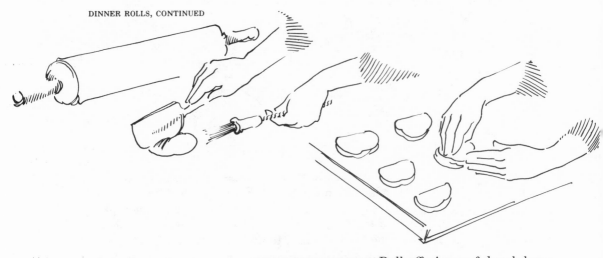

PARKER HOUSE ROLLS: Pull off pieces of dough large enough to make balls of about 2½ inches in diameter. Flatten these and then make a crease down the middle with a floured spatula. Butter one half and fold the other half over, pressing the edges together securely. Set on greased baking sheets 1 inch or more apart. Brush with butter.

BOW-KNOTS OR TWISTS: Pull off pieces of dough and roll out into ropes about ½ inch in diameter. To make bow-knots cut off 6-inch pieces and tie into bows as illustrated. For twists take two ropes 4 inches long and twist them, pinching the ends together. Place on greased baking sheets an inch apart. Brush with milk.

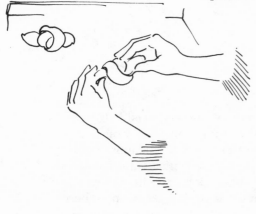

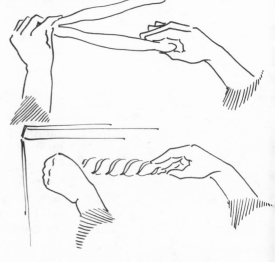

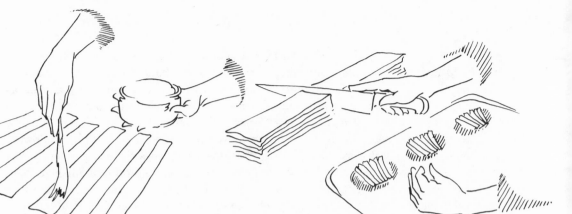

FAN-TANS: Divide the dough in half and roll into 2 squares ⅛ inch thick. Cut into strips 1½ inches wide. Brush each strip with melted butter, then make a stack of 6. Cut into 1-inch pieces and place in buttered muffin pans, cut side up.

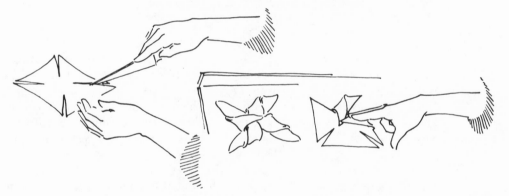

PINWHEELS: Divide the dough in half and roll out into 2 squares ½ inch thick. With a ruler mark off 3-inch squares, then cut and separate them. Now make a 1½-inch cut at each point going toward the center. Pull each corner toward the center and fold over to the right, pressing down in the center to secure.

For the second rising, allow the formed rolls to rise, lightly covered with waxed paper, in a warm place for 45 minutes. Paint lightly again with the prescribed glazes. Bake in a preheated 375° oven for about 25 minutes until golden. Remove from pans and serve warm.

Icebox Rolls

Like icebox cookies, these sweet yeast rolls suggest "old-fashioned cooking" and the pleasure, perhaps, had by a farmwife when she had in her ice-cooled food chest a bowlful of dough that could last a week as she pulled off just enough for an immediate need—exactly the amount to make rolls for supper each night. In our Vermont kitchen we've used the recipe below to make a batch of small round rolls simply brushed with butter; on a following night a new batch was sprinkled with sesame seeds; on a third night we shaped the same dough in twists, brushed them with egg glaze, and embellished them with poppy seeds that dotted the seams. From the same lot of dough one night we made a small, thin French-style loaf, put it in an oval clay dish, and baked it outdoors in a domed barbecue grill. What remained, finally, we used to make cinnamon rolls (page 185). And of course the original dough can be varied with the addition of whole wheat flour, or a liberal seasoning of herbs, or a choice of grated cheese or fresh cheese to give flavor. The dough keeps well for one week and would furnish enough for a small family for that long; if your family is larger, double or triple this recipe.

Makes 4–5 dozen rolls, depending on size

*2 tablespoons active
  dry yeast*
⅓ cup sugar
2 cups warm water
*2 teaspoons coarse salt
  or 1 teaspoon table
  salt*
1 egg, well beaten
*3 tablespoons melted
  butter or vegetable
  shortening*
*5½–6 cups white flour,
  preferably
  unbleached*

Mix the yeast and sugar and warm water together in a large bowl. When dissolved, add the salt, the beaten egg, and melted butter or shortening. Mix in enough of the flour until the mixture becomes hard to stir. Then turn the dough out onto a floured working surface and let rest while you clean out the bowl.

Knead the dough, adding more flour as necessary, for about 6–7 minutes until it is smooth and elastic. Grease the cleaned bowl and put the dough into it, turning to coat. Cover with plastic wrap and let rise until double in volume—about 1–1½ hours.

Punch the dough down, cover with floured plastic wrap, put a plate on top, and store in the refrigerator until ready to use. It will keep for a week.

To make rolls, simply tear off as much dough as you think you'll need for your purposes. Form into whatever shapes you want to make, warming up the dough a little in your hands as you shape the roll. Place on a greased baking sheet an inch or two apart if you want rolls with a crust, or if you want soft ones, snuggle them close to each other in a greased pie or cake pan. Cover lightly with a kitchen towel and let rise until double in volume.* Bake in a preheated 425° oven for 15–20 minutes until golden.

*Just before baking, brush with an egg glaze (1 egg beaten with 1 teaspoon water) if you wish, and add whatever topping you may want to use.

Canadian Buttermilk Honey Rolls

With buttermilk and honey readily available on a Quebec farm, these rolls could be easily whipped up for supper. The secret of the method here is that no first rising is called for, so that the rolls take less than 1½ hours from start to finish. You can substitute sour cream thinned with a little milk if buttermilk isn't readily available.

Makes 20 large rolls

2 cups buttermilk
1 tablespoon active dry
  yeast
2 tablespoons honey
2 teaspoons coarse salt
  or 1 teaspoon table
  salt
2 tablespoons butter or
  lard
¼ teaspoon baking
  soda
4–4½ cups white flour,
  preferably
  unbleached
Melted butter

Heat the buttermilk to lukewarm. Pour ⅓ cup of it into a medium-size bowl and sprinkle in the yeast. Let stand until the yeast is dissolved and starts to swell.

Meanwhile melt the honey, salt, and butter or lard in the rest of the buttermilk. Add the baking soda and let cool to lukewarm, then mix in with the yeast. Add the flour 1 cup at a time, beating thoroughly after each addition.

Turn the dough out onto a lightly floured surface and knead for 2–3 minutes until smooth and resilient; the dough should not be sticky, so add a little more flour if necessary. Roll the dough out to ¾-inch thickness and with a floured cutter or glass 2½ inches in diameter, cut out circles and place on a greased baking sheet about 1 inch apart. Cover with a porous towel and let rise until double in bulk—about 1 hour.

Brush the tops generously with melted butter and bake in a preheated 400° oven 20 minutes; the rolls will be golden-topped puffy cushions and should be eaten warm.

Graham Bran Rolls

Earthy, slightly chewy, these are so tempting you'll find you can easily become addicted to them.

Makes 18 rolls

1½ cups milk
1 tablespoon active dry
  yeast
2 tablespoons butter
1 tablespoon dark
  brown sugar
1 tablespoon molasses
1 teaspoon coarse salt
  or ½ teaspoon table
  salt
¼ teaspoon baking
  soda
¾ cup graham flour
1¼ cups bran
1½–2 cups white flour,
  preferably
  unbleached
Melted butter

Warm the milk and when lukewarm remove ¼ cup and pour over the yeast in a large mixing bowl.

Melt the butter with brown sugar, molasses, and salt in the remaining milk, then cool to lukewarm. Pour into the bowl with the yeast. Stir in the baking soda, then the graham flour, the bran, and as much white flour as you need to make a soft dough. Cover the bowl with a towel and set into a pot of tap-hot water. Let rise (it will only take 30–40 minutes).

Punch the dough down, cover, and let rise again the same way until double in bulk (even less time this round).

Turn the dough out onto a floured working surface, knead a few turns, and work in what flour is necessary so that the dough isn't too sticky and can be rolled to a thickness of ½ inch. Cut circles with a 2½–3-inch floured cookie cutter or glass and place them at least an inch apart on a greased baking sheet; if they stick to your surface, simply use a dough scraper to get them up. Now brush the circles with melted butter and fold over so that the upper lip slightly overlaps the lower. Cover loosely with a towel, place the baking sheet over the pot of warm water, and let rise until double—about 30–40 minutes.

Bake in a preheated 375° oven 18–20 minutes until nicely browned on top. Remove and brush with melted butter. Serve hot.

Potato-Celeriac Rolls

You can make a plain potato roll simply by using unadulterated mashed potatoes here, but the combination of potato and celeriac makes an unusual subtly-flavored roll. You could also use puréed rutabaga or carrots in combination with potatoes.

Be sure to save the water that you cook the potatoes and celeriac in. This recipe also makes a good bread; double it if you want two 8-inch loaves, or make one free-form round loaf.

Makes 16 rolls

1 tablespoon active dry yeast
¾ cup warm potato-celeriac cooking water
1 tablespoon nonfat dry milk
1 teaspoon sugar
2 cups or more white flour, preferably unbleached
½ cup warm mashed potatoes mixed with equal part mashed celeriac
2 tablespoons soft butter
1½ teaspoons coarse salt or 1 teaspoon table salt

Dissolve the yeast in a medium bowl with the potato-celeriac water, dry milk, sugar, and 1 cup of the flour. Cover with plastic wrap and let sit until it froths and bubbles up—about 20–30 minutes.

Beat the ½ cup of warm potato-celeriac purée with the butter, and most of the remaining cup of flour. Add the yeast sponge and salt. Mix until it becomes hard to stir, then turn the dough out onto a floured working surface and let rest while you clean and butter the bowl. Knead, adding a little more flour as necessary until smooth and elastic—7–8 minutes. Return to the bowl, cover with plastic wrap, and let rise until double in bulk—about 1 hour.

Tear off small hunks of the dough, a little bigger than a golf ball, form into rolls as described on page 157, and place about an inch apart on a greased baking sheet. Cover loosely with a towel and let rise 40 minutes.

Bake in a preheated 400° oven 15–18 minutes until lightly browned on top. Serve warm.

Honeyed Wheat Hamburger Rolls

If good-quality well-seasoned ground beef perks up your taste buds, nothing can do more to make the all-American snack really satisfying than the bun on which you put the meat. Anyone who knows the joy of making bread will find this an easy recipe and one that can be shaped to hold hot dogs just as winningly as hamburgers.

Makes 12 hamburger buns

1 tablespoon active dry yeast
1 ¼ cups warm water
1 tablespoon honey
2 tablespoons vegetable oil
2 teaspoons coarse salt or 1 teaspoon table salt
3 tablespoons nonfat dry milk
½ cup wheat germ
3–3 ½ cups white flour, preferably unbleached
Melted butter

In a medium-size bowl dissolve the yeast in ¼ cup of the warm water and the honey. Add the oil, salt, the remaining warm water, and the dry milk. Stir in the wheat germ and add 3 cups of the flour, a little at a time. When the dough begins to leave the sides of the bowl, turn out onto a floured surface and let rest while you clean and grease the bowl. Knead until it is smooth and elastic, adding any remaining flour as necessary. Return the dough to the bowl, cover with plastic wrap, and let rise about 1 ½ hours, until doubled in bulk.

Punch down the dough and knead briefly. Pat the dough into a round about the size of a Frisbee. Use a floured knife to cut the dough first into quarters; then cut each quarter into 3 wedges. Cover and let rest 15 minutes.

Flour your hands and shape the wedges of dough into 12 balls. Flatten the balls with your hand and arrange, well spaced, on a large greased cookie sheet. Cover the buns and leave to double in bulk.

Spread tops with melted butter. Bake in preheated 400° oven for 25–30 minutes.

Parsnip (or Pumpkin or Squash) Rolls

Even if you think you hate parsnips, try these rolls. The flavor is so delicate that it merely tantalizes, and the puréed vegetable makes the rolls particularly tender and moist. In the same recipe either pumpkin or squash can also be good, and they give a pleasing color. But we think parsnips with their surprising flavor are tops. This amount will also make two nice 8-inch loaves of bread, or you can vary and make about 20 rolls plus one of those small crusty loaves which country inns like to serve these days on a small board with a knife alongside to cut it.

Makes about 30 rolls

1 pound parsnips (or
  pumpkin or squash)
¼ cup light brown
  sugar
Nutmeg
2 teaspoons coarse salt
  or 1 teaspoon table
  salt
1 cup milk
6 tablespoons butter
2 teaspoons grated
  lemon peel
1 tablespoon active dry
  yeast
¼ cup warm water
4½–5 cups white flour,
  preferably
  unbleached
Melted butter

Scrape the parsnips and chop roughly. Cook in about 2 cups salted water for 15–20 minutes until they can be pierced easily with a fork. Drain thoroughly and mash (you should have about 1 cup) or spin in the food processor, beating in the brown sugar, several gratings of nutmeg (or about 1/16 teaspoon if you do not have a whole nutmeg and a little grater), the salt, milk, butter, and lemon peel. (If you are using pumpkin or squash, it will be easier to use the canned or frozen form, not seasoned or sweetened, unless, of course, you happen to have about 1 cup of leftover mashed pumpkin or squash in the refrigerator.)

In a medium bowl dissolve the yeast in the warm water. Add the puréed mixture and then stir in the flour cup by cup until the dough starts to come away from the sides of the bowl. Turn the dough out on a floured surface and knead for 4–5 minutes until smooth, adding more flour as necessary.

Clean the bowl, grease it, and return the dough to it, turning to coat. Place the bowl covered with plastic wrap over a pan of hot but not boiling water, and let rise until double in volume—30–40 minutes.

Turn the dough out and form into rolls as shown on page 157. Place on a buttered baking sheet an inch apart and cover lightly with a towel. Let rise until double in size. (Or form into two 6-inch loaves or one large loaf for a 9–10-inch bread pan.)

Bake in a preheated 375° oven 15–20 minutes until golden on top (25 minutes for a small loaf; 40 for the 9-inch size). Remove and brush with melted butter. Serve warm.

Sweet Potato Ginger Rolls

Sweet potato biscuits and rolls are as old as Virginia's Old Dominion—and they're particularly delicious with country ham. In colonial kitchens, powdered ginger might have been more commonly used.

Makes about 3 dozen rolls

1 tablespoon active dry
   yeast
1¼ cups warm water
2 tablespoons sugar
2 tablespoons nonfat
   dry milk
1 teaspoon grated
   fresh ginger root*
1 teaspoon grated
   orange rind
1 teaspoon coarse salt
   or ½ teaspoon table
   salt
⅛ teaspoon freshly
   grated nutmeg
2 tablespoons soft
   butter
¾ cup mashed sweet
   potatoes
3½ cups white flour,
   preferably
   unbleached

In a medium-size bowl dissolve the yeast in ¼ cup of the warm water. Stir the sugar and dry milk into the remaining water and add to the yeast along with the grated ginger, orange rind, salt, and nutmeg. Whip the butter into the mashed sweet potatoes and add. Stir in the flour and then beat the mixture for 1 minute. Cover the bowl with plastic wrap and place over a pan of warm water to rise until double in volume—about 45 minutes.

Turn out onto a floured work surface, punch down, and knead very lightly a few turns. Pull off pieces of dough slightly smaller than Ping-Pong balls and, since they will be very sticky, just roll lightly with floured hands to form a ball. Place in one or two greased pans large enough to hold the 3 dozen rolls side by side without crowding and cover with a kitchen towel to let rise in a warm place for 30 minutes. Paint with the egg glaze and sprinkle sesame seeds on top.

Bake in a preheated 350° oven for 25 minutes. Serve warm.

GLAZE:

1 egg beaten with 1
   teaspoon water
Sesame seeds

* To grate fresh ginger, peel the skin from half of a piece of ginger root and then grate, using the fine holes of a grater set over a plate or a piece of waxed paper.

Spiced Cranberry Rolls

The tradition of cranberries as an accent to Thanksgiving dinner may belong to Cape Cod, and such delights as cranberry muffins may seem authentically Yankee, but the red berries grow abundantly in Wisconsin, where deep-fried "cranberry burrs," a sort of doughnut to accompany the meat course, seem to have originated. On the West Coast also, the indigenous fruit is a big crop in Oregon and Washington, and orange-flavored cranberry quick bread is often baked to celebrate the annual Bandon Cranberry Festival. Cranberry rolls, made with yeast and accented by ginger as well as cinnamon, can be served at any meal—hot from the oven, of course.

Makes 2 dozen rolls

1 cup milk
4 tablespoons (½ stick) butter
¼ cup sugar
1 teaspoon coarse salt or ½ teaspoon table salt
2 tablespoons active dry yeast
¼ cup warm water
2 eggs, lightly beaten
½ teaspoon ground ginger
1 teaspoon cinnamon
4½–5 cups white flour, preferably unbleached
½ cup chopped fresh cranberries

Heat the milk to the boiling point and dissolve the butter, sugar, and salt in it. Let cool to lukewarm.

In a large bowl dissolve the yeast in the warm water. Add the cooled milk mixture, eggs, ginger, and cinnamon. Stir in almost all the flour until the dough starts to come away from the sides of the bowl.

Turn out and knead about 3–4 minutes, adding more flour as necessary. Sprinkle some flour over the cranberries, then knead them into the dough. Clean your bowl and butter it. Return the dough to it; let rise, covered with plastic wrap, until double in volume.

Turn out and roll the dough to a thickness of ½ inch. Cut into 2½-inch circles, plump the dough up by pulling the sides under and pinching together on the bottom, and place on buttered baking sheets an inch apart, seam side under. Cover with a kitchen towel and let rise about 30 minutes.

Bake in a preheated 350° oven 25 minutes. Serve warm.

Onion Rolls

Breads enriched with onions have been popular in many cultures since ancient Egyptians convinced themselves of the mystic value of pungent bulbs. In this somewhat unusual version, best when absolutely fresh and warm, the small amount of rye flour gives a slightly chewy texture, and by tucking the onions and poppy seeds mostly inside, you don't get the burnt taste that afflicts many onion rolls.

Makes 12 rolls

1 tablespoon active dry yeast
1 tablespoon brown sugar
¾ cup warm water
2 tablespoons nonfat dry milk
2 teaspoons coarse salt or 1 teaspoon table salt
2 tablespoons rye flour
About 2 cups white flour, preferably unbleached
1½ cups chopped onions (3 medium onions)
3 tablespoons butter
2 tablespoons poppy seeds

GLAZE

1 egg beaten with 1 tablespoon water

In a medium-size bowl dissolve the yeast and the brown sugar in the warm water. Stir in the dry milk, salt, rye flour, and as much of the white flour as can be easily absorbed.

Turn the dough out on a floured work surface and let rest while you clean out and grease the bowl. Knead the dough, adding more flour as necessary, for 8–10 minutes until it is smooth and elastic. Return to the greased bowl, cover with plastic wrap, and let rise until double in volume—about 1 hour.

Meanwhile sauté the onions in the butter about 3–4 minutes until translucent.

Turn the dough out on a floured surface and pat and/or roll into a circle 9 inches in diameter. Spread the onions on top, then sprinkle with poppy seeds. Cut into quarters, then cut each quarter into three even wedges. Roll each wedge

from the outside toward the center and place on a greased baking sheet an inch or so apart. Cover lightly with a towel and let rise until almost double in volume—about 30–40 minutes.

Brush the tops with the egg glaze and bake in a preheated 350° oven about 20–25 minutes or until golden brown on top. Serve fresh and warm.

Brazilian Beer Rolls

When Brazilian men are out drinking the draft beer they call *chopp* (which they, like most South Americans, do in vast quantities), the cooks at home may be using beer as a liquefier in preparing bread dough. These dinner rolls are often also served at breakfast with *café con leche*. They are very light, with a quality reminiscent of sourdough.

Makes 12 rolls

1 package active dry
  yeast
1 tablespoon sugar
¼ cup warm milk
½ cup lager beer, at
  room temperature
About 2½ cups white
  flour, preferably
  unbleached
2 eggs, separated
4 tablespoons softened
  butter
2 teaspoons coarse salt
  or 1 teaspoon table
  salt

Make a sponge: put yeast, sugar, and milk in a large bowl and add the beer. When the yeast bubbles, stir in 1 cup flour to make a smooth mixture. Cover and let the dough rise about 1 hour, until double in bulk.

Beat the egg whites until stiff. Beat the yolks until thick and pale; add the butter and continue beat while adding the sponge and enough flour to make a soft dough. Add the salt. Fold in the beaten egg whites. When well blended scrape the dough into a large greased bowl, cover with plastic wrap, and let rise 1 hour.

On a floured surface turn the dough out and knead for 2–3 minutes, working in more flour as necessary. The dough should be soft but firm. Cut it into 12 equal pieces, and form these into balls. Put in buttered muffin pan, cover with plastic wrap, and let rise for 12 minutes.

Bake for 20–25 minutes in a preheated 400° oven, until pale brown. Serve warm.

Papaya Bread Rolls

Some tropical vegetables like plantains and cassavas are turned into flour for use in baking, but the melonlike papaya adds its exotic flavor to these rolls when the fibrous flesh itself is beaten with a sweetener like honey, then blended with wheat flour. The texture is accentuated by shiny black papaya seeds.

Makes 20 rolls

1 tablespoon active dry yeast
⅔ cup warm water
1 very ripe papaya
2 tablespoons honey
1 teaspoon coarse salt or ½ teaspoon table salt
1 tablespoon soft butter
2½–3 cups white flour, preferably unbleached

Sprinkle the yeast into the container of a food processor and pour the warm water over it. Let sit a couple of minutes, then insert the metal blade and give it a spin to blend.

Split the papaya and scoop out the seeds, reserving them. Scrape out the flesh and put into the food processor along with the honey, salt, and butter. Blend until thoroughly smooth. Then through the funnel add flour and keep processing until the dough leaves the sides of the bowl. Turn out onto a floured surface and knead a minute or two. Place in a greased bowl and refrigerate overnight, or until ready to use, covered with plastic wrap with a plate on top.

Scrape the dough out onto a floured surface and knead until it warms up. Form into a roll and lop off 20 equal pieces. Flatten each one and tuck a half dozen or so papaya seeds into the dough. With your cupped hands form each of these into a roll, pinching the seam at the bottom, and place 2 inches apart on a greased baking sheet (or 2 if needed), if you want rolls that are crusty; otherwise place side by side in a large buttered pie plate. Cover lightly with a towel and let rise until double in volume—about 40 minutes.

Bake in a preheated 400° oven for 20 minutes. Rub the tops with butter while still warm.

Earl Grey Tea Rolls

These delicate rolls made with Earl Grey tea taste surprisingly spicy and are at their best when served fresh from the oven.

Makes about 30 small rolls

1 tablespoon Earl Grey tea
1 cup boiling water
1 tablespoon active dry yeast
2 tablespoons sugar
2 tablespoons melted butter
1 teaspoon coarse salt or ½ teaspoon table salt
Grated rind of 2 limes
3–3¼ cups white flour, preferably unbleached
Soft butter

Put the tea in a warm pot and pour the boiling water over it. Let steep, covered, for 15 minutes, then strain and cool.

Put the yeast and sugar in a medium-size bowl and pour the lukewarm tea over them. When dissolved, stir in the melted butter, salt, lime rind, and enough of the flour until it becomes hard to stir.

Turn the dough out onto a lightly floured surface and let rest while you clean and butter the bowl. Knead the dough, adding more flour as necessary, until it is smooth and resilient—about 6–7 minutes. Return it to the bowl, cover with plastic wrap, and let rise until double in volume.

Turn the dough out onto a floured surface and punch down. Tear off pieces of dough the size of Ping-Pong balls and form into small rolls. Place 1½ inches apart, on a buttered baking sheet, cover lightly with a towel, and let rise for about 25 minutes.

Bake the rolls in a preheated 375°oven for 15 minutes. Remove and brush with soft butter. Serve warm.

VARIATION: Use lemon tea instead of Earl Grey and the grated rind of 1 lemon instead of lime rind. Add ¼ teaspoon lemon juice as well.

Avocado Rolls

In ancient South America the Incas cultivated avocados, often cooking them (some weighing as much as four pounds) as a vegetable course. It is the buttery, musky texture and flavor that intrigues and, in the recipe below, makes the resulting rolls so rich. The dough is a lovely pale green so delicate it virtually disappears when baked. You'll find that all can be done by hand, but that using a food processor makes the preparation easy.

Makes 12 rolls

1 tablespoon active dry yeast
⅓ cup warm water
1 small ripe avocado or ½ very large one
1 tablespoon sugar
1 teaspoon coarse salt or ½ teaspoon table salt
¼ cup plain yogurt
2½–2¾ cups white flour, preferably unbleached
Soft butter

Sprinkle the yeast on the bottom of a food processor container. Pour the warm water over. Let rest a minute or two, then insert the metal blade and spin a second to blend.

Peel the avocado and add to the yeast. Blend until thoroughly puréed. Blend in the sugar, salt, and yogurt and start adding the flour through the funnel with the motor going, incorporating just enough so that the dough starts to leave the sides of the bowl and balls up. Remove and knead on a lightly floured surface a minute or two, adding a little more flour if necessary.

Place the dough in a buttered bowl, cover with plastic wrap, and let rise until double in volume—about 1 hour or so.

Tear off pieces of dough slightly larger than Ping-Pong balls and form into round, plump rolls, pinching together the seams at the bottoms. Place on a greased baking sheet 2 inches apart and cover lightly with a towel. Let rise until double in volume—about 45 minutes.

Bake in a preheated 400° oven for 20 minutes. Rub the tops with butter while still hot. Serve warm.

Rye Twists

A very chewy, substantial twisted roll, made in a small size so it doesn't overwhelm as a dinner bread. The rolls don't keep well, so freeze immediately any you don't use the first night. As a variation try brushing a few with honey and sprinkling them with pine nuts just before baking—lovely with morning coffee.

Makes 20 rolls

2 tablespoons active
   dry yeast
1 cup warm water
1 cup plain yogurt, at
   room temperature
2 teaspoons coarse salt
   or 1 teaspoon table
   salt
1⅓ cups rye flour
1 cup gluten flour
1½–2 cups white flour,
   preferably
   unbleached

GLAZE

1 beaten egg white

TOPPING

A sprinkle of kosher or
   other coarse salt
Caraway seeds

In a medium-size bowl dissolve the yeast in the warm water. Stir in the yogurt, salt, rye and gluten flours, and about 1½ cups of the white flour until it becomes hard to stir.

Turn the dough out on a floured work surface and let rest while you clean and oil the bowl. Knead the dough—it will be quite sticky—adding more flour as necessary until you have a smooth dough that has lost its tackiness. Return to the bowl, cover with plastic wrap, and let rise until doubled in volume; this will be a slow rise—2 hours or more.

Turn the dough out on a lightly floured surface and divide into 20 pieces. Cut each piece in half and then roll each half out to a length of 5–6 inches. Pinch the ends of the two strands together, twist one over the other several times, then pinch the opposite ends together. Repeat with the rest. Place the twists either in crescent shapes or in circles, overlapping the ends and pinching them together, 1½ inches apart on greased baking sheets. Cover lightly with towels and let rise 1 hour.

Paint the twists with egg white, then sprinkle coarse salt and caraway seeds on top. Bake in a preheated 375° oven for 20 minutes. Serve warm.

Khachapuri (Georgian Cheese Cushions)

In the bestselling memoir of his youth in southern Russia, George Papashvily points out that learning to cook was as much a masculine prerogative as it was feminine, and he vividly remembers the weekly baking days and the making of cheese-filled *khachapuri* and other Georgian breads. Similar memories are recorded by Sonia Uvezian in her book on Russian food. As other ethnic groups do also, Georgians consider all bread sacred, and much dedication traditionally goes into its preparation. Their cheese breads are made in numerous shapes and sizes, often as small molten cushions like these. In the method given below we found that fresh Monterey Jack from the supermarket could be substituted for the more commonly used muenster, and that it is improved when combined with an accent of ground aged Monterey Jack; but similar combinations of mild and sharp cheese will do as well.

Makes 16 cushions

1 tablespoon active dry yeast
1 cup warm water
1 tablespoon honey
¼ cup nonfat dry milk
2 teaspoons coarse salt or 1 teaspoon plain salt
6 tablespoons melted butter
2¾–3 cups white flour, preferably unbleached
10 ounces Monterey Jack or muenster
3 tablespoons grated aged Monterey Jack or Parmesan
1 egg
2 tablespoons soft butter

GLAZE

1 egg, beaten

In a medium-size bowl (or in the bowl of the food processor) dissolve the yeast in the warm water. Stir in the honey, dry milk, salt, and melted butter. Add flour until it becomes difficult to stir, then turn out to knead (or knead in the food processor) until the dough forms a ball.

When the dough is smooth and elastic—if you are hand-kneading, after 5–6 minutes—put it in a clean bowl that you have warmed first with hot water, dried, and buttered. Turn to coat all over, and cover with plastic wrap. Let rise until double in volume.

Turn the dough out, punch it down, lightly cover, and let rest while you prepare the cheese filling.

Grate the soft cheese coarsely and mix it with the hard. Lightly beat the egg, then mix in the cheeses and the soft butter.

To make cushions: divide the dough in half, covering one half while you work with the other. Roll the one half out on a lightly floured surface to an 18-inch square or a little more, as the dough tends to contract. Using a 4½-inch cutter make eight circles. Place a generous tablespoon of cheese filling in the center of each, then draw up the two opposite sides and pinch them firmly together in the middle. Do the same with the other two sides; pinch together the seams, too, and to be sure they are secure—otherwise the filling will ooze out— drizzle a little of the egg glaze along the seams, then pinch again with well-floured fingers. Place 2 inches apart on a greased baking sheet. Paint the tops all over with the egg glaze.

TOPPING

About 2 tablespoons grated aged Jack or Parmesan

Let rest, uncovered, for about 20–25 minutes until they are beginning to swell slightly. If any seams have sprung open, pinch them back together.

Form the other half of the dough in the same manner.

Just before baking, paint the tops again with egg glaze and sprinkle grated topping cheese over. Bake for 20 minutes in a preheated 375° oven. Let rest a few minutes before eating—if you can hold off—then enjoy them fresh and warm. To reheat, wrap in foil.

8 · Sweet Breakfast and Tea Breads, Rolls, and Buns

Sweet Saffron Bread
Portuguese Sweet Bread
  with Macadamia Nuts
Mennonite Streuselkuchen
Coffee Cake Ring
Orange Rolls with Glaze
Philadelphia Cinnamon Buns
Butterscotch Rolls
Bath Buns and Chelsea Buns
Kolache
Brioches—Hand Method,
  Food Processor Method
Croissants
Danish Pastries
Pisticcini

The story of sweet breads that satisfy the morning palate runs from pre-Christian times to the contemporary fix in which we find ourselves. Some American schoolchildren today are persuaded to accept as breakfast snacks an "engineered food" that looks natural but is packed with synthetic vitamins and proteins centered on a prefab filling designed to seem creamy and appetizing. Long before such modern laboratory products, according to George Lang in *The Cuisine of Hungary,* yeast dough coffee cakes originated centuries ago as pre-Christian burial offerings—some were sweet breads that had been braided like hair, and others were made in pretzel shapes like arm bracelets. Hot cross buns became associated with Good Friday after the Reformation. Before that, dough was customarily slashed with a cross to ward off evil spirits that might at any time prevent the leaven from working. Other sweet breads as we know them today are often playfully marked, and they vary from plain and simple brioches in the French manner to the sticky buns of Philadelphia. Generations of youngsters have known how naturally good such honest sweet breads really are—and it's a real satisfaction to share them now with your own small fry, to say nothing of adults.

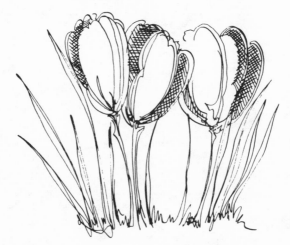

Sweet Saffron Bread

The Spanish still use saffron in several kinds of cooking, but in most of the rest of Europe the colorful seasoning is confined to baking cakes and breads—even though it remains discouragingly expensive.

Makes one 9-inch loaf

½ teaspoon saffron
   threads
2 tablespoons boiling
   water
1 tablespoon active dry
   yeast
1 cup warm milk
¼ cup raisins
¼ cup currants
½ teaspoon coarse salt
   or ¼ teaspoon table
   salt
3½ cups white flour,
   preferably
   unbleached
½ cup (1 stick) butter
½ cup light brown
   sugar
1 egg
2 tablespoons ground
   almonds
½ teaspoon almond
   extract

GLAZE

1 egg yolk
Sugar
Sliced almonds

In a small cup steep the saffron threads in boiling water and let cool.

In a medium-size mixing bowl dissolve the yeast in ¼ cup of the warm milk and let stand. Toss the raisins and currants and salt with the flour.

In another bowl beat the butter until creamy, then add the brown sugar and finally the egg. When well blended add the ground almonds and almond extract.

Stir the saffron and its deep orange-colored water into the yeast; scrape up every bit of this precious liquid—in fact, rinse out the cup with the rest of the milk, then add to the yeast mixture. Beat in the flour mixture, continuing to beat for almost a minute. Cover the bowl with plastic wrap and set over a pan of warm water to rise until the dough is light and doubled in volume—about 45 minutes.

Uncover the bowl and now beat in the butter-sugar mixture; beat hard for several minutes. Turn the dough onto a floured surface and knead until smooth and shiny—about 5 minutes. Divide the dough in half and roll out into thick rolls 1½ inches in diameter and a little longer than the bread pan. Twist the 2 rolls together and place in a well-buttered 9-inch loaf pan. Brush the top with egg yolk and let rest, then brush again after a minute. Sprinkle sugar all over the top and then sliced almonds liberally—as many as manage to stick. Lightly cover with a towel; let rise in a warm place until double in volume.

Bake in a preheated 375° oven for 40 minutes. Let cool in the pan 5 minutes, then turn out carefully onto a rack.

Portuguese Sweet Bread
with Macadamia Nuts

Macadamia nuts, known to the Western world for only a century, sometimes accent fried fish in Australia; and Hawaiians have devised a splendid chiffon pie that gets its sweet elusive flavor from the nuts named for Dr. John Macadam, a South Pacific botanist. Because of the difficulty of processing, macadamia nuts are expensive, and we've been able to discover few breads making use of them. Here is an adaptation of a Portuguese sweet bread introduced in Honolulu by the first colonists.

Makes 1 round loaf

*1 tablespoon active dry
  yeast
¾ cup warm water
2 tablespoons nonfat
  dry milk
⅓ cup sugar
½ teaspoon coarse salt
  or a pinch of table
  salt
2 eggs at room
  temperature, beaten
3–3¼ cups white flour
  preferably
  unbleached
4 tablespoons soft
  sweet butter
1 cup macadamia nuts,
  roughly sliced*

In a medium-size bowl dissolve the yeast in the warm water. Stir in the dry milk, sugar, salt, and beaten eggs. Mix in 1 cup of the flour, then beat in the soft butter a tablespoon at a time until it is absorbed. Add enough more of the flour to make a manageable dough.

Turn the dough out on a floured work surface and let rest while you clean and butter the bowl. Knead the dough lightly for a few minutes, adding more flour as necessary, then return it to the bowl, cover with plastic wrap, and let rise in a warm place until double in volume—about 1 hour.

Turn the dough out, punch down, and knead in the nuts. Let rest, covered with a towel, for 10 minutes.

Punch the dough down again and form into a round. Place in a buttered 9-inch cake pan, cover with a towel, and let rise again until double in volume—about 45 minutes.

Bake in a preheated 350° oven for 45 minutes. Turn out and cool on a rack.

Mennonite Streuselkuchen

"Streusel," coming from the German word for sprinkling or strewing, is an accepted American term for coffee or breakfast breads that are made from sweetened dough and are topped with a mixture of sugar crumbs and nuts. Wherever Germans gather there are bound to be coffee cakes, and some of the best come from Mennonite kitchens in various parts of the U.S. This makes three cakes. If you choose to freeze one, you'll find it reheats well when wrapped in foil.

Makes three 8-inch cakes

CAKE DOUGH

1 tablespoon active dry
   yeast
½ cup warm water
6 tablespoons butter
⅔ cup sugar
1 egg, separated
1 teaspoon coarse salt
   or ½ teaspoon table
   salt
1½ cups warm milk
¼ cup heavy cream
About 5 cups white
   flour, preferably
   unbleached

STREUSEL TOPPING

½ cup sugar
1 teaspoon cinnamon
¼ cup white flour,
   preferably
   unbleached
3 tablespoons soft
   butter
½ teaspoon vanilla
   extract
¼ cup chopped
   walnuts

Stir the yeast in a cup with the water and let rest until dissolved.

In a large bowl cream the butter and the sugar together. Then beat in the yolk of the egg, the salt, the dissolved yeast, the milk, and the cream. Stir in enough of the white flour to make a soft dough.

Beat the egg white until it forms soft peaks, then stir and fold gently into the dough. Cover with floured plastic wrap, put a plate on top of the bowl, and let rise slowly overnight in the refrigerator.

Remove the dough, turn out onto a floured working surface, and divide into 3 parts. Form into cakes, adding just a little more flour if necessary to make manageable, although this should remain a soft dough, and pat into 3 greased 8-inch cake tins. Cover with towels and let rise in a warm place for 1½ hours.

Mix together the streusel ingredients and sprinkle evenly over the tops of the 3 pans of dough. Bake in a preheated 400° oven for 20 minutes. Let sit a few minutes in the pans, then remove and cool on racks. Serve warm.

Coffee Cake Ring

The basic coffee cake dough given here can be filled with almost anything you like—apples, prunes, cottage cheese and raisins (see fillings, pages 204–206). Just follow the proportions of this filling and play with the ingredients.

Makes 1 large ring

CAKE DOUGH

*1 tablespoon active dry
   yeast
¼ cup warm water
⅓ cup sugar
½ cup sour cream
½ teaspoon grated
   lemon rind
½ teaspoon coarse salt
   or ¼ teaspoon table
   salt
½ teaspoon almond
   extract
2 eggs
2½–2¾ cups white
   flour, preferably
   unbleached
⅓ cup soft butter*

FILLING

*2 tablespoons melted
   butter
3 tablespoons sugar
1 tablespoon cinnamon
¼ cup yellow raisins
2 tablespoons currants
⅓ cup chopped
   walnuts
1 egg, beaten
Powdered sugar*

In a medium bowl soak the yeast in the warm water until dissolved. Add the sugar and mix well. If the sour cream is refrigerator-cold, warm it, then add to the yeast mixture along with the lemon rind, salt, and almond extract. Beat in 2 eggs. Add enough of the flour to make a soft dough, then beat in the butter.

Turn out on a floured work surface and knead until the dough is shiny and smooth—about 6–7 minutes. Clean out the bowl, butter it lightly, and return the dough to it. Cover with plastic wrap and let rise until double in bulk—45–60 minutes.

Turn the dough out, flatten it, then roll out on a lightly floured surface to a rectangle 28 by 8 inches.

Brush the dough surface with the melted butter, then scatter the remaining filling ingredients over. Roll up jelly-roll fashion quite tightly and pinch together the final seam securely. Now pull the

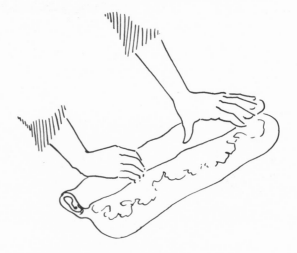

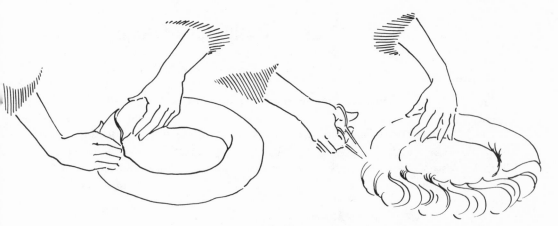

ends toward each other to make a circle, overlap
the end pieces, and pinch together firmly. Transfer
to a greased cookie sheet. With a pair of sharp
scissors, snip gashes all around the top circle of
dough, 1 inch apart. Cover with a towel and let
rise until double—about 45 minutes.

Paint the surface with beaten egg and bake in a
preheated 375° oven 10 minutes, then lower the
heat to 350° and continue baking 20 minutes until
nicely browned. When cool, sprinkle with
powdered sugar.

Orange Rolls with Glaze

This recipe makes a panful of soft, sticky rolls with a lovely orange flavor. If you like a roll that's not too gooey, don't put the rounds of dough in the glaze to rise, but form small balls instead; bake about 2 inches apart for a crustier surface, then paint with glaze for the last few minutes of baking. You'll need only half the amount of glaze if you do them this way. To make a loaf of orange bread, put the dough after the first rising into an 8-inch greased bread pan and let it rise once more. Bake 10 minutes in a preheated 400° oven, reduce heat to 350°, and bake 35–40 minutes longer.

Makes 20 rolls

DOUGH

1 tablespoon active dry yeast

⅓ cup light brown sugar

¼ cup warm water

1¼ cups fresh orange juice

3 tablespoons butter, cut up

1½ teaspoons coarse salt or ½ teaspoon table salt

2 tablespoons grated orange rind

3½–4 cups white flour, preferably unbleached

GLAZE

2 tablespoons butter

1 tablespoon cornstarch

1 cup fresh orange juice

2 tablespoons grated orange rind

½ cup sugar

½ cup water

Put the yeast and brown sugar in a medium-size bowl and pour warm water over. Let stand while you heat ½ cup of the orange juice and the cut-up butter; dissolve salt in the hot juice, then stir in the orange rind and the remaining orange juice. Stir in the yeast, add 3½ cups of the flour a little at a time, and beat with an electric beater at least 3 minutes. Cover the bowl and place in a pot of hot tap water; let rise until the dough is light and almost double in bulk—about 1 hour.

While the dough is rising, prepare the glaze: melt the 2 tablespoons butter in a saucepan, then add all the other ingredients, whisking well to smooth as they heat up. Boil rapidly for 3–4 minutes, until thickened. Allow to cool; when tepid, spread the glaze over the bottom of a 10-by-14-inch baking pan.

When the dough is ready, turn out onto a floured surface and roll out to ⅓-inch thickness. (It is easier to work with half the dough at a time, keeping the other half covered.) Add flour as necessary to keep the dough from sticking. With a floured cookie cutter or a glass about 2 inches in diameter, cut circles of dough and place them nearly touching on top of the glaze. Cover with a towel and let rise over the pot of hot water until double in bulk—45 minutes or so.

Bake 20 minutes in a preheated 375° oven. Serve warm from the pan.

Philadelphia Cinnamon Buns, Sticky Buns, or Pecan Rolls

Various names, as above, are attached to this American sweet bread that probably derives from a confection Mrs. William Penn and other Pennsylvania ladies called "whig." Other parts of the country called them as they saw them.

Makes about 20 buns

1 tablespoon active dry yeast

1¼ cups warm water

¼ cup nonfat dry milk

½ teaspoon coarse salt or ¼ teaspoon table salt

1 cup sugar

4 tablespoons vegetable shortening, melted

4 cups white flour, preferably unbleached

½ cup (1 stick) sweet butter, softened

1 cup brown sugar

¾ teaspoon cinnamon

½ cup raisins

⅔ cup roughly chopped pecans

In a large bowl dissolve the yeast in a little warm water. When it swells, add the dry milk, remaining water, salt, sugar and melted shortening, stirring until smooth. Add the flour a little at a time, beating thoroughly. Cover with plastic wrap and let rise for 1 hour or more in a warm place, until the dough doubles in bulk.

Turn the dough out onto a floured surface and roll out ¼ inch thick to form a rectangle about 30 by 8 inches. Spread with half the softened butter. Mix the brown sugar with the cinnamon and raisins; sprinkle half this mixture over the buttered dough, then roll up like a jelly roll, starting with a long end. Pinch edges to seal. Cut crosswise into sections 1½ inches wide.

Mix the remaining butter with remaining sugar-cinnamon-raisin mixture and scatter this along with the pecans over the buttered surface of 2 eight-inch round cake pans. Place sections of the rolled dough, the wide side down, in the pans so they almost touch. Cover lightly with towels and let rise to double in size.

Bake in a preheated 375° oven for 25–30 minutes, until golden. Ease the rolls out of the pans and serve warm, bottom side up.

Butterscotch Rolls

We advise using nonstick muffin pans to make these very sticky rolls. Serve while still warm.

Makes 24 rolls

2⅓ cups cake flour
2 teaspoons baking
  powder
½ teaspoon baking
  soda
1 teaspoon coarse salt
  or ½ teaspoon table
  salt
¼ cup sugar
1 egg
½ cup buttermilk
5 tablespoons
  shortening
⅔ cup melted butter
1¼ cups brown sugar

Sift the flour, baking powder and soda, salt, and sugar together. Beat the egg thoroughly, then whisk in the buttermilk. Cut the shortening into the flour. Now pour the wet ingredients into the dry, mix, turn out onto a lightly floured surface, and knead 20 strokes. Roll out into a rectangle 12 by 6 inches.

Put 1 teaspoon melted butter and 2 teaspoons of the brown sugar in the bottom of 24 muffin forms. (If you want to bake in two batches, prepare only 12 now, reserving ¼ cup melted butter and about ½ cup brown sugar.)

Spread the remaining butter (you should have about 2 tablespoons) over the dough and sprinkle with the remaining brown sugar. Roll up jelly-roll fashion. Then slice the roll into pieces ½ inch thick. Place the slices, cut side down, in the bottom of the prepared tins. Bake in a preheated 375° oven for 15–20 minutes until lightly browned and gooey. Remove from the muffin cups while still hot.

BATH BUNS AND CHELSEA BUNS

Some years ago, on a visit to a friend in Exeter after a drive through Somerset, we were told that we'd made a mistake in not eating a Bath bun in the town that gave that confection its name. Bath buns, said our hostess, were invented by the health resort's chief physician, Dr. William Oliver, along with Bath Olivers, the crackers famous in England for the way in which they complement such good things as cheese. Bath buns first appeared about 1750, and for generations they have been sold by Fortts and other local bakeries; traditionally they are also made in Somerset farm kitchens on baking days, being put into the oven after the bread is taken out. Strewn with bits of orange peel, these favorite buns of Bath became so popular with England's smart set during the Georgian period that the Old Chelsea Bun House, in southwest London, developed a rival recipe that acquired among its devotees George III and his queen. In a single day, Theodora FitzGibbon has recorded, the Bun House on Pimlico Road sold as many as a quarter million of these small sweet breads.

> Prelates and princes, and lieges and Kings,
> Hail for the bellman, who tinkles and sings,
> Bouche of the highest and lowliest ones
> There's a charm in the sound which nobody shuns,
> Of 'smoking hot, piping hot, Chelsea Buns!'

Basic Bun Dough

Makes 18 buns

*3½ cups white flour,
  preferably
  unbleached*
*1 teaspoon coarse salt
  or ½ teaspoon table
  salt*
*2 tablespoons active
  dry yeast*
¼ cup sugar
½ boiling water
½ cup milk
*6 tablespoons soft
  butter*
1 egg, lightly beaten

BUN WASH

*¼ cup sugar mixed
  with ⅓ cup water*

Toss the flour and salt in a warm bowl to warm them up.

In a medium-size mixing bowl mix the yeast and 1 tablespoon of the sugar together. Pour the boiling water on top of the cold milk to make up 1 cup, then pour this over the yeast. Stir in a tablespoon of flour and whisk until you have a smooth batter. Cover with plastic wrap and let it foam up—15–20 minutes.

Mix the rest of the sugar and all but ⅓ cup of the flour together and then rub the butter into it. Make a well in the center and put the egg and the yeast mixture in. Mix thoroughly, then turn out on a floured work surface and knead for 8–10 minutes, adding more flour as necessary, until the dough is elastic and doesn't stick to your hands, though it will still be a little tacky.

Wash out the bowl with hot water, dry, and butter it. Put the dough in, turning to coat, and cover with plastic wrap. Let rise until double in volume.

Meanwhile boil the ingredients for the bun wash together for 2 to 3 minutes until syrupy. Reheat before using.

Use for Chelsea or Bath Buns:

♦ CHELSEA BUNS

*Basic Bun Dough (see
  above)*
*4 tablespoons (½
  stick) melted butter*
*⅓ cup dark brown
  sugar*
½ cup raisins
*¼ cup chopped
  candied orange peel*

Turn the risen dough out onto a floured working surface, punch it down, and roll out into a rectangle 12 by 18 inches. Brush all over with melted butter. Sprinkle the brown sugar, raisins, and candied peel over the top. Roll the dough up tightly jelly-roll fashion, then cut it into 18 even pieces. Place the coiled pieces cut side down on 2 buttered pans, 1 inch deep; there should be a space of ½ inch between the rolls and in from the sides of the pans. Brush the buns with beaten egg and let them rise, uncovered, for about 25 minutes.

GLAZE

Beaten egg
*Bun wash (preceding
recipe)*
Granulated sugar

Bake in a preheated 450° oven for 10–15 minutes. Remove and, while still hot, brush the buns with bun wash (see dough recipe) and sprinkle sugar all over. Leave them to cool in their pans, but serve them warm and separated; they will have "a characteristically white torn appearance, which contrasts with the sticky brown sugared top."

◆ BATH BUNS

*Basic Bun Dough
  (preceding recipe)*
⅔ cup yellow raisins
*¼ cup chopped
  candied orange peel*
1 egg, beaten
*About 20 small lumps
  sugar**

Turn the risen dough out onto a floured working surface; knead in the raisins and candied peel just enough to distribute them evenly. Form into a long sausage and cut into 18 even pieces. Form these into buns and place on buttered baking sheets 1½ inches apart. Brush with beaten egg.

Put the sugar lumps between two pieces of waxed paper and with a rolling pin crush them into smallish rough pieces. Strain out the powdered bits so that you have only the pieces and sprinkle these over the buns. Let rise for 25 minutes, uncovered.

Bake in a preheated 450° oven for 10–15 minutes. Remove and while still hot brush gently with bun wash (see dough recipe). Serve warm.

*Jane Grigson, from whom we have borrowed the bun recipes, writes: "This crunchy sugar scattered over today's Bath buns is a last souvenir of the crushed caraway seed comfits which were used to flavour wigs and buns as late as the eighteenth century. Comfits were made by dipping aromatic seeds over and over again in boiling sugar, until they were thickly coated— there is a most carefully set out recipe for making them, complete with a list of equipment, given in Sir Hugh Plat's *Delight for Ladies* of 1605."

Kolache

We first tasted kolaches at a street fair in a Minnesota town established by Bohemian immigrants, just as travelers have sampled them in other Mississippi basin towns like Prague, Oklahoma, where ancestral customs are also annually celebrated. At least once a week in Czechoslovakia, kolaches are served in many homes, warm from the oven—a dab of homemade fruit preserve surrounded by a pillow of airy bread.

We find them good for breakfast, tea, or even for dessert with a dollop of sweetened whipped cream.

Makes about 20

1 tablespoon active dry yeast
¼ cup warm milk
⅓ cup sugar
2½ cups white flour, preferably unbleached
6 tablespoons sweet butter
2 eggs, separated
¼ cup heavy cream
1 teaspoon grated lemon rind
¼ teaspoon mace
1 teaspoon coarse salt or ½ teaspoon table salt

GLAZE

1 egg yolk mixed with 1 tablespoon cream

FILLING

Plum, apricot, or raspberry jam

Make a sponge in a small bowl by dissolving the yeast in the warm milk, then stirring in 2 tablespoons each of the sugar and the flour. Let sit covered for about 10 minutes.

In a medium-size bowl cream the butter, then slowly beat in the remaining sugar until smooth. Stir in the egg yolks, cream, lemon rind, mace, salt, the sponge, and the remaining flour. Beat 100 strokes. In a separate bowl beat the egg whites until stiff, then mix them into the dough by cutting through the batter with a spatula and folding the whites in as best you can; this is more difficult with an elastic yeast dough, and you won't incorporate them completely. Now cover the bowl with plastic wrap and place over a bowl of warm water. Let rise for 1 hour.

With a spatula cut through the dough to break it down. Using well-floured fingers, pull off pieces of dough about the size of Ping-Pong balls and slap them down onto a floured surface; the dough will be soft and *very* sticky. Pat gently—always with well-floured fingers—to make rough circles and place them 2 inches apart on greased baking sheets. Paint the tops with egg glaze. Then make an indentation with the back of a floured spoon in the center of each round and fill with about 1 teaspoonful of jam. Let rise for 30 minutes in a warmish place.

Bake in a preheated 375° oven for 15–20 minutes. Serve warm.

BRIOCHES AND CROISSANTS

The French eat a light breakfast, often no more than *café au lait* and a sweet bread. Small wonder—a warm croissant or brioche fresh from the bakery is so delicious, one wants little else. Without a neighborhood boulangerie from which to bring back these treats still warm from the oven, it is worth making them and freezing for tomorrow what you don't eat today. Brioches are considerably easier to master than croissants, and if you have a food processor, you can use the second even easier method given below.

Brioches

To make real French brioches with the fluted base and saucy topknots, one must get little French brioche tins—1½ inches in diameter on the bottom, 3 inches at the top; they also come in a larger size, but brioches made thus are used primarily for scooping out and stuffing with a delicate filling like creamed chicken or lobster. If the small tins can't be found, you could use gem-size muffin tins, although they won't produce the real thing with the fluted base.

Makes 12 brioches

2 teaspoons active dry
  yeast
2 teaspoons nonfat dry
  milk
3 tablespoons warm
  water
2¼ cups white flour,
  preferably
  unbleached
3 eggs, at room
  temperature
2 tablespoons sugar
1 teaspoon coarse salt
  or ½ teaspoon table
  salt
10 tablespoons (1¼
  sticks) melted sweet
  butter

GLAZE

1 egg mixed with 1
  teaspoon water

In a medium-size mixing bowl stir the yeast and the dry milk together in the warm water until thoroughly dissolved. Beat in ⅓ cup flour and 1 egg (all the eggs must be at room temperature; if they're refrigerator-cold, before cracking them soak in hot water for 5 minutes) and beat for 30 seconds with an electric mixer. Sprinkle 1 cup of the flour on top. Cover tightly with plastic wrap and let stand in a warm place for 1½–2 hours until more than double in volume.

Uncover; stir in the sugar, salt, remaining eggs, and flour. Beat thoroughly for a good minute or so, then start adding the melted butter (the butter should not be sizzling hot—just warm), beating all the time with the electric mixer. When all the butter has been absorbed, cover the bowl again tightly and let rise for an hour.

Now scrape the dough out onto a floured surface and pat into a rectangle. Fold the dough in thirds, wrap in floured plastic wrap, and refrigerate for at least 30 minutes; if you don't want to bake right away—for instance, you may want to refrigerate overnight and finish making the brioches in the morning—put a plate on top to weight the dough (it will keep 3 days this way; to keep longer, freeze).

To form the brioches, with well-floured hands tear off pieces slightly larger than golf balls and shape into balls, as you would for rolls (see page 157). Reserve about one eighth of the dough for the topknots. Carefully butter the brioche tins, making sure that you get butter into all the crevices, and place balls of dough inside, flattening slightly. Now make the topknots by pulling off a piece of dough about the size of a grape. Slap it to get a smooth surface, then shape in a ball. Pinch one end, elongating it ½ inch. With a well-floured finger poke a deep hole into each brioche and insert the tapered end of the topknot. Repeat until all are done and place tins on a baking sheet. Lightly cover with buttered plastic wrap and let rise in a warm place until double in volume and swelling over the tops.

Preheat the oven to 425° about 10 minutes before baking, and 5 minutes before, paint the tops of the brioches with egg glaze, taking care not to let the glaze spill down into the tins. Let rest a minute or so and paint again.

Place the sheet of brioche tins in the oven and bake 5 minutes, then reduce the heat to 375° and bake another 12 minutes, covering loosely with foil if the brioches seem to be turning too brown—they should be shiny and mahogany-colored on top. If you're uncertain as to whether they are done, insert a straw at the rim of one of the tins and if it comes out clean, the brioches are done. Turn out and cool on racks. Serve warm.

♦ FOOD PROCESSOR METHOD FOR MAKING BRIOCHE

Put the flour, dry milk, sugar and salt in the container of the processor and spin for a few seconds. In a small cup stir the yeast and warm water together and let sit until dissolved.

Now with the motor on pour the melted butter through the feed tube; when the flour has absorbed it, add the dissolved yeast, and, one by one, the eggs. Continue to process about 30 seconds or until the dough masses around the central shaft. Remove the dough to a medium-size warm, buttered bowl; turn to coat and then cover the bowl with plastic wrap. Let the dough rise in a warmish place until almost triple in volume— about 1½ to 2 hours or more.

Turn the dough out, punch it down very thoroughly, then gather it into a ball, flatten it, and wrap loosely in floured plastic wrap. Refrigerate with a heavy plate or lid on top for at least ½ hour or longer, even overnight.

Proceed as above.

Croissants

The ability to produce your own light, flaky croissants may seem to be a professional baker's art. But the sense of achievement derived from making these crescent-shaped French breakfast treats is reward enough for mastering the challenge. The secret behind the flakiness characteristic of croissants lies in the layers of firm butter sandwiched between the layers of dough. This is accomplished by keeping the butter intact—rolling dough over it, turning, folding, and rolling again, each time increasing the number of butter-filled layers. It is imperative that the butter stay cold (don't try to make croissants on a warm muggy day) and that the dough also remain chilled and yet so pliable it rolls out easily. The dough must have periodic rests in the refrigerator to cool off, and to relax the gluten. Most European white flour does not have as much gluten in it as that of America does and as a result it is more malleable. To counteract the effect of gluten, we add a small amount of cake flour.

Makes 16 croissants

2 teaspoons active dry
  yeast
2 cups warm water
¼ cup nonfat dry milk
2 teaspoons coarse salt
  or 1 teaspoon table
  salt
2 tablespoons sugar
½ cup cake flour
3¾ cups white flour,
  preferably
  unbleached
½ pound (2 sticks)
  chilled sweet butter

In a medium bowl dissolve the yeast in ¼ cup of the warm water. Mix the dry milk, salt, and sugar in the remaining water, stir to dissolve, then add to the yeast. Stir in the cake flour and 1½ cups of the all-purpose flour. Beat steadily for 1½ minutes. Stir in the remaining flour; you should have a soft dough, which, in this instance, will not be kneaded because you do not want to overactivate the gluten. Cover with plastic wrap and let rise slowly in the refrigerator for 1½ hours.

A few minutes before removing the dough, take out the well-chilled butter, cut the 2 sticks lengthwise in half and place the 4 pieces snugly side by side on a large piece of waxed paper. On a second sheet of waxed paper draw a rectangle 9 by 6 inches and place this on top of the butter. Using a heavy rolling pin, whack the butter all over to start it moving, then alternately whack and roll out to the dimensions you have traced. You may have to trim and patch the edges to get a precise 9-by-6-inch piece; refrigerate it, wrapped in its waxed paper.

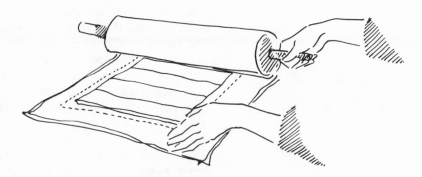

Remove the dough and turn out on lightly floured, cool work surface. Roll the dough out into a rectangle 15 by 8 inches, picking it up now and then and reflouring the work surface to make sure it doesn't stick. Remove the butter from the refrigerator, peel off the waxed paper, and place the butter at one end of the dough, leaving a 1-inch border; it will cover approximately two-thirds of the dough. Lift the unbuttered third up and

fold it over the middle third; then fold the remaining buttered third over that. You will now have a neat folded package 8 by 5 inches; make sure with each fold that all the corners are squared off and carefully aligned. Give the dough a turn so that now the shorter side faces you and roll again to a 15-by-8-inch rectangle, flouring as necessary. (If at any point the dough seems to be getting soft and the butter melting and breaking through, stop and refrigerate for at least 15 minutes before continuing.) Fold the top third of the dough over, as before, and then the bottom third over that. You have now given the dough 2 turns, so make an imprint with 2 fingers to remind yourself (in case you want to forget it and go off to the movies). Wrap the dough in lightly floured plastic wrap, then enclose in a plastic bag, and refrigerate for at least 1 hour, a few hours longer if convenient, even overnight but not longer.

Remove the dough and roll out and fold 2 more times, exactly as you have done before. Make an imprint with 4 fingers, and wrap as before and

GLAZE

*1 egg beaten with 2
teaspoons milk*

refrigerate for at least 2 hours or longer (it can be
overnight if you want to get up a couple of hours
earlier and have hot croissants ready for breakfast;
don't hold the dough any longer than that).

Before taking the dough out, mix the glaze so it
is ready. Unless you have a very large work surface
(40 inches), it will be simpler to cut the dough in
half now and refrigerate one half while working
with the other. On a floured surface roll out one
half to a rectangle 20 by 5 inches. With your ruler
mark off four 5-inch squares. Cut them with a
sharp knife, then cut each square diagonally into
two 5-inch triangles. Roll each triangle to stretch
one point to about 7 inches from the base. Then
starting at the base, roll the triangle up, stretching
the base points as you roll and finally bring the
top point up and over; it should just rest on the
work surface, not tuck under; if necessary to
secure the flap, wet it with a little of the glaze.

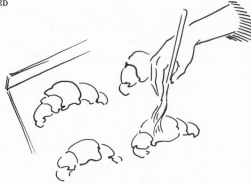

Wipe a baking sheet with a cold, wet cloth and arrange the croissants with plenty of room between them. Pull down the pointed ends to form crescents and paint each croissant with the egg glaze. Repeat with the remaining dough. If your oven doesn't hold 2 baking sheets, it is wise to wait about 20 minutes before forming the second batch, so the rising time is staggered. Let rise, uncovered, in a warm place in the kitchen until they are more than double in size, almost triple, and look puffy and light—about 1½ hours for each batch.

Brush with the glaze again and bake in a preheated 450° oven for 16–18 minutes or until a deep golden color. Check after 10 minutes and turn the baking sheet if necessary to ensure even browning. Cool on racks for 15 minutes, and serve still warm from the oven. If you are going to keep the croissants more than 24 hours, freeze them, wrapped securely in plastic, after they have cooled. To restore to life again, simply heat, still frozen, in a 400° oven for 5 minutes.

Danish Pastries

For thousands of Americans "coffee and a danish" is the ultimate in short-order breakfasts, but in Denmark the word for these lush pastries is *Wienerbrød,* or Vienna bread. As Inger Hahn told us the story one day in Copenhagen, the Danish term derives from the fact that a young Austrian baker traveled north to set up shop more than a hundred years ago, quickly establishing a reputation among the Danes for his pastrymaking secrets. Danish bakers proudly mastered his techniques, and eventually some of them introduced the pastries in various American regions. For the serious home baker, producing a successful batch may seem the highest form of culinary accomplishment. Aside from preparing the butter-layered dough (very close to croissant dough), requiring much rolling and folding and long rests in the refrigerator, there are creams and fillings and icings to be made, as well as different shapes and combinations of flavors. As with croissants, don't try to do the dough in hot or sticky weather, and give yourself plenty of time—this is a project for a leisurely day.

Makes 16 snails and/or 16 packages, cockscombs, pinwheels and/or coffee ring and/or 1 braid and/or 1 lattice-work strip

DANISH PASTRY DOUGH

½ teaspoon cardamom seeds

½ cup boiling water

2 tablespoons nonfat dry milk

2 tablespoons active dry yeast

3 tablespoons sugar

¼ cup warm water

2 eggs

1 teaspoon coarse salt or ½ teaspoon table salt

½ cup cake flour

2½ cups white flour, preferably unbleached

10 ounces (2½ sticks) sweet butter

Crush the cardamom seeds (you may have to extract them from their husks first, if you have bought them whole), using a rolling pin or mortar and pestle. Pour the boiling water over them, mix in the dry milk, and let them steep until cooled to lukewarm.

Dissolve the yeast and sugar in the ¼ cup warm water in a medium-size bowl. Lightly beat the eggs, then stir them in, along with the cooled, strained cardamom milk, the salt, and the two flours. Beat steadily until thoroughly mixed and dough comes away from the sides of the bowl. This can be done with an electric mixer, or you can put everything together and blend in a food processor until the dough comes away from the sides of the container. Cover the bowl with plastic wrap and let rest to rise slowly in the refrigerator for 1½ hours.

Now follow paragraphs 2, 3, and 4 of the preceding croissant recipe, except—because you will have an extra half strip of butter—make the butter rectangle 10 by 7 inches and the dough rectangle 9 by 16 inches.

After returning the dough to the refrigerator and letting it rest 2 hours, repeat the rolling, folding, and resting process 2 more times (you should be able to reduce your resting periods to an hour each for these 2 final turns). Now you are ready to shape and fill the pastries, and there are a variety of traditional ways to do this. It's more fun to make at least two shapes and fillings, so decide which ones you want to do and prepare ahead the fillings and cream and glaze you have selected.

♦ SNAILS

Makes 16 pastries

*½ above Danish
    Pastry Dough
Vanilla Cream (½ of
    recipe on page 204)
Hazelnut or Prune
    Filling (½ of recipe
    on page 205)*

GLAZE

*1 egg beaten with 1
    teaspoon milk
Icing (about ½ of
    recipe on page 206)*

Roll the dough out on a lightly floured surface to a rectangle 8 by 16 inches. Spread the vanilla cream over it, then distribute the hazelnut or prune filling on top. Roll up firmly, jelly-roll fashion, then cut into sixteen 1-inch pieces. Place on a lightly greased baking sheet 2 inches apart. Cover with waxed paper and let rise 45 minutes. Brush with some of the egg glaze and bake in a preheated 400° oven 12–14 minutes until puffy and golden. Cool on racks and drizzle icing over the snails while still warm.

◆ COCKSCOMBS

Makes 8 pastries

½ above Danish Pastry Dough
Hazelnut, Prune, or Apricot Filling (½ of recipe on page 205)
1 egg beaten with 1 teaspoon milk

GLAZE

Some of above egg

Icing (½ of recipe on page 206)

Roll the dough out on a lightly floured surface to a rectangle 8 by 16 inches. Cut into 8 4-inch squares. Across the center of each square spread about a tablespoon of filling. Paint the surrounding dough with egg glaze, then fold over, pressing the edges securely together. Now make cuts about ¾ inch apart along the wide end, cutting in almost as far as the filling. Remove to a lightly greased baking sheet and spread each package open into a semicircle so the cuts open out; leave at least 1½ inches between each cockscomb. Cover with waxed paper and let rise for 45 minutes. Brush with the remaining egg and bake at 400° for 10 to 12 minutes. While still warm, drizzle icing on top.

◆ PACKAGES

Makes 16 pastries

½ *above Danish*
  Pastry Dough
Cheese, Prune, or
  Apple Filling (½ of
  any of the recipes on
  pages 205–206)

GLAZE

1 egg beaten with 1
  teaspoon milk
Icing (almost all of
  recipe on page 206)

Roll the dough out on a lightly floured surface to a
16-inch square and then cut into sixteen 4-inch
pieces. Place in the center of each square a
teaspoonful of whatever filling you are using. Draw
the 4 corners of the square to the center so that
the points just overlap. Press down firmly to
secure them, painting the edges with a little egg
glaze if necessary to make them stick. Place on an
ungreased baking sheet 1½ inches apart, cover
with waxed paper, and let rise 45 minutes. Brush
with egg glaze and bake in a preheated 400° oven
12–14 minutes until golden. Remove to racks and
drizzle icing over while still warm.

◆ PINWHEELS

Makes 8 pastries

Roll out ½ recipe for Danish Pastry Dough to a
rectangle 8 by 16 inches, cut out 8 4-inch squares,
and make pinwheels as described on page 159.
Place a teaspoon of jam or any of the fruit fillings
that follow in the center of each square before
folding in the four points. Paint with egg glaze and
bake at 400° for 10 minutes.

◆ BRAID

Makes 1 braid

*½ above Danish
  Pastry Dough
Vanilla Cream (½ of
  recipe on page 204)
Hazelnut Filling (½ of
  recipe on page 205)*

GLAZE

*1 egg beaten with 1
  teaspoon milk
½ cup sliced almonds
Icing (almost all of
  recipe on page 206)*

Roll the dough out on a lightly floured surface to a rectangle 9 by 24 inches. Using a ruler, cut into three 3-by-24-inch strips. Carefully spread the vanilla cream over each strip, then distribute the hazelnut or poppy seed filling as evenly as you can on top. Now roll each strip lengthwise and pinch the seams together firmly. Braid the three strips together, starting at one end and pinching together the three strands; repeat the pinching when you have braided to the other end. Place the braid, seam side up, on an ungreased cookie sheet, tuck the ends under, and cover with plastic wrap. Let rise for 1 hour. Brush with the egg glaze, scatter the almonds on top, and bake in a preheated 400° oven about 15 minutes until nicely browned. Cool a little and then drizzle icing over the top while still warm.

◆ COFFEE RING

Makes 1 ring

*½ above Danish
  Pastry Dough
Vanilla Cream (½ of
  recipe on page 204)
Prune, Apple, or
  Cheese Filling (½ of
  recipes on pages
  205–206)*

GLAZE

*1 egg beaten with 1
  teaspoon milk
½ cup sliced almonds
Icing (almost all of
  recipe on page 206)*

Roll the dough out to a rectangle 8 by 28 inches. Spread vanilla cream over and then the prune, apple, or cheese filling. Tightly roll up jelly-roll fashion and pinch the final seam together securely. Pull the ends toward each other to make a circle, overlap the end pieces, and pinch together firmly. Transfer to an ungreased cookie sheet. With a pair of scissors, snip gashes all around the top of the circle of dough, 1 inch apart. Cover with a kitchen towel and let rise about 40 minutes. Paint the surface with the glaze, scatter almonds on top, and bake in a preheated 400° oven 15 minutes. When somewhat cooled drizzle icing over the top.

◆ LATTICE-WORK STRIP

Makes 1 strip

*½ above Danish
  Pastry Dough
Vanilla Cream (½ of
  recipe that follows)
Apple, Prune, or
  Apricot Filling (½
  of recipe that
  follows)*

GLAZE

*1 egg beaten with 1
  teaspoon milk*

*Optional icing (about
  ½ of recipe on page
  206)
2 tablespoons slivered
  almonds (for Apple
  Filling)*

Roll the dough out on a lightly floured surface to a rectangle 8 by 16 inches, then transfer it to a lightly greased baking sheet. Spread vanilla cream in a 2-inch strip down the center lengthwise. Then spoon the fruit filling on top. Now make diagonal cuts ½-inch wide on either side of the dough, cutting to within ½ inch of the filling. Draw the strips alternately from one side and then the other toward the center, overlapping them where they meet. When you get to the two final strips, tuck them under. Paint the dough with egg glaze, cover lightly with waxed paper and let rise for 45 minutes. Paint again and bake in a 400° oven 12–14 minutes until pastry is golden. Let firm up for about 10 minutes before attempting to transfer to a rack. Drizzle optional icing on top while still warm. If you used apple filling, sprinkle almonds on top.

◆ VANILLA CREAM

*4 tablespoons sweet
  butter
½ cup confectioner's
  sugar
1 tablespoon vanilla
  extract*

Blend everything together until smooth. A food processor will do the job well.

♦ HAZELNUT FILLING

1 cup hazelnuts
1 cup sugar
2 tablespoons butter
1 egg

Chop the hazelnuts quite fine. Work in the sugar, butter, and egg. The food processor will work well: put the hazelnuts in first to chop them, then add the rest of the ingredients.

♦ PRUNE FILLING

1 cup cooked prunes
1 teaspoon grated
  lemon rind
1 teaspoon grated
  orange rind
⅛ teaspoon freshly
  grated nutmeg
3 tablespoons sweet
  butter
½ cup chopped walnuts
2 tablespoons sugar

Remove the pits from the prunes, mash, and then blend with the rest of the ingredients. It can all be done in the food processor.

♦ APRICOT FILLING

1 cup cooked dried
  apricots
2 tablespoons Grand
  Marnier
⅓ cup chopped walnuts
Sugar to taste

Purée the apricots with the Grand Marnier and walnuts, which can be easily done in the food processor. Taste and add additional sugar if desired.

♦ POPPYSEED FILLING

½ cup poppyseeds,
  ground*
4 tablespoons soft
  sweet butter
¼ cup honey
½ cup finely chopped
  walnuts
1–2 tablespoons sour
  cream
3 tablespoons currants

Mix the ground poppyseeds, butter, honey, and walnuts together. Add a little sour cream to make the mixture spreadable and fold in the currants.

---

* You can get poppyseeds already ground in shops specializing in Middle European baking materials. Otherwise prepare your own by pouring boiling water over the poppyseeds and soaking them overnight, then grinding in a spice grinder.

3 apples, grated
½ teaspoon grated
lemon rind
½ teaspoon vanilla
3 tablespoons sugar
1 teaspoon cinnamon
¼ cup currants
1 teaspoon lemon juice

♦ APPLE FILLING

Mix all of the ingredients together thoroughly.

♦ CHEESE FILLING

2 tablespoons yellow
raisins
1 tablespoon orange
juice
1 cup farmer cheese or
cream cheese
softened with 1
tablespoon sour
cream
¼ cup sugar
1 tablespoon flour
1 egg yolk
1 teaspoon melted
butter
½ teaspoon grated
lemon rind
½ teaspoon vanilla

Blend all of the ingredients together. A food processor will do the job quickly.

♦ ICING

1 cup confectioner's
sugar
2 tablespoons lemon
juice
½ teaspoon vanilla
1–2 drops almond
extract

Mix everything together until you have a smooth paste.

Pisticcini

In various parts of the world when grains have been unavailable, bakers have made flour from nuts. Just as American Indians often turned acorns into meal, Corsicans left without grain by Genoan and Pisan overlords ground the annual harvest of chestnuts to make it a vital part of their cooking. Chestnut meal handles something like corn meal and is often substituted in recipes originally calling for ground corn. But because there is a natural sweetness in chestnuts, more often *pisticcini* is regarded as a sweet bread or cake, to be eaten with coffee or tea. Personally we love to eat this bread, with its accent of rosemary and pine nuts, along with a good fresh goat cheese and a glass of red wine.

Makes 1 8–9-inch round

2 cups chestnut flour
1¼ cups water
2 plus a little more
   tablespoons olive oil
1 teaspoon coarse salt
   or ½ teaspoon table
   salt
2 tablespoons yellow
   raisins
2 teaspoons chopped
   fresh rosemary or 1
   teaspoon dried
1 tablespoon pine nuts

Mix together thoroughly the chestnut flour, water, 2 tablespoons olive oil, salt, and raisins. Oil a shallow casserole or pie plate no more than 2 inches deep and about 8–9 inches in diameter and pour the batter into it. Sprinkle the rosemary and pine nuts over the top.

Bake in a preheated 375° oven for 50–60 minutes, until the bread has shrunk from the sides of the pan and the surface is cracked. Drizzle just a little more olive oil over and serve warm directly from the pan.

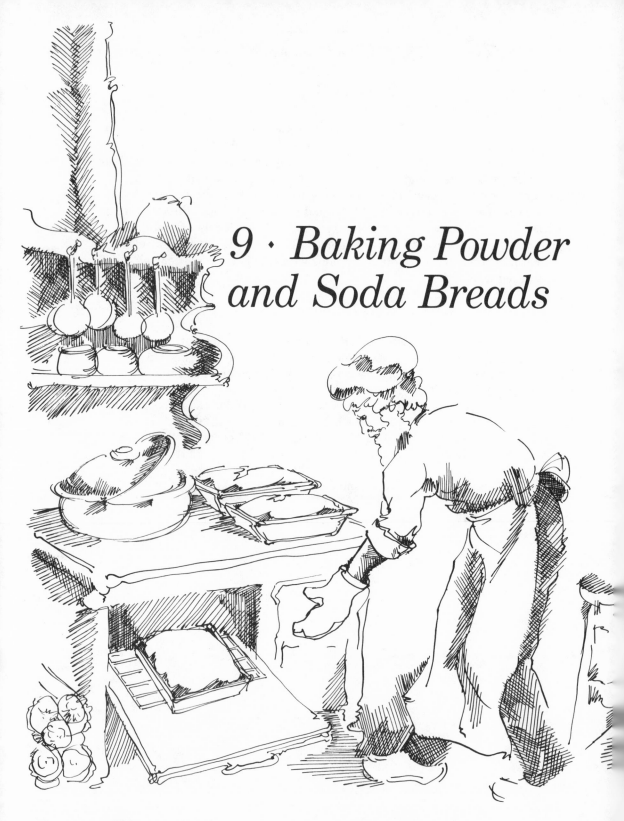

9 · Baking Powder and Soda Breads

Wheat Honey Loaf with Pecans

Banana Bread

Banana Carrot Bread

Blueberry Orange Bread

Apricot and Toasted Almond Bread

Bronwyn's Orange-flavored
  Zucchini Bread

Green Mountain Green Tomato Bread

Pumpkin Bread

Carrot Bread

Macadamia Nut and Maple Syrup Bread

Strawberry Almond Breakfast Bread

Quince and Black Walnut Bread

Grandma McLeod's Gingerbread

Mustard and Caraway Seed Loaf

Cousin Ed's Irish Soda Bread

Black Walnut, Prune, and
  Spiced Tea Bread

Sour Cream or Buttermilk
  Corn Bread

209 ♦

Breads made with baking powder or baking soda are often called quick breads—you don't have to knead them and you don't have to wait around while the dough rises. They have a more cakelike texture than yeast-risen breads, and are apt to dry out faster. That's why inventive cooks have often worked in fruits and vegetables, as well as different fats, to keep the dough moist. For the most part these quick breads—or "tea breads"—are sometimes a little sweet and enhanced with nuts and raisins. In addition, there are savory quick breads, made without sweetening, that run a gamut from the legendary Irish soda bread baked in a hanging pot to one we love that combines the essences of mustard and caraway seed. Quick breads that aren't sweet should be eaten the day they are baked, whereas the fruity, nutty ones develop more flavor if they wait twelve hours or more before you serve them.

Wheat Honey Loaf with Pecans

Even before the Athenians made their first claims that the best honey came from Mount Hymettos and the people of Delphi held out for the product of their local bees, bread doughs have been sweetened with honey in basic ways that bakers have known for centuries. One of the favorite loaves of France, *pain d'épice* (page 355), has many spices, in addition to honey.

Makes one 8-inch loaf

1 ½ cups white flour
1 cup whole wheat flour
2 teaspoons baking powder
½ teaspoon baking soda
1 teaspoon coarse salt or ½ teaspoon table salt
⅔ cup honey
1 cup buttermilk
3 tablespoons vegetable oil
2 eggs, beaten
1 cup chopped pecans
½ cup raisins or chopped dates

Thoroughly mix the flours with the baking powder and soda and the salt. In a separate bowl blend the honey, buttermilk, and oil with the beaten eggs. Add the dry ingredients to the liquid, stirring just enough for them to become moistened. Fold in the pecans and raisins or dates.

Turn the batter into a well-buttered 8-inch loaf pan and bake in a preheated 325° oven for 1 hour or until a straw inserted in the center comes out clean. Cool for 5 minutes in the pan, then turn out on a rack.

Banana Bread

Next time you pick up a bunch of bananas, put three of them aside to ripen thoroughly so that you can treat yourself to this fragrant yogurt-enriched bread. Or try the banana-carrot loaf that follows.

Makes one 9-inch loaf

4 tablespoons (½ stick) butter
¾ cup sugar
3 medium-size ripe bananas, peeled and roughly chopped
1 egg
⅓ cup yogurt
2 cups white flour
1½ teaspoons baking powder
½ teaspoon baking soda
1 teaspoon coarse salt or ½ teaspoon table salt
1 cup chopped pecans

Cream the butter either in a food processor or electric mixer and add the sugar, blending thoroughly. Add the bananas and process until thoroughly mashed and blended. Beat in the egg and yogurt.

Mix the remaining ingredients together thoroughly and then add the wet mixture to them, stirring to mix until all the flour is moistened.

Turn the batter into a buttered 9-inch loaf pan and bake in a 350° oven for 1 hour. Let rest in the pan 10 minutes before turning out and cooling on a rack.

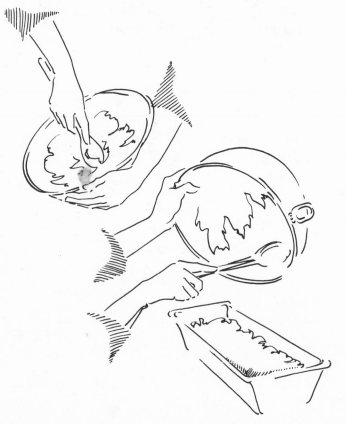

Banana Carrot Bread

This banana bread is spicier and has a less pronounced banana taste than the preceding bread.

Makes one 9-inch loaf

4 tablespoons (½ stick) sweet butter, softened
¾ cup sugar
2 large eggs
1 very large or 2 small ripe bananas (to make 1 cup mashed)
2 cups white flour
2 teaspoons double-acting baking powder
½ teaspoon cinnamon
1 teaspoon coarse salt or ½ teaspoon table salt
¼ teaspoon baking soda
⅛ teaspoon ground cloves
1 cup chopped nuts
¾ cup grated carrots
1 teaspoon vanilla extract

Cream the butter and the sugar together in a bowl until fluffy. Beat in the eggs, one at a time, and beat until well combined. Mash and stir in the bananas.

In another bowl sift together the flour, baking powder, cinnamon, salt, baking soda, and cloves. Gently add the dry mixture to the banana mixture. Add the nuts, carrots, and vanilla. Mix the batter very well.

Pour in a well-buttered 9-inch loaf pan and bake in a preheated 350° oven for 1 hour or until a cake tester inserted in the center comes out clean. Allow the bread to cool in the pan for 15–20 minutes. Turn it out of the pan and onto a rack and let it cool completely before serving.

Blueberry Orange Bread

Once in Maine, a state that makes much of its bountiful blueberry crop, we ran across a flavorsome blueberry gingerbread, but the combination of two fruits in this recipe from the Hotel Anderson in Minnesota's Hiawatha Valley seems something special. In the hotel's kitchen one helper's chief job is to station herself at the ovens so that the hot breads, meal after meal, are transferred immediately to the bread trays that are continually passed in the dining room.

Makes one 9- or 10-inch loaf

3 cups white flour
3½ teaspoons baking
*   powder*
¼ teaspoon baking
*   soda*
1½ teaspoons coarse
*   salt or 1 teaspoon*
*   table salt*
½ cup sugar
1 cup blueberries,
*   preferably fresh*
1 egg
1 cup milk
⅓ cup orange juice
1 tablespoon grated
*   orange rind*
½ cup vegetable oil

In a large bowl mix the dry ingredients together
thoroughly. Toss in the blueberries and with your
hand stir them around to coat them with the flour.

In another bowl beat the egg lightly, then add
the remaining ingredients. Combine this liquid
with the flour mixture, stirring just enough to
moisten all the dry ingredients.

Turn into a well-buttered 9- or 10-inch bread
pan and bake in a preheated 350° oven for 1 hour
and 10 minutes. Cool in the pan for 5 minutes,
then turn out onto a rack to cool thoroughly
before slicing.

Apricot and Toasted Almond Bread

A little different from the usual apricot bread—the
apricots for this one are soaked in orange juice, the almonds are toasted, and we
use some oat flour, all of which gives this loaf an almost exotic flavor.

Makes one 9-inch loaf

1½ cups (about 7
*   ounces) dried*
*   apricots*
½ cup orange juice
½ cup light brown
*   sugar*
3 tablespoons
*   vegetable oil*
¾ cup chopped
*   almonds*
2 eggs

Chop up the apricots (a food processor will do the
job very efficiently). Heat the orange juice until it
boils, then stir in the apricots—you should have a
heaping cupful chopped—and the brown sugar.
Let sit for at least 15 minutes.

Meanwhile, using 1 tablespoon of the oil, brown
the almonds in a medium frying pan, stirring and
tossing them so that they toast evenly and are
lightly browned all over.

Beat the eggs until frothy, then mix in the
remaining oil and buttermilk. Thoroughly blend

½ cup buttermilk
1½ cups white flour
1 cup oat flour
2½ teaspoons baking
  powder
½ teaspoon baking
  soda
1 teaspoon coarse salt
  or ½ teaspoon table
  salt

the two flours, baking powder and soda, salt, and toasted almonds. Add to the egg mixture, then stir in the apricots and their juice.

Turn the batter into a buttered 9-inch baking pan and bake in a preheated 350° oven for 50 minutes. Let rest in the pan 5 minutes before turning out onto a rack to finish cooling.

Bronwyn's Orange-flavored Zucchini Bread

Our daughter, Bronwyn, loves to make this bread for a party because the loaf looks so attractive sliced, with flecks of green showing, along with a touch of orange, all marbled with walnuts. It also tastes so good it disappears quickly. So if you are having more than six or eight friends in, you'd better double the recipe and make two loaves.

Makes one 9-inch loaf

1½ cups white flour
1 cup sugar
2 teaspoons baking
  powder
½ teaspoon baking
  soda
½ teaspoon coarse salt
  or ¼ teaspoon table
  salt
¼ teaspoon ground
  ginger
2 eggs
½ cup oil
1½ cups grated
  zucchini
1 teaspoon chopped
  orange peel
½ cup chopped
  walnuts

Mix the flour, sugar, baking powder, baking soda, salt, and ginger together thoroughly. In a medium-size bowl beat the eggs, then add the oil and the grated zucchini. Stir in the dry ingredients, the orange peel (be sure to strip off the peel from the orange and chop it, not grate it—it has more crunch this way), and the walnuts.

Scrape the batter into a buttered 9-inch bread pan and bake in a preheated 375° oven for 50 minutes. Let cool in the pan 5 minutes, then turn out onto a rack.

Green Mountain
Green Tomato Bread

As we indicated in Chapter 2, some of our Vermont acquaintances know how to circumvent Jack Frost by using unripened tomatoes in a bread that is mysteriously delicious.

Makes one 9-inch loaf

2¾ cups white flour
1½ teaspoons baking
  powder
1 teaspoon baking soda
¾ teaspoon coarse salt
  or ½ teaspoon table
  salt
¾ teaspoon cinnamon
½ teaspoon ground
  ginger
¼ cup chopped
  crystallized ginger
¾ cup chopped
  walnuts
2 eggs
⅓ cup maple syrup
⅓ cup melted butter
⅔ cup cider
1 large or 2 small
  green tomatoes,
  chopped (to make 1–
  1¼ cups)

Mix the dry ingredients together thoroughly. Toss in the crystallized ginger, then the walnuts, separating and coating each piece.

In a medium-size bowl beat the eggs until light and slightly thickened. Add the maple syrup, butter, and cider, mixing well. Fold the dry ingredients into the bowl, add the green tomatoes, and stir until just mixed.

Spoon into a buttered 9-inch loaf pan and bake in a preheated 350° oven for 60–65 minutes, until the edges are browned and start to leave the sides of the pan. Cool in the pan for 10 minutes, then turn out. It's better to let this bread settle and slice it the next day.

Pumpkin Bread

"Stew and strain some pumpkin, stiffen it with Indian meal," Catharine Beecher, Harriet Beecher Stowe's talented sister, wrote in 1842, "add salt and yeast, and it makes a most excellent kind of bread." Today's methods make use of either yeast or baking powder, and the vegetable purée base can be made from winter squash as well as pumpkin.

Makes one 9-inch loaf

1¾ cups white flour
1 teaspoon coarse salt
   or ½ teaspoon table
   salt
1¼ cups sugar
2 teaspoons baking
   soda
1 cup pumpkin purée
⅓ cup vegetable oil
¼ cup water
2 eggs, beaten
½ teaspoon cinnamon
¼ teaspoon nutmeg
Pinch each of mace
   and ground cloves
½ cup chopped nuts
   or toasted sunflower
   seeds (optional)

Combine the flour, salt, sugar, and baking soda. Mix the pumpkin, oil, water, eggs, and spices. Stir the dry ingredients into the wet ones enough to mix. Fold in nuts or sunflower seeds, if desired.

Turn into a buttered 9-inch loaf pan and bake in preheated 350° oven 50–60 minutes. Turn out and cool on racks.

Carrot Bread

Carrot bread and cake (and there's little difference between them except for some overwhelming frostings on cakes) have come back into popularity again. And no wonder—the carrot flavor makes for a tantalizing, moist loaf that keeps very well. Double this recipe if you have a houseful of carrot bread addicts.

Makes one 9-inch loaf

*12 tablespoons (1½
   sticks) sweet butter*
1 cup sugar
⅓ cup honey
½ teaspoon cinnamon
¼ teaspoon nutmeg
*1 teaspoon grated
   orange peel*
3 eggs
1¼ cups grated carrots
¼ cup lemon juice
1¾ cups white flour
*¼ teaspoon coarse salt
   or a pinch of table
   salt*
*1 teaspoon baking
   powder*
*2 teaspoons baking
   soda*
*½ cup chopped
   hazelnuts*

Cream the butter in a food processor or with a
beater and add the sugar, beating until well
incorporated. Add the honey, cinnamon, nutmeg,
and orange peel, and beat in the eggs one by one.
Mix in the grated carrots and lemon juice.
Thoroughly mix the dry ingredients and the nuts,
then blend with the wet mixture until all the flour
is moistened.

Turn the batter into a buttered 9-inch loaf pan
and bake in a preheated 350° oven for 45 minutes.
Let rest in the pan 10 minutes before turning out
and cooling on a rack.

Macadamia Nut and
Maple Syrup Bread

This is another bread recipe we devised using mac-
adamia nuts (see Portuguese Sweet Bread, page 180). Here the nutty flavor is
enhanced by maple syrup, the sweetener brought to Hawaii by other early settlers from New England. "This is the bread," said one of its first tasters, "I'd
like to take to a desert island."

Makes one 9-inch loaf

2 cups white flour
*1 teaspoon baking
   powder*
1 teaspoon baking soda
*1 teaspoon coarse salt
   or ½ teaspoon table
   salt*

Mix the flour, baking powder, soda, and salt
thoroughly in a medium-size bowl. Make a well in
the center, break the egg into it, then, using a fork,
mix the yolk and the white together. Add the
maple syrup, buttermilk, and butter, and mix all
the ingredients until blended. Stir in the
macadamia nuts. Scrape the batter into a greased

1 egg
⅓ cup maple syrup
¾ cup buttermilk
3 tablespoons melted
   butter
1 cup roughly chopped
   macadamia nuts

9-inch bread pan and bake in a preheated 350°
oven for 50 minutes. Let the bread cool in the pan
for 10–15 minutes before turning out onto a rack.
Let it rest at least several hours before slicing.

Strawberry Almond Breakfast Bread

Each time we've visited California's Napa Valley,
we've been increasingly impressed with the quality of the wine, naturally
enough, but also with the food a traveler can find—it gets better, too. In gathering material for a little book on country inns we were given the following
recipe by Ned and Marge Smith of the Wine Country Inn at St. Helena. Homemade breads are their specialty, and this colorful loaf is only one of many original breads they serve at the "harvest table" in their attractive common room,
or outdoors on the deck. The strawberries disintegrate, becoming more like jam
when baked in the bread, so it is really not worth using fresh berries here unless
you happen to have an overabundance.

Makes one 8-inch loaf

10-ounce package
   frozen sliced
   strawberries
2 eggs
½ cup cooking oil
1 cup sugar
1½ cups white flour
1½ teaspoons
   cinnamon
½ teaspoon baking
   soda
½ teaspoon coarse salt
   or ¼ teaspoon table
   salt
⅔ cup chopped
   almonds

Defrost strawberries. Beat eggs in a bowl until
fluffy. Add oil, sugar, and strawberries. Sift
together flour, cinnamon, soda, and salt into a
large mixing bowl. Stir in strawberry mixture,
mixing until well blended; stir in almonds.
   Scrape dough into a greased and floured 8-inch
loaf pan. Bake in preheated 350° oven for 1 hour
and 10 minutes, or until done. Cool in pan 10
minutes, then turn out onto a rack to cool.

Quince and
Black Walnut Bread

If you have a quince bush in your backyard, save some to make bread after the canning season. Black walnuts with their musty flavor are just the right complement, but if they are too difficult to come by (there are black walnut trees in many parts of the country, but the nuts are mighty hard work to extract from their shells—hence their high price in specialty shops), you can substitute California walnuts to produce an almost equally unusual bread. (See also Black Walnut, Prune, and Spiced Tea Bread, page 224.)

Makes one 9-inch loaf

2¼ cups white flour
¾ cup sugar
2 teaspoons baking
  powder
½ teaspoon baking
  soda
¼ teaspoon ginger
½ teaspoon coarse salt
  or ¼ teaspoon table
  salt
1 egg
¾ cup buttermilk
3 tablespoons
  vegetable oil
1 cup chopped cooked
  quince*
¾ cup chopped black
  walnuts

Combine the flour, sugar, baking powder and soda, ginger and salt and mix well. In a medium bowl beat the egg, then add the buttermilk, oil, and ¼ cup of the syrup from the cooked quince (if you do not have quite that much, add additional buttermilk to make up ¼ cup). Stir the dry ingredients into the wet mixture, then fold in the chopped quince and black walnuts.

Turn the batter into a buttered 9-inch bread pan and bake in a preheated 350° oven for 55 minutes. Let rest in the pan 10 minutes, then turn out and cool on a rack.

* To cook quince, quarter and core but do not peel the quince. Use 1 cup sugar per pound of quince and cover by an inch of water. Let cook slowly until the fruit is tender but not mushy and water has reduced to a syrup—about 40 minutes. It will take about ¾ pound quince to make 1 cup cooked and chopped.

Grandma McLeod's Gingerbread

In *The Cook's Own Book,* published in Boston in 1832, a distinction is made between traditional gingerbread and what the author calls "American Gingerbread"—chiefly in the fact that the New World version uses twice as much powdered ginger and calls for brown sugar instead of a combination of confectioner's sugar and treacle. The following recipe is traditional, related to the gingerbreads that go back to Shakespeare's time and were eaten as a true bread, with butter. Old recipes vary greatly; some in colonial Virginia called for either ale yeast or potash, and for the addition of nuts, dates, orange or lemon peel, and sometimes nutmeg or cloves. No indulgence of whipped cream, or synthetic whips.

Makes one 8-inch-square cake

½ cup sugar
¼ cup shortening
¾ teaspoon baking soda
½ cup molasses
¾ teaspoon baking powder
1 teaspoon cinnamon
1 teaspoon ground ginger
¼ teaspoon ground cloves
¼ teaspoon coarse salt or a pinch of table salt
1½ cups white flour
¾ cup boiling water
1 egg, beaten

Cream together sugar and shortening. Beat ½ teaspoon of the baking soda into molasses until fluffy and light; combine with shortening and sugar. Blend baking powder, cinnamon, ginger, cloves, and salt with the flour. Mix boiling water with remaining ¼ teaspoon of baking soda, then gradually add it to the molasses mixture, alternating with dry ingredients. Stir thoroughly, adding beaten egg as you do so.

Grease and flour an 8-inch-square baking pan and pour in gingerbread mixture. Bake about 20 minutes in a preheated 325° oven.

Mustard and Caraway Seed Loaf

Seeds in great variety have been used in many countries to sprinkle the top crusts of bread and to be worked into the dough for added texture as well as seasoning. The combination of mustard and caraway seeds give this quick bread a tangy quality of its own.

Makes one 9-inch loaf

3 cups white flour
¼ cup sugar
2 tablespoons baking
  powder
1 tablespoon caraway
  seeds
1 tablespoon mustard
  seeds
1 tablespoon coarse
  salt or 2 teaspoons
  table salt
3 eggs, beaten
1¾ cups milk
¼ cup vegetable oil

In a large bowl combine flour, sugar, baking powder, caraway and mustard seeds, and salt. Stir in beaten eggs, milk, and oil, mixing only enough to moisten the flour.

Scrape the dough into a well-oiled or buttered 9-inch bread pan. Bake in preheated 350° oven 65–70 minutes, or until done. Cool on rack 15 minutes before removing from pan.

Cousin Ed's Irish Soda Bread

When an Irish lass thinks of the Auld Sod, she sometimes thinks of the Irish soda bread that she might serve with tea were she living in Ireland. Our friend Kathy Hourigan contributed this way of baking a soda loaf, just as it came from Cousin Ed.

Makes 1 round loaf

2 cups white flour
2 teaspoons baking
  soda

In a large bowl mix the flour, baking soda, baking powder, salt, and sugar. Using two knives or a pastry blender, cut the butter into the dry mixture

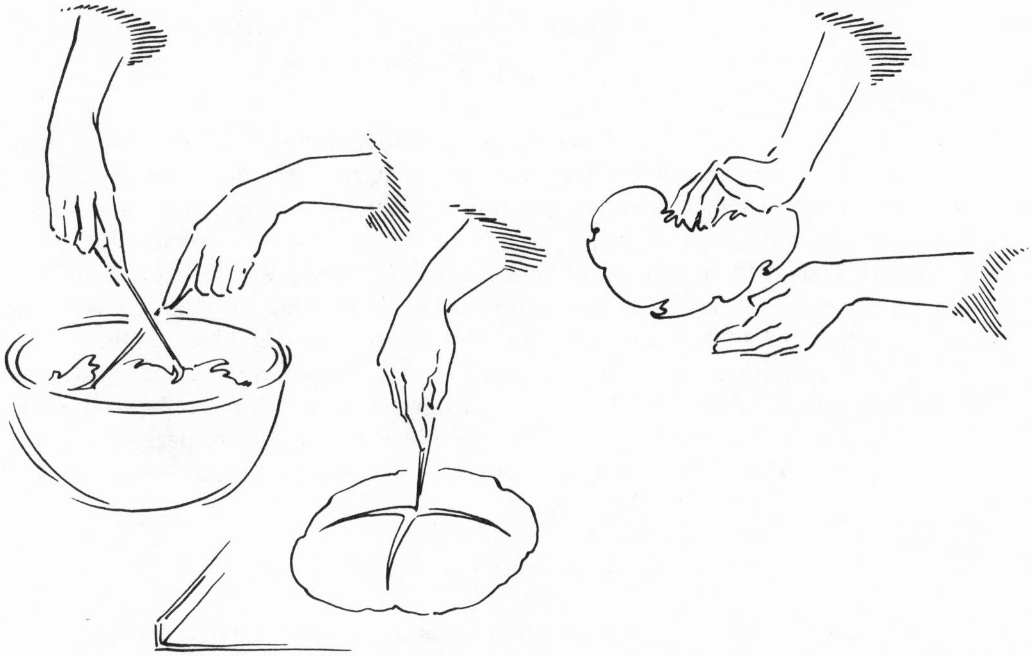

2 teaspoons baking
  powder
1 teaspoon coarse salt
  or ½ teaspoon table
  salt
3 tablespoons sugar
3 tablespoons butter,
  softened
1 cup buttermilk
½ cup raisins
2 tablespoons caraway
  seeds
Confectioner's or
  granulated sugar

until it consists of pea-size bits. Add the buttermilk, raisins, and caraway seeds, and mix until just moist. Gather quickly into a ball; place on a lightly floured surface, and knead 1 minute. Roll into a ball and pat down to form a round, rather flat loaf. With a floured knife, cut a large cross approximately 1½ inches deep into the dough. Top with a sprinkling of sugar, and bake on an ungreased cookie sheet in a preheated 375° oven for 35 minutes.

Black Walnut, Prune, and Spiced Tea Bread

The cakelike persimmon bread of Kentucky is said to descend from the prune bread that helped to nourish the followers of Hernando DeSoto when he crossed the South to the Mississippi River, and Cumberland pioneers who first baked such bread were equally resourceful when they thickened their dough—in times when corn meal was in short supply—with black walnut meats. Today good cooks know that no other nut contributes so much flavor to baked goods, and the combination of black walnuts and prunes is used in various southern breads. In this variation from our apartment kitchen, the blended flavors turned out to be almost exotically enhanced when an infusion of Twining's Spiced Tea was added to the dough; perhaps a good strong tea and your own combination of spices would produce something almost as wonderful?

Makes one 8-inch loaf

1 cup dried prunes
1½ cups strong spiced tea, hot
¼ cup orange juice
1 egg, beaten
2 tablespoons melted butter
2 cups white flour
2 teaspoons baking powder
½ teaspoon baking soda
½ teaspoon coarse salt or ¼ teaspoon table salt
1 cup black walnuts, broken up

Steep the prunes in the tea for about 1 hour.

Scrape the prunes from the pits, breaking into rough pieces as you do so. Measure out ½ cup of the liquid in which they were steeped and stir that into the prunes along with the orange juice, egg, and melted butter. In a bowl mix together the flour, baking powder, soda, and salt very thoroughly, then stir in the prunes and liquid ingredients long enough to blend. Fold in the walnuts.

Scrape the batter into a buttered 8-inch loaf pan. Bake in a preheated 350° oven for 1 hour. Let rest in the pan for about 10 minutes before turning out.

Sour Cream or Buttermilk Corn Bread

This recipe will give you a corn bread that is light and yet doesn't have that slight chemical taste that so many do that use too much baking powder. If you want to spice it up with some hot peppers, just chop up a few of the small bottled green variety and work them into the dough. Or make the Soft-as-Pie Texas Corn Bread on page 295. Another delicious variation is the addition of about ¾ cup diced tart apples to the dough just before baking.

Makes one 9-inch round

¾ cup white or yellow corn meal
1 cup white flour
1 teaspoon baking powder
1 teaspoon baking soda
1 teaspoon coarse salt or ½ teaspoon table salt
3 tablespoons brown sugar
1 egg
2 tablespoons melted butter
1 cup sour cream plus ¼ cup milk, or 1¼ cups buttermilk

Sift together the corn meal, flour, baking powder and soda, salt, and brown sugar. Sift again.

Beat the egg thoroughly, then add the melted butter, sour cream and milk, or buttermilk, and beat them all together. Stir the dry ingredients into the wet mixture and beat thoroughly. Pour the batter into a buttered round 9-inch shallow earthenware dish or cake pan. Bake in a preheated 425° oven for 20 minutes. Serve warm from the pan.

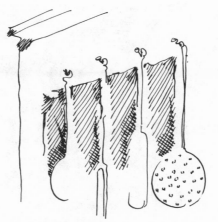

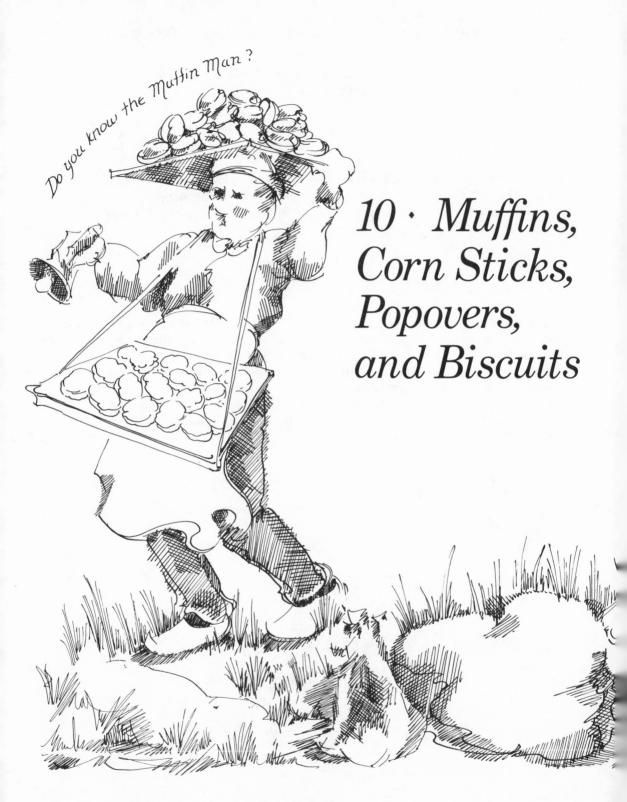

Do you know the Muffin Man?

10 · Muffins, Corn Sticks, Popovers, and Biscuits

Blueberry Muffins
Bran Muffins
Apple Muffins
Nancy Hill's Elderberry Muffins
Jerusalem Artichoke Flour
  and Raisin Muffins
Meal-in-a-Muffin
Tofu and Spinach Muffins
Tofu, Carrot, and Soy Milk Muffins
Hominy Grits Muffins
Date-Nut Muffins
Bacon and Peanut Butter Muffins
Pumpkin Corn Meal Muffins
Rhubarb Oatmeal Flour Muffins
Karen's Biscuit Muffins
Corn Meal and Corn Kernel
  Corn Sticks
Peanut Butter Corn Sticks

Crackling Bread Sticks
Popovers
Cheese Popovers
Buttermilk Biscuits
Buckwheat Biscuits
Tepertös Pogácsa
  (Crackling Biscuits)
Sourdough Biscuits

We have it from Louis P. DeGouy, as knowledgeable a chef as ever composed a cookbook, that "a muffin is a gem and a gem is a muffin." (In another less domestic context, Isabella Bird, author of *A Lady's Life in the Rocky Mountains,* wrote of girls who might innocently agree to join a young man for some fun that "when she acquiesces she is called 'a muffin.'") Having cooked in U.S. kitchens, DeGouy decrees that any good muffin must be baked in old-fashioned cast-iron gem molds, but the variety used for producing muffins may be less interesting than the lore of the "muffin man," a common sight on streets in England and in this country during the last century. In *London Labour and the London Poor,* Henry Mayhew quoted a fourteen-year-old muffin man on his trade:

"I turns out muffins and crumpets, sir, in October, and continues until it gets well into spring, according to the weather. I carries a first-rate article; werry much so. If you was to taste 'em, sir, you'd say the same. If I sell three dozen muffins at ½ d. each, and twice that in crumpets, it's a werry fair day, werry fair. . . . If there's any unsold, a coffee-shop gets them cheap, and puts 'em off cheap again next morning. My best customers is genteel houses, 'cause I sells a genteel thing. I likes wet days best, 'cause there's werry respectable ladies what don't keep a servant, and they buys to save themselves going out. We're a great convenience to the ladies, sir—a great convenience to them as likes a slap-up tea."

A great convenience today to cooks who like freshly made breads is various muffin tins that work well for most of the recipes in this chapter. The assortment ranges from filled muffins that are typically Yankee in character to tiny crisp muffins, corn sticks, popovers, and biscuits, as well (crumpets are to be found in the chapter on Skillet-Baked Breads).

Blueberry Muffins

This recipe makes extra-good blueberry muffins because it calls for a healthy proportion of blueberries. Make them when the berries are at their ripest and full of flavor.

Makes 10 gem-size or 8 larger muffins

1 cup blueberries
2 cups white flour
1 teaspoon baking
  powder
½ teaspoon baking
  soda
1 tablespoon sugar
½ teaspoon coarse salt
  or ¼ teaspoon table
  salt
1 egg
½ cup buttermilk
2 tablespoons melted
  butter

Wash the blueberries and shake dry in a strainer. Spread ½ cup of the flour on waxed paper and toss the blueberries in the flour to coat. Mix the remaining flour, baking powder, soda, sugar, and salt together thoroughly.

In a mixing bowl beat the egg lightly and add the milk and melted butter. Then stir in the dry ingredients and the blueberries with their flour, mixing just enough to moisten the dry ingredients.

Grease a gem pan or muffin pan liberally and spoon in the batter to fill the cups two-thirds full. Pop into a preheated 375° oven and bake 20–25 minutes. Check after 20 minutes to see if the muffins have turned golden brown and the batter has shrunk from the sides of the cups. If so, they're done; otherwise bake 4–5 minutes more. Run a knife around the sides of each cup and turn the muffin tin over onto a rack; the muffins should fall out easily. Serve hot with lots of butter.

Bran Muffins

Bran is considered the best source of dietary fiber but these muffins are so particularly good that you don't have to be persuaded to eat them for health reasons.

Makes 8 large, 10 gem-size, or 30 tiny muffins

1 cup buttermilk
1 cup bran
2 tablespoons melted
   butter
1 egg, separated
⅓ cup maple syrup or
   honey
1 cup flour
2½ teaspoons baking
   powder
½ teaspoon coarse salt
   or ¼ teaspoon table
   salt
Rind of 1 orange,
   coarsely grated
½ cup yellow raisins

Pour buttermilk over the bran and soak for 5 minutes. Stir in melted butter, the egg yolk, maple syrup or honey. Mix flour, baking powder, and salt, and combine with bran mixture.

Beat the white of egg until it forms soft peaks. Fold into the batter along with the orange rind and the raisins. Spoon mixture into well-greased muffin tins and bake in preheated 375° oven about 30 minutes, or until lightly brown. Serve warm.

VARIATION: Eliminate the orange rind and raisins and instead add to above mixture 1 cup ground ham, 1 minced scallion, 1 tablespoon chopped parsley, and freshly ground pepper. Instead of maple syrup or honey use 1 tablespoon sugar and add about ¼ cup additional buttermilk for extra moisture.

Apple Muffins

Be sure to use tart, firm apples—not a soft type like McIntosh—so that the pieces hold their shape and give the muffins a good appley contrast.

Makes 10–12 large muffins

1 egg
¼ cup safflower or vegetable oil
½ cup light brown sugar
2½ cups white flour
½ cup graham flour
4 teaspoons baking powder
½ teaspoon coarse salt or ¼ teaspoon table salt
1 cup milk
2 medium apples, peeled, cored, cut in small dice

TOPPING:

2 teaspoons sugar mixed with ½ teaspoon cinnamon

Beat the egg and then add the oil and sugar, continuing to beat until well blended. Mix the dry ingredients together thoroughly. Add them to the egg mixture alternately with the milk, stirring just enough to mix. Fold in the diced apples. Spoon the batter into greased muffin tins, filling the cups two-thirds full. Sprinkle topping evenly over all the muffins and bake in a preheated 375° oven 20 minutes. Serve warm.

Nancy Hill's Elderberry Muffins

Lewis Hill tells in his book *Successful Cold Climate Gardening* a good many helpful hints about growing elderberries, and Nancy Hill, his wife, has traced the origin of traditional Yankee recipes such as elderflower fritters (sometimes made by soaking petals in brandy), as well as letting us share her method of making elderberry muffins. The elderberry bush is a member of the huckleberry family; found throughout the U.S., it bears flowers and berries from May through November. When the fruit has ripened to dark purple-black it is ready for this recipe, every bit as good as blueberry muffins.

ELDERBERRY MUFFINS,
CONTINUED

Makes 12 large muffins

1 cup sugar
2½ tablespoons butter
3 cups white flour
2 teaspoons baking
   powder
½ teaspoon coarse salt
   or pinch table salt
1 egg
1 cup milk
1 cup elderberries

Cream together sugar and butter. Sift flour with baking powder and a pinch of salt. Blend the creamed mixture with the egg, then add milk alternately with the flour mixture. When the batter is thoroughly mixed add berries. Pour into greased muffin tins, and bake in a preheated 350° oven approximately 20 minutes.

Jerusalem Artichoke Flour and Raisin Muffins

Here's another way to use Jerusalem artichoke flour (see page 105), and the elusive flavor will mystify anyone sampling these for the first time. We find these muffins taste best absolutely fresh with lots of sweet butter.

Makes 12 large muffins

1 cup Jerusalem
   artichoke flour
1 cup white flour
3 tablespoons brown
   sugar
½ teaspoon coarse salt
   or ¼ teaspoon table
   salt
1 teaspoon baking
   powder
½ teaspoon baking
   soda
1 egg
1¼ cups buttermilk
3 tablespoons melted
   butter
½ cup raisins

Mix together thoroughly the two flours, sugar, salt, baking powder, and soda. In a separate bowl beat the egg lightly, then stir in the buttermilk and butter. Pour the dry ingredients into the wet mixture, add the raisins, and stir until mixed. Distribute the batter evenly into a well-greased 12-cup muffin pan and bake in a preheated 375° oven for 20 minutes. Serve warm.

Meal-in-a-Muffin

A traditional "ploughman's lunch" in England consists of cheese and rolls and sometimes fruit. This combination of cheese (we would use an aged Cheddar), apples, and nuts in quick bread dough results in a delicious and filling muffin.

Makes 12–15 large muffins

4 tablespoons (½ stick) softened butter
½ cup sugar
2 large eggs
1½ cups sifted white flour
1 teaspoon baking powder
1 teaspoon baking soda
½ teaspoon kosher salt or ¼ teaspoon table salt
¾ cup rolled oats
1 large tart apple, cored and peeled
⅔ cup grated cheese
½ cup chopped nuts
¾ cup milk
1 apple, sliced thin
¼ cup melted butter
2 tablespoons sugar mixed with 1 tablespoon cinnamon

Blend softened butter with sugar and add eggs, beating the mixture thoroughly. Sift together flour, baking powder, soda, and salt, then stir into butter-sugar mixture. Stir in oats. Chop the large peeled apple into small bits and add to dough with cheese and nuts. Gradually add milk, stirring lightly.

Fill buttered muffin tins two-thirds full. Brush apple slices with melted butter and coat with sugar-cinnamon mixture, then top batter in each muffin tin with 1 apple slice. Sprinkle remaining sugar-cinnamon mixture evenly over top. Bake for about 25 minutes in a preheated 400° oven.

Tofu and Spinach Muffins

Of all plant foods tofu has the highest ratio of protein to calories, and it is considered a good source of iron, phosphorus, calcium, and B and E vitamins. It's been pointed out that until recently so few Americans (in a country that grows forty-nine billion acres of soybeans) have tasted tofu that it's a little like living in a wheat-growing country where no one eats bread. Here are two recipes to help dispel that irony.

TOFU MUFFINS, CONTINUED

Makes 10–12 large muffins

½ cup cooked drained
  spinach, chopped
1 cup spinach cooking
  water plus skim milk
1 egg
¼ cup honey
2 tablespoons safflower
  oil
1 cup whole wheat
  flour
½ cup white flour,
  preferably
  unbleached
½ cup bran flakes
1 teaspoon coarse salt
  or ½ teaspoon table
  salt
3 teaspoons baking
  powder
Freshly ground
  nutmeg
1 cake (about 5
  ounces) tofu or bean
  curd, medium
  texture
1 tablespoon sesame
  seeds

In a medium-size bowl mix together the spinach and its water (plus enough milk, if necessary, to make a full cup) along with the egg, honey, and oil. On a large piece of waxed paper toss together the flours, bran flakes, salt, baking powder, and several gratings of nutmeg until everything is very well mixed. Make a funnel of the waxed paper and pour the dry ingredients into the wet ones, mixing sufficiently to moisten them.

Distribute the batter evenly among 10 or 12 oiled muffin cups, depending on the size of your tins. Slice up the tofu cake into 10 or 12 even slices and press these on top of each cupful of batter. Sprinkle with sesame seeds.

Bake the muffins in a preheated 375° oven for 20 minutes.

Tofu, Carrot, and Soy Milk Muffins

Makes 10–12 large muffins

⅓ cup raisins
¾ cup warm soy milk*
1 cup whole wheat
  flour

Soak the raisins in the warm soy milk for 30 minutes or longer.

Mix the flour and bran flakes together, then stir in the soy milk and raisins, the honey, salt, oil,

*Soy milk powder may be purchased in some health food stores. You can also make your own: see Madhur Jaffrey's *World-of-the-East Vegetarian Cooking*.

1 cup bran flakes
4 tablespoons honey
½ teaspoon salt
2 tablespoons
  vegetable oil
1 egg
½ cup coarsely grated
  carrots
1 cake (about 5
  ounces) tofu or bean
  curd

egg, and carrots. Cut the bean curd into ½-inch dice and gently fold into the batter. Pour into oiled muffin tins, filling the cups about two-thirds full.

Bake in a preheated 375° oven for 20 minutes. Eat warm.

Hominy Grits Muffins

Although soya grits are becoming popular, grits to most Americans mean hulled dried corn kernels that have been coarsely ground. Southerners love these muffins with a breakfast of ham and eggs.

Makes 12 gem-size, 8 large, or 30 tiny muffins

3 tablespoons hominy
  grits
1 cup boiling water
⅛ teaspoon kosher
  salt or a pinch of
  table salt
2 teaspoons active dry
  yeast
2 tablespoons warm
  water
4 tablespoons (½
  stick) butter, cut up
1 tablespoon sugar
⅓ cup scalded milk
1½–1¾ cups white
  flour, preferably
  unbleached

Cook hominy grits by sprinkling into the boiling water; add the salt, turn down heat, cover pan, and let it simmer, stirring occasionally, for 25 minutes. You should have about ½ cup of cooked grits.

Dissolve yeast in warm water in a large bowl. When it swells, add warm grits, cut-up butter, sugar, milk, flour, and a dash of salt, and stir thoroughly. Turn out onto floured surface and knead a few minutes, adding a little more flour if necessary. Your dough should be moist. Cover with plastic wrap and let rise in a warm place until dough doubles in bulk.

Punch down dough. Butter muffin tins or gem pan, then fill each cup two-thirds full. Let rise, uncovered, for 1 hour.

Bake in top third of preheated 375° oven for 25–30 minutes.

A COVEY OF MUFFINS

To come to the end of the subject of muffins—James Beard in *American Cookery* makes clear his lack of enthusiasm for them and George Bernard Shaw summed up the specious argument in *Man and Superman* when one character tells another, "Marry Ann and at the end of a week you'll find no more inspiration in her than in a plate of muffins." To make it easy for you to make up your own mind, here are four more recipes that will appeal to different appetites. We find all of them much more crisp and delicious made in the muffin pans with the tiny cups.

Date-Nut Muffins

Makes 10 gem-size or 8 larger muffins

2 eggs
3 tablespoons light
  brown sugar
4 tablespoons melted
  butter
1 cup milk
2 cups white flour
1 tablespoon baking
  powder
½ teaspoon coarse salt
  or ¼ teaspoon table
  salt
1 cup pitted, chopped
  dates
¾ cup chopped walnuts

Beat the eggs until fluffy, then beat in the brown sugar, butter, and milk. Thoroughly mix the flour, baking powder, and salt together. Add the dates and nuts and toss lightly to coat them. Combine the dry ingredients with the liquid mixture enough to moisten the flour. Turn into a greased muffin pan. Bake in a preheated 375° oven about 25 minutes or until lightly browned.

Bacon and Peanut Butter Muffins

Makes 12 large or 30 tiny muffins

2 cups white flour
1 tablespoon baking
  powder
1 tablespoon sugar
1 teaspoon coarse salt
  or ½ teaspoon table
  salt
1 egg
1 cup milk
2 tablespoons melted
  bacon fat or butter
3 strips of cooked
  bacon, finely
  chopped
About 4 tablespoons
  peanut butter

Mix thoroughly flour, baking powder, sugar, and salt. In a medium-size bowl beat the egg; add milk, melted fat, and chopped bacon. Stir in the flour mixture, but do not beat; mixture should be just moistened. Pour a little batter into each well-greased muffin tin, then drop in about ⅓ teaspoon of peanut butter before filling tins three-fourths full. (If you are using the very small size muffin tins, you'll need only a tiny dot of peanut butter, the cups may be filled to the brim). Bake in a preheated 400° oven for 20–25 minutes.

Pumpkin Corn Meal Muffins

Makes about 24 large muffins (halve recipe to make about 30 tiny muffins)

2 cups white flour
2 cups yellow corn
  meal
2 tablespoons baking
  powder
1 teaspoon baking soda
2 teaspoons coarse salt
  or 1 teaspoon table
  salt
3 eggs
1 cup cooked pumpkin
½ cup honey
½ cup light molasses
2 cups buttermilk
8 tablespoons (1 stick)
  butter, melted

Sift dry ingredients together. Beat eggs thoroughly, then add pumpkin, honey, molasses, and buttermilk. Combine with dry ingredients and mix well. Stir in melted butter. Grease muffin tins and fill two-thirds full with batter. Bake in a preheated oven at 425° about 20 minutes, until golden brown.

Rhubarb Oatmeal Flour Muffins

Makes 12 muffins

¾ cup lightly cooked
  rhubarb*
1 cup juice from the
  rhubarb plus milk
1⅓ cups oatmeal flour
⅔ cup white flour
1 teaspoon coarse salt
  or ½ teaspoon table
  salt
2 teaspoons baking
  powder
½ teaspoon baking
  soda
1 egg
2 tablespoons brown
  sugar
3 tablespoons melted
  butter

Drain the cooked rhubarb. Collect the juice in a measuring cup and add enough milk to make a full cup.

Sift the flours together with the salt, baking powder, and soda. Beat the egg, then beat in the brown sugar and melted butter. Combine the dry ingredients with the wet ones just enough to moisten them. Fold in the rhubarb and turn into buttered muffin tins, distributing the batter evenly among the cups and filling them about three-quarters full.

Bake in a preheated 375° oven for 25 minutes.

* To cook rhubarb it's best to bake it so it doesn't get mushy. For 1 pound cut-up rhubarb use ½ cup sugar. Place in covered nonmetallic casserole and bake in a 350° oven only 15 minutes if you want it lightly cooked, still holding its shape.

Karen's Biscuit Muffins

Karen Hubert is a gifted cook whose numerous adaptations of American recipes (as well as those from other cuisines) are served at the Manhattan restaurant called Hubert's. These small dinner breads, part biscuit, part muffin, are a variation on the classic Southern baking powder biscuit, but they make a very special crisp, buttery mouthful when baked this way in tiny muffin (really cupcake) tins.

Makes about 3 dozen tiny muffins

¼ pound sweet
  whipped butter

Break up the butter and place in the bottom of a medium-size bowl. Sift the flour, baking powder,

2 cups white flour, unbleached preferred
3 teaspoons baking powder
1½ teaspoons kosher salt or 1 teaspoon table salt
Several grinds pepper
1 tablespoon sugar
⅔ cup milk*
2 teaspoons minced chives and dill
¼ cup clarified butter

salt, pepper and sugar over it. Then mix lightly with your fingers or a pastry blender until the butter and flour is about the texture of coarse meal. Stir in the milk and the herbs.

Turn the dough out on a lightly floured surface and knead just for 6 or 7 turns—enough to smear the butter and make the dough hold together. Brush with clarified butter the bottom of a muffin or cupcake tin with tiny cups—only 1 ounce size— and then pluck off small fingerfuls of dough and plop into each cup, letting the piece of dough retain its rough shape. (If you don't have more than one of the muffin tins, you'll have to bake in 3 batches but the dough keeps perfectly well, covered.) Drizzle a little more clarified butter over the top of the biscuits and bake in a preheated 350° oven for 20–25 minutes, until golden and crisp. Serve warm.

*If you want to use buttermilk instead of regular milk, substitute 1 teaspoon baking soda for the baking powder.

Peanut Butter Corn Sticks

Baked in old-fashioned cast-iron corn stick pans (page 365), these peanut-flavored corn sticks are delectable when served sizzling hot from the oven.

Makes 10 corn sticks

1 cup white flour
¼ cup corn meal
½ teaspoon coarse salt or ¼ teaspoon table salt
1 tablespoon sugar
1 tablespoon baking powder
¼ cup peanut butter
1 egg
¾ cup milk
Bacon fat

Mix the flour, corn meal, salt, sugar, and baking powder together thoroughly. Using a pastry blender or two knives, cut the peanut butter into the dry ingredients until the mixture resembles a coarse meal. In a separate bowl beat the egg until fluffy, then beat in the milk. Combine the dry ingredients with the milk and egg just enough to moisten, making sure to incorporate all the flour from the bottom of the bowl. Liberally grease the corn stick pans with bacon fat and fill the sections about three-quarters full with the batter. Bake in a preheated 425° oven for 12 minutes. Serve warm.

Corn Meal and Corn Kernel Corn Sticks

These are especially good if you use a cast-iron corn stick mold, which makes this golden bread look like small ears of corn and gives you plenty of crusty exterior. The addition of corn kernels makes for a moist interior and adds a touch of sweetness; no other sugar is needed, we feel. You can use the same batter to make muffins; the tiny muffins described in the preceding recipe are particularly good and would require the same cooking time.

Makes 14 cornsticks

1 cup yellow corn meal
1 cup white flour,
   preferably
   unbleached
2 teaspoons coarse salt
   or ½ teaspoon table
   salt
1 tablespoon baking
   powder
2 eggs
1 cup milk
¾ cup corn kernels,
   cooked or canned
   and drained
2 tablespoons melted
   butter
Bacon fat

Mix the corn meal, flour, salt, and baking powder together thoroughly. In a separate bowl beat the eggs until fluffy, then beat in the milk. Combine the dry ingredients with the milk and egg, making sure to incorporate all the flour. Stir in the corn kernels and melted butter. Liberally grease the corn stick pans with bacon fat (if you have only one pan, bake in two batches). Fill molds almost to the top with batter. Bake in a preheated 425° oven for 20 minutes. Serve warm.

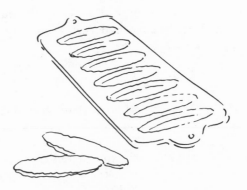

Crackling Bread Sticks

In the old days hog killing time was an important part of the lives of farmers who raised pigs, giving rise to the old saw about using everything but the squeal. Inevitably, perhaps, various ethnic bread loaves were benefited by porcine by-products, and among the most American of these are breads studded with cracklings. "When the lard was rendered and strained," Edna Lewis recalls in *The Taste of Country Cooking,* "little defatted pieces were left which we called cracklings. Cut into small pieces and mixed into cornmeal batter they made a bread which was deliciously crispy and chewy." Mrs. Lewis has given us her recipe for these crackling bread sticks. "Eat them with soups and stews, eat them plain, but make sure you eat them good and hot!" she says firmly.

Makes about 8-10 bread sticks

1 cup water-ground white corn meal
2 teaspoons coarse salt or 1 teaspoon table salt
½ cup crisp cracklings (see below)
1½ cups cold water

Mix together the meal, salt, and cracklings. Stir in the water and mix by hand. Add a few extra spoonfuls of water if the dough is not holding together well.

Pinch off a piece of dough the size of a small egg, then pinch it into a small rectangular bar. Grease a cookie sheet and on it roll the bars of dough into sticks about 3 inches long. Roll each bar away from you until it is thin enough.

Bake in a preheated 375° oven for 12–15 minutes, until golden in color.

♦ CRACKLINGS

Cut pork fat from the loin into 1-inch pieces; there should be no lean bits on the fat. Put them into a heavy iron skillet or pot over low heat, stirring often to prevent sticking. As they heat up and begin to cook they will rise and float on their own melted fat. When done, all the cracklings will be floating, turning crisp and brown. Strain the fat into a heatproof bowl, and drain the cracklings on absorbent paper. When they have cooled, cut them into ¼-inch pieces.

Popovers

Here is an example of a bread—served piping hot from the oven—that rises on egg power alone. No baking powder or soda is used. It is simply the exposure of the eggs to heat that makes a popover pop, rising well above its container, usually at a jaunty, lopsided angle. Theories about how to make popovers abound: the muffin tins should be red hot—cast iron considered the best kind—and the butter should be already sizzling in them. But the truth is that popovers rise just as spectacularly started in a cold oven and that individual Pyrex cups are far better than a muffin pan because the glass generates so much heat. So if you have an oven that can be set to turn on by itself at a specified time, prepare the batter the night before, put it in the oven in well-greased Pyrex custard cups, set the timer—and bring on crisp, golden, sky-high popovers for breakfast.

Makes 8 popovers

1 cup white flour
1 teaspoon coarse salt
  or ½ teaspoon table
  salt
3 eggs
2 tablespoons melted
  butter
1 cup milk

Use either a blender or a food processor and dump all the ingredients into its container. Blend until thoroughly mixed, scraping down any flour clinging to the sides. Or put the flour and salt in a bowl, make a well in the center, and add the rest of the ingredients, beating until smooth. Fill well-greased 5-ounce Pyrex cups between half and two-thirds full. Place in a cold oven, turn heat to 400°, and bake 35 minutes. Run a knife around the edge of the cups to loosen the popovers and serve immediately with lots of butter and jam.

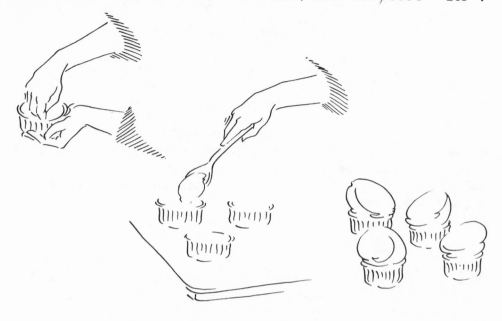

Cheese Popovers

The British for centuries have been making cheese baps, and the French often add Gruyère to their brioche dough; cheese adds flavor and subtle smoothness to the texture of breads. An American variation on this theme may be found in the following recipe from *The World of Cheese.*

Makes 8 popovers

1 cup white flour
½ teaspoon coarse salt or ¼ teaspoon table salt
2 eggs
1 cup milk
Tabasco
1 cup freshly grated sharp cheese (Cheddar, Asiago, or Romano)

Sift flour and salt into a bowl. Beat eggs and milk together, then add to flour, beating until quite smooth. Add a few drops of Tabasco. Lightly oil eight 5-ounce Pyrex custard cups. Spoon a tablespoon of the batter into each, then a tablespoon of grated cheese, alternating until both are used up and cups are about half full. Place in cold oven, then immediately turn heat to 400°. After 30 minutes lower heat to 350° and bake another 10 minutes. Serve right away.

Buttermilk Biscuits

A good biscuit is supposed to be crisp and flaky on the outside, rich and moist within. There is a tendency today to emphasize the height of the baked biscuit and, as a result, many recipes add too much baking powder, which not only gives the biscuits a chemical baking powder taste but makes them too dry. Biscuits in the South were often made with naturally soured milk and required only a little baking soda to achieve the proper height—which should be only about an inch. Because the milk we get now doesn't sour naturally, we like to use buttermilk (or yogurt) and a small amount of baking powder along with soda.

Makes about 18 small biscuits

2 cups white flour
1½ teaspoons baking
   powder
½ teaspoon baking
   soda
1 teaspoon coarse salt
   or ½ teaspoon table
   salt
4 tablespoons (½
   stick) butter or fresh
   lard, chilled
¾ cup buttermilk

Mix all the dry ingredients together thoroughly. Cut the cold butter or lard into small (roughly ½ inch) pieces and toss with the dry ingredients. Then with your fingertips (or using a pastry blender or two knives) lightly and quickly rub the fat into the flour until the mixture resembles coarse meal; don't overmix. Make a well and pour in the buttermilk, then mix with a fork to make a soft dough. Turn out onto a lightly floured board and knead lightly for 5 or 6 turns—no more than 30 seconds. Roll out to ½-inch thickness and cut the dough into rounds with a floured cookie cutter

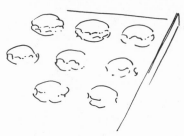

or the rim of a glass approximately 1¾ inches in diameter. Place biscuits on an ungreased baking sheet ¾ inch apart and bake in a preheated 450° oven for 12–15 minutes.

Buckwheat Biscuits

Makes 18 biscuits

1 tablespoon active dry
  yeast
1½ cups warm water
⅔ cup melted butter
⅔ cup lukewarm milk
2 tablespoons molasses
1½ cups buckwheat
  flour
3½ cups white flour,
  preferably
  unbleached
2 tablespoons sugar
2 teaspoons coarse salt
  or 1¼ teaspoons
  table salt
2 egg whites, lightly
  beaten
½ cup chopped nuts

In a large bowl mix the yeast with ½ cup warm water. Mix 4 tablespoons of the melted butter with milk, molasses, and remaining warm water, blending thoroughly; combine with yeast mixture and leave in warm place, covered, for 30 minutes or more.

Sift buckwheat flour and mix with white flour, sugar, and salt, then stir into yeast-molasses mixture. When dough becomes a little sticky, turn out on a floured surface and knead 4–5 minutes, until smooth and velvety. Put dough in a buttered bowl, cover with plastic wrap, and let rise until doubled in bulk.

Punch dough down and let it double again.

Punch dough down again, then pinch off small balls about 1½ inches in diameter and roll lightly in flour, then in remaining melted butter. Arrange in rows on ungreased baking sheet and let rise 10 minutes, then bake in preheated 400° oven for 20–25 minutes. Remove from oven and brush tops with egg white, then sprinkle with chopped nuts. Put under broiler and brown.

Tepertös Pogácsa
(Crackling Biscuits)

To boast of using every part of the pig except the squeal seems to be common wherever pork is eaten. Romanians, for instance, make a thin crackling bread without yeast that is scored in squares, then broken in pieces when served. Our Viennese sister-in-law makes this Hungarian version in her Prinz Eugenstrasse apartment as well as when she visits us. It is wonderful to serve with drinks, and she often makes a large amount so she can freeze enough to use on occasions when there isn't time to start from scratch. Some Hungarian cooks also make *tepertös pogácsa* with goose fat as a substitute for the pork cracklings.

Makes about 30 biscuits

1 tablespoon active dry
  yeast
¼ cup warm water
1 egg
2 teaspoons coarse salt
  or 1½ teaspoons
  table salt
¾ cup sour cream
¼ cup yogurt
About 3½ cups white
  flour, preferably
  unbleached
2 cups cracklings (see
  page 241)

GLAZE

1 egg beaten with 1
  teaspoon water

In a medium bowl dissolve the yeast in the warm water. Beat in the egg, salt, sour cream, yogurt, and enough of the flour to make a soft dough. Cover with plastic wrap and let stand ½ hour.

Put the cracklings in a food processor to chop them finely or else chop them up with a sharp knife.

Turn the dough out onto a floured surface and knead ⅓ of the cracklings into it. Cover and let stand until the dough swells to approximately half again its size—about 30 minutes.

Knead ⅓ more of the cracklings into the dough, cover again, and let rise for about 30 minutes.

Punch the dough down, pat it out, and spread the remaining crackling over it. Fold in the sides and let stand again, covered, for 30 minutes.

Now roll the dough out to a thickness of ¾ inch. Cut out circles with a 2-inch cookie cutter, place on an ungreased baking sheet an inch apart, cover with a kitchen towel, and let rise for 30 to 40 minutes until double in size.

Brush the tops with the egg glaze and bake in a preheated 450° oven for 12 minutes.

Sourdough Biscuits

Be sure you have on hand some sourdough starter that hasn't lost its kick. You can use either a plain sourdough starter, page 67, or the rye one, page 113, which will deepen the color of these biscuits.

Makes about 18 small biscuits or 12 larger

2 cups white flour
1 teaspoon baking
  powder
½ teaspoon baking
  soda
1 teaspoon coarse salt
  or ½ teaspoon table
  salt
⅓ cup shortening or
  lard
½ cup sourdough
  starter
About ½ cup
  buttermilk or yogurt

Mix the dry ingredients together thoroughly. With your fingertips or with a pastry blender, cut in the shortening or lard until the mixture resembles coarse meal. Add the starter and enough buttermilk or yogurt to make a soft dough. Knead lightly for a dozen turns or so on a floured surface. Then roll out or pat to a thickness of ½–¾ inch. With a cookie cutter or the rim of a glass cut biscuits the size you want and place ½ inch apart on an ungreased cookie sheet. Bake in a preheated 450° oven for 10–12 minutes until lightly browned.

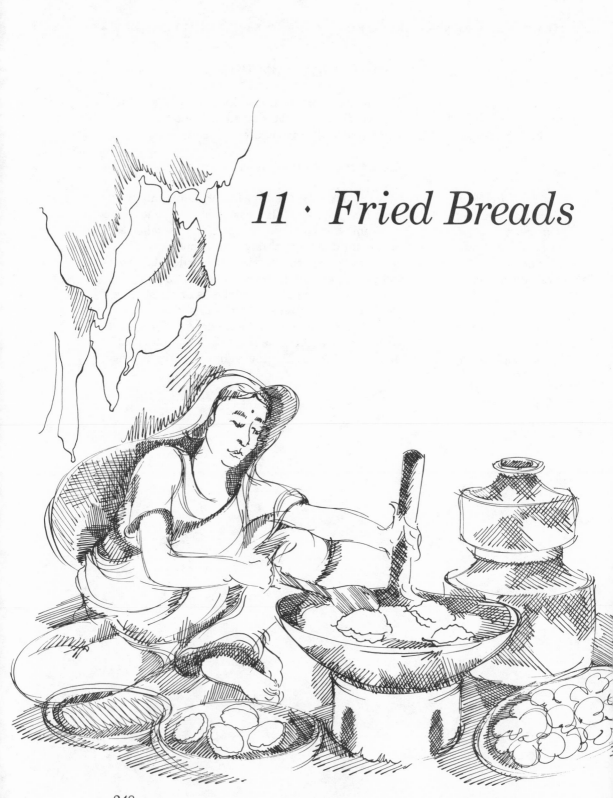

11 · Fried Breads

Doughnuts—Plain, Buttermilk,
  Brown Sugar
Raised Doughnuts, Jellied
Fastnachts
Navajo Fried Bread
Sopaipillas
Puris
Hush Puppies
Wild Rice Beignets or Fritters
Helen Brown's Fly-Away Rolls
Chinese Fried Scallion Bread

Fried breads can include anything from *pain perdu* (i.e., the breakfast dish we call French toast or, as an Englishman might say, "poor knights of Windsor") to doughnuts. In India the bread called *puri* puffs out when the flat dough is immersed in hot deep fat. In Holland crisply fried crullers (or *olie bollen*) are the forerunners of America's doughnut. It is sometimes said that a visit to New Orleans is a waste of time without a visit to the French Market for breakfast doughnuts. Less famous in this country outside the Southwest, however, are the fried breads called *buñuelos* or *sopaipillas.* In California, where they are known as a sort of Mexican popover, these fried breads are sometimes shaped like rosettes and sometimes come out of the bubbling fat as "a sweet hollow pincushion." They are closely related to Navajo fried bread, and are often served with honey, or with cinnamon-flavored syrup. Made of corn meal like hush puppies, or of whole wheat flour like some *puris,* fried breads are fun—to cook and to serve.

DOUGHNUTS

It might be said that the doughnut is ethnically Dutch, but the hole that gives it character is American. A monument to Hanson Gregory of Maine commemorates the day in 1847 that he persuaded his mother to shape them in rings to eliminate uncooked centers. A few generations later John Bergner invented the machine that loops out doughnuts in endless numbers, but not one of the doughnut shops of the automated world can deliver what you can make with ease in your own kitchen. It's the fresh fat you use in the frying that ensures the burst of flavor that brings contentment to palates jaded by junk food. Here are some good rules to follow:

1. Don't overmix the dough.

2. Don't add too much flour. Dough should be slightly sticky, and letting it rest at least 30 minutes in the refrigerator makes it manageable.

3. After you've shaped the doughnuts, let them rest about 10 minutes before frying.

4. Use fresh oil for frying, keep the frying oil at 365° or the recommended temperature and have at least 3 inches in your frying kettle. Use a frying thermometer if you do not have a thermostatically controlled fryer or skillet.

5. Don't crowd doughnuts. Fry only three or four at a time. If you turn them several times during the cooking, you'll have fewer cracks.

6. To thaw frozen doughnuts, be sure to remove them from their wrapping and heat in a moderate oven; otherwise they'll be soggy.

Plain Doughnuts

Makes about 24 doughnuts

1 cup milk
1 cup sugar
4 teaspoons baking
    powder
1 teaspoon coarse salt
    or ½ teaspoon table
    salt
1 egg
2 tablespoons butter,
    melted
½ teaspoon freshly
    grated nutmeg
3½ cups white flour
Frying oil: fresh pure
    pork fat, vegetable
    oil, or shortening
Confectioner's sugar

Combine the milk, sugar, baking powder, salt, egg, butter, and nutmeg. Stir in the flour just enough to mix and to form a soft, barely handleable dough. Cover the bowl and refrigerate for 30–60 minutes.

Roll or pat out dough on a board floured enough so that it won't stick. When dough is ½ inch thick, using a well-floured doughnut cutter, cut out doughnut shapes and let them rest on slightly floured surface (remove the holes but save them to fry along with the doughnuts—they're delicious). Heat enough fat or oil to fill your frying kettle to a depth of at least 3 inches. When it reaches 365° (or as old-fashioned cooks would say, "when it is hot enough to set a match aflame") drop in three or four doughnuts. As soon as they float to the surface and are holding their shape, turn them. Fry until golden brown on both sides—about 2–3 minutes. Drain on absorbent paper and dust with confectioner's sugar after they have cooled a little.

SUGAR

Buttermilk Doughnuts

Makes about 30 doughnuts

2 eggs
1 egg yolk
1 cup sugar
1 cup buttermilk
4 cups white flour
1 teaspoon baking
  powder
½ teaspoon soda
1 teaspoon coarse salt
  or ½ teaspoon table
  salt
About ½ teaspoon
  freshly grated
  nutmeg
1 tablespoon melted
  butter
Frying oil

Beat the eggs and egg yolk together, then gradually add the sugar and buttermilk. Sift the flour, baking powder, soda, and salt together, and stir into the egg mixture. Grate in the nutmeg and add the melted butter. This batter should not be refrigerated, so cut doughnut shapes, let them rest about 5 minutes on a lightly floured surface, and then fry as in the preceding recipe.

Brown Sugar Doughnuts

Makes about 20 doughnuts

2 cups brown sugar
2 cups cake flour
1 cup all-purpose flour
3 teaspoons baking
  powder
¼ teaspoon nutmeg
¼ teaspoon cinnamon
1 teaspoon coarse salt
  or ½ teaspoon table
  salt
1 cup milk
2 eggs
1 egg yolk
¼ cup melted butter
Frying oil

Sift all the dry ingredients together. Whisk the milk, eggs, and yolk together until well blended and light. Combine dry and liquid ingredients, then add melted butter. Let dough rest, refrigerated, and proceed as in Plain Doughnuts (opposite page).

Raised Doughnuts

These are yeast doughnuts and therefore light and airy. They are best eaten immediately, so if you want them fresh for breakfast, let them rise in the refrigerator overnight and then get up early enough to form them and let them rise again—about 40 minutes if they are cold. It takes less than 5 minutes to fry a batch in deep fat. If you like the surprise of sweet jelly in the center of a warm doughnut, try the variation of jelly doughnuts.

Makes 18 doughnuts

2 tablespoons butter
½ cup milk
1 tablespoon active dry yeast
⅓ cup sugar
¼ cup warm water
About 2¼–2½ cups white flour, preferably unbleached
1 egg, lightly beaten
1 teaspoon coarse salt or ½ teaspoon table salt
¼ teaspoon ground cardamom
¼ teaspoon cinnamon
¼ teaspoon mace
Oil or shortening for frying
Confectioner's sugar

Heat the butter with the milk, bringing it just to the boil, then let cool. In a medium bowl dissolve the yeast and the sugar in the water. When the milk mixture has cooled to lukewarm, stir it in. Beat in 2¼ cups of the flour, the egg, salt, and spices. You should have a soft but manageable dough; add a little more flour if necessary. Turn out and knead lightly on a floured work surface for 1 minute. Clean and grease the bowl and return the dough to it. Cover with plastic wrap and let rise until double in volume or overnight in the refrigerator.

Turn out on a lightly floured surface and pat or roll the dough out to ½-inch thickness. Cut with a doughnut cutter (don't throw away the centers—they are delicious, too, fried into small puffy balls), cover lightly with a towel, and let rise until almost double—about 25 minutes or 40 if cold.

Heat 3 inches of frying oil in a frying kettle to 370°. Slip in doughnuts one by one, but do not fry more than four at a time. Almost immediately they will rise to the surface and swell up gloriously. Poke them around if they try to nudge each other. After 2 minutes turn with a spatula and fry about the same amount of time on the other side. Remove with a slotted spoon to paper towels and place in warming oven; proceed with the rest, making sure that the frying fat comes back up to 370° before frying each new batch. When all are done, sprinkle with confectioner's sugar or put sugar in a paper bag and shake the doughnuts in it to coat all over. Serve still warm.

VARIATION: To make *jelly doughnuts,* pat out the risen dough to ¼-inch thickness and cut in 2½-inch circles. Place a heaping teaspoon of jelly or jam in the center of half the circles. Wet the rim with egg white and place an empty circle on top. Pinch the edges securely together. Continue with the rest and fry as above.

Fastnachts

In German the name means "night before fasting," and the fried breads now so called were produced as a way of using up the last of the fat that was banned during Lent. Fastnachts are still popular in Pennsylvania, as well as other areas where German Americans settled, and they are made in various shapes. Here they are diamond-shaped with a slash through the middle.

Makes about 24 fastnachts

2 teaspoons active dry
  yeast
⅔ cup sugar
⅓ cup lukewarm water
1 medium potato,
  boiled and mashed
  (to make ⅓ cup)
About 2¼–2½ cups
  white flour,
  preferably
  unbleached
⅓ cup lukewarm milk
1 egg, lightly beaten
¼ cup melted butter
½ teaspoon kosher
  salt or ¼ teaspoon
  table salt
¼ teaspoon mace
Oil or shortening for
  frying

Make a sponge: put the yeast and ⅓ cup of the sugar in a medium-size bowl, pour the warm water over, and let dissolve. Beat in the mashed potato and ⅓ cup flour, then cover the bowl with plastic wrap and let stand 1–3 hours.

Stir the milk, the egg, the melted butter (cooled to lukewarm if it is hot), the remaining sugar, the salt, and mace into the sponge. Add enough flour until the dough becomes hard to stir.

Turn the dough out on a floured surface and knead lightly a few minutes, adding a little more flour as necessary, but keep the dough light and quite moist. Clean the bowl, butter it, and return the dough to it. Cover with plastic wrap, let rise for 1 hour, then refrigerate anywhere from 30 minutes to overnight (it can even be kept a few days if you want to do a small batch of fastnachts one day and some doughnuts a day or so later).

Roll the dough out to ¼-inch thickness. Using a ruler, mark off diamond shapes, about 2 inches at their widest point, then cut them, using a knife that you have just run under very hot water and dried. With the leftover pieces, make twists or bows or whatever. With a spatula transfer the shapes to a floured baking sheet and let them rise, covered lightly with a towel, for 30–40 minutes.

Before frying, preheat the oil or shortening to 360°; you should have 2 inches in the pan. Using a hot sharp knife, slash each fastnacht once on top. Fry for 2 minutes on each side, being sure not to crowd the pan. Remove and drain on paper towels.

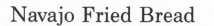

Navajo Fried Bread

Our first taste of Indian fried bread was at a glass-and-chrome roadside place on the high-desert highway to Monument Valley. We stopped because of a sign that said "Navajo Food," and because we were curious. Among the featured specialties was fried bread, and when it came it was as large as a dinner plate—in fact, the warm, flaky, golden bread served as a plate to hold a mound of shredded lettuce, chopped tomatoes, strips of sweet peppers, and Monterey Jack cheese. The bread was so unusually good we wanted to know how it was made, and the paunchy Navajo proprietor directed us to an Indian woman who lived nearby. She not only showed us how the bread was made but scooped out some blue corn meal which she had ground while we watched (see page 282).

This is how she made her fried bread. She had some fresh pork lard on hand, but she assured us we could use a vegetable shortening and the result would be almost as good. It is.

Makes 6 rounds

2 cups white flour
2 teaspoons baking
  powder
2 teaspoon coarse salt
  or 1 teaspoon table
  salt
1 tablespoon lard or
  shortening
About ¾ cup
  lukewarm water
3 cups lard,
  shortening, or oil for
  frying

In a medium-size bowl mix the dry ingredients, stirring thoroughly. With the tips of your fingers or with a pastry blender cut in lard or shortening until mixture has the texture of corn meal. Slowly add the water, stirring with a fork, using just enough liquid for the dough to hold together.

Turn the dough out onto a floured surface and knead gently for about 3 minutes. Cover it with a piece of plastic wrap or towel and let it rest 10–15 minutes.

Divide the dough into six round balls and let these rest, lightly covered, while you start heating the fat in a frying kettle or electric fryer or skillet.

Roll out the first ball of dough to a round 6–7 inches in diameter. Make a 3-inch cut down the center of the circle with a sharp knife. By now the fat should be hot; if you have a deep-frying fat thermometer test its temperature—it should be about 380°; if you don't, test with a small pinch of the dough—it should sizzle and float to the top but not darken too quickly. When ready, slip the first round of dough into the hot fat. It will puff up immediately; cook it on one side for a minute or so, then turn it with a slotted spatula and cook on the other. Remove and drain on paper towels and prepare the next round of dough. Watch the fat to make sure it stays hot enough but doesn't start to smoke. The fried bread may be kept warm in a low oven, but it should be eaten as soon as possible, either strewn with shredded lettuce, tomatoes, chilies, cheese, and hot sausage, if you like, or it can be eaten with honey.

Sopaipillas

This New Mexican fried bread is very much like Navajo bread except that *sopaipillas* are cut in squares that are rolled very, very thin, and when each one hits the hot frying oil it puffs up like a pillow. They are served golden and warm with honey.

Makes 12 sopaipillas

2 cups white flour
*2 teaspoons baking
powder*
*1 teaspoon kosher salt
or ½ teaspoon table
salt*
*2 tablespoons
shortening*
⅔ cup warm water
Oil for deep frying

Mix all the dry ingredients together thoroughly. Cut in the shortening, using the tips of your fingers or a pastry blender. Gradually add the water, stirring with a fork, using just enough to moisten the flour.

Turn the dough out onto a lightly floured surface and knead for 3–4 minutes. Make a ball of the dough, cover with plastic wrap, and let rest 10–15 minutes.

Divide the dough in half and start slowly heating enough oil to cover the bottom of a frying kettle by 1 inch. Roll the first half of the dough out to a rectangle 6 by 9 inches. If it is too springy and resists you, stop and let the dough rest a minute, covered lightly with plastic wrap, then start rolling again. Keep the surface lightly floured and pick up the dough and turn it a few times as you are rolling it out to make sure it isn't sticking. Now cut the rectangle into six even squares. Just before frying roll each piece again, stretching it another couple of inches to about 5 by 4 inches.

When the oil is almost smoking (it should be about 380°), slip one or two of the squares in, depending on the size of the pan—don't crowd. It will sink and rise immediately, puffing up into a pillow. Turn it when it is golden on one side—less than a minute—and fry the other side until golden. Drain on paper toweling. Repeat with the remaining pieces. Then proceed with the second batch of dough in the same manner. Serve immediately.

Puris

Cooks in India make breads like chapati that are baked on a griddle called a *tava* or those that sizzle in deep fat and are known as *puris* (or *pooris*). Rolled very thin, *puris* burst into balloons when they're plunged into very hot fat, and they collapse, of course, the moment they're torn open. Chapati and *puris* are both unleavened, as is the Indian bread *naan* on page 290.

Makes 15 puris

1 cup whole wheat
    flour
⅓ *cup white flour*
2 *tablespoons cake*
    flour
1 *teaspoon coarse salt*
    or ½ *teaspoon table*
    salt
2 *tablespoons*
    vegetable oil
½ *cup or slightly more*
    water
Oil for deep frying

In a bowl mix ½ cup of the whole wheat flour with the two white flours and the salt. Pour the oil over. Slowly add the water, mixing until you have moistened all the flour; you may need a few drops more than ½ cup. Turn the dough out onto a lightly floured surface and knead it until smooth and resilient, although it will never be as bouncy as a yeast dough—about 8 minutes.

Return to the cleaned but ungreased bowl and cover with plastic wrap to rest at least 1½ hours.

Start heating the oil in an electric skillet or frying kettle; it should be 2–3 inches deep.

Sprinkle some of the remaining whole wheat flour over your working surface. Turn the dough out and divide it into 15 small balls. Cover the remaining balls with floured plastic wrap as you work with one of the balls. If there are two of you in the kitchen, it is helpful at this stage if one can do the rolling out, while the other fries each *puri* as it is shaped. Roll the ball into a circle 3½ inches in diameter; the dough will be resistant, but roll firmly from the center out, turning the dough and flouring the work surface as necessary.

When the oil is almost smoking—about 385°—slip one of the disks of dough in. It will sink, then rise to the surface. Working quickly, with a slotted spoon keep pushing it down and also splash a little hot oil over the surface. In about 30 seconds it will have puffed up like a balloon. Turn it over and cook the other side 30 seconds. Continue with the rest. When all are done, serve immediately.

Hush Puppies

Indoors or out, hush puppies are traditionally fried in the same fat with freshly caught fish; in some parts of the South they are also closely linked to pork barbecue. Old recipes sometimes call for corn meal only, but white flour makes for easier handling, and some recipes require self-rising flour. If you're cooking them outdoors, drop a cube of bread into the seething fat—if it browns in 60 seconds the temperature is about 375°.

Makes about 30 hush puppies

1 ½ cups yellow
  cornmeal
1 ½ cups all-purpose
  flour
2 tablespoons sugar
1 tablespoon baking
  powder
1 teaspoon coarse salt
  or ½ teaspoon table
  salt
¾ cup water
⅓ cup evaporated
  milk
2 tablespoons
  vegetable oil
1 egg, beaten
Vegetable oil or
  shortening for frying

Combine the dry ingredients. Add water, evaporated milk, 2 tablespoons vegetable oil, and beaten egg. Stir thoroughly.

Use a tablespoon to scoop up the batter and drop into oil or shortening heated to about 370°. Don't cook too many at a time. Turn hush puppies once, cooking them altogether about 3–5 minutes, until golden brown—time depends on size. Drain well.

Wild Rice Beignets or Fritters

Long before the American Revolutionary War, voyageurs of the fur trade brought the rudiments of French cuisine to America, and they were also the first to discover Indians who cooked wild rice. This recipe is based on an ancient way of making beignets, which more prosaic Americans call fritters.

Makes about 24 fritters

1 tablespoon active dry
  yeast
½ cup warm water

In a good-size bowl mix yeast and warm water, add wild rice, and set aside for about 3 hours (or longer), covered with plastic wrap.

1¼ *cups cooked wild*
  rice
3 *eggs, well beaten*
3 *tablespoons sugar*
1 *cup all-purpose flour*
1 *teaspoon coarse salt*
  or ½ teaspoon table
  salt
Freshly ground
  nutmeg
Vegetable oil for frying
Maple syrup

Stir in beaten eggs, sugar, flour, salt, and a
liberal grating of nutmeg. Blend well and leave in
a warm place about 30 minutes.

When the mixture has developed tiny bubbles
on the surface, heat at least 2 inches of oil in a
skillet or frying kettle to about 325°. To test
temperature of oil, drop ½ teaspoon of the batter
in; it should sizzle actively. Cook the batter by
dropping in separate spoonfuls, making sure they
do not touch. Fry about 3 minutes to a side. They
should be light brown, so adjust the heat to
prevent burning and to ensure cooking through.
Drain on paper and serve hot with maple syrup.

Helen Brown's Fly-Away Rolls

In culling nineteenth-century small-town cook-
books for her own *West Coast Cookbook,* Helen Evans Brown retrieved this
recipe, which we in turn have found makes a hit when prepared in Vermont's
hill country. Fly-Away Rolls are so called, Mrs. Brown wrote, "for obvious reasons." They disappear in short order.

Makes about 30 rolls

2 *tablespoons active*
  dry yeast
3 *tablespoons sugar*
½ *cup warm water*
4 *tablespoons butter*
1 *cup milk*
2 *teaspoons coarse salt*
  or 1 teaspoon table
  salt
2 *eggs*
1 *teaspoon ground*
  coriander
3–3½ *cups white flour,*
  preferably
  unbleached
Oil for frying

In a medium-size bowl dissolve the yeast and the
sugar in the warm water.

Heat the butter in ½ cup of the milk and stir in
the salt until both are dissolved. Add the rest of
the milk to cool the mixture. Separate the eggs
and whisk the yolks into the milk mixture. In a
separate bowl beat the egg whites until they form
peaks.

Add the milk-egg mixture to the yeast. Stir in
the coriander and 3 cups of the flour. Now fold in
the beaten egg whites. It's not too easy to fully
incorporate stiff egg whites into a bread dough and
still keep them light, but cut and fold as best you
can; you will have a soft dough. Now gently work
in almost all of the remaining flour, then cover the
bowl with a piece of floured plastic wrap and
refrigerate for about 2 hours—or longer if
convenient.

Turn the dough out on a lightly floured board, pat down, and pull off pieces of dough just a little smaller than Ping-Pong balls. Form into balls, handling gently. Place on a lightly floured board and allow to rise, uncovered, until double in size.

Heat at least 3 inches of oil in a frying kettle to 370°. Scoop up the rolls one at a time with a slotted spoon and drop gently into the hot oil. Don't crowd the pan. Fry them on one side about a minute until golden, then turn and fry on the other. Drain on paper towels, and keep hot while you do the rest. Serve the fly-away rolls in a napkin-lined basket with lots of sweet butter.

Chinese Fried Scallion Bread

"Breakfast doesn't seem right without this" is a sentiment expressed by one of our friends from China, where bread as we know it is uncommon. We are more apt to serve it as a lunch or supper bread with cold meats or eggs and salad.

Makes 3 rounds about 10 inches in diameter

1¾ cups white flour plus more for dusting
¼ cup cake flour
1 cup water
2 teaspoons coarse salt or 1 teaspoon table salt
3 tablespoons lard or shortening, at room temperature
¾ cup chopped scallions, including ½ of the greens
⅓ cup peanut oil

Mix 1¾ cups white flour with the cake flour and water until well blended. Put on a lightly floured working surface and knead until smooth, adding just a little more flour to keep the dough from sticking. Form into a ball, cover with plastic wrap, and let rest about 10 minutes.

Tear off one-third of the dough, re-covering the remaining. Lightly flour an area of at least 12 inches and pat the piece of dough into a circle. Then, using a floured rolling pin, roll it out into a large circle 11–12 inches in diameter, turning, lifting, and dusting as necessary. Sprinkle the round with salt, then spread a tablespoon of the lard or shortening over the surface evenly, and finally distribute ¼ cup of the scallions evenly on top. Now roll the circle up jelly-roll fashion. Pick up this roll and twist it several times as you would a rope. Plop one end of the roll down and let the dough sink down, finally pressing the top down firmly to make a cake. Roll this cake out again, first dusting your work surface with flour, to a circle about 10 inches in diameter. Place between waxed paper while you prepare the remaining 2 cakes in this same manner.

Heat a large heavy skillet and pour in 2 tablespoons oil. Swirl around to spread evenly and when good and hot, slip one of the rounds in. Fry over medium heat for about 2 minutes, pressing down here and there lightly with the spatula so it cooks evenly, then turn and fry on the other side, 1½–2 minutes, until golden-pocked. Drain on paper towels and keep warm between foil in a low oven while you make the other 2 breads. Serve very warm and cut in quarters at table.

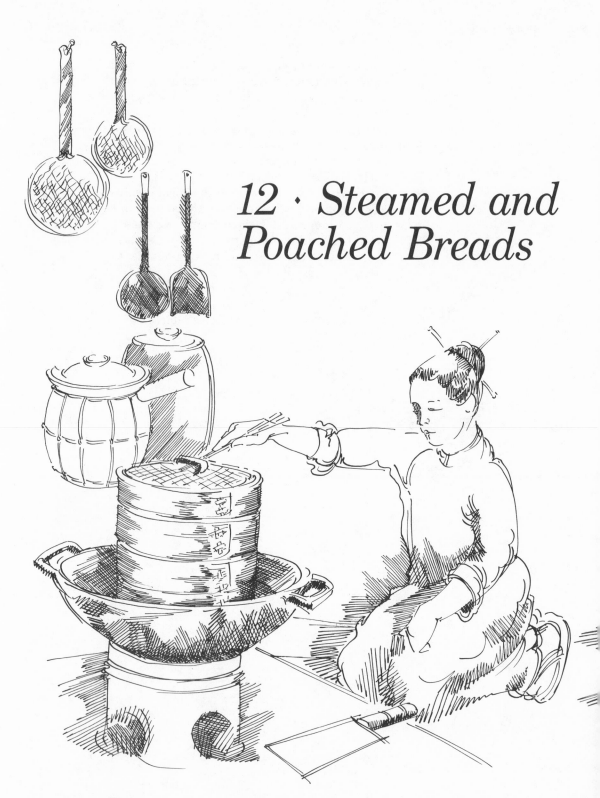

12 · Steamed and Poached Breads

Bagels
Dumplings
Bread Dumplings
Steamed Boston Brown Bread
Yankee Togus Bread
Madhur Jaffrey's Cream of Wheat Idlis
Chinese Steamed Buns
Filled Meat Buns

I n this country the best-known bread that is cooked by steam undoubtedly is Boston brown bread, of which there are several variations. When this traditional cylindrical loaf is rich with molasses and bursting with raisins, it isn't hard to see how closely it is related to the Christmas plum pudding.

In other regions steamed bread that combines corn meal and white flour is an old favorite of plantation cooks. For their part, dumplings are a sort of embryo form of bread almost as old as Chinese civilization; Chinese children still eat steamed buns, sometimes with fillings, as after-school pick-me-ups.

Today dumplings are particularly associated with the cooking of Czechoslovakia, Austria, and Hungary, and in Czechoslovakia one of the most famous of dumplings is made with cubes of bread embedded in cooked dough that is light as a feather. In the cooking they sometimes rest on top of the meat of a stew; sometimes they're suspended over the steam in a napkin.

Bagels, much to the surprise of some of us, are doughnut-shaped dumplings that are poached and then baked; or, sometimes, first browned under a broiler and then steamed until done.

Bagels

We've heard it said that it was America's Jewish comedians who brought nationwide popularity to bagels. For us, it's the word of Molly Goldberg, one of radio's most famous funny women, that is definitive. "Bagels is a roll," she wrote almost thirty years ago in her cookbook. "It's more of a varnished doughnut made with a special bread dough. It is a thing of beauty to behold, especially on a cold Sunday morning in the winter. The bagel is a lonely roll to eat all by yourself because in order for the true taste to come out you need your family. One to cut the bagels, one to toast them, one to put on the cream cheese and the lox, one to put them on the table, and one to supervise." Bagels also are great fun to make at home, for the whole act is different from other baking performances. Although bagels do have a final baking in the oven, it's the poaching in simmering, slightly sugared water that seems almost contradictory for a final product that is as crusty as a turtle. Bagels keep well—in fact, those with a passion for them say the staler the bagel the better. Lox (smoked salmon) and bagels is such traditional Jewish fare that there are those of us growing up in New York who thought loxanbagel was all one word, one dish. Of course cream cheese also is a must with bagels that are split and toasted.

Makes 18 bagels

1 tablespoon active dry
   yeast
2½ tablespoons sugar
1 cup warm skim milk
2 tablespoons
   vegetable oil
2 teaspoons coarse salt
   or 1 teaspoon table
   salt
2 eggs
3¾–4 cups white flour,
   preferably
   unbleached
1 egg white

Put the yeast and 1 tablespoon of the sugar in a medium-size mixing bowl and pour half the warm skim milk over them. Let stand to dissolve. Add the oil, salt, and eggs, and beat thoroughly. Stir in 3½ cups of the flour until you have a firm dough.

Turn the dough out on a floured work surface and knead, adding flour as necessary, until you have a smooth, bouncy dough. Clean out the bowl, grease it, and return the dough to it to let rise, covered, until double in bulk—about 40 minutes.

Turn the dough out and divide into 18 pieces. Cover them lightly with a towel.

One by one form each piece of dough into a ring by shaping it first into a round, then flattening it to a circumference of about 2½ inches; now make a hole by thrusting your index finger, well floured, into the center. Twirl the circle around your finger to stretch the hole, then widen it further by gently

pulling back the edges and evening and plumping the roll as you do so. Let the rolls rest for 20 minutes.

Meanwhile put 3 quarts of water with the remaining sugar into a large pot and bring to a boil. Starting with the first of the circles you shaped, drop them gently, 3 at a time, into the simmering water. They will rise quickly to the surface and swell up. Poach the first side 3–4 minutes, then turn to cook the other side 3 minutes. If the holes start to close up, ease them open with the handle of a wooden spoon.

Remove the bagels with a slotted spatula and place on a greased cookie sheet. Paint the tops with egg white. If you want some—or all—of the bagels sesame-covered, press ½ teaspoon of sesame seeds over the glazed tops. If you want some with onions, 10 minutes before they have finished baking, spread 1 teaspoon chopped onions, which have been sautéed in butter until translucent, over the top of each and return to the oven.

OPTIONAL

1 teaspoon–½ cup chopped onions sautéed in butter

½ teaspoon–¼ cup sesame seeds

Bake the bagels in a preheated 375° oven for 30 minutes.

Dumplings

"A dish for Lucullus" is what Joseph Wechsberg called them. Dumplings are produced in bewildering variety, and the simplest may be those made from a baking powder dough that is dropped by the spoonful into hot broth or the juices of a stew. It is then both simmered and steamed at the same time until it cooks through and swells to more than twice its original size. Dumplings should be light and airy, and it's important for the liquid to simmer ever so gently; fast boiling will cause the egg in the dough to harden and you'll end up with a stodgy lump. (Dumplings are great for camp cooking when you're apt to have room for only one pot on the fire.) Wherever you're cooking, you can make a hearty soup or stew and bread at the same time by floating dumplings on top for the last 10 minutes of cooking.

Makes 8 dumplings

1 cup cake flour
2 teaspoons baking
  powder
¾ teaspoon coarse salt
  or ¼ teaspoon table
  salt
1 egg
¼ cup milk
2 tablespoons chopped
  parsley
1 tablespoon chopped
  fresh dill, marjoram,
  or tarragon
  (optional)
1 tablespoon finely
  minced scallions

Sift the dry ingredients together into a bowl. Lightly beat the egg and the milk together and stir into the dry ingredients along with the parsley, another herb if you like, and scallions.

Dip a teaspoon into the hot liquid in which you'll be cooking the dumplings—either soup or the juices of a stew—and then scoop up a rounded spoonful of the dough. Drop it onto the simmering liquid and continue with the remaining dough, distributing the dumplings on the top of your cooking pot a good 1½ inches apart to allow for swelling. Be sure that the pot remains just at a simmer, cover, cook 5 minutes on one side, then turn the dumplings carefully and cook another 5 minutes. Serve immediately floating on soup or on top of stew.

Bread Dumplings

Austrians and Czechoslovakians have devised over the centuries a fine way to give new life to stale bread—rolls, especially—by incorporating the cut-up pieces in dumplings sometimes called *semmelknoedel*, sometimes *houskove knedlicky*. Whether slices are lopped off from a long rolled dumpling or the dough shaped in individual dollops, bread dumplings

BREAD DUMPLINGS, CONTINUED

are excellent accompaniments to goulash, or other meats served with gravy, and they are traditional with roast goose. Working with our Viennese sister-in-law, we have adapted an old recipe to American ingredients.

Makes two 7-inch rolls to serve 6–8

4 tablespoons melted butter
3 cups stale bread, cut in ½-inch cubes
4 scallions with some green, minced
3 tablespoons minced parsley
¼ cup milk
2 eggs
About ¾ cup white flour
Freshly grated nutmeg
1 teaspoon coarse salt or ½ teaspoon table salt
Freshly ground pepper

Drizzle 3 tablespoons of the butter over the bread cubes and toast them under the broiler, set about 10 inches below the heat. Turn so that all sides are toasted light brown.

Sauté the scallions in the remaining butter until just soft. Toss in the parsley. Sprinkle the milk over the toasted bread, toss, and let stand only 2–3 minutes. Beat the eggs lightly and stir into the bread along with the scallions and parsley. Then add enough flour to make a soft, barely manageable dough—it will be sticky. Season with several gratings of fresh nutmeg (or, if you must, ¼ teaspoon already powdered nutmeg); add salt and pepper to taste. Turn the dough out onto a floured surface and knead very lightly with well-floured hands. Divide in 2 and roll each half to a length of 7 inches. Wrap loosely in cheesecloth, twisting the ends, and place the 2 dumpling rolls in a large pan of salted simmering water a couple of inches deep. Poach for 20–25 minutes, turning once, and keep covered, but be sure the water is only at a simmer. To test for doneness, extract one of the dumpling rolls and slice off a piece.

Cut in ½-inch slices to serve, and be sure to have lots of gravy.

Steamed Boston Brown Bread

Looking back to childhood in New England, or Minnesota, there is no failing the memory of Boston brown bread—it was served a thousand miles away from its home city just as it was on Bailey Avenue in Montpelier, and the traditional accompaniment was a pot of baked beans that had bubbled all night in the oven. As early as the mid-seventeenth century, one local historian has reported, "the most famous cornbread was the Boston brown bread of Mr. Latly Gee, and Mrs. Bennett." It was popular because of the difficulty of getting yeast. Never mind the stories that steamed brown bread is on the indigestible side—it is a fragrant tasty example of food that kept the colonies alive when ovens to bake bread were scarce.

Makes 1 loaf

½ *cup warm molasses*
½ *cup rye flour*
½ *cup whole wheat*
  flour
½ *cup yellow corn*
  meal
½ *teaspoon baking*
  soda
½ *teaspoon baking*
  powder
½ *teaspoon coarse salt*
  or ¼ teaspoon table
  salt
1½ *cups buttermilk*

To make pouring easier, put the molasses bottle in warm water while measuring the flours and corn meal; combine them with the baking soda, baking powder, and salt in a large bowl. Mix warm molasses with buttermilk and beat into flour mixture. Butter the inside of a 1-quart melon mold, or a 1-pound coffee can, and fill with bread mixture. Put the cover on the mold or cover the coffee can with foil and tie it tightly. Put the bread container on a rack in a pot containing sufficient boiling water to come halfway up. Cover the pot and steam for 3 hours. After 2¾ hours, preheat oven to 300°. Remove lid of mold and put the bread in the oven for 5–6 minutes to dry. Use a length of hard string to slice the steamed loaf.

Yankee Togus Bread

The novelist and culinary writer Sophie Kerr recommended the loaf she called togus bread as "fine for ski or skating parties." Other food historians have related the basic recipe with the Algonquin Indian method of producing steamed bread from a mixture of corn meal and a sweetener of maple syrup or wild berries that was adapted by early Yankees before ovens were common. In its consistency, if not in color, it might be considered a collateral relative of Boston brown bread—a tall coffee can makes the handiest mold.

Makes 1 cylinder-shaped loaf

Soft butter
½ cup buttermilk
1½ cups milk
⅓ cup maple syrup
1½ cups yellow corn meal
½ cup white flour
½ teaspoon baking soda
½ teaspoon coarse salt or ¼ teaspoon table salt

Butter a 1-pound coffee can thoroughly. Combine buttermilk and milk, and stir in maple syrup. Stir together corn meal, flour, baking soda and salt until thoroughly combined with all lumps eliminated. Add liquid mixture a little at a time and blending well to prevent lumping. Pour this soft dough into the coffee can, cover the top with aluminum foil, and tie securely with string. Put the can on a trivet in a deep pot and put a heavy cover on top so it won't tilt or float. Pour in boiling water to within 1–2 inches of the top of the can. Return water to a rolling boil, cover the pot, and steam with water at a steady boil 3–4 hours; add boiling water as necessary to maintain original level.

Madhur Jaffrey's Cream of Wheat Idlis

As she says in *World-of-the-East Vegetarian Cooking,* the steamed round cakes Madhur Jaffrey describes as somewhat like Madeleines are served all over South India for breakfast and at snack times. Her recipe below calls for the use of easily available cream of wheat breakfast cereal that is given an interesting texture by the addition of shredded coconut and is tantalizingly seasoned with black mustard seeds and fresh hot green chilies. Lacking the idli molds that an Indian cook would use, you can improvise with a steaming trivet inserted in a steamer or colander. As the procedure indicates, you will have large cakes that may be cut in the shape of diamonds or wedges.

Makes four 6-inch rounds or 12 small idli-mold cakes

2 tablespoons
  vegetable oil
1 teaspoon whole black
  mustard seeds
1 cup commercial
  cream of wheat
  cereal
3 tablespoons freshly
  grated coconut
1½ teaspoons coarse
  salt or ¾ teaspoon
  table salt
1–2 fresh hot green
  chilies, minced
1½ cups plain yogurt
  (the sourer the
  better)

Heat the oil in a 7–8-inch skillet over a medium flame. When hot, toss in the mustard seeds and as soon as they pop, lower the heat to medium low and add the cream of wheat. Sauté it, stirring, for 2–3 minutes; it should not brown. Remove from the heat and stir in the coconut, salt, and chilies. Let cool, then add the yogurt. You should have a thick batter.

Place a double layer of wet cheesecloth over a standard metal steaming trivet. If you have an electric steamer with a basket the trivet can go right inside that; if not, place it in a colander. The point is not to have the water touch the steamer. Bring the water in your steaming apparatus to a rolling boil. Pour half an inch of batter into the cheesecloth-lined trivet and steam, covered, for 20 minutes. Repeat, making 4 cakes in all. Or if you happen to have the Indian idli molds, lightly oil 12 of them and fill them with batter; then set into a steamer, covered, for 20 minutes.

Serve hot, presenting the smooth underside up.

Chinese Steamed Buns

The Chinese, who seldom use ovens, steam their buns, often by improvising a steam device in a wok or employing a tiered bamboo steamer. The simplest way to set up a steamer that can accommodate all these buns is to use a large covered roasting pan, put about 2 inches of boiling water in the bottom, then put a flameproof platter above the water by setting it up on a trivet or some empty cans; put the top on and you'll have an "oven" of steam. These buns actually taste rather bland, but they're used primarily as a vehicle for mopping up sauce. Since they are steamed, they have no crust. Frankly we find them more delicious and satisfying stuffed; evidently Chinese children do, too—they consider them after-school snacks, according to Irene Kuo, whose recipe this is.

Makes 12 buns

1 teaspoon active dry
    yeast
1 cup plus 2
    tablespoons warm
    water
3½ cups white flour,
    preferably
    unbleached
1 tablespoon sugar
1 teaspoon baking
    powder

Dissolve the yeast in 2 tablespoons of the warm
water, letting it sit for 5 minutes. Put the flour in
a large bowl and stir in the sugar. Make a well in
the center and pour in the dissolved yeast and the
remaining water; stir with chopsticks or a wooden
spoon until a lumpy mass forms. Press and knead
the mass to form a large ball. Turn the dough onto
a floured work surface and knead it for 5 minutes,
dusting with more flour if it is too sticky, until the
dough is smooth and springy. Return to the bowl,
cover, and let sit in a warm place for about 2
hours, or until double its bulk.

Turn the dough out on a lightly floured work
surface, and flatten with the palm of your hand to
make an oblong shape. Sprinkle the baking powder
over the surface, fold over, and knead vigorously
for 5 minutes until smooth, satiny, and firm, with
plenty of bounce.

Divide the dough in two, shaping each half into
a smooth log 6 inches long, using the palms of
your hands to roll it out. Cut each roll crosswise
into 6 even pieces, making 12 in all. Dust a baking
sheet with flour, place the buns a good 1½ inches
apart on it, cover with a kitchen towel, and let rise
until double in size—about 45 minutes.

Set up your steamer. If it is large enough and
you have a big enough heatproof platter or baking
sheet to accommodate all 12 rolls, not touching,
line that platter with a damp cloth and place the
buns on it; otherwise you will have to steam them
in two batches. When the water is boiling
vigorously, place the platter inside, cover, and
steam over high heat for 15 minutes. Turn off the
heat and allow the steam to subside for a few
seconds before uncovering. Serve warm. If you
need to reheat, simply return the buns to the
steamer.

◆ FILLED MEAT BUNS

Makes 20 buns

1 pound ground pork
1 large scallion, finely
   chopped
2½ tablespoons soy
   sauce
1 tablespoon dry
   sherry
¼ teaspoon salt
¼ teaspoon black
   pepper
3 tablespoons sesame
   oil
1 tablespoon
   cornstarch dissolved
   in 5 tablespoons
   water
Yeast dough from
   Chinese Steamed
   Buns (preceding
   recipe)

Chop the ground pork to loosen it, then toss and mix it with the scallions, all the seasonings, and the oil and cornstarch until well blended. Refrigerate for 30 minutes to firm it. Then divide into 20 portions.

Divide the dough in half and, using the palms of your hands, roll into two 10-inch-long sausages. Cut into 1-inch pieces. Dip the cut side in flour and press the piece with your palm to flatten slightly. Roll into a 4½-inch circle, making the center thicker than the rim, then put in your cupped hand and place 1 portion of the filling in the center. Pleat the edge firmly all around the filling and bring the folds together at the top. Pinch and twirl them into a tiny knot. Repeat until all 20 buns are made. Place them, knot side down, on a lightly floured baking sheet, cover with a kitchen towel, and let them puff up for almost 30–40 minutes in your warm kitchen.

Transfer them, turned knot side up now, to your heatproof steaming platter covered with a damp cloth and steam them as in the master recipe for 20 minutes.

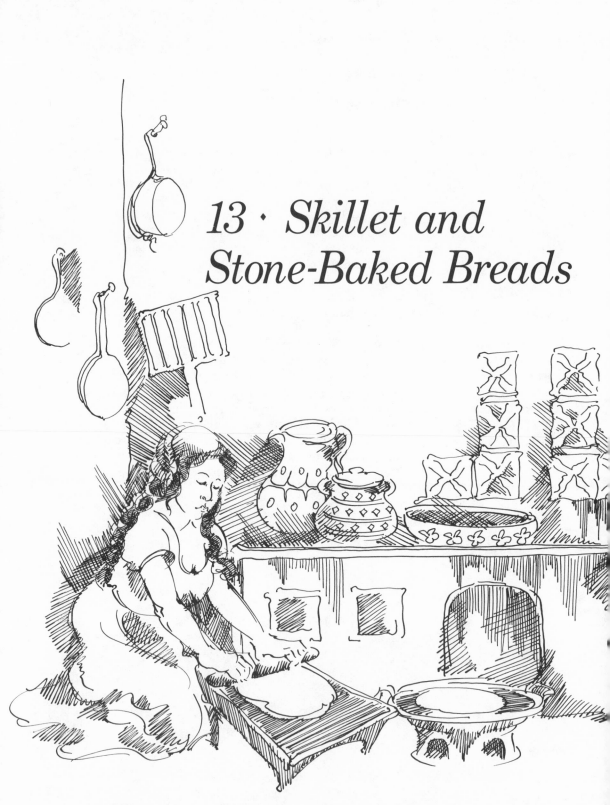

13 · Skillet and Stone-Baked Breads

Buttermilk Pancakes
Blueberry Griddle Cakes
Freshly Ground Wheat Griddle Cakes
Cottage Cheese Pancakes
Sunflower Pancakes
Blue Corn Pancakes
Buckwheat Blinis
Welsh Planc Bread
Oatmeal Scones
Tortillas
English Muffins
Naans or Nans
Skillet Scallion Bread
Stuffed Parathas
Hoe Cakes
Skillet-baked Sesame Seed Cheese Corn Bread
Soft-as-Pie Texas Corn Bread
Crumpets
Madhur Jaffrey's Hoppers

In the South, traditional cooks still bake corn pones and hoe cakes on a griddle, or they use a heavy cast-iron skillet to effect the old means of cooking. As dictionaries have it, the process of baking means to cook by dry heat acting by conduction, either in a closed space—an oven—or on a heated surface like a bakestone or a griddle. In Wales today, for instance, the word bakestone is used for the flat round utensil made especially for baking traditional breads, and new cast-iron bakestones are being brought home by tourists.

In Scotland, where the word "griddle" is common, breads, bannocks, and scones are baked on carefully heated griddles over peat fires, and the typical oat cake is as large as a skillet and is cut into quarters, or *farls,* for cooking. The fourteenth-century traveler Jean Froissart tells of Scottish cavalry soldiers who fed themselves—"they truss on a broad plate of metal, and behind the saddle they will have a sack full of oatmeal . . . and they lay the plate on the fire, and when the plate is hot they cast the thin paste thereon, and make a little cake, in the manner of a cracknel or biscuit, and that they eat to the comfort of their stomachs. . . ." Lacking ovens, cooks in most countries have been resourceful in devising breads as various as English muffins, Indian *naans,* or the blue corn breads of the American Southwest. They may lack yeast in some cases, but all the breads in this chapter offer special reasons for duplicating them in home kitchens.

Buttermilk Pancakes

You can use yogurt or sour cream instead of buttermilk here. The principle is the same: as long as there is something sour, the baking soda interacts and will make the pancake puff up when it is baked (no need of baking powder). To our minds, this makes a more subtle-tasting pancake.

Makes 12 pancakes 3–4 inches in diameter

1 cup buttermilk
2 tablespoons melted
  butter
1 egg
1 cup white flour
1 teaspoon baking soda
2 tablespoons sugar
¾ teaspoon coarse salt
  or ¼ teaspoon table
  salt

Beat the liquid ingredients together. Thoroughly mix the dry ingredients and add them to the liquid, stirring only long enough to moisten the flour. Spoon a small ladleful onto a hot, lightly greased skillet, using enough batter to let the pancake spread to 3–4 inches, as you like them; if you wish them even thinner, add more buttermilk to the batter, although the above formula makes for a fairly loose batter. Bake until golden on the bottom, less than a minute; bubbles will appear on the top, which tells you to check and see if the bottom is golden, then turn with a spatula to brown the other side. Serve immediately.

Blueberry Griddle Cakes

We think this note from *The Martha's Vineyard Cookbook,* a fine guide for Yankees and other aristologists by Louise Tate King and Jean Stewart Wexler, is worth repeating here: "Whatever name you call them by—high-bush, low-bush, early sweet, late low, or sour-top blueberries, whortleberries, huckleberries, dangleberries, whorts, hurts, bilberries—the fruit of the twenty or more species of *Vaccinium* and *Gaylussacia* are popped into almost every mouth on the Vineyard during blueberrying time.... There are acres of them on the Vineyard, but don't expect a berry picker to tell you where they are." We know secret places in the Green Mountains, and this recipe for traditional New England blueberry griddle cakes is a result of our first picking expeditions. Serve with hot melted butter and real maple syrup. Other ways with blueberries are on pages 213 and 229.

Makes about 24 cakes

2 cups white flour
2 eggs, beaten
2 cups milk
3 teaspoons sugar
2 teaspoons baking
   powder
½ teaspoon coarse salt
   or ¼ teaspoon table
   salt
1 tablespoon melted
   butter
¼ teaspoon freshly
   grated nutmeg
1–2 cups fresh
   blueberries

In a large bowl stir flour with the beaten eggs, milk, sugar, baking powder, and salt. When smoothly mixed stir in butter and nutmeg. Spoon batter on lightly greased hot griddle or skillet, and after 2 minutes drop as many blueberries as you like on top of each cake; turn over, then cook until golden.

Freshly Ground Wheat Griddle Cakes

The first time we ever tasted pancakes made of freshly ground wheat we were having breakfast in a Vermont farmhouse. Our hostess slipped in to the storeroom, where she kept her flour grinder, and came out with the fragrant freshly ground wheat, still warm. As she made these delicious cakes for us, she used her own maple syrup as a sweetener, and then served yogurt with her own freshly sprouted mung beans on the side. It was a memorable repast.

Makes 8–10 cakes

1 cup whole wheat
  flour
½ teaspoon baking
  soda
½ teaspoon coarse salt
  or ¼ teaspoon table
  salt
1 egg
1 cup buttermilk
2 tablespoons maple
  syrup
2 tablespoons melted
  butter

Mix the flour, soda, and salt together. Add the egg, buttermilk, maple syrup, and melted butter, and beat until smooth. The batter may be mixed in a blender or food processor, throwing everything in together and blending until smooth, scraping down the sides, if necessary, when the flour sticks. Ladle a couple of tablespoonfuls onto a hot greased skillet and bake until bubbles begin to appear on the surface, then turn and bake the other side until lightly browned; this batter is quite moist, so turn gently. You can keep the cakes warm in a low oven until all are done. Then serve immediately on hot plates with plenty of butter and maple syrup.

Cottage Cheese Pancakes

Years ago, delicate pancakes like these could be made only by sieving the cottage cheese through a strainer, but with blenders and food processors in most kitchens, you can make a perfectly smooth cheese batter with just a whirl of the machine. Let the batter rest 10 minutes or longer before pan-baking them.

Makes 12 cakes 3 inches in diameter

1¼ cups cottage
  cheese
3 eggs
2 tablespoons melted
  butter
⅓ cup white flour
¼ teaspoon coarse salt
  or a pinch of table
  salt

Spin all ingredients in a blender or food processor until smoothly mixed. Let batter rest 10 minutes. Heat a lightly greased skillet until a drop of water sizzles on its surface. Spoon in a couple of tablespoons of batter—enough so that as you tilt the pan to encourage spreading you have a round cake about 3 inches in diameter. Turn heat to medium and cook less than a minute on each side, until golden. Don't try to cook too many cakes at the same time; leave enough space between them so you can turn them carefully with a spatula— these are more fragile cakes than some others. Serve immediately on hot plates.

Sunflower Pancakes

An elusive nutty flavor (see page 92, on making sunflower meal) makes these pancakes something special. Because they are quite soft, they're difficult to turn, so it's easier to make them somewhat smaller than the usual pancake. Serve with butter and maple syrup or crushed berries and sour cream or yogurt.

Makes 20 small pancakes

¾ cup sunflower meal
¾ cup whole wheat
  flour
1 teaspoon baking
  powder
½ teaspoon baking
  soda
¾ teaspoon coarse salt
  or ¼ teaspoon table
  salt
2 eggs
1 tablespoon honey
3–4 tablespoons melted
  butter
1½ cups buttermilk

Mix all the dry ingredients throughly together. In a medium bowl beat the eggs until well blended, then add the honey, 2 tablespoons of the butter, and buttermilk. Mix the dry ingredients into the liquid, stirring just enough to moisten the flours. Brush a skillet generously with melted butter and heat over a medium flame. Spoon small amounts of the batter into the skillet to make cakes about 3 inches in diameter. Bake until brown on one side—about a minute—and turn gently to brown the other. Continue with the rest, buttering the skillet with each round.

Blue Corn Pancakes

The Pueblo Indians of the Southwest cultivated red, yellow, blue, and white corn, in a number of varieties, and the Hopis of Arizona have been called by their neighboring tribes "the people of the short blue corn." Southwest cooks make a cornmeal mush dish known as *chauquehue,* as well as using finely ground dried blue corn in other tasty ways. Navajos produce "kneel-down bread" by wrapping dough in green husks and baking it in hot ashes. Our first blue corn pancakes were made with flour a Navajo grandmother had ground for us on the reservation near Flagstaff. Hopi women reduce the hard bluish gray kernels to a fine powder which is mixed with water to make paper-thin bread; this looks like rolls of parchment when it is baked, and it is called *piki.* At a Hopi-owned restaurant at Second Mesa, Arizona, we could buy *piki* or blue-corn griddle cakes that were dyed the color of turquoise for tourists. But when we cooked them at home we made our blue corn cakes without the coloring—the unique flavor is more impressive than the looks. (Simply substitute regular corn meal to make ordinary corn meal pancakes.)

Makes about 16 pancakes

1 egg
¾ cup milk
2 tablespoons melted
 butter or lard
½ cup finely ground
 blue corn meal
½ cup white flour
2 teaspoons baking
 powder
2 tablespoons sugar
½ teaspoon coarse salt
 or ¼ teaspoon table
 salt

Lightly beat the egg and add the milk and melted butter or lard. Mix together the dry ingredients thoroughly and add them to the liquid, mixing just enough to dampen the flour. Heat a lightly greased heavy skillet or nonstick frying pan to the point where a drop of water sizzles and splutters. Then ladle in 2–3 tablespoonfuls of the batter for each pancake, leaving room for them to spread. You may want a thinner pancake, particularly if you are going to wrap it around a filling; if so, add more milk to the batter. Bake until the top side starts to look dry and bubbles form, then turn and bake the other side until lightly browned. Serve warm with syrup.

Buckwheat Blinis, or Thin Pancakes

Americans often wax nostalgic for buckwheat cakes, and certain Frenchmen dream moodily of *crêpes Breton*. We've had these Brittany delicacies on the Quiberon peninsula and several times at a displaced Breton restaurant near the market square in Grasse, the French perfume capital. There batter was spread on the round griddle with a hoelike wooden gadget, and the thin cakes were turned by fingers, dolloped with butter, and topped with fresh Gruyère ground in a mouli, along with a slice of *jambon;* the cakes were then folded envelope-fashion and served hot and crisp as *croques monsieur* might be. These diaphanous buckwheat blinis are even more delicate, and they became an American favorite after Russian immigrants began to arrive in large numbers. This is the way we make blinis in our kitchen, to be served with inexpensive red caviar or, sometimes, with herring in sour cream.

Makes about 10 cakes

*1 tablespoon active dry
    yeast*
2¼ cups warm water
1 cup buckwheat flour
*1 cup white flour,
    preferably
    unbleached*
*1 teaspoon coarse or ½
    teaspoon table salt*
*1 tablespoon melted
    butter*
*¼ teaspoon baking
    soda*

About 12 hours before serving, dissolve the yeast in 2 cups of warm water in a large bowl; when yeast swells, stir in buckwheat and white flour and the salt. Cover bowl with plastic wrap and set in a warm place.

Just before using, stir in remaining ¼ cup of water, the melted butter, and soda; the batter should have the consistency of heavy cream. Brush a heavy 8-inch skillet with softened butter, and heat until you can see a haze rising from the pan. Pour in just enough of the batter to cover the bottom of the pan, tilting the pan to distribute evenly. Turn when bubbles appear on the tops of the cakes and bake until lightly browned on the other side.

Welsh Planc Bread

It's said that there are more than twenty indigenous Welsh loaves differing in shape and kind, and that women of the principality have not in the least neglected the art of baking. On visits to this ancestral land we've found shops selling *bara Abertawe* (Swansea bread), *bara Genith bara brith* (see page 147), *bara fflat* (batch bread), *bara Carwe Sir Fon* (caraway), *bara surgeirch* (sour oatmeal), and *bara tun* (baked in a tin or can). *Bara planc* is sometimes translated as bakestone or griddle bread and is as old as the Welsh nation, going back to days when a flat stone over the outdoor fire was used as a cooking surface. Nowadays the cast-iron plank, or baking iron of Wales, is placed over the top of a clear fire on the hearth, and it's important it should never get too hot or the dough will scorch rather than bake slowly and thoroughly. Traditionally, the loaf was flattened on the griddle by hand and when baked was kept warm beside the fire. To give a semblance of the Welsh fireplace in the sense that its walls reflect heat onto the top and sides of a bread loaf, we make use of the bell-shaped clay top of La Cloche (page 365), placing it over our planc bread to contain as much of the stovetop heat as possible. The result is a slightly spongy but firm and delicately flavored loaf. Two hundred years ago a Welsh cottager might have served this bread with smoked goat ham, and buttermilk or whey to drink.

Makes 1 round loaf

1 tablespoon active dry
  yeast
¾ cup warm water
¾ cup warm milk
1 teaspoon coarse salt
  or ½ teaspoon table
  salt
3–3½ cups white flour,
  preferably
  unbleached
1 tablespoon lard

In a small bowl dissolve the yeast in the warm water. Stir in the milk and the salt.

Warm 3 cups of the flour in a medium-size preheated bowl. Rub the lard into the flour with the tips of your fingers. Now make a well and pour the yeast mixture in. Stir to mix well, then turn out onto a floured working surface and knead, adding more flour as necessary, until you have a smooth dough—about 7–8 minutes.

Wash out your bowl, rinse it with very hot water to have it warm, dry it, and grease it with a little lard or butter. Put the dough in, turning to coat all sides. Cover with plastic wrap and let rise until double in volume—at least 1½ hours.

Turn the dough out and punch it down. Pat into a round no more than 1 inch thick. Place in a lightly greased heavy iron skillet. Cover with a towel and let rest in the pan for 20 minutes.

Remove the towel and turn the heat on to moderate until the pan is hot. Then lower heat and bake bread slowly on one side for 20 minutes; turn and bake 20 minutes on the other side. Unless you have a lot of things cooking on the stove all around the bread so that heat is circulating, as it would if this were being cooked the traditional Welsh way in an open fire, we've found that you should give each side an extra 5 minutes of cooking while covered; either use a domed top or make a tent of aluminum foil—you don't want to seal, just to trap some of the heat.

The bread will rise considerably during the cooking and when done it will be speckled deep brown on both sides. Remove and cool on a rack.

Oatmeal Scones

The word "scone" derives from the Gaelic *sgonn* and rhymes with "gone." Scottish cooks bake scones by dropping small amounts of dough on a hot griddle, and seldom use either baking powder or soda to help them rise. In the eighteenth century when Johnson and Boswell made their famous Highlands tour, wheat flour was scarce, so scones ("very good cakes baked with butter," as Boswell characterized them) were often made with *bere* (barley meal), oatmeal, or peasemeal. This recipe produces scones that are very rich and "short"; they are crumbly and therefore difficult to split. Serve them as warm as possible, with butter, honey, or raspberry jam.

Makes 8 scones

1¼ cups white flour
1 teaspoon baking
  powder
½ teaspoon baking
  soda
½ teaspoon coarse salt
  or ¼ teaspoon table
  salt
¼ cup sugar
4 tablespoons (½
  stick) butter
¼ cup vegetable
  shortening
1 cup oats
⅓ cup raisins
⅓ cup buttermilk
Melted butter

In a medium bowl, thoroughly mix together the flour, baking powder, soda, salt, and sugar. Then work in the butter and shortening with a pastry cutter or two knives until the dough has the texture of oatmeal. Stir in the oats and the raisins. Add the buttermilk, mixing just enough to moisten the dry mixture. Turn out onto a floured working surface and knead lightly for only 7–8 turns.

Roll or pat the dough out into a circle about 7 inches in diameter. Then cut into 8 equal-size wedges. Transfer these wedges to an ungreased baking sheet and brush the tops with melted butter. Bake in a preheated 375° oven for 15 minutes.

Tortillas

As the increasing interest in Hispanic-American influences in this country has coincided with casual eating at home and on highways and byways, tortillas have come to be recognized as the basic bread form they have always been in the southwestern states as well as south of the border. The new recognition has resulted in simplified recipes—a tacos restaurant in Scottsdale, Arizona, admits that it uses a dough of prepared biscuit mix, and throughout the region large fried tortillas with various adornments are called "crisps." With one basic piece of equipment—the tortilla press or *comal*—at

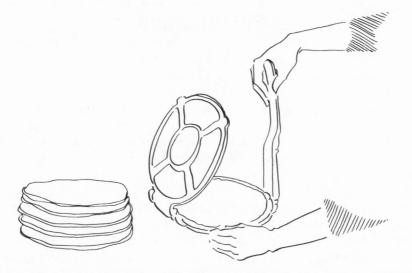

the ready, this flat bread is very much worth making at home. Use the specially ground *masa harina,* which is widely distributed in most of the States, or use the finely ground blue corn meal from the Southwest, which will give your tortillas a special flavor and mauve color.

Makes about 12 tortillas

2 cups Quaker masa
   harina or 2¾ cups
   blue corn meal
1⅓ cups cold water

Stir *masa harina* or blue corn meal and water together, mixing quickly and lightly. Set the dough aside for about 20 minutes. Meanwhile heat 2 heavy skillets so a drop of water sizzles when it touches the hot metal. Open the tortilla press and lay an 8-inch square piece of plastic wrap across the bottom plate. Tear off a piece of the dough and make a ball about 1½ inches in diameter; flatten it slightly. Put it on top of the plastic wrap, positioned slightly toward the handle of the press; cover the dough with a second sheet of plastic wrap. Bring the top handle of the press forward, using your weight to push it on top of the plastic covering the ball, so that the dough spreads evenly into a round flat cake about 5 inches in diameter. Peel off the plastic, and carefully transfer the tortilla to the hot skillet. If the heat of the skillet is right, it will take about 2 minutes to cook. Flip it over and cook for a somewhat longer time, then flip back to the first side and finish—it should puff into attractive blisters. Repeat until you have used up all the dough.

English Muffins

Long before you plan to make English muffins, start collecting tuna fish or kitty food cans—the 6½-ounce size—to save yourself the unnecessary expense of buying special baking rings. Once the contents of the can have been devoured, rescue it before it is thrown away, wash it out well, and then with a can opener remove the top and bottom so that you have a smooth ring. When you've collected a minimum of four rings, you're ready to make English muffins; if you have eight and use two skillets, the baking will go faster.

This recipe calls for part whole wheat or graham flour, which makes for a tastier and more wholesome muffin. If you prefer the traditional white, simply substitute white flour for the whole wheat. You may also add additional sweetening—3–4 tablespoons of honey or brown sugar—but since English muffins are eaten split (they should be pried apart, not cut with a knife), toasted, and usually swimming with butter and marmalade or jam, we prefer the traditional unsweetened muffin—a carrier for the sweet rather than a sweet bread itself. English muffins are great fun to make, and you'll get extra applause these days when your family realizes that you've produced for about 35 cents a dozen English muffins that would cost close to $2 in the supermarket.

Makes 12 muffins

1 tablespoon active dry yeast
1 tablespoon sugar
1½ cups warm water
3 tablespoons nonfat dry milk
1 tablespoon coarse salt or 2 teaspoons table salt
1 cup whole wheat or graham flour
1¾–2 cups white flour, preferably unbleached
¼ teaspoon baking soda dissolved in 2 tablespoons warm water

In a medium-size mixing bowl dissolve the yeast and sugar in ½ cup of the water. Stir the dry milk and salt into the remaining cup of water and combine with the yeast. Add the whole wheat flour and 1¾ cups of the white flour and beat, either by hand or with an electric mixer, for several minutes. The dough should be like thick pancake batter but more gummy, and should just begin to leave the sides of the bowl. Add a little more white flour if needed to reach this consistency. Then cover the bowl with plastic wrap and set in a warm place for 1¼–1½ hours or until double in bulk.

Now uncover the bowl and beat in the dissolved baking soda thoroughly. Let the dough rest, covered, while preparing the baking setup.

Thoroughly grease the inside of the rings with shortening or butter. Heat one or two large heavy skillets until almost smoking, then brush with shortening or oil, and set rings inside (a large skillet should hold 4). Lower the heat and ladle

about ¼ cup of dough into each ring. The dough
will still be very elastic—more like chewing gum or
Silly Putty—and you may find you'll have to chop
off your ladleful from the bowl with a knife. Try
to even out each portion of dough by poking with
your finger so that it fills the whole ring. Bake
over low heat 5 minutes, occasionally moving each
ring a little once the dough has set. The top
surface should now have lost its moist look; lift the
ring off and turn each muffin over to bake on the
other side 5 minutes. Repeat this procedure,
greasing the rings and the skillet again, until you
have used up all the dough.

Cool the muffins on racks, and store in plastic
wrap until you are ready to eat them. Then tear
them apart and toast them, either in a toaster or
under the broiler.

Naans or Nans

A flattish bread from India, *naans* ordinarily are made by slapping leaf-shaped pieces of dough against the hot interior wall of a tandoor, an oven of clay the shape of a huge olive oil jar sometimes sunk halfway into the ground. The crackly, bubbled bread can also be baked on a heavy skillet, or a baking stone if you have one, or—as we have done—on a 10-inch Teflon-coated fry pan. What gives this recipe its special flavor is the finely chopped onion; this touch is sometimes achieved by using onion seed, but we find fresh minced onions add a pleasant texture as well as flavor. Warm *naans* are delicious served with something tart, as they would be in the East. Yogurt, or a mixture of grated cucumber and yogurt, or cottage cheese is good; and we've also included bean sprouts or for the less vegetarian-minded a piquant cold beef salad. It makes a fine lunch just to wrap the warm *naan* around these fillings and dispense with forks and knives.

Makes 8 naans

*3 medium onions,
  finely chopped
  (about 1 cup)*
3 tablespoons butter
½ cup warm water
*1 teaspoon coarse salt
  or ½ teaspoon table
  salt*
1¾–2 cups white flour

Sauté the onions slowly in the butter in a 10-inch skillet until they become translucent, but not browned. Remove from the heat and let cool to lukewarm. Scrape into a mixing bowl and add the water and salt.

Stir in the flour ½ cup at a time—as much as the liquid will absorb. Turn out onto a floured working surface and knead for 2 minutes, incorporating more of the flour as needed. Divide into 8 balls and let rest, covered with plastic wrap, for 5 minutes.

Roll the balls into 7–8-inch circles, working with 2 at a time; the dough will resist you, so let one piece rest when it gets too stubborn and work with the other. It is important to keep dusting the surface and your rolling pin lightly with flour and to pick up the circle of dough, turn it, and let it stretch; after is has rested, you will always find that the gluten is more relaxed so the dough stretches more readily. Sometimes as you're rolling the *naans* you'll feel the crunch of a piece of onion as the pin rolls over it and sometimes you'll make a hole; no matter, you're supposed to have a rather lacy-looking round before you're through and a tear won't hurt.

Now wipe out your skillet and heat it to almost smoking (or heat up your baking stone); test with a drop of water, which should sizzle and splutter. Drop in one of the circles and let bake for about 2 minutes. Turn up a corner to see if the bottom has browned (it will brown unevenly, leaving little blisters here and there). Turn before it turns black and adjust the heat so it is always high but not smoking.

Continue with the rest of the *naans.* Serve immediately in a napkin-lined basket.

Skillet Scallion Bread

An American version of a Chinese classic (see page 262.) This is a bread that could also be prepared over a campfire using a prepared biscuit mix.

Serves 6–8

4 tablespoons butter
1 teaspoon sugar
5 scallions
Batter for Buttermilk
  Biscuits (page 244)

Put half the butter and the teaspoon of sugar in a 10-inch skillet, and heat and swirl the butter around. Remove from the heat. Chop the scallions quite fine, using about two-thirds of the green part, and scatter half on the bottom of the skillet.

Prepare the biscuit dough as directed, and cut into 1¾–2-inch rounds. Place the rounds on top of the butter-scallion mixture, letting them overlap slightly to fill the whole skillet. Cover and cook over medium-low heat 5–6 minutes, until golden on the bottom. Put a large plate on top of the skillet and quickly flip the nest of biscuits over onto it. Melt the remaining butter in the skillet, sprinkle on remaining scallions, and slip the biscuits back into the skillet, uncooked side down. Cover and cook 5 minutes on this side. Remove to a warm serving plate.

Stuffed Parathas

In northern India, where more wheat is grown than in other parts of the subcontinent, common breads include the chapatis familiar to many westerners and the puffy griddle baked bread called parathas, usually "stuffed" with a vegetable. However, because they are rolled flat after the filling is inserted, the word "stuffing" may seem misleading. Used as an eating tool, both chapatis and parathas are often served with curries, lentil dishes, and *pellaos,* the Indian version of rice pilafs. Parathas are sometimes stacked in several layers and filled with such grated vegetables as potatoes and onions, or they may be filled with green peas, cauliflower, and Indian, Chinese, or red-skinned radishes. A filling pleasing to any who love spicy things may be made by mixing mashed potatoes, onions, parsley, chives, mint, chili powder, and ginger. Two mixtures we've used below are both excellent with a sprightly curry.

Makes 6 parathas

DOUGH

*1½ cups whole wheat
  flour
¾ teaspoon kosher
  salt or ½ teaspoon
  table salt
1½ tablespoons
  vegetable shortening
½–¾ cup warm water*

Put the flour in a medium-size bowl and mix in the salt. Rub in the shortening (an Indian cook would do this by rubbing the flour and shortening between the palms of the hands). Add enough of the water, stirring, until the dough forms a mass; add the last few drops slowly and stop before the dough gets at all sticky, reserving some of the water.

Turn the dough out on a lightly oiled surface and start kneading—Indian style, if you wish, which means punching the dough all over with your knuckles, folding, and turning, and punching again. If the dough seems dry as you are kneading, sprinkle a little more warm water over it and wet your hands. Knead for at least 10 minutes. (Or toss the dough into the food processor and let it do the work in a minute or two; the dough should form a mass around the central shaft.) Clean your bowl and return the dough to it, cover with plastic wrap, and let rest anywhere from 30 minutes to several hours.

Meanwhile make one of the stuffings:

FILLING I

1 cup grated radishes

*1 teaspoon coarse salt
or ½ teaspoon table
salt*

*¼–½ small hot green
pepper, seeded and
chopped fine, or ¼
teaspoon red pepper
(according to taste)*

*½ teaspoon curry
powder*

*1 teaspoon minced
fresh ginger*

*2 teaspoons dried
crushed
pomegranate seed
(optional)*

FILLING II

*1 cup grated raw
cauliflower*

*½ teaspoon coarse salt
or ¼ teaspoon table
salt*

*2 tablespoons
vegetable oil*

*½ teaspoon curry
powder*

*1 teaspoon minced
fresh ginger*

*¼–½ small hot green
pepper, seeded and
minced (according to
taste), or ¼ teaspoon
red pepper*

FILLING I: Put the grated radishes in a strainer and sprinkle the salt over them. Let stand 30 minutes, then press down on them to extract the water and pat dry. Mix in the remaining ingredients.

FILLING II: Sauté the grated cauliflower sprinkled with salt in the vegetable oil for 4–5 minutes, stirring, until dry and just beginning to turn tan at the edges. Mix in the remaining ingredients and let cool.

Turn the dough out on a lightly floured surface and divide it into 6 equal pieces. Work with one piece at a time and keep the remaining pieces covered. Pat the piece into a 4-inch circle, then pick it up in one hand, making a cup of it as you hold it, and spoon about one-sixth of the stuffing into the center, or as much as the paratha will comfortably hold. Pull the edges up around the stuffing and pinch them together firmly at the top, giving a small twist to secure a seal. Cover with plastic wrap and proceed with the rest.

Now slap the stuffed cushion down on a floured surface; turn and slap the other side. Then roll out to an even circle 6 inches in circumference, reflouring your surface and rolling pin as you do so.

Heat a cast-iron skillet over medium heat until hot but not smoking. Place one paratha disk in it and bake on one side for about 2 minutes (you can be preparing the second paratha while the first is cooking). Usually the paratha will have puffed up when it is ready to turn. Flip over, brush the top with oil, and bake on the other side for 30 seconds. Flip over again and give the oiled side a final browning of about 20 seconds. Put on a warm platter and cover while you do the rest. Serve immediately when all are done.

Hoe Cakes

In early New England and the colonial South the most primitive form of corn bread was called an ash cake or a hoe cake, for the cooking was done in hot ashes and the most convenient contrivance to hold the dough was a straight garden hoe. "Hoe cakes," according to one cook's memory, "was made of meal. You mix a cup of meal with water, and pat it into small cakes. Grease it if you've got grease—that keeps it from sticking. Then you rake out the ashes, and stick it on the hoe into the bottom of the fire, and cover it up. Let it cook about five minutes then take it out, rub the ashes off, and pick out the splinters. Wash it off with warm water, and eat it before it cools. Don't taste like nothin' if you let it get cold." Nowadays, a method almost as simple and one that results in less grit and better flavor requires an iron skillet, a little fat, and a quick fire. If you want to add real Yankee flavor, stir a tablespoon of maple syrup into the ingredients given below.

Makes about 12

2 cups corn meal
1 teaspoon salt
About 2 cups boiling
   water
1 tablespoon maple
   syrup (optional)
Fat for frying

Stir the corn meal and salt together and pour in enough boiling water to make a stiff dough. Add maple syrup, if using it. Heat enough fat in a skillet to cover the bottom of the pan by about ⅛ of an inch. Shape the dough into small cakes, and when the fat is sizzling fry each side until crusty and brown. Turn once. Serve very hot.

Skillet-baked Sesame Seed Cheese Corn Bread

Easy and utterly delicious—here is another skillet bread that can be made over a campfire. Make two jarfuls of batter if you are serving more than six people.

Makes one 10-inch round

3 tablespoons sesame
   seeds
4 tablespoons (½
   stick) butter
1 egg
¾ cup milk

Toast the sesame seeds in a dry 10-inch skillet over medium heat, shaking the pan frequently until they are lightly toasted (sometimes they will pop and splutter). Set aside.
   Melt the butter slowly in the skillet. Meanwhile beat the egg well, then add the milk, 3 tablespoons

1 cup grated Cheddar
   cheese
¾ cup yellow corn
   meal
¾ cup white flour,
   preferably
   unbleached
1 tablespoon sugar
1 tablespoon baking
   powder
1 teaspoon coarse salt
   or ½ teaspoon table
   salt

of the butter, the cheese, and the toasted sesame seeds. Mix the remaining dry ingredients thoroughly and add them to the bowl, stirring enough to blend them well. Pour the batter on top of the remaining tablespoon of melted butter in the skillet. Cover and cook over low heat for 20 minutes until firm on top. Serve hot directly from the pan in wedges or loosen the edges and slip onto a warm plate.

Soft-as-Pie Texas Corn Bread

Many southerners were among the early settlers of Texas and they brought with them a taste for traditional plantation food. This recipe for batter bread may seem a little ornate to purists, but it's a delicious meeting of two worlds—simple Anglo-Saxon batter bread ornamented with south-of-the-border accents and the hot seasonings of the Southwest.

Makes about 6 servings

1 thin slice of bacon,
   cut in squares
¾ cup coarse stone-
   ground corn meal
1 cup boiling water
2 tablespoons melted
   butter
2 tablespoons bacon
   fat
3 eggs, beaten
2 teaspoons baking
   powder
1 cup buttermilk
1 tablespoon molasses
1–2 small canned chili
   peppers, chopped

Preheat oven to 350°; in it put an 8-inch iron skillet containing the bacon slice, and let the bacon cook while preparing the corn meal dough.

In a mixing bowl, scald the corn meal with boiling water and let it steep 5 minutes. Add melted butter and 2 tablespoons of the fat from the bacon and mix well. Stir in the beaten eggs, baking powder, buttermilk, and molasses. Add chopped chili pepper, blend well, and pour mixture on top of bacon in the hot skillet. Bake for about 30 minutes. Serve with a spoon.

Crumpets

In Brittany and Wales, where Celtic influences are strong, the words *krampoch* and *crempog,* respectively, identify thin baked breads made of batter that may be antecedents of the English crumpets served with tea by early American colonists. As they were prepared in Virginia during Jefferson's lifetime, crumpets for either tea or breakfast were baked on a griddle without being turned. Mrs. Randolph's recipe, dated 1831, suggests you "Take a Quart of Dough from your bread at a very early Hour in the morning," and after adding to it beaten egg yolks and frothy whites, "set it to rise till Breakfast Time. . . ." Here we use a dough following British tradition with no eggs but we do add some cake flour to temper the high gluten content of American white flour. The traditional crumpet is very similar to our English muffins; they are baked in crumpet rings, which are a little smaller and shallower than English muffin size, and you can substitute 7½-ounce tuna fish cans with tops and bottoms removed if you don't fill them too full—less than ½ inch. And we prefer to turn our crumpets so both sides are baked.

Makes 12 crumpets

2 teaspoons active dry yeast
½ cup warm water
1 cup warm milk
1 teaspoon coarse salt or ½ teaspoon table salt
⅔ cup cake flour
2 cups white flour, preferably unbleached
¼ teaspoon baking soda mixed with 2 tablespoons warm water
Lard or shortening

Put the yeast in a medium-size bowl and pour warm water over it. When dissolved, stir in the milk, salt, and both flours. Beat 100 strokes by hand; it's better not to use an electric mixer because the beating is so violent it tends to make the dough turn gummy. Cover with plastic wrap and let sit in a warm place until double in volume and bubbly on top—about 45 minutes.

Stir the baking soda and water into the batter thoroughly. Grease both the insides of your ring molds and the bottom of a large skillet. Set the rings on the skillet and heat over a moderate flame. When hot enough so that a drop of water sizzles just slowly on the surface of the pan, spread about 2 to 3 tablespoons of batter into each ring to fill it just under ½ inch; if it doesn't spread to all the edges, poke with a floured finger to even out the circle. Bake about 5 minutes, until the tops have blisters and the edges are firm. Turn, remove the rings, and bake another 3–4 minutes on the other side. Clean and grease the rings again and repeat until the batter is used up.

Cool on racks. When ready to serve, split the crumpets, toast them, and spread liberally with butter.

Madhur Jaffrey's Hoppers

Ceylon may have changed its name to Sri Lanka, but hoppers remain one of the more popular of the island dishes. Hoppers are yeast pancakes based on a leavener produced from the sweet sap of various palms of the East, fermented into a mildly alcoholic drink that used to be the common rising agent. The name is said to derive from *appa*, a word in the Tamil language for small rice flour cakes eaten at breakfast time. Madhur Jaffrey describes a hopper as a marriage between a French crêpe and an English muffin and points out that the hopper isn't baked, but is cooked under cover in a wok, "which allows it to be thicker, whiter, and softer in the center and crisp around its delicate browned edges." Serve hoppers with butter and honey or jam. Incidentally, don't use one of the new flat-bottomed woks or you won't achieve the right hopper shape.

Makes 8 hoppers

1 teaspoon active dry
  yeast
1 cup lukewarm water
1 tablespoon sugar
2 teaspoons coarse salt
  or 1 teaspoon table
  salt
1½ cups white flour
½ cup rice flour
1 cup coconut milk, at
  room temperature
About 3 tablespoons
  vegetable oil

In a large bowl dissolve the yeast in the water. Stir in the sugar and salt, mixing well. Sift the white flour and rice flour together, then add them slowly to the yeast, stirring. You will have a thick, pasty dough. Cover with plastic wrap and leave in a dark warm place for 10 hours. An oven with a pilot light is a good spot.

Now add the coconut milk to the risen, bubbly batter, stirring well. Let sit for 10 minutes.

Heat a wok over low heat (or if you have 2, use them so you can be baking 2 hoppers at once); brush the center with oil, covering a diameter of about 7 inches. Pour in ⅓ cup of the batter and immediately pick up the wok by its handles and swirl the batter around in a circular motion to extend its circle by about ¾ inch. Cover the wok and let the hopper cook on low heat for about 11–12 minutes or until the center looks like a slightly puffed-up English muffin and the edges are light brown and crisp. Remove to a warm plate and cover with another warm plate, as you make the rest of the hoppers. Serve immediately.

14 · Flat Breads

Pita

Pizza

Zata or Pideh

Socca

Hapanleipa—Flat Finnish Sour Rye Bread

Vorterkaker

Flatbröd

Flat circles of bread take us back in time to the earliest efforts at baking, and even perfection in the use of yeast has not changed in otherwise fundamental ways the breads of some cultures. Wheat and barley are still the staples of Syria and Lebanon; the round thin loaves of Syrian bakers are called *khobaz arabee* and their thicker bunlike bread is known as *talamee*. Travelers who have strolled in the bazaars of Damascus have tasted the sweet cherry and anise buns called *ka'ick,* and pita or pocket bread has overflowed the ovens of the Middle East into supermarkets almost everywhere. Scandinavian flat breads (often using rye flour) sometimes seem *de rigueur* at cocktail and buffet parties and on American cheese trays. American fast-food entrepreneurs have made the pizza their own—it is even now advertised as at its best when the base is transformed into a French baguette. All the breads in this chapter are as rewarding to make at home as any of the loaves that sentimentalists associate with great-grandmother's black wood stove and baking day.

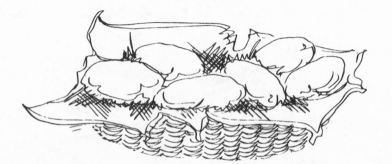

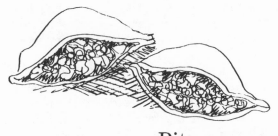

Pita

Bakeries are common enough throughout the Middle East, but many housewives prefer to make their own bread and send it out to be baked in the village ovens. In *A Book of Middle Eastern Food,* Claudia Roden gives this glimpse of family life: "Children rushing through the streets balancing a large wooden tray or a flat wicker basket on their heads are a common daily sight. The trays hold rounds of flattened dough laid on a cloth, and covered by another cloth. At the bakery, the children stand close to the big oven, watching where their bread is put down so as not to lose it among the other loaves. People often mark their loaves with a pinch or brand it with a sign drawn with a stick in order to be able to recognize and claim their own when it comes out of the oven." She adds, "Sometimes it is cut in half and the pocket filled with hot shish kebab and salads. . . ." To be sure the pita you eat is your own and needs no distinguishing pinch or brand, here is how to bake it yourself. We favor whole wheat pita, but if you prefer white, simply substitute 1 cup white flour for the 1 cup whole wheat.

Makes twelve 6-inch pita

1 tablespoon active dry
   yeast
1½ cups warm water
2 teaspoons coarse salt
   or 1 teaspoon table
   salt
1 tablespoon olive oil
1 cup whole wheat
   flour
About 2½ cups white
   flour

In a large bowl mix the yeast in ½ cup of the warm water. When completely dissolved and foamy, stir in remaining warm water mixed with salt and olive oil. Mix well, then stir in the flours, holding back a little of the white.

Turn the dough out onto a floured surface, and knead for about 10 minutes, adding more flour as necessary to make a firm, elastic dough. Clean out the bowl and rub with additional oil, put the dough in, turning to coat, and cover with plastic wrap. Let rise in a warm place until doubled in volume—about 1½ hours.

Put the dough on a large, lightly floured surface and roll into a long cylinder; then cut off 12 equal sections. Form each section into a ball about the size of a Ping-Pong ball, stretching the dough with the palms of your hands, gently pulling the sides down; pinch the ends together where they meet underneath.

As each ball is formed, set it aside on a floured surface and cover lightly with a kitchen towel. Let rest about 5 minutes; then, with a heavy rolling pin, roll each ball, one by one, flattening it into a disk 6 inches in diameter. The dough will be resistant, so you will have to roll firmly, turning the dough on the floured surface so it does not stick; use weight on the rolling pin to help shape the flat dough into even rounds.

Lift the disks onto a floured surface and cover while forming others. The pita shapes should rest 20 minutes as you heat the oven, lined with tiles or a baking stone, to 500°, the highest temperature. If you have a paddle, transfer two of the rounds to it and slide them onto the hot tiles or stone; otherwise gently pick up disks with your fingers and toss them carefully onto tiles one at a time. (If you have tiles, you can probably manage to bake 6 at a time without touching; a stone may take only 2 at a time.) Work quickly—to retain the heat in the oven, shut the door and don't peek for 1 minute; then open it slightly and you will see that the rounds of dough have puffed up like balloons. (Of course, if you have a glass door you can watch it all happen.)

Continue baking for 2 minutes, then remove one by one with a spatula, resting them on a cool surface while you bake your remaining disks. Gradually, they will deflate as they cool. Pita bread can be eaten by breaking it open and buttering while still warm, or with a filling stuffed in the pocket. To keep pita, stack them and put them in a plastic bag, squeezing out the air and tightly closing the open end of the bag. Store in the refrigerator, or freeze them. You'll find they are also good when toasted.

◆ A FILLING FOR WARM PITA

You can fill this pocket bread with just about anything. If you have some cheese on hand, you'll find it adds an extra fillip to almost any filling combination—just stuff the pita and return it to the oven until the melting cheese spreads over the rest of the pita filling and oozes out to make a temptingly gooey snack. For example, here's a way to dress up your pita as a very satisfying lunch:

To fill 6 pita

½ *pound mushrooms,
  sliced*
6 *scallions, sliced, with
  some of the green
  tops*
½ *large red pepper,
  seeded and chopped*
2 *tablespoons butter*
2 *tablespoons olive oil*
⅓ *cup chopped
  country ham*
4 *eggs, lightly beaten*
Salt
*Freshly ground black
  pepper*
Cayenne pepper
¼ *cup sliced green
  and black olives*
3 *tablespoons chopped
  parsley*
¼ *cup freshly grated
  Parmesan or other
  cheese*

Sauté mushrooms, scallions, and chopped red pepper in butter and oil for 5–6 minutes, until lightly cooked. Stir in the ham and cook 1 minute longer. Stir in beaten eggs and cook over moderate heat until the eggs set. Season with salt, pepper, and cayenne. Toss in the olives and parsley. Open the warm pitas with your fingers and stuff with the cooked mixture, adding grated cheese. Put in a hot oven just long enough for cheese to melt. Serve immediately.

Pizza

According to a Gallup poll, the embellished Italian bread called pizza has become the favorite informal food of Americans between the ages of twenty-one and thirty-three. Any interested cook can make his or her own, and recipes abound. Our unorthodox version uses some whole wheat flour to make the dough more stretchable, more olive oil than is usually called for and some dry milk to make the crust more tender.

PIZZA, CONTINUED

Makes 4 8–9-inch pizzas or 2 18–20-inch

1 tablespoon active dry
   yeast
1½ cups warm water
¼ cup nonfat dry milk
1 tablespoon coarse
   salt or 2 teaspoons
   table salt
¼ cup olive oil
⅔ cup coarsely ground
   whole wheat flour
2–2½ cups white flour,
   preferably
   unbleached
Corn meal

Dissolve the yeast in a large bowl with ½ cup of the water. Stir the dry milk and salt together with the rest of the water until dissolved, then pour over the yeast. Add the olive oil, whole wheat flour, and about 2 cups of the white flour, stirring to mix, then turn out on a floured surface and let rest while you wash out and oil the bowl.

Knead the dough until smooth, adding more flour as necessary—about 6–8 minutes. Return the dough to the bowl, cover with plastic wrap and let rise until doubled in volume.

Preheat oven lined with baking tiles or stone to 450 degrees.*

To make 9-inch pizzas, divide the dough in quarters (if you don't want to make 4 pizzas immediately, freeze remaining dough). To make two 18–20-inch pizzas, divide the dough in half.

Start stretching the piece of dough you are working with by kneading a bit first, then flattening it out and coaxing it out from the center toward the edges. It will be bouncy and resistant, so you must work at it, pulling lightly and stretching, concentrating on the areas that remain thick, twirling it over your fist the way they do in pizza parlor windows. The important thing is to get it as thin and even as possible.

*If you do not have a baking tile or stones, we have found the next best thing is to bake on a heavy black baking sheet.

Sprinkle either a paddle or a cookie sheet with corn meal. Place the stretched dough for one pizza on top of the corn meal, patting it into a round of the desired circumference. Now spread on the filling, leaving a ½-inch border. Your oven and tiles or baking stone should be piping hot now. Open the oven door and with a quick gesture (as though you were pulling the tablecloth out from under a table setting), slide the pizza off the paddle onto the tiles. Bake just about 12 minutes, a little more if it isn't quite as brown at the edge as you want.

♦ PIZZA FILLING FOR 18-INCH PIZZA

3 cups canned plum tomatoes, drained and chopped
1 teaspoon dried oregano or basil
8 strips anchovy fillets or ham or Italian salami
½ cup black olives, pitted
1 cup diced mozzarella cheese
Olive oil
About 2 tablespoons freshly grated Parmesan cheese

Spread half of the drained tomatoes over the pizza dough and sprinkle with oregano or basil. Arrange anchovies or meat strips like spokes, and scatter olives attractively. Sprinkle with mozzarella, drizzle a little olive oil over, and top with 1 tablespoon or more of Parmesan.

Zata or Pideh

These are ancient flat breads from the Middle East that may have been a forerunner of pizza. The toppings vary; sometimes it is simply mahleb—ground cherry pits; sometimes a combination of ginger, sesame, cumin, poppy seeds, aniseed and a bit of dry grated cheese is sprinkled on top. The following recipe called zata is our version of a bread made by Middle Eastern bakeries in the New York area and is topped with thyme, black pepper, and sesame seeds.

Makes two 8–9 inch disks

*1 teaspoon active dry
  yeast*
¾ cup warm water
*1 tablespoon vegetable
  oil*
*1 teaspoon coarse salt
  or ½ teaspoon table
  salt*
½ cup cake flour
*1½–2 cups white flour,
  preferably
  unbleached*
*4 tablespoons sesame
  seeds*
Olive oil
3 teaspoons thyme
Freshly ground pepper

In a medium bowl dissolve the yeast in the warm water. Stir in the oil, salt, cake flour, and enough of the unbleached flour to make a cohesive dough. Turn out onto a floured work surface and let rest while you clean the bowl.

Knead the dough, adding more flour as wanted, until it is smooth and resilient—about 7 or 8 minutes. Return it to the bowl, cover with plastic wrap, and let rise until double in volume—about 1½ to 2 hours.

Meanwhile toast the sesame seeds in a large skillet over medium heat, stirring occasionally as they heat up, then steadily as they pop and turn brown. Remove from the heat.

Turn the dough out and punch it down. Divide it in two, then punch each half out into a round of about 8 or 9 inches, using your knuckles and rotating the dough to enlarge the circle. Transfer them to a paddle or baking sheet sprinkled with corn meal, if you are using a baking stone or tiles; otherwise, place at either end of an oiled baking sheet. Be sure to preheat your oven at this stage to 450° so that the baking surface can get hot.

Rub the disks with olive oil, then crush the thyme in your hands and rub it on top, adding a little more oil, if necessary to make the herb and oil a little smeary. Grind pepper generously over the tops and then sprinkle on the sesame seeds. Let sit 5 minutes.

Bake for 10 minutes. Remove and eat warm.

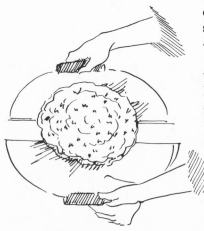

Socca

Chickpeas or garbanzos are among the oldest legumes of the Mediterranean. (Westerners may know them best as the foundation of wonderful soups or transformed into a cocktail dip known in the Middle East as *hummus*.) Flour is also made from chickpeas, and the *panisses* of the Riviera are deep-fried matchlike chickpea bread sticks that are eaten as a snack or served like French fried potatoes with a meat course. Socca is hot bread, a crisp pancake often more than a foot in diameter. It is sold on the streets of Nice in the way hot dogs are in America, but we sampled it first at a Provençal inn called La Maillane. In this country, we find socca easy enough to make at home. Chickpea flour is available at ethnic markets, or if you have an electric flour mill, you can grind your own from dried chickpeas—don't try to do it in a blender. Socca with a glass of chilled California Pinot Chardonnay is a fine idea.

Makes one 10-inch socca

⅔ *cup chickpea flour*
½ *teaspoon coarse salt*
   or ¼ teaspoon table
   salt
Freshly ground pepper
¼ *cup olive oil*
1 *cup water*

Mix the flour, salt, and several turns of pepper grinder with the oil, adding enough of the water for a batter the consistency of the average pancake. Stir well and set aside for about 30 minutes.

Preheat oven (lined with tiles or a baking stone, if you have them) to 450°. Oil a round shallow pan about 10 inches in diameter. Pour on the batter in a layer about ⅛ inch thick. Bake for 5 minutes, then brush the top of the socca with a little oil and put the pan under the broiler as close as possible to the heat source. Broil about 3 minutes, until crisp and golden. Slide onto a large serving plate and sprinkle lightly with salt and pepper before cutting into wedges.

Hapanleipa—Flat Finnish Sour Rye Bread

In western Finland this bread was always shaped into a round flat loaf with a hole in the center so that the bread could be hung up to dry. It was then stored in an outdoor granary and would keep for months; it would be dry but still chewable. This version worked out by Beatrice Ojakangas uses some wheat flour and is, she feels, more to American tastes, but it does dry out quickly, so if you're not planning to eat both loaves immediately, freeze the second one. The large, shiny, golden-brown disks look splendid on a supper table, and when we serve it, we place it in the center of a basket tray and let our guests tear off pieces.

Makes two 12-inch disks

2 tablespoons active dry yeast
2 cups lukewarm potato water*
1 teaspoon sugar
2 cups rye flour
2 teaspoons coarse salt or 1 teaspoon table salt
About 3 cups white flour, preferably unbleached
Melted butter

In a medium-size ceramic or glass bowl mix the yeast in ½ cup of the warm potato water with the sugar and let stand until it starts to swell. Add the rest of the potato water and the rye flour and beat until smooth. Cover with plastic wrap and leave the bowl in a warm place for 24 hours. The sponge will bubble up and rise, then subside, and will acquire a good sour smell.

Transfer to a larger bowl and add the salt and 2½ cups of the white flour, a little at a time, stirring to make a stiff dough. Turn out on a floured surface and let rest, covered, for 10 minutes.

Start kneading, incorporating as much of the remaining flour as required; the dough will be very sticky, but adding flour helps, and after 10 minutes it should become smooth and resilient. Clean the mixing bowl and butter it. Form the dough into a ball and return it to the bowl, turning it to coat with butter. Let rise, covered with plastic wrap, for 1½–2 hours until doubled in bulk.

Turn the dough out, punch down, and knead a few more minutes, then divide in two. Roll each half out into a 12-inch round, trying to keep the

---

* Potato water is simply water in which several peeled potatoes have been cooked.

thickness as even as possible, and place on
buttered baking sheet. With a 2-inch cookie cutter
or the rim of a glass, cut out a circle in the center
of each round. Prick the bottoms of the rounds all
over with a fork and let them rise, covered loosely
with a towel, for about 1 hour until they are
almost doubled in bulk.

Bake the loaves in a preheated 375° oven for 30
minutes. Remove to racks and brush them with
melted butter. Let them cool covered lightly with
a towel.

Vorterkaker

All the Scandinavian countries are famous for crisp,
thin breads, and on the Danish island of Bornholm one autumn we discovered
its crackerlike biscuits to be among the world's best—but it's hard to choose.
This Norwegian rye flat bread has quite a different flavor from the Finnish
Hapanleipa; for instance, it is slightly sweet with a tantalizing taste of anise,
and while it is meant to be a dry crisp bread (incidentally, don't store it in
plastic wrap or it will stay soft), it is also delicious just warm from the oven and
served with sweet butter and/or a chunk of Swiss, Cheddar, or Esrom cheese.

Makes 2 large flat rounds

*1 tablespoon active dry
   yeast*
⅓ cup warm water
½ cup lard
1 cup milk
¼ cup dark corn syrup
*1 tablespoon coarse
   salt or 2 teaspoons
   table salt*
*1½ teaspoons fennel
   seeds*
1½ teaspoons aniseed
3 cups rye flour
*1¼–1½ cups white
   flour, preferably
   unbleached*

Put the yeast in a large bowl and cover with the warm water. Let stand while you melt the lard in a medium saucepan. When melted, mix in the milk, corn syrup, and salt. Crush the fennel and aniseed by rolling a rolling pin over them, then add to the saucepan. When cool, pour this mixture into the yeast. Stirring, add 1¼ cups of the rye flour and ¾ cup of the white. Beat for a minute, then gradually mix in the rest of the rye until it is all incorporated. This should be a stiff dough. Now cover the bowl with plastic wrap and let rise until double in bulk—about 1 hour.

Turn the dough out onto a floured work surface and knead, adding the rest of the white flour as necessary, until the dough is no longer sticky and the surface is smooth, compact, but resilient. Cut in half and roll each half out into a circle 12 inches in diameter. Transfer to greased baking sheets, then cut a hole in the center with a 2-inch cookie cutter or the rim of a glass, floured. Prick all over with a fork, cover lightly with a towel, and let rise again until double—about 45 minutes.

Bake in preheated 425° oven for 20 minutes until browned. Brush with warm water as soon as you remove the rounds from the oven and let cool on racks.

Flatbröd

One day on a train we met an elderly Englishman who struck up a conversation about his pleasure in bread baking. He'd traveled around this country a lot, usually in a camper, and he said he always met with a warm welcome in any household if he presented his hosts with a loaf of the bread he baked himself in his camper oven. During such travels, he also took long hikes in the wilderness, and he told us he wished he had a recipe for a dry Scandinavian flat bread that would keep well for long periods. Learning of our prospective book on bread, he got our promise to provide him with the kind of recipe he sought—so here it is:

Makes twenty-four 6-inch squares

1 cup boiling water
1 tablespoon butter
½ teaspoon coarse salt or ¼ teaspoon table salt
1 cup rye flour
½ cup whole wheat flour
½ cup white flour

Pour the boiling water over the butter and salt in a medium-size mixing bowl, stirring until melted. Let cool.

Combine the rye, whole wheat, and white flours and beat 1½ cups into the water mixture. Gradually add enough of the remaining flour, mixing thoroughly, until you have a fairly firm dough that holds together.

Turn the dough out onto a floured working surface. Tear off a piece about the size of a golf ball and roll it out, turning it and dusting your surface with flour as needed, until you have a thin piece about 6 by 6 inches. Trim it to make a neat square, and with the tines of a fork prick the surface all over every ½ inch.

Heat an ungreased heavy skillet until hot but not smoking. Pick up a dough square with a spatula and slip it into the skillet. Let cook almost a minute, then check the underside to see if it has dried and turned lightly tanned; there will be a few dark spots on its surface, too. Turn and cook another minute on the other side, then transfer to a baking sheet. Meanwhile roll out the next square, but before you put it in the skillet, wipe the bottom of the pan with a paper towel to remove any burnt flour. Continue with the rest of the squares, and when all are done, place the baking sheets (you'll probably need two so the pieces don't touch) in a preheated 300° oven and bake 20 minutes or until dry and crisp. Cool and store in an airtight container.

15 · Shaped Breads

Pennsylvania Dutch Poppy Seed Twists
Sicilian Twist
Bubble, Monkey, or Pull-Apart Bread
Flowerpot Breads
Free-form Sculptured Breads
Mushroom Bread
Wheat Sheaf Bread
Grissini or Crisp Bread Sticks

One of the old folk rituals of Ukrainian life in the U.S.S.R. is that of baking bread for a wedding. Seven bridesmaids grind flour from wheat grown in seven different fields, and the results are sifted together and made into bread dough; the good-luck loaf is ornamentally formed by the bride's friends. Always there are rosettes and other flower shapes molded from dough as decorations, and on top of the *korovai*—as this wedding bread is called—the skillful breadmakers sculpt nesting doves and cupid's hearts. Simply twisting and braiding, you can turn simple dough into wonderful forms. And by using your imagination, you can create your own fanciful menagerie. Every Western culture has traditions of sculptured breads, and you'll find a dough that is elastic and firm is easier to work with than modeling clay. The festive breads you make can be used as edible centerpieces for parties, just as you'll find them to be most acceptable gifts to take to good friends on almost any occasion.

Pennsylvania Dutch
Poppy Seed Twists

It's been said that the women who helped to settle the Pennsylvania Dutch country were the first really talented cooks to come to America, and their descendants still prove their skills in making handsome shaped loaves. Their art may have been an antidote for boredom. At any rate, in 1975 it was estimated that the average Pennsylvania Dutch housewife annually baked as many as 1,200 separate breads for her family.

Makes 4 twists about 12 inches long

3 medium potatoes
1 cup potato water
1½ tablespoons active
    dry yeast
1 teaspoon sugar
3 tablespoons butter
1¼ cups warm water
1 tablespoon coarse
    salt or 2 teaspoons
    table salt
4½–5 cups white flour,
    preferably
    unbleached
Milk
2–3 tablespoons poppy
    seeds

Peel and quarter the potatoes and drop them into boiling water to cover. Cook about 25 minutes until soft. Drain, reserving the potato water, and cool (you should have at least 1 cup). In a large mixing bowl dissolve the yeast in ½ cup of the lukewarm potato water with the sugar.

Mash the potatoes with the butter until fluffy (you will want to use only 1 cup of the mashed potatoes, so if you have extra, set aside for another purpose). Add the remaining ½ cup of potato water plus 1¼ cups warm water, the mashed potatoes, which should be tepid by now, and the salt to the yeast and mix well. Add the flour a cup at a time until the dough becomes hard to stir, then turn out onto a floured surface. Let rest a few minutes, then knead for about 10 minutes, adding more flour as necessary, until the dough is smooth and satiny.

Clean out the mixing bowl and grease generously with lard or butter; put the dough in, turning to coat all sides, rubbing a little more grease on top. Cover with plastic wrap and leave in a warm place until dough doubles in bulk—about 1½ hours.

Turn out the dough and divide it into 4 pieces; then as you work with 1 piece, cover the other 3 lightly so they don't crust on the surface. Divide each piece into thirds and roll out each third into a 14-inch roll. Place the 3 rolls close together on one side of a buttered baking sheet. Squeeze the 3 strands together at the top and tuck them under; then start braiding. When the 3 strands are all braided, pinch the ends together at the bottom and tuck under. Cover lightly with a towel and repeat this process with the other 3 sections of dough until you have 4 rather slender braided loaves—you'll need 2 cookie sheets. Let rise in a warm place until double in bulk—about 45 minutes.

Brush the twists liberally with milk and sprinkle poppy seeds all over the tops and sides. Bake in a preheated 375° oven 35–40 minutes until browned. If you have to bake the sheets on two levels of your oven, switch them halfway through the baking time. Cool the loaves on racks.

Sicilian Twist

"As for the blended savors which are the major characteristic of Sicilian cooking," Gaetano Falzone wrote after a visit to the island, "the field in which it beats all other cuisines, it derives from the mixing not only of the different races which have come onto Sicilian soil, of the different civilizations, of the different cultures, but also of the different cuisines." This loaf reflects a fondness for the sesame seeds that may have been brought first by Arab immigrants in the eighth century. As made by Mediterranean bakers in America, this bread from Sicily has not only an attractive twisted shape but a slash down its length that adds to the crust, forming a trough in which the sesame seeds cling.

Makes 1 large loaf

*2 teaspoons active dry
   yeast*
1½ cups warm water
*2 teaspoons coarse salt
   or 1½ teaspoons
   table salt*
*3–3½ cups white flour,
   preferably
   unbleached*
1 tablespoon olive oil

In a medium bowl dissolve the yeast in the warm water. Stir in the salt and as much of the flour as can be absorbed. When it becomes hard to stir, turn the dough out and let rest while you wash the bowl.

Knead the dough, adding more flour as necessary, until it is smooth and bouncy—about 8 to 10 minutes. Return it to the bowl and brush the top with olive oil, letting a little run down the sides. Cover the bowl with plastic wrap and let the dough rise slowly until almost triple in volume—several hours or longer in a cool place.

GLAZE

*1 egg beaten with 1
teaspoon water*

TOPPING

*2 tablespoons sesame
seeds*

Punch the dough down, cover and let rise again until double in volume—about an hour or so.

Turn the dough out and deflate it thoroughly. Roll it out into a long, thickish roll almost a yard long. Leaving a 12-inch base, start twisting the dough around that base, looping it around about four times. Place on a greased baking sheet and with a sharp knife make a ¾-inch-deep slash the length of the loaf. Cover with a kitchen towel and let rise until double in size—about 50 minutes.

Brush the top and the gash where it has opened up with the egg glaze and sprinkle sesame seeds all over. Bake in a preheated 425° oven for 10 minutes, then lower the heat to 375° and bake 25 minutes more. Cool on a rack.

Bubble, Monkey, or Pull-Apart Bread

A couple of generations of Americans have found entertainment in making this fun bread. When it rises and later when it comes forth from the oven, it may look like a festive glistening crown, full of gooey bubbles.

Makes one 10-inch crown

2 tablespoons active
   dry yeast
1⅓ cups warm water
⅓ cup nonfat dry milk
½ cup sugar
1 teaspoon coarse salt
   or ½ teaspoon table
   salt
4 tablespoons (½
   stick) butter, melted
2 eggs
4½–5 cups white flour,
   preferably
   unbleached

GLAZE:

1½ cups dark brown
   sugar
⅓ cup evaporated
   milk or cream
2 tablespoons corn or
   maple syrup
5 tablespoons butter
1 cup currants
¾ cup chopped pecans

In a large bowl dissolve the yeast in ⅓ cup of the warm water.

Mix the remaining water with the dry milk, sugar, and salt, then pour over the dissolved yeast. Stir in the melted butter (be sure it is only lukewarm). Beat in the eggs, then stir in about 4½ cups of the flour until the mixture gets hard to stir.

Turn the dough out onto a floured working surface and let rest while you clean your bowl.

Scrape up the dough and knead for 6–8 minutes, adding more flour as necessary, until it is smooth and bouncy.

Grease the bowl and return the dough to it. Cover with plastic wrap and let rise in a warm place until double in bulk—about 1 hour.

A few minutes before the dough seems to have doubled, prepare the glaze. Put the brown sugar, evaporated milk or cream, corn or maple syrup, and butter in a saucepan and heat until sugar and butter are dissolved, stirring now and then. Set aside to cool.

Punch the dough down and turn out onto a floured surface. Tear off pieces of dough the size of golf balls and roll them around in your lightly floured hands to form round bubbles.

After you have formed about 10 balls thoroughly grease a 10-inch cake tube pan (be sure that it does *not* have a removable bottom or the glaze will leak out) or a Bundt pan. Spread about ¼ of the glaze over the bottom, then sprinkle on a fourth of the currants and pecans. Now place the first layers of bubbles on top, nestled close together, making more as you use the first ones up.

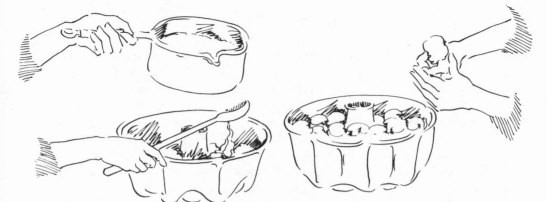

Drizzle on the top another fourth of the glaze, currants, and nuts, then cover with another layer of bubbles. Repeat until all is used up, finishing off with glaze on top.

Cover the pan with waxed paper and let rise in a warm place until the bubbles have risen to the top of the pan—about 30 minutes.

Bake in a preheated 350° oven for 45 minutes until the top of the crown is caramel-colored. Peek after the first half hour to make sure the top isn't turning too dark; if so, make a tent of aluminum foil and cover.

Remove from the oven and let rest 10 minutes before turning out onto a rack. Serve warm.

Flowerpot Breads

The familiar tapered red clay flower pots—large, small, shallow, window-box-shaped—all are intrinsically ovenproof and ready for breadmaking once their terra cotta interiors have been treated (see below) to keep the dough from sticking. The loaves they turn out may seem a little odd in shape, but they're modern reminders of the bread once produced in the old-fashioned brick ovens that were built into fireplaces in colonial days and for decades afterward. Some cooks are convinced that the texture and flavor of bread baked in a clay pot are superior because the clay absorbs moisture from the dough as it bakes. "It's sort of alive, when you compare it to metal or glass," one devotee told us. "The result is like the loaves they used to bake in outdoor ovens."

Treating the Flowerpots

Use very clean clay flowerpots and generously rub the insides all over with vegetable oil.

Place the pots in a 450° oven and let them bake for 1 hour (do this, if possible, alongside something else that may be baking so as not to waste fuel).

After this treatment the pots need simply be washed in warm water after you've baked in them. If you notice any sticking, repeat the treatment.

Doughs to Use

Almost any yeast dough will bake well in a flowerpot, but these are the ones we've found particularly good:

BUBBLE BREAD DOUGH (page 318) (using the currants but eliminating the chopped nuts and sticky glaze) and the sweet dough for FREE-FORM SCULPTURED BREAD that follows. Both of these make nice sweet breakfast breads, particularly baked in small individual flowerpots. Sprinkle the tops with sesame or poppy seeds after glazing just before baking, or sprinkle powdered sugar over the little breads after baking.

CHEESE BREAD DOUGH (page 134). This turns beautifully golden and crusty. Sprinkle the tops with grated Parmesan before baking, if you like.

WHOLE WHEAT BREAD DOUGH (page 77). This is nice baked in a larger pot so that you can slice the bread crosswise for round sandwiches after you've eaten the topknots, particularly good if dusted with cracked wheat just before baking.

Forming and Baking

Use the dough after it has had its first rising. Punch it down and form into shapes roughly half the size of the flowerpots you'll be using.

Most flowerpots have a hole in the bottom, so stuff that with a wad of crumpled aluminum foil. Thoroughly oil the sides and bottoms of the pots and have the pots slightly warm when you put the dough in.

Fill the pots only half full. Clay makes dough expand more readily, so if they are more than half full the bread will mushroom over the top too much and fall over to one side. To make topknots, form rounds of dough the size of golf balls. Make indentations in the dough in the pots and, elongating one side of each ball to a point, fit it into its hole. Very small flowerpots will take only one topknot—and in this case the ball should be about half the size of a golf ball; wider pots will take 2 or 3 snuggled close together.

Cover the filled pots with a kitchen towel and let the dough rise until it is almost to the top—about 45 minutes.

Just before baking, paint the tops with a glaze of 1 egg beaten with 1 teaspoon water.

Bake in a preheated 425° oven for 15 minutes, then lower heat to 350°; small pots will need only an additional 5–10 minutes; medium size 10–15 minutes; and a large pot an additional 30 minutes, particularly if you are using whole wheat dough.

Slip the baked breads out of their pots and let them sit a few minutes in the turned-off oven, then cool on racks.

Free-form Sculptured Bread

A shape of more than about 10 inches will be hard to handle, particularly if it has any fragile parts. If you are working with children and they all want to make different shapes, simply double or triple this recipe so there is lots of dough to play with.

Makes 2 shapes, depending on size

1 tablespoon active dry
  yeast
¼ cup warm water
⅓ cup sugar
2 eggs
1 teaspoon vanilla
  extract
¼ cup light cream or
  milk
½ teaspoon coarse salt
  or ¼ teaspoon table
  salt
¼ cup melted butter
1 teaspoon grated
  orange peel
2½–3 cups white flour,
  preferably
  unbleached

Put the yeast in a medium bowl and mix with the warm water and sugar. When dissolved, add the eggs, vanilla, cream or milk, salt, butter, and orange peel, and beat until thoroughly mixed. Stir in 2½ cups of flour, then turn out onto a floured working surface and knead until smooth, about 6–7 minutes, adding more flour as necessary.

Clean the bowl, grease it, and return the dough to it. Cover with plastic wrap and leave in a warm place until double in volume—1½–2 hours; the higher proportion of sugar and eggs will make this dough slower to rise, and it does need a warm place, in an oven with a pilot light or near a radiator.

Turn the dough out and divide in half. If you want to make a long shape, roll one half out a bit to flatten it. The dough will have a will of its own and may suggest a form to you—perhaps a fish, or a bird, or a rabbit, or some fanciful prehistoric creature. If you want to make legs and tails, pinch off a bit of dough and roll it out, then attach to

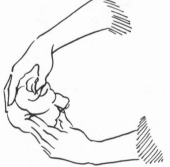

GLAZE

*1 egg mixed with 1
teaspoon water*

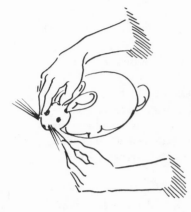

the main body of your dough by wetting the edges and pinching firmly; round balls of dough can be used for ears and noses. Use raisins or currants for eyes, strips of orange peel for fins and whiskers perhaps, wheatberries or pine nuts for teeth— whatever strikes your fancy. Do your final shaping on a well-greased baking sheet, cover lightly with a towel, and let rise again for 45 minutes. Paint the surface on your sculpture with the egg glaze and bake in a preheated 350° oven 20–25 minutes, depending on how thin your sculpture is. Watch carefully, and if some of the extremities seem to be browning too much, cover them with foil. Remove from baking sheets while still warm, using one or two spatulas to lift off the shapes carefully.

Mushroom Bread

As early as the eighteenth century cooks might scoop out the crumb of a soft brioche and fill the empty center with mushrooms in a sauce, but there seems little to be learned from former times about bread dough in which mushrooms are as vital as pumpkin in pumpkin bread. This recipe, devised not far from our Vermont woods where mushroom lovers hunt in season, is based on a sauté of minced mushrooms with a couple of soaked dried mushrooms added for flavor; use wild mushrooms if you are lucky enough to have some. We have shaped this loaf to look something like a large toadstool by baking it in a 2-pound 10-ounce can opened so that the dough mushrooms over the top. We've tried to make small mushroom shapes as well with the dough, but stem and cap seem to merge in the baking, so if you want rolls—and they are delicious—just make conventional shapes.

Makes 1 large mushroom shape

2 dried mushrooms
1 cup hot water
¼ pound fresh
   mushrooms, minced
6 scallions, minced
   (white plus half
   green part)
2 tablespoons butter
2 tablespoons fresh
   chopped tarragon or
   1 teaspoon dried
1 tablespoon active dry
   yeast
1 teaspoon honey
1 teaspoon coarse salt
   or ½ teaspoon table
   salt
About 2 cups white
   flour, preferably
   unbleached

GLAZE
Heavy cream

Soak the dried mushrooms in the hot water for 30 minutes.

Sauté the fresh mushrooms with the scallions in the butter. Squeeze out the dried mushrooms, straining and reserving the water; remove any hard stem, chop, and add to the pan. Sauté all together for about 3 minutes. Mix in the tarragon and let cool.

In a medium-size bowl dissolve the yeast in the mushroom water, measuring first to be sure you have ¾ cup; if not, add enough warm water to bring it up to that measure. Stir in the honey, salt, the cooled sautéed mushroom mixture, and enough flour to form a soft dough.

Turn the dough out on a floured surface and let rest while you clean out the bowl. Knead, using a light hand and adding more flour as necessary, until you have a smooth, elastic dough—about 4–5 minutes. Butter the bowl and return the dough to it. Cover with plastic wrap and let rise until double in volume—about 1 hour.

Prepare a 2-pound 10-ounce can as a mold: remove the top and bottom and butter the inside very thoroughly. Set on a buttered cookie sheet. Now punch down the risen dough and put inside the can (it should come at least two-thirds of the way up the sides). Let rise for about 40 minutes.

Bake in a preheated 350° oven for 25 minutes. Pull the rack out and brush the mushroomed top with cream, then bake another 10 minutes. Remove by running a knife around the inside of the can and pushing the loaf out from the bottom. Let cool on a rack.

Wheat Sheaf Bread

Because this is such a very wheaty dough, shaping it into a beautiful wheat sheaf gives added meaning. It's an attractive symbol to make for your family's Thanksgiving table.

Makes 1 sheaf

2 tablespoons active
   dry yeast
2 cups warm water
4 tablespoons (½
   stick) butter
2 tablespoons honey
2 tablespoons molasses
2 teaspoons coarse salt
   or 1 teaspoon table
   salt
2 shredded wheat
   biscuits
¼ cup toasted wheat
   germ
2½ cups whole wheat
   flour
2–3 cups white flour,
   preferably
   unbleached

GLAZE

1 egg beaten with 1
   teaspoon water

Dissolve the yeast in a large bowl with ¼ cup of warm water. Break up the butter and stir into the remaining warm water until dissolved. Mix in the honey, molasses, and salt and stir into the yeast. Crush the shredded wheat biscuits and add to the bowl, stirring along with the wheat germ, whole wheat flour, and about 2 cups of the white flour. Turn out the dough and let rest while you clean the bowl.

Now start kneading, adding more white flour as necessary, for about 10 minutes, until you have a smooth, elastic, and relatively nonsticky dough. Grease the bowl and return the dough to it. Cover with plastic wrap and let rise until double in bulk.

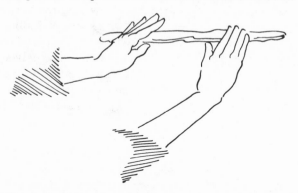

Turn the dough out onto a large working surface sprinkled with flour. Divide the dough into 15 pieces and roll each one out to a length of about 16 inches. Cut one of these in half, twist the two strands together, and set aside. Now place 4 ropes close together in the center of a well-greased baking sheet. Pile other ropes on top and around to form a bunch at the bottom and bend the tops at varying angles as illustrated. Place the twisted strand in the middle and tuck the ends under. Cover loosely with a kitchen towel and let the dough rise again for about 40 minutes.

Now snip the ends of the bent portion of the "stalks" with scissors to make them look like wheat. Paint the entire surface with the egg glaze and bake in a preheated 350° oven for 25 minutes. If the ends of the stalks seem to be browning too much, cover them with foil. Remove from the baking sheet, using spatulas, while still warm.

Grissini or Crisp Bread Sticks

Bread sticks, which are known all over today whether they be coated in sesame, caraway, poppy, or fennel seeds and coarse salt, originated in Turin. Napoleon was so taken with them that he dubbed them "les petits batons de Turin." Nowadays more often we see them displayed upright in vases in Italian restaurants. That fine cook from the West Coast, Mildred Knopf, suggests breaking a long stick in threes and wrapping prosciutto around each piece to serve as an appetizer. She prefers them fresh, as we do—and the best way to ensure freshness is to make your own. They turn crunchy within the first twenty-four hours but are good for several days. You can also freeze them as soon as they have cooled after baking. The length you want to make them is up to you. If you have an oven 30 inches or wider, it is amusing to produce really long batons.

Makes 8 sticks about 17 inches long

1½ teaspoons active
    dry yeast
1 cup warm water
½ teaspoon coarse salt
    or ¼ teaspoon table
    salt
½ cup cake flour
1½–2 cups white flour,
    preferably
    unbleached

GLAZE:

1 egg white beaten
    with 1 teaspoon
    water

TOPPING:

2–3 tablespoons
    sesame, caraway,
    poppy, or fennel
    seeds
2–3 tablespoons coarse
    salt, preferably sea
    salt

In a medium bowl dissolve the yeast in the warm water. Stir in the salt, cake flour, and enough of the unbleached flour to make a fairly stiff dough. Turn out on a floured surface and let rest while you clean the bowl.

Knead the dough, adding more flour as necessary, until smooth and elastic. Return it to the bowl, cover with plastic wrap, and let rise until almost triple in volume—2 to 3 hours or overnight in a cool place.

Punch the dough down and let rise again 30 to 40 minutes, or an hour if it is cold.

Turn the dough out onto a large, lightly floured work surface. Divide into 8 pieces (or fewer if you want to make really long sticks). Pat each piece into an oval, fold over, securing the seam, then roll out to a length of about 17 inches; the roll should be about ½ inch in diameter and as even as possible. When rolled out, let it hang for a second from your hand to keep its length, because it will want to pull back. Place on greased baking sheets several inches apart. Cover with kitchen towels and let sit 30 minutes.

Be sure to preheat your oven (lined with tiles, if possible) to 450° and put a pan of boiling water on the oven floor 15 minutes before baking.

Paint the top and sides of each stick with egg white glaze. Sprinkle whatever seeds you want to use over the glaze and then add some sea salt; the latter can be eliminated—and often is, particularly when using sesame seeds. Bake for 10 minutes, then remove the pan of steaming water and bake another 6 to 7 minutes. Let cool on the sheets a minute, then carefully lift, gently prying loose any stuck areas with a spatula. Prop up the sticks so air circulates to cool them. Whatever seeds and salt may have spilled off—and some are bound to—can be stored for future use.

16 · Breads as Casings

Pollo in Pane
Whole Ham in a Bread Cozy
Luncheon Pizza Roll
Calzone Alicia
Bubbat
Pâté in Brioche
Armen's Chicken Boereg

T he roasting technique of surrounding a
game bird with a damp clay shell may have
originated because careless cooks too often
burned the outside of the meat before it was thoroughly done inside. Clay,
scooped up and patted onto the raw bird, would seal in juices as it cooked.
Only a step away from this medieval custom is the use of dough as a
protecting layer (in some Oriental cuisines paper serves a similar purpose). As
with carapaces of baked earth, bread casings can be thrown away when used
only as a container—or, unlike clay, crusty moist bread with seasoned juices
can be eaten with appreciation. Bread thus cooked is closely related to the
trenchers of baked dough that served as eating utensils before the
introduction of forks. In those days, slabs of bread were especially made to
hold piled-on food and were sometimes consumed by the diner and sometimes
passed on to servants, or to the poor in the streets who had little or no bread
of any kind and rarely if ever tasted meat, fowl, or fish.

Our recipes for breads in casings are all designed by cooks of the past as
compatible matings of bread and meat. We've found that house guests to
whom we've served ham baked in bread have asked for it the next morning in
place of toast to go with eggs. The Tuscan Pollo in Pane is an equally
impressive dish, but it takes a little more careful attendance to be sure the
bird roasting inside is done to a turn. (Scooping up the stuffing with pieces of
casing is an extra treat.) The Bubbat is a simple version of the same general
idea, but the rolled pizza is a recent innovation with special qualities of its
own.

Pollo in Pane

This large, fresh-from-the-oven Italian bread is cut open at the table to reveal a whole unboned chicken that has been stuffed with *odori*, a tossed assembly of aromatic vegetables, chicken livers, red wine, and prosciutto. The bread absorbs meat and vegetable juices and is a perfect complement for the chicken—it may be served in chunks torn off rather than more conventional slices.

The Italian method of making country loaves may seem a reversal of more ordinary ways. Instead of adding flour to liquid and stopping when the mixture becomes a mass of dough, many Italian country cooks favor adding liquid gradually to the flour, kneading as more liquid is incorporated. In our experience, the flour seems to tighten up and kneading the dough is difficult. American flour is higher in gluten content, and that may account for the difficulty. Moreover, the Italian method most often used for this recipe calls for putting all the flour on the work surface, making a well in which the dissolved yeast is poured, along with a gradual addition of water, then mixing and kneading in more and more of the flour from the outer rim of the well.

This is much the same method as used in pasta making, but the eggs usually called for in pasta dough make a more manageable dough than this watery mixture that tends to run away and causes hands to become almost impossibly sticky.

Our first introduction to this breadmaking procedure was on a reporting assignment in Florence in 1976. In a fourteenth-century convent, before a restored fresco of the Last Supper, Giuliano Bugialli was at work on the dough when we joined his American students. As we took careful notes so we could try to achieve the same result at home, he deftly kneaded and mixed the sticky dough.

If you're an inveterate breadmaker and like to develop new techniques, do try his method. What follows evolved from numerous versions of Pollo in Pane turned out in our apartment kitchen. To make things easier, we recommend using a food processor.

You'll notice that these Italian breads tend to be drier than most, and they require longer baking, according to Mr. Bugialli, whose *The Fine Art of Italian Cooking* is a source of great value on the subject. (So, too, is Marcella Hazan's *More Classic Italian Cooking*.) Tuscan breads use little or no salt—they are intended chiefly as a vehicle for mopping up sauces and, indeed, they predate Italy's gift to diners everywhere, the fork. One of Tuscany's simplest and most delicious snacks—or it can be an appetizing first course—is a crusty slice of country bread bathed in olive oil and strewn with chopped fresh tomatoes.

POLLO IN PANE, CONTINUED

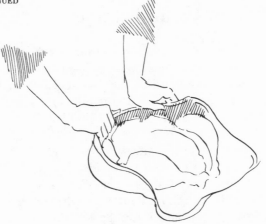

Serves 4–5 with extra bread

THE BREAD

*2 tablespoons active
  dry yeast
2⅓ cups warm water
6 cups white flour,
  preferably
  unbleached
1 teaspoon coarse salt
  or ½ teaspoon table
  salt*

In a small bowl dissolve the yeast in ⅓ cup of the warm water. Stir in 4 tablespoons of the flour, mixing well. Sprinkle a little more flour over the top, cover the bowl with a kitchen towel, and let stand until the sponge has swollen to twice its size.

To mix the dough the Italian way: Dump all the flour on your working surface and make a well in the center. Scrape the yeast sponge into it. Add the salt and ⅓ cup more water and start mixing gently with your hand, incorporating a little of the flour along the wall of the well into the liquid. Continue to add water, a little at a time, and to absorb more of the flour each time by folding it in with your hand in a circular motion until all is incorporated. Knead the dough until it is entirely smooth.

Or use our standard method: Combine the sponge with the remaining water, then add the flour, cup by cup, until you have a fairly stiff dough. Turn out and knead.

Flour the kitchen towel and place the dough inside, covering loosely. (Or place in an ungreased bowl and cover with plastic wrap.) Let rise until double in volume—1½ hours or more.

Prepare the chicken as soon as you set the dough to rise because you will want it to have cooled before you wrap the dough around it.

THE CHICKEN

1 chicken, about 4
   pounds
¼ pound chicken
   livers
2 carrots
1 large rib celery
1 medium-size red
   onion
2 ounces prosciutto
1 clove garlic
¼ cup olive oil
Salt and freshly
   ground pepper to
   taste
4–5 gratings nutmeg
   (about ¼ teaspoon)
½ cup red wine

Rinse out the cavity of the chicken and dry. Reserve the liver and add enough extra livers to make ¼ pound. Chop each piece in thirds.

Chop the carrots, celery, onion, and prosciutto in good-size, rough pieces; mince the garlic. Sauté all together in the olive oil in a cast-iron cocotte or a deep heavy pan with a cover for 5 minutes. Remove with a slotted spoon and reserve. Sauté the whole chicken now in the same pan, turning to brown all sides—about 15 minutes. Salt and pepper all over and grate nutmeg on top, then add wine to the pot. Cook uncovered until the wine has almost evaporated, then cover and cook 10 minutes. Sauté the chicken livers in the pan juice, stirring and tossing for a minute or two. Mix in the reserved vegetables and cook covered for 10 minutes. Remove the chicken and let cool.

Turn out the risen dough, punch down, and roll out on a floured surface into a piece that will be large enough to encompass the chicken. Salt and pepper the cavity and stuff with the sautéed vegetables and livers, reserving a little to tuck in between the joints. Rub the chicken all over with the residue in the pan, salt and pepper again, and place breast side down in the center of the dough. Pull the sides of the dough up, pinch the seams together, then flip the chicken over onto a greased baking sheet. Let stand for about 20 minutes—or 30–40 minutes if the dough is cold.

Bake in a preheated 375° oven for 1½ hours.

Let rest 5–10 minutes before serving. To carve, first cut off a large oval of bread from the top so you can get at the chicken to disjoint and slice the breast. Give everyone a good hunk of the delicious bread along with a portion of chicken and vegetable stuffing.

Whole Ham in a Bread Cozy

A century ago in the South it wasn't uncommon to seal a country ham in dough to prepare it for baking. An old Texas method calls for making a dough of corn meal and water to pat on the ham to a depth of three-quarters of an inch, and it has been reported that at meetings of the Colonial Dames at the Powder Magazine in Charleston, South Carolina, "ham baked in a dough blanket" was often served. The Carolina casing was a mixture of flour seasoned with brown sugar and spices and made into a paste with cider or peach pickle juice. Mrs. S. R. Dull, long the *Atlanta Journal*'s food writer, described how to mix flour and water to a "very stiff" consistency, then to apply it to the ham, patting on flour to cover, and putting it in a hot oven long enough for the dough to harden. After finishing in a slow oven, she said, "a ham cooked in this way is very juicy and most delicious." All these southern ways end with the casings discarded. Such a waste is not the result in our recipe—the dough makes real bread, which is redolent of honest ham seasoning.

3 tablespoons active dry yeast
7 cups warm water
4 teaspoons coarse salt or 2½ teaspoons table salt
½ cup whole wheat flour
4 cups rye flour
About 12 cups white flour, preferably unbleached
1 whole precooked ham

In a very large bowl—at least 5 quarts—dissolve the yeast in 1 cup of the warm water. Stir in the rest of the water, the salt, wheat flour, rye flour, and as much of the white flour as you can manage.

Now dump the dough out onto a well-floured surface and start scraping and kneading to incorporate as much more flour as the dough will absorb. You want to have quite a dry dough. Knead for at least 10 minutes until the dough is smooth and bouncy. Place it in a large kettle, big enough to allow it to double in volume (we use a big soup kettle), cover with plastic wrap, and let rise until double. It will be quite a slow rising—2 hours or more.

Turn the dough out onto a floured surface and punch down. Now pat or roll it about 1 inch thick, to a circumference that will envelope the whole ham. Place the ham on top, pull the sides of the dough up to meet, and pinch the ends securely together. Place seam side down on a lightly greased cookie sheet. Let rest for 25 minutes.

Spray the dough with water, then bake in a preheated 350° oven for 1½ hours. Let rest at least 15 minutes before serving. To serve, cut or tear off hunks of bread, put a piece on each diner's plate, then carve slices of ham against the bone.

Luncheon Pizza Roll

Food historians have traced the Neapolitan pizza (the word means pie) to Rome in the first century B.C. and say it is cited in a poem by Virgil. Always a bread designed to contain a filling, pizza changes at the whim of imaginative cooks. This version is a flavorsome pizza that is elegantly rolled to make an attractive luncheon dish, eaten with knife and fork.

Makes one 12-inch roll, serving 6

THE DOUGH

1½ teaspoons active dry yeast
1 cup warm water
2 tablespoons olive oil
1½ teaspoons coarse salt or 1 teaspoon table salt
¼ cup cake flour
About 2 cups white flour, preferably unbleached

THE FILLING

4–5 ripe tomatoes, peeled, seeded, and roughly chopped, or the equivalent amount canned, drained
1 medium onion, chopped
½ clove garlic, minced
1 tablespoon olive oil
10–12 black Mediterranean style olives, pitted
2–3 ounces peperoni, thinly sliced
4 ounces mozzarella, sliced

In a medium-size bowl dissolve the yeast in the warm water. Stir in the olive oil, salt, cake flour, and as much of the white flour as can be absorbed without the dough's getting too stiff to stir.

Turn the dough out and let it rest while you clean and oil the bowl. Knead the dough about 7–8 minutes, adding more flour as necessary, until it is smooth and bouncy. Return it to the bowl, cover with plastic wrap, and let rise until double in volume. Or put in a cool place and leave to rise overnight or all day.

In the meantime prepare the base of the filling: Sauté the tomato, onion, and garlic in the oil for about 5 minutes. Don't let it cook to a mush; the tomatoes should still hold their shape.

Turn the dough out on a large lightly floured surface. Punch it and spread it out, then roll it into a rectangle 12–13 inches by 8 inches. Distribute the tomato-onion mixture evenly all over, then add olives, peperoni, and mozzarella. Roll the dough up jelly-roll fashion, starting on a long side, pinch the seam together on the bottom, and place on an oiled cookie sheet, seam side down. Cover with a towel and let rise for 20 minutes.

Bake in a preheated 450° oven for 20 minutes. Serve hot.

Calzone Alicia

Another filled bread originating in Naples, calzone pizza (calzone means "pants leg"), is sometimes shaped like a crescent that is crimped around the edges like a Cornish pasty. It is more authentic, perhaps, shaped like a small football or stubby submarine as it is produced in brick ovens at Alice Waters' Chez Panisse in Berkeley. "Cut through this roomy pastry igloo, drinking in the heady scent of garlic," wrote the restaurant reporter Arthur Bloomfield, "and out runs a luxuriant river of cheese, both goat and mozzarella, aromatically harmonized with bits of prosciutto and a medley of herbs." Our last visit with Alice set us to adapting her professional methods to our own facilities. One Neopolitan recipe we encountered calls for chopped chicory hearts, unsalted anchovy fillets chopped fine, capers, black olive slices, currants, garlic, and an egg yolk. Marian Morash, the Victory Garden cook, favors a filling of chopped kale sautéed in garlic and oil with diced Genoa salami and slices of mozzarella.

Makes 3 calzones 6–7 inches to serve 6

1 recipe Rolled Pizza
  dough (p. 335)
¼ pound goat cheese
2–3 tablespoons cream
  (optional)
4 ounces mozzarella,
  coarsely grated
3 tablespoons grated
  cheese, ½ Swiss and
  ½ Parmesan or dry
  Jack
½ teaspoon minced
  garlic, or more if
  desired
½ teaspoon or more
  coarse salt
3 tablespoons chopped
  fresh herbs: Italian
  parsley, chives, basil,
  pinch rosemary or
  savory
¼ pound prosciutto or
  country ham, thinly
  sliced and chopped
Freshly ground pepper

Punch the dough down thoroughly after its first rising and cover with plastic wrap while you prepare the filling. Be sure to preheat your oven to 400° at least 15 minutes ahead; line it with tiles or a stone so that the baking surface gets hot.

Mash the goat cheese with the optional cream if it is rather dry, then work in the other cheeses. Mash the garlic with the salt and mix with the herbs and cheeses, along with the prosciutto or ham. Add pepper; taste and adjust seasonings.

Divide the dough into 3 parts. Roll each section, one at a time, into an oval about 7 inches long and 5 inches at its widest. Try to get the dough as thin as ¼ inch. Distribute the filling down the center of each oval. Paint the edges of the dough with the egg mixture, bring up the sides and ends to meet,

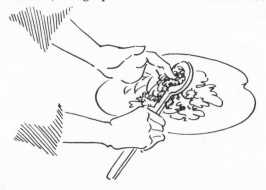

*1 egg beaten with 1
teaspoon water*
Corn meal

pinch them together securely, and then fold over. Paint the tops and sides with egg, adding extra around the seams and pressing down firmly to avoid leakage. Place on a corn-meal-sprinkled paddle or baking sheet and let rise 5 minutes. Slip the calzones onto hot oven tiles or a baking stone, seam side up (or if you don't have them, bake the calzones on your baking sheet).

Bake for 15 minutes at 400°, then turn the calzones, paint with egg, and prick in 2 or 3 places, lower heat to 350° and bake another 15 minutes. Serve warm.

Bubbat

Bubbat is a simple country-cooking way of baking bread dough with pieces of sausage tucked into it; as the bread rises and bakes, the dough swells up, almost enveloping the meat. It is a Russian Mennonite recipe introduced to America during the Mennonite immigration in the Plains States; you may use any firm smoked sausage, but we find that cooked Polish kielbasa seems just right. Serve bubbat hot with mustard and pickles.

Makes one 10-by-14-inch loaf to serve 6–8

*1 tablespoon active dry
yeast*
1½ cups warm milk
3 tablespoons sugar
1 egg, lightly beaten
*1 tablespoon coarse
salt or 1 teaspoon
table salt*
*3½–4 cups white flour,
preferably
unbleached*
*1 pound precooked
smoked sausage*

Put the yeast in a large bowl, stir in the warm milk and sugar, and let dissolve. Add the beaten egg, salt, and enough of the flour until the dough can barely be stirred with a spoon (you want a stiff dough). Cover the bowl with plastic wrap and let rise until double in volume—about 1 hour.

Punch the dough down, turn it out on a floured working surface, and knead lightly for just a few turns. Press into a 10-by-14-by-2-inch greased pan. Press 3-inch lengths of sausage at 3-inch intervals into the dough. Cover lightly with a towel and let rise again until the dough swells up around the sausages—about 30–40 minutes.

Bake in a preheated 400° oven for 10 minutes, then lower the heat to 350° and bake 20 minutes more.

Pâté in Brioche

A pâté blanketed in rich brioche dough makes a very elegant presentation—and tastes so good. There is no need to follow exactly the pâté recipe we give below. Play with the flavors and vary the ingredients, if you like. Or use instead your own well-seasoned meat loaf or even a store-bought pâté, since it must be cooked ahead of time anyway, then cooled, before you wrap the brioche dough around it.

Makes 1 large loaf to serve 8–10

¼ *pound chicken livers*

4 *shallots or whites of 6 scallions, chopped*

½ *cup cognac*

2 *pounds pork*

½ *pound pork fat*

3 *cloves garlic*

½ *teaspoon thyme*

½ *teaspoon rosemary*

1 *tablespoon coarse salt or 2 teaspoons table salt*

½ *teaspoon savory*

Freshly ground pepper

1 *teaspoon quatre épices (optional)*

¼ *cup chopped parsley*

1 *egg*

Pork fatback, cut in thin pieces

¼ *pound ham, cut in long strips*

3 *bay leaves*

Brioche recipe, page 192, doubled

1 *egg beaten with 2 teaspoons cream*

Marinate the chicken livers overnight in the shallots or scallions and cognac.

Put the pork, pork fat, and garlic through the medium blade of a meat grinder or chop them in a food processor. Mix in the thyme, rosemary, salt, savory, about ½ teaspoon of freshly ground pepper, the optional *quatre épices,* and parsley. Remove the chicken livers from their marinade. Beat the marinade and the egg into the ground meat mixture. Mix together thoroughly.

Line the bottom and sides of a 12-cup loaf pan with pieces of fatback. Spread half the meat mixture over the bottom, then distribute the chicken livers down the center and surround them with ham strips. Spread the remaining meat on top and lay 3 bay leaves evenly across its surface. Press strips of fatback on top and around the sides to meet the other pieces so the whole pâté is enveloped in fat. Cover with a double layer of aluminum foil tucked snugly around the pan and place it in a pan of boiling water that comes two-thirds of the way up the sides of the loaf pan. Bake in a preheated 350° oven for 1½ hours. Remove and put a weight on top of the foil (such as a couple of heavy cans). Let cool overnight.

Prepare the brioche dough and allow to rise in the refrigerator as directed. Cut off about three-quarters of the dough (wrapping and returning the remaining dough to the refrigerator for another use). Roll it out into a rectangle large enough to encompass the pâté. Remove the pâté from its pan, scrape off most of the fat, and place in the

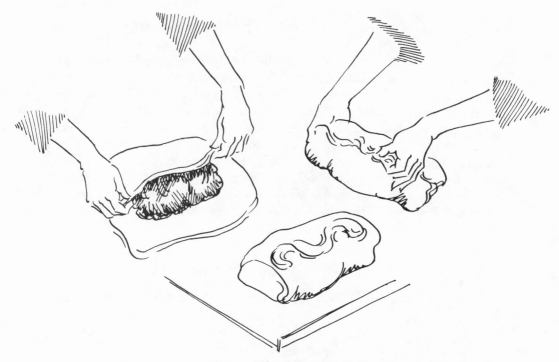

center of the dough. Pull the sides up all around and pinch the seams together, trimming any areas, such as the corners, where the dough is too thick. Turn over and place on a buttered baking sheet, seam side down. Roll out any scraps or pinch a small piece off the remaining dough and make decorations—either crescents or a rope you can coil into an elongated S-shape or whatever you like. Paint the brioche with the egg glaze, place decorations on top, and paint again. Let rest 10 minutes, then bake in a preheated 375° oven for 35–40 minutes until golden-crusted.

VARIATION: Sausage in brioche: Poach a 1-pound garlic sausage in simmering water to cover for 30 minutes. Remove, peel off the casing, and cool. Wrap in brioche dough (the amount reserved above or ½ the recipe on page 192 will be enough), pinch the seams together, and place, seam side down, on a buttered baking sheet. Glaze with egg, decorate with pastry bits if you wish, and bake in a preheated 375° oven for 35 minutes.

Armen's Chicken Boereg

In Armenia the word *boereg* describes stuffed and baked or fried pies of varying sizes that can be served as an hors d'oeuvre, main course, or dessert; it's the term also for a stuffed vegetable. The same word, spelled differently, is used in Turkey and other parts of the Middle East, and the dough in one region may be a simple bread mixture, a flaky paste, or it may be paper-thin filo. Meat fillings are often made of lamb, and combinations of spinach and cheese are very common. Savory fillings are sometimes accented by mint, as well as other herbs. We seem to remember the Levantine taste of mint (see below) in the first *boereg* we sampled, years ago, at Armen Bali's restaurant in San Francisco. Serve these crescents hot with lentil soup and a garden salad.

Makes 6 filled crescents

2 cups vegetable oil
(optional)

THE DOUGH

1 package active dry
  yeast
¾ cup warm water
1½ teaspoons coarse
  salt or 1 teaspoon
  table salt
1½–2 cups white flour,
  preferably
  unbleached

Boereg may be cooked in a skillet or fryer at 360°, or in a 350° oven; heat either the oil or the oven while preparing the dough. (The filling may be mixed in advance.)

Dissolve the yeast in lukewarm water, and stir in the salt and flour to make a fairly stiff dough. Knead on a floured surface, adding more flour as necessary, until the dough is smooth and resilient but still firm. Put the dough in an oiled bowl, cover with plastic wrap, and let stand 45 minutes.

To make the filling, mix all the ingredients and set aside.

When the dough has risen, knead for 2–3

THE FILLING

1 cup finely chopped
   cooked chicken
2 tablespoons minced
   parsley
4 scallions with some
   of the green, minced
1 teaspoon dried mint
⅓ cup finely chopped
   walnuts
1 slightly beaten egg
2 tablespoons yogurt
Salt and freshly
   ground pepper to
   taste

minutes and divide into 6 pieces of the same size. Roll out each with a rolling pin to form circles about ¼ inch thick.

Spoon the chicken filling onto the centers of each round of dough, dividing the mixture equally. Wet the rim of one side of each piece of dough and fold the other over to form a stuffed half-moon. Pinch the edges of the dough securely to hold filling in. Put the stuffed half-moons on a floured baking sheet, cover, and let stand for about 15 minutes.

If you are baking, slide the *boeregs* into the preheated 350° oven; bake 45 minutes.

To fry, cook the *boeregs* in preheated oil 2 or 3 at a time. Turn after 3–4 minutes and fry the same amount of time on the other side. Drain on paper towels.

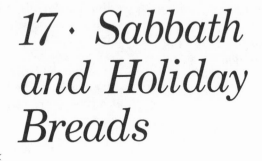

17 · Sabbath and Holiday Breads

Kings' Day Ring
Hot Cross Buns
Lussekatter or St. Lucia's Buns
Christmas Stollen
Greek Easter Bread—Lambrópsomo
Choereg
Christmas Wreath
Pain d'Epice
Minnesota Swedish Christmas Twists
Pannetone
Challah
Scotland's Black Bun

On an island near Hong Kong the wives of
fishermen make thousands of buns to be
piled together as slender towers in
gratitude for the sea's bounty, and the towers are climbed by young boys who
race to see who can bring down the bread that forms the peak. It is a festival
of bread which echoes the mood of many others in various parts of the world.
Bread seems always to have been celebrated, either at harvest time or on
religious days, and there is evidence that the hot cross buns that are baked for
English Easter eating go back to pagan rites of ancient Greece. Christstollen,
the sweet Christmas bread now so popular in this country, was made first
about A.D. 1400 in Dresden. Italy's pannetone is equally old. In many cases, as
time passed, such loaves became works of art, with recipes passed from one
generation to another. In this chapter we've chosen a few from various places
for you to try.

Kings' Day Ring

On the twelfth day of Christmas . . . on El Dio de Los Santos Reyes, Mexicans mark the arrival of the Three Kings in Bethlehem, and this bread of the kings is traditionally baked with a porcelain doll hidden in it. Whoever gets the piece of the bread containing the doll must give a party on Candlemas Day. Recipes for the bread ring vary—sometimes orange flower water is used, sometimes small figures made of dough are shaped on top of the ring, and usually there are citrus fruits or maraschino cherries in the dough.

Makes 1 large ring

1 tablespoon active dry
  yeast
¼ cup warm water
2½ cups white flour,
  preferably
  unbleached
½ teaspoon coarse salt
  or ¼ teaspoon table
  salt
¼ cup sugar
2 eggs, well beaten
4 egg yolks
8 tablespoons (1 stick)
  butter, softened
Grated rind of 1 lemon
1½ cups coarsely
  grated or finely
  chopped candied
  fruits and citron
1 tiny china doll
Melted butter

GLAZE

1 cup confectioner's
  sugar
2 tablespoons light
  cream

TOPPING:

Additional candied
  fruits and citron
Maraschino cherries,
  cut in half

In a large bowl add yeast to warm water and let it soften. Add 1¼ cups of the flour, the salt, sugar, beaten eggs, egg yolks, butter, and lemon rind, and beat until well blended. Stir in remaining flour to make a soft dough, adding a little extra flour if sticky. Turn out on a floured surface and knead about 5 minutes, until smooth and elastic.

Clean the bowl and butter it. Return the dough to the bowl, cover with plastic wrap, and let rise in a warm place until double in volume—about 1½ hours.

Turn the dough out, punch it down, knead in fruits, and shape into a ring, burying the tiny doll. Put ring on a greased baking sheet, and cover with plastic wrap; leave in a warm place for 2 hours, or until double in volume.

Brush ring with melted butter, and bake 30 minutes in preheated 350° oven. Allow to cool. Combine the confectioner's sugar and the light cream, and paint the top of the ring. Sprinkle top with additional fruits and citrus peel, and arrange cherry halves decoratively.

Hot Cross Buns

Baked in the old days on Good Friday and signed with a cross, hot cross buns were believed by many Britons never to get moldy, and they were often hung in kitchens as lucky charms.

Makes 18 buns

1¼ cups milk
2 tablespoons active dry yeast
3½–3¾ cups white flour, preferably unbleached
2 teaspoons coarse salt or 1 teaspoon table salt
2 tablespoons light brown sugar
1 teaspoon cinnamon
¾ teaspoon nutmeg
¼ teaspoon allspice
¼ teaspoon ground cloves
2 eggs
2 tablespoons butter, softened
½ cup currants

GLAZE
½ cup confectioner's sugar mixed with 2 teaspoons warm milk (optional)

Heat the milk just to lukewarm and pour it over the yeast in a cup.

In a large warm bowl mix 3½ cups flour with the salt, sugar, and spices. Make a well in the center and pour in the dissolved yeast. Stir and add the eggs, one at a time, and beat in the softened butter. Add a little more flour if necessary to make a firm dough. Fold in the currants, mixing them evenly through the dough.

Cover with plastic wrap and let rise until double in volume—about 2 hours.

Punch down the dough, turn it out onto a floured surface, and knead briefly—less than a minute. Lightly roll the dough out into a cylinder and with a knife cut off 18 even-size pieces. Shape

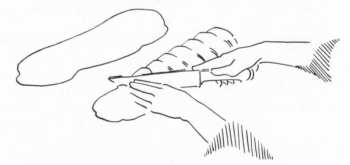

these into buns by rounding them with your two cupped hands, tucking under the sides, and pinching the seams together at the bottom. Place them on greased baking sheets 2 inches apart.

Cover the buns lightly with waxed paper and let them rise in a fairly warm place until double their size—about 35 minutes.

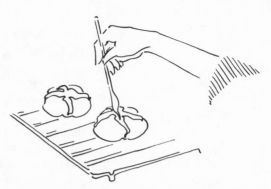

Just before baking, make a cross in each bun using scissors, snipping quite deep. Put them immediately into a preheated 425° oven for 10–15 minutes until golden.

The cross will have opened up in baking, but if you want to emphasize it and give a little flavor of sweet frosting, dip a chopstick or the wrong end of a wooden spoon into the sugar glaze and drizzle a little over the buns after they have cooled a bit, following the lines of the cross.

If you don't eat all the hot cross buns right away, they can be reheated or split and toasted.

Lussekatter, or St. Lucia's Buns

On December 13, when Scandinavians celebrate St. Lucia's Day, these fanciful buns known as Lucia's cats are baked in many households. As a part of the Christmas holiday, a young daughter of the family dons a long white dress and a crown of lingonberry twigs and lighted candles and joins with others in visiting neighbors to serve ginger cookies and saffron buns. Often the twisting of the sweet dough results in shapes that remind you of nestled kittens.

LUSSEKATTER, CONTINUED

Makes 24 buns

4–5 threads saffron
1 cup hot water
1 ½ tablespoons active
    dry yeast
½ cup warm water
¼ cup nonfat dry milk
⅔ cup sugar
1 teaspoon coarse salt
    or ½ teaspoon table
    salt
1 teaspoon grated
    orange rind
2 eggs
10 tablespoons (1 ¼
    sticks) melted butter
5 ½–6 cups white flour,
    preferably
    unbleached

Steep saffron in the hot water for 5–10 minutes.

In a large bowl dissolve the yeast in the warm water. When the saffron liquid is lukewarm, add that to the yeast along with the dry milk, sugar, salt, and grated orange rind. Beat in the eggs and the melted butter—making sure that it is only lukewarm. Stir in the white flour a cup at a time until it becomes hard to stir.

Turn the dough out onto a floured working surface to rest while you clean out and butter the bowl, keeping it in a warm place. Knead the dough, adding more flour as necessary, until you have a smooth and elastic dough—about 7–8 minutes. Return it to the bowl, turning to coat, cover with plastic wrap, and let rise in a warm place; it will take longer than the usual dough because of the butter and eggs—1 ½ hours or more.

GLAZE

1 egg beaten with 1
    teaspoon water
About ½ cup raisins
2 tablespoons sugar

Turn the dough out on a floured surface, punch it down, and divide it in 24 equal-size pieces. Then roll each one out into a strand about ¾ inch thick and coil it into a shape, such as those illustrated, always curling up the end pieces. Brush the *lussekatter* with the egg glaze, then tuck raisins in among the curlicues. Place on buttered baking sheets at least 1 ½ inches apart, cover lightly with towels, and let rise until double—about 30 minutes. Brush again with egg glaze, poke back any raisins that may have sprung loose, and sprinkle with sugar.

Bake in a preheated 400° oven for 20 minutes. Cover with a towel while cooling.

Christmas Stollen

Stollen is a traditional German Christmas bread that's made in a long loaf folded over like a pocketbook or giant Parkerhouse roll, studded with candied fruits and nuts and raisins, and glazed lightly with a snowy sugar frosting. Stollen keeps well and, in fact, tastes almost better a little dry, sliced and spread with sweet butter, so you can make these loaves several days before Christmas as gifts; they also freeze well.

Makes 3 large or 4 medium stollen

¾ cup candied orange peel

¾ cup candied lemon peel

¾ cup yellow raisins

¾ cup currants

½ cup hot water (with 2 tablespoons brandy, if wanted)

2 tablespoons active dry yeast

1 cup warm water

3 eggs, at room temperature

¼ cup nonfat dry milk

¾ cup sugar

2 teaspoons coarse salt or 1 teaspoon table salt

Grated peel of 2 lemons

1 teaspoon vanilla extract

6–6¾ cups white flour, preferably unbleached

10 tablespoons (1¼ sticks) softened sweet butter

1 cup slivered almonds

6 tablespoons melted sweet butter

Slice the orange and lemon peel into ½-inch pieces, unless it comes already diced. Toss with the raisins and currants in a bowl and cover with the hot water, tossing well to mix. Let stand about 45 minutes.

In a large bowl dissolve the yeast in ½ cup of the warm water. One by one beat in the eggs and continue beating until mixture is fluffy. Mix together the remaining water with the dry milk, suger, salt, grated lemon peel, and vanilla and beat into the yeast-egg mixture. Now drain the juices from the raisin-fruit mixture into the yeast and eggs, shaking your strainer to get all the liquid. Spread the fruits onto a piece of waxed paper and sprinkle ½ cup of the flour over them. Stir the cooled milk mixture into the yeast-egg bowl, then the remaining flour, cup by cup, until the dough thickens, holding back about ½ cup. Beat in the softened butter a little at a time.

Now turn out onto a well-floured surface and knead lightly—the dough will be sticky and you'll have to use your scraper—gradually adding the flour-coated fruits until all are absorbed. Knead about 10 minutes in all, adding more flour as necessary. Set aside ⅓ cup of the slivered almonds; chop up the rest roughly and work them into the dough. Clean the bowl, butter it well, and return the dough to it, turning to coat. Cover with plastic wrap and leave in a draft-free place to rise; be sure that it doubles in bulk, which can take at least 2 hours, maybe more, depending on how warm your kitchen is.

STOLLEN, CONTINUED

GLAZE

1 cup confectioner's
   sugar
2 tablespoons lemon
   juice
½ teaspoon vanilla
   extract

Turn the dough out on a floured surface and divide into 3 (or 4) parts. Pat into ovals about 10 inches long and 6 inches at the widest point (if making 4 stollen, the ovals will be about 7½ inches). Paint each oval generously with melted butter, sprinkle remaining sugar and slivered almonds over the surfaces, and fold over lengthwise, bringing the upper half only about two-thirds of the way over (see illustrations or see Parkerhouse Rolls). Press the edge down securely and brush the surface again with melted butter. Place on greased baking sheets, cover lightly with waxed paper, and let rise for 40 minutes or until the dough has spread by about 4 inches in length (this is not a dough that rises high). Bake in a preheated 350° oven for 45 minutes or until golden on top. Remove to cool on racks.

Prepare the glaze by mixing all the ingredients together and adding a few drops of water if it doesn't seem spreadable. Drizzle over the still warm stollen. Wrap when cool in plastic wrap or foil, sealing tightly, and refrigerate; it will keep a week to 10 days.

Greek Easter Bread— Lambrópsomo

Wherever Greeks have settled in America many of the housewives still mark the end of Lent by producing several kinds of traditional breads, including Lambrópsomo, or Easter bread. Lambrópsomo may or may not incorporate eggs that have been hard-boiled and dyed red; usually one egg is centered in a round leaf with a cross formed over it, or four red eggs will be nestled into a braided loaf. Our recipe calls for one loaf of each of these shapes. In some households the same bread without the red egg decoration is baked and served on Sunday throughout the year.

Makes 2 round loaves

2 tablespoons active
   dry yeast
½ cup warm water

In a large bowl mix yeast with warm water, then stir in milk, butter, and salt. Add the aniseed, the beaten eggs, the sugar, grated orange peel, and

1 cup warm milk
½ cup melted butter,
  at room temperature
2 teaspoons coarse salt
  or 1 teaspoon table
  salt
1 ½ teaspoons aniseed,
  crushed
3 eggs, beaten
½ cup sugar
1 tablespoon grated
  orange rind
¼ teaspoon mahleb
  (optional)
About 6 cups white
  flour, preferably
  unbleached
2–5 hard-boiled eggs,
  dyed red

GLAZE

Soft butter
Sesame seeds
  (optional)

optional mahleb. Keep stirring while adding the flour. When the mixture is stiff, turn out on a floured surface and knead about 10 minutes, until smooth and satiny.

Clean the bowl and grease it well. Put the dough in the bowl, and turn so all surfaces are oiled; cover with plastic and let rise about 2 hours, until doubled.

Punch the dough down, knead briefly, and divide in half to make the two different shapes (or make two loaves of the same shape if you prefer).

To make a round loaf with a cross with one half of the dough, first tear off a piece of dough—about one-fifth the whole amount. Form the larger piece into a round and put it on a greased baking sheet. Center one red egg on the top of the round. Divide the reserved piece in half and roll out 2 long strips. Place these over the egg in the form of a cross, tucking the ends under the loaf.

To make a braided crown with the other half, divide the dough in thirds and roll out into ropes at least 24 inches long. Braid the ropes together, pinching the ends securely, and then form into a circle on a greased baking sheet, pinching again the ends where they overlap. Nestle 4 red eggs in among the braids.

Cover both loaves with a kitchen towel and let rise 1 hour.

Bake in a preheated 350° oven for 30 minutes. Remove and brush immediately with butter, then sprinkle on optional sesame seeds.

Choereg

We used to get occasional culinary bulletins from a brother living in Moscow, and they were often tied to his strolls from his news bureau on Kutuzovsky Prospekt to Gastronom #1, the imposing food store founded by Ivan Filippov that sells everything from black bread to brandy from Armenia. In the old days, according to one bulletin, rye bread and buns baked by Filippov were shipped daily to the imperial court in St. Petersburg. "They tried to bake them near the palace but the results were unacceptable, and Filippov told everyone it was because the water used, from the Neva River, was bad. In addition, Filippov always froze his bread for shipping by a secret method when it was steaming hot—just before serving it was thawed in wet towels." Another casual bulletin from Tbilisi, Georgia, included the recipe below for choereg, the Easter bread that is often flavored with the essence of black cherry kernels. It is commonly either braided or formed into snail-shaped rolls. When *mahleb* (derived from black cherry pits) is unavailable, choereg may be seasoned with vanilla and anise, or grated lemon or orange rind.

Makes 4 small loaves or 8 snails

⅓ cup warm water
1 tablespoon active dry
   yeast
1¼ cups sour cream,
   at room temperature
2 eggs, slightly beaten
1 cup soft sweet butter
⅓ cup sugar
1½ teaspoons coarse
   salt or 1 teaspoon
   table salt
1 teaspoon vanilla
2 teaspoons ground
   aniseed
½ teaspoon baking
   soda
5½–6 cups white flour,
   preferably
   unbleached

GLAZE
1 egg, beaten
Sesame seeds or finely
   chopped almonds

In a large bowl mix warm water and yeast. Add sour cream, 2 beaten eggs, butter, sugar, salt, vanilla, aniseed, and baking soda, and mix thoroughly. Gradually stir in flour to make a soft dough. Scrape out onto a floured surface and knead until smooth. Clean the bowl and oil it lightly, put in the dough, and turn it so it is lightly greased. Cover and let rise in a warm place about 2 hours, until double in bulk.

Punch down the dough, and transfer to a floured work surface. Divide in 4 equal parts, then divide each of these in 3. To shape each loaf, roll 3 pieces of dough into ropes about 12 inches long. Braid these together and pinch the ends. To make snails, divide each of the 4 pieces in half. Roll each piece into a rope about 7 inches long. Coil each into a snail shape, starting with outside and coiling toward the center—it should hump up slightly in the middle. Arrange shapes on greased baking sheets, cover, and let rise in a warm place about 45 to 50 minutes, until doubled.

Brush the braids and/or snails with beaten egg; sprinkle with sesame seeds or almonds. Bake in preheated 350° oven about 30 minutes, until golden. Serve warm.

Christmas Wreath

Shaped into a large wreath and decorated with gla-céed red and green cherries, here is a handsome sweet bread that's nice to have around for the holidays.

Makes 1 large wreath

2 tablespoons active
   dry yeast
½ cup warm water
3 eggs, at room
   temperature
⅓ cup light brown
   sugar
½ teaspoon coarse salt
   or ¼ teaspoon table
   salt
½ cup sour cream, at
   room temperature
8 tablespoons (1 stick)
   sweet butter,
   softened
About 4 cups white
   flour, preferably
   unbleached
1 teaspoon vanilla
   extract
½ teaspoon almond
   extract
1 teaspoon grated
   lemon rind
½ cup currants

In a large bowl dissolve the yeast in the warm water. Beat in the eggs, one at a time, then the sugar, salt, and sour cream. Alternately beat in tablespoonfuls of softened butter and half cups of flour until the butter has been absorbed and you have a dough that starts to come away from the sides of the bowl. Stir in the vanilla and almond extract.

Turn the dough out onto a floured working surface and let rest while you clean and butter your bowl. Knead the dough lightly, adding more flour as necessary, for about 3 minutes; it will be a relatively soft dough and you shouldn't push down too hard on it as you knead. (Incidentally this is a good dough to mix and knead in the food processor, but reverse the process, spinning the flour first, then adding the butter, and finally the liquid ingredients, starting with the dissolved yeast.) Put the dough in the buttered bowl, cover with plastic wrap, and let rise in a warm place—it will take about 2 hours.

Turn the dough out on a floured surface and pat down. Pinch off a piece about the size of a lemon and reserve. Spread the currants over the bulk of the dough, knead lightly to incorporate, then divide into 2 pieces. Roll each piece out into a strand 24 inches long. Twist the 2 strands together and form into a circle on a buttered baking sheet,

CHRISTMAS WREATH, CONTINUED

GLAZE

*1 egg beaten with 1
  teaspoon cream*

TOPPING

*1 dozen glacéed red
  and green cherries
Angelica
1 dozen almond halves
  (optional)*

ICING

*½ cup confectioner's
  sugar
2 teaspoons water
½ teaspoon almond
  extract*

overlapping the ends and pinching them together securely. Enlarge the circle in the center as much as you can. Now roll out about half the reserved piece of dough into a long strand and make a bow with it. Flatten the remaining reserved dough, roll out thin with a rolling pin, and make small cutouts to resemble leaves. Paint the circle of dough all over with the egg glaze, then place the bow over the joined area, distribute leaves here and there and paint again. Let rise for 30 minutes and paint again.

Bake the wreath in a preheated 350° oven for 25 minutes. Remove and distribute the red and green cherries and/or pieces of angelica attractively around and, if you like, make stars of almond halves in 3 places on the surface (you may need to paint again with glaze to make your decorations stick). Return the wreath to the oven and bake another 5–8 minutes. Remove and cool a few minutes. Combine icing ingredients, then dab icing all over except on the bow, which you may want to rub with a little butter to bring up its contrasting color. Serve slightly warm with lots of sweet butter.

Pain d'Épice

This pungent spiced loaf, authentically based on rye flour and honey, goes back to the Crusades and the increase in the use by European cooks of spices from the Orient. Rivalry between Flemish bakers and those of Dijon was such that in A.D. 1595 Henri IV gave *lettres patente* to the latter, and the recipe the Burgundians perfected was accepted for some time as definitive. Ours is not definitive, perhaps, but it is as close to the *pain d'épice* we first tasted in Paris at Christmastime as we can come in an American kitchen.

Makes one 9-inch loaf

1 tablespoon active dry yeast
1½ cups warm water
1 teaspoon coarse salt or ½ teaspoon table salt
¾ cup dark honey (such as buckwheat or avocado)
2 teaspoons aniseed
1½ teaspoons allspice, freshly ground if possible
1½ teaspoons ground ginger
2¼–2½ cups rye flour
2¼–2¾ cups white flour, preferably unbleached
Soft butter

In a large bowl dissolve the yeast in the warm water. Stir in the salt, honey, spices, and 2 cups each of the rye and white flours.

Turn the dough out on a floured surface and let it rest while you wash out the bowl and oil it lightly. Scrape up the dough and start kneading, adding more rye and white flour as necessary; it will be very sticky. Knead for about 6–7 minutes until the dough becomes cohesive and loses most of its tackiness.

Place in the oiled bowl, turning to coat. Let rise in a fairly warm place—it will probably take about 3 hours.

Punch down the dough thoroughly and form into a 9-inch loaf. Place in a well-oiled bread pan, cover with a towel, and let rise until it reaches the top of the pan—about one-third again its original volume.

Bake in a preheated 325° oven 1 hour; cover lightly with foil, turn oven to 300° and bake 40 minutes longer. Rub soft butter over the top while hot, let rest in the pan 10 minutes, then turn out and cool thoroughly on a rack. Wrap securely in foil, then in a plastic bag to keep moist. Store in a cool place. It will keep several weeks.

Minnesota Swedish
Christmas Twists

Many cooks of Scandinavian heritage annually mark the holidays by deep-frying these small sweet breads known as *klenater* that are often flavored with brandy. Others make *fattigman,* which get their pronounced taste from cardamom seeds.

Makes about 40 twists

6 egg yolks
6 tablespoons
   confectioner's sugar
4 tablespoons soft
   butter
1 tablespoon brandy or
   rum
1 tablespoon grated
   lemon rind
2 cups white flour
Fat for deep frying

In a large bowl beat the eggs, stir in sugar and butter, then add the brandy or rum and the lemon rind. Add flour a little at a time and blend the mixture thoroughly. Cover and chill. Turn the dough out on a floured surface and roll until it is about ¼ inch thick. Cut into strips about 6 inches long and ¾ inch wide. Cut a long gash in the center of each strip and twist one end through it. Heat the fat to 375° and fry the twists 2–3 minutes, until golden brown.

Pannetone

This creation of Lombardy is one of those Christmas breads that is so rich some cooks call it cake. It is made and sold commercially now all over Italy, and we first tasted it during the blizzard of 1970 that struck the Mediterranean littoral just after Christmas. Savoring it for tea in the restaurant of Savona's Hotel Astoria may have been the only cheering thing on an aborted attempt to drive from Plascassier near Cannes to a farmhouse south of Florence. In the U.S., pannetone often helps to celebrate the Yuletide in California's Napa Valley, as well as in other localities settled by Italian families. Sometimes it is baked with a collar, like a soufflé, and its puffed-out top has been likened to the domes of northern Italian churches.

Makes 2 loaves, 7–8 inches high and 5 inches at the base

2 tablespoons active
    dry yeast
½ cup warm water
1 tablespoon nonfat
    dry milk
¾ cup sugar
1 teaspoon coarse salt
    or ½ teaspoon table
    salt
6 egg yolks
2 eggs
½ pound (2 sticks)
    sweet butter,
    softened
5½–6 cups white flour,
    preferably
    unbleached
1 cup yellow raisins
½ cup finely diced
    candied lemon peel
2 tablespoons finely
    chopped lemon peel
Confectioner's sugar
    for topping

In a large bowl dissolve the yeast in the warm water. Stir in the dry milk, sugar, salt, and then, one by one, beat in the egg yolks and the eggs. Alternately beat in large blobs of the soft butter and a cup of flour until all the butter has been absorbed and enough of the flour to make a soft dough.

Turn the dough out onto a floured working surface and let it rest while you clean and butter the bowl. Start kneading the dough, adding more flour as necessary, but use a light hand. Don't press down heavily on the dough; 5 minutes of kneading should be sufficient for it to become pliant and alive, though more sluggish than the usual dough. Return it to the bowl, cover with plastic wrap, and let rise in a warm place. You really will need a warm spot of over 80° for this dough, and still it may take as much as 3 hours for it to double in volume.

Punch the risen dough down, spread it out, and distribute the raisins, candied lemon, and chopped peel evenly over the surface. Then roll up and divide in half. Knead lightly and form each half into a plump ball less than 5 inches in diameter. Place in 2 small soufflélike baking dishes 5 inches in circumference, buttered on the bottom, into

PANNETONE, CONTINUED

which you have inserted a foil collar 7 inches high, buttered on the inside; have the end of the collars overlap and pin them together to make secure frames for the bread to rise in—otherwise the loaves can burst through the seams. Cover lightly with a kitchen towel and let rise in a warm place until double in volume—at least 1 hour.

Bake in a preheated 350° oven for 45 minutes. If the tops seem to be browning too much, cover with foil. When done, let cool in their baking dishes for 5 minutes, then remove the foil collars, and turn out. Sprinkle the tops with confectioner's sugar and let cool on racks.

Challah

Commonly available in Jewish delicatessens, this egg bread is at least as delicious when made at home. Because the use of stoves is forbidden on the Sabbath, it is traditional to bake challah on Thursday or Friday so that it is sure to be ready before sundown at the beginning of the holy day. At the Sabbath table the head of the family removes the cloth that covers the bread and says grace before slicing the loaf. Challah is most often braided, but it may be baked in various other shapes.

Makes 1 large loaf

1¼ tablespoons active dry yeast
¾ cup warm water
1 tablespoon sugar
2 teaspoons coarse salt or 1 teaspoon table salt
2 eggs, lightly beaten
2 tablespoons vegetable oil

Dissolve yeast in warm water in a large bowl. When dissolved, add sugar, salt, eggs, oil, and as much flour as can be stirred into the liquid 1 cup at a time. Turn out onto a floured board and knead at least 10 minutes, adding more flour as wanted, until dough is smooth and elastic. Put in oiled bowl, cover, and leave in a warm place until doubled in bulk.

Punch dough down, knead in a little more flour if too moist to handle, then divide into 2 portions.

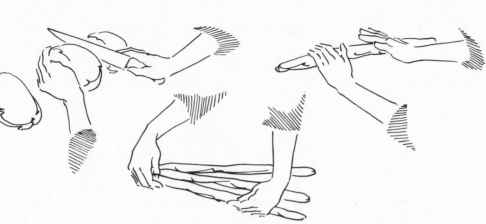

3½–3¾ *cups white flour, preferably unbleached*

GLAZE:

1 egg yolk mixed with ⅓ teaspoon water
Poppy seeds

Portion 1: cut into 3 equal parts, rolling each into ropes about 10 inches long. Pinch one end of each rope together, then braid, and pinch together other ends, to make one braided piece. Portion 2: divide into 2 pieces, one larger than the other; make braids of each piece as in Portion 1. Take first large braid and put it on a large cookie sheet; place next largest braid on top of first braid; top with smallest braid, each braid centered on the other. Press dough together at intervals to help braids remain in place. Cover and let rise at room temperature until double in bulk. Brush the braided loaf all over with egg glaze, and sprinkle with poppy seeds. Bake 10 minutes in a preheated 400° oven, then reduce oven heat to 375° and continue baking 35–40 minutes longer. Cool on rack.

Scotland's Black Bun

Grandfather McLeod's library was founded on the collected works of Sir Walter Scott in uniform bindings, and his Highland chauvinism generally was of such intensity that Hogmanay, or New Year's, must be marked by the serving of the traditional rich currant and raisin studded black bun. The family recipe was an adaptation, from a deteriorating copy of Mrs. Rundell's 1841 cookbook, in which Louisiana dark molasses was substituted for treacle. In the Hebrides and various other parts of Scotland recipes vary a great deal—especially when it comes to shape. Some think the term "bun" is used because proper loaves resemble giant buns. Cooks of Skye and Harris, however, often shape this holiday bread like a *pâté en croûte;* in Edinburgh and such places as Ecclesfechan, it is apt to look like a loaf of sandwich bread. Purist versions have interiors the color of a Christmas pudding, but our recipe, minus the molasses of the heritage instructions, relies on the dense, natural taste of dried fruits and almonds, sometimes with a splash of brandy. The bread crust surrounding the black bun is what keeps the interior so moist.

Makes 1 large round bun

1½ tablespoons active dry yeast
2 cups warm water
2 tablespoons sugar
¼ cup nonfat dry milk
1 tablespoon coarse salt or 2 teaspoons table salt
6½–7 cups white flour, preferably unbleached
12 tablespoons (1½ sticks) sweet butter, softened
1 cup chopped orange peel
¾ cup whole almonds
4 cups currants
1 cup black raisins
3 cups yellow raisins
¼ cup brandy (optional)
2 eggs

In a large bowl dissolve the yeast in the water. Stir in the sugar, dry milk, salt, and 1 cup flour. Add the softened butter a tablespoon at a time, alternating with ½ cup more flour. Continue until all the butter has been absorbed and enough of the flour added to make a dough that begins to leave the sides of the bowl.

Turn the dough out onto a floured working surface and let rest while you clean the bowl and butter it. Knead the dough about 8–10 minutes, adding more flour as necessary, to make a smooth, pliable dough. Return to the bowl, cover with plastic wrap, and let rise until double in volume—2 hours or more because of the considerable amount of butter.

Meanwhile prepare the black bun filling. Soak the orange peel in warm water to cover if the peel is very dry. Then drain and mix it with the almonds, currants, raisins, and optional brandy.

When the dough has doubled, turn it out and punch down thoroughly. Reserve a third of it, covered, while you mix the other two-thirds portion with the eggs and the dried fruit and nut

mixture. Knead to incorporate all the filling, and add a little more white flour, if necessary, to make a firm dough. Form into a bun about 7 inches in diameter, (or, if you prefer into two or three smaller buns) flattening it on top. Now roll the remaining dough out into a piece large enough to encompass the bun. Place the bun in the center and draw the sides of the dough up all around it. Where there is heavy overlapping of seams, trim the dough so it will not be too thick. Squeeze together the seams, and then turn the whole thing over into a 9-inch shallow buttered round casserole or a buttered ring (approximately 9 inches in diameter) placed on a greased baking sheet. Using a skewer, prick deep holes in the top about 2 inches apart, piercing straight through to the bottom. Let rest 10 minutes.

Bake the bun in a preheated 350° oven for 1 hour and 45 minutes. (If you have made smaller buns 1½ hours will be enough). Turn out of its casserole or ring and let cool on a rack. Wrapped in foil and then in plastic wrap, it will keep for a couple of weeks, to be brought out at teatime all through the holidays.

Helpful Equipment

Helpful Equipment for Mixing, Kneading, Shaping

MIXING BOWLS: You will need one or two nests of bowls made of stainless steel or pottery; plastic may be substituted if you don't mind the texture. Straight sides tend to make dough rise faster—not necessarily a desirable quality, however. The nests should include:

A large 5-quart bowl
A medium-size (7–8 cup) bowl
A small 3–4 cup bowl

SPATULAS: Hard plastic spatulas are very helpful for scraping sticky dough from sides of bowls; rubber spatulas are better for folding batter mixtures or cleaning viscous ingredients from a bowl. Metal spatulas are good for spreading icing.

MARBLE SLAB: A marble slab measuring at least 20 inches by 12 inches is very useful for making croissants and Danish pastries because the marble remains cool.

CROISSANT CUTTER: Just roll it over your croissant dough and you have the necessary perfect triangles. They come in various sizes, so check to get one that conforms with the size called for in our recipe.

BANNETON: A bowl-shaped form with ridges used for the second rising. Flour the banneton first and then the dough will slip out easily and hold the form as it bakes.

SPOONS: Large wooden spoons are by far the best for mixing bread dough.

DOUGH SCRAPER: Shaped something like a painter's scraper but more blunt, with a sharp edge for trimming dough, dough scrapers are most useful, the bigger the better. There is a huge 13-inch blade dough scraper from France—packaged two to the box—worth sending for (see mail order sources, p. 367); it scrapes the counter clean in a few sweeps and flips a large, sticky dough over with one easy flip. You can, of course, in a pinch use a painter's tool. (We have in our kitchen a small beautiful eighteenth-century cast-iron scraper probably made for a colonial bride—it has etched on its face a heart surrounding two pairs of initials, which proves that this has been a cherished home baker's tool for a long time.)

ROLLING PIN: Use a heavy ball-bearing pin. (In lieu of this, use a large round glass bottle.)

TORTILLA PRESS: Essential for making tortillas (see page 286 for details).

PASTRY BRUSHES: A soft brush is best for glazing risen dough; even nicer is a feather especially treated (as a matter of fact, in a pinch you can use any good-size clean feather or, as we've done in the country, a dried wheat stalk).

PASTRY BLENDER: Useful for cutting fat into flour when making biscuits, but two knives will do.

THERMOMETERS: A bar model thermometer is very useful for deep frying. We don't recommend thermometers for dissolving yeast; you should learn to gauge the temperature of the solution by sticking a finger in, but if you're really in doubt you can always use the fat thermometer.

PLASTIC WRAP: Essential, we find, for covering bowls of rising dough. Use a heavy wrap for freezing breads.

KITCHEN TOWELS: To cover formed loaves, a kitchen towel is best because it is less apt to stick. Any material, except terry cloth, is fine.

Helpful Equipment for Baking

BREAD PANS: 9 inches by 5 inches by 3 inches (6 cups) 8½ inches by 4½ inches by 2½ inches (5 cups) 4¾ inches by 3¼ inches by 2¼ inches (2 cups) The higher-priced blue steel, or black metal, pans are recommended to give a crustier loaf; these pans can be bought with a slide-in top to make pullman loaves, measuring 7 inches by 3½ inches by 3½ inches, and in other odd sizes (recipes must be adjusted accordingly).

FRENCH BREAD PLAQUES: 18-inch-long double trough shapes, usually in black metal, to make 2 French loaves about 2¼ inches wide. To improvise your own, see suggestion page 60.

BAKING SHEETS: You'll need two, 17½ inches by 13½ inches. The heavy blue steel or black metal ones are excellent. Nonstick surfaces are good, too, but be sure to get top quality or the surface will wear off.

MUFFIN PANS: Standard large size have cups that measure 2¾ inches across the top with a ½ cup capacity. Get pans that will take a dozen muffins. Nonstick pans are good for sticky buns. Cast-iron gem pans hold slightly less but they give a good crust and the muffins stand higher; however, they are heavy and hard to clean. Muffin pans with very small cups measuring 1¾ inches across the top with only 1 ounce capacity—usually identified as small cupcake pans—are highly recommended for miniature crusty muffins. Get two if you like the results as much as we do.

CAST-IRON CORN STICK MOLD: Made of heavy iron, this will give you 7 crusty cornsticks about 5 inches long.

BUNDT PAN: These are sold with non-stick interior; they are nice for making bubble breads, but a tube cake pan will do.

ROMERTOPF CLAY COOKER: The largest size provides a clay oven for baking smallish oval loaves (the risen dough should not touch the clay) giving them a lovely crust. Better still is . . .

LA CLOCHE: A large unglazed earthenware circular platter with a bell top, in which you can bake good-sized round loaves. When put in a hot oven, La Cloche—like the Romertopf—becomes a clay oven within an oven, and the loaf thus baked rises beautifully and evenly, forming a splendid crust.

STEAMING DEVICE: A plant atomizer is excellent when spraying loaves in the oven. Another way to make steam calls for a shallow pan of water to be set in the oven, in which a very hot metal object (we use an old-fashioned iron) can be placed, thus creating billows of steam.

TILES OR BAKING STONES AND WOODEN PADDLE: To line the rack of the oven so that you can bake directly on this hot surface for the same effect that bakers get when they shovel loaves directly onto a hot brick floor. Tiles can be obtained from a building supply company. Baking stone and paddle can be obtained from Creative Kits, see source list that follows.

For the Finished Loaf

BREAD KNIFE: A good long, serrated knife is essential for cutting bread.

PIZZA CUTTER: Helpful also in cutting strips of dough.

ENGLISH MUFFIN BREAKER: Fashioned so that two sets of prongs can be inserted into the center of an English muffin and pulled apart, tearing the muffin gently in half.

ALUMINUM FOIL: For freezing loaves or individual shapes, wrap each separately first in plastic wrap and then foil for added protection. Foil is particularly good for thin French loaves because you can wrap it tightly around, thereby helping to eliminate the ice crystals that sometimes form between the bread and the crust.

Electrical Appliances

STANDING MIXER WITH DOUGH HOOK: As you may have read in Chapter 2, the making of bread dough by hand can be a beautiful experience; but it can certainly be simplified in terms of effort by the use of a heavy duty electric mixer with a specially designed dough hook. Before buying one of the mixers made by various manufacturers, be sure that the bowl is a large one with a rounded bottom and that the model is equipped with a pouring shield or splash cover, a kneading hook, and balloon whip.

FOOD PROCESSOR: The food processor is also helpful in mixing and kneading limited amounts of bread dough and in puréeing, chopping, etc., some of the ingredients that go into our doughs. Be sure you have a model with a strong motor. For information about bowl capacity and a dome top to increase the capacity, see page 39.

ELECTRIC FRY PAN: Good for making doughnuts and other fried breads. We like the models that have stainless steel or simple chrome finishes that can be kept clean easily; the heat control should be detachable so the pans can be immersed for washing. Heat settings should be from 250° to 420° with control to maintain a steady temperature during frying.

Mail Order Sources

STONE-GROUND FLOUR AND MEAL

Buck's General Store
  (for blue cornmeal)
P.O. Box 13567
Albuquerque, N.M. 87112

Byrd Mill,
Louisa, Virginia 23093

DeBole's Nutritional Food, Inc.
  (for Jerusalem artichoke flour)
2120 Jericho Turnpike
Garden City Park, N.Y. 11040

Edwards Mill,
School of the Ozarks,
Point Lookout, Missouri 65726

Elams,
2625 Gardner Road,
Broadview, Illinois 60153

El Molino,
Box 2250,
City of Industry, California 91746

Kenyon Mill,
Usquepaugh, Rhode Island 02836

Moore's Flour Mill,
1605 Shasta Street,
Redding, California 96001

Vermont Country Store,
Weston, Vermont 05161

Walnut Acres,
Penns Creek, Pennsylvania 17862

HOME GRAIN MILLS

Magic Mill,
235 West 200 South,
Salt Lake City, Utah 84101

R & R Mill Company,
45 West North,
Smithfield, Utah 84335

Retsel Corporation,
McCammon, Idaho 83250

SPECIAL BREADMAKING EQUIPMENT

The Bridge Company,
214 East 52nd Street,
New York, New York 10022

Cross Imports,
P.O. Box 128,
Newton Highlands, Massachusetts
02161–0128

Creative Kits,
P.O. Box 351,
Medford Lakes, New Jersey 08055

Sassafras Enterprises Inc.,
P.O. Box 1366,
Evanston, Illinois 60204

Williams-Sonoma,
576 Sutton Street,
San Francisco, California 94102

Index

"A.B.C." (aerated) bread, 24
African breads:
  Arab, 99–100
  turmeric and black caraway seed, 150
  yams, dried and ground, discussed,
    142
alfalfa sprouts:
  in soy and graham bread, 137
  sprouting method, 137
all-purpose flour, 29
almond(s):
  and apricot bread, 214–15
  in black bun, 360–61
  on *choereg* (Easter bread), 352
  in Christmas stollen, 349–50
  on saffron sweet bread, 179
  -strawberry breakfast bread, 219
Anadama bread, 85–86
anchovies, in pizza filling, 305
animal-shaped bread, 322–23 and *illus.*
aniseed:
  in *choereg* (Easter bread), 352
  in Greek Easter bread (*lambrópsomo*),
    350–51
  in *limpa* (Swedish rye bread), 116
  in Moroccan or Tunisian bread, 99–
    100
  in *pain d'épice*, 355
  in *vorterkaker* (Norwegian rye flat
    bread), 310
apple(s):
  filling for Danish pastry, 206
  in meal-in-a-muffin (with cheese,
    nuts), 233
  muffins, 231
apple cider, in applesauce and hazelnut
    bread, 127–28
applesauce and hazelnut bread, 127–28

apricot:
  and almond bread, 214–15
  filling:
    for Danish pastry, 205
    for kolache, 190
Armen's chicken boereg, 340
ash cakes (or hoe cakes), 294
avocado rolls, 172
Azouz, Fatima, 99

bacon and peanut butter muffins,
    237
bagels, 267–68 and *illus.*
  discussed, 266, 267
baguette, 15–16, 43
  of cheese bread, 134
  shaping, 45
  see also French bread
baker's oven:
  ancient, 15 and n.
  for French bread, 64–65
  steam in, *see* steam
  tandoor (Indian, of clay), 290
baker's stone, 47, 365
baking bread, 47
  testing for doneness, 47
baking powder, 25–26
  breads, *see* quick breads
  see also soda bread
Bali, Armen, 340
banana:
  bread, 212
  -carrot bread, 213
  flour, mentioned, 150
Bandon (Oregon) Cranberry Festival,
    167
bara brith (Welsh raisin bread), 147
bara planc (Welsh planc bread), 284–85

barley:
    ancient cultivation of, 14
    bread:
        with malt syrup, 101
        with pearl barley, 102–103
        Welsh, 101–102
barley malt, homemade, 36
    in barley bread, 101
    in Jewish rolled raisin bread, 119–20
    in *limpa* (Swedish rye bread), 116
    in pumpernickel bread, 114
    in tofu bread, 72
basic white bread, 55–57
    sponge method, 57
basil:
    in calzone Alicia, 336–37
    in herb wheat bread, 78–79
    in pizza filling, 305
Basque bread, discussed, 48–49
Bath buns, 189
    discussed, 187
Bath Olivers, discussed, 187
batter bread, 73
Bedouin breads, discussed, 15
bean curd, 34
    bread, 72
    and carrot and soy milk muffins, 234–
        35
    and spinach muffins, 233–34
Beard, James, 99, 136
    American Cookery, 236
Beecher, Catharine, 217
beer:
    bread (rye), 112–13
    rolls, Brazilian, 169
beet and carrot bread, dill-flavored, 136
beignets (fritters), of wild rice, 260–61
Belle, Nelle Key, 69 n.
Bergner, John, 251
berries, *see* blueberries; cranberry; elder-
    berry; strawberry
Bird, Isabella: *Lady's Life in the Rocky
    Mountains, A*, 228
birnbrot, discussed, 126
biscuit muffins, Karen's, 238–39
biscuits, 244
    buckwheat, 245
    buttermilk, 244–45
    crackling (*tepertös pogácsa*), 246
    sourdough, 247
black bread, 16, 110
    American, 120
    darkening agents for, 120
    see also pumpernickel bread
black bun, Scottish, 360–61 and *illus.*
black walnut(s), 224
    and prune and tea bread, 224

black walnut(s) (*cont.*)
    and quince bread, 220
    and rosemary round loaf, 140
blinis, buckwheat, 283–84
Bloomfield, Arthur, 336
blueberry/ies, 280
    muffins, 229
    -orange bread, 213–14
    pancakes, 280
blue corn:
    pancakes, 282–83
    tortillas, 286–87
boereg, chicken, 340–41
bolting (winnowing), 28
Bornholm, Denmark, 121
Boston brown bread, 271 and *illus.*
    discussed, 16, 49, 266, 271
Boswell, James, 286
bowl, buttering (or oiling) of, 37
braided or twisted loaf, 44, and *illus.*
bran:
    and buckwheat bread, 92
    in Danish wheat-rye bread, 121
    graham rolls, 162
    in mixed grains bread, 84–85
    muffins, 230
    in pumpernickel bread, 115
    in whole wheat bread with ham and
        cheese, 148
Brazilian beer rolls, 169
bread crumbs:
    freezing of, 55
    from white bread, 54–55
    bread dumplings, 269–70
bread flour, 29
bread sticks (grissini), 326–27
brewer's yeast, 24
brick ovens:
    New England, 118
    Palermo bakery, 130
brioches, 192–93 and *illus.*
    discussed, 191
    food processor method, 194
    pâté in, 338–39 and *illus.*
    sausage in, 339
    tins for, 192
broa (Portuguese corn bread), 88–89
Bronwyn's orange-flavored zucchini
    bread, 215
Brown, Helen Evans: *West Coast Cook-
    book,* 261
brown bread, Boston, 271 and *illus.*
    discussed, 16, 49, 266, 271
brown rice:
    bread, 96–97
    flour, in bread, 96–97
brown sugar doughnuts, 253

bubbat (sausage in bread dough), 337
bubble bread, 318–19 and *illus.*
  as flowerpot bread, 320
buckwheat, 91
  biscuits, 245
  blinis (thin pancakes), 283–84
  with bran, 92
  bread, 91
  flour, 92
Bugialli, Giuliano: *Fine Art of Italian
    Cooking, The,* 331
bulgur (cracked wheat), 32, 90
  and honey bread, 90
Bun House, Pimlico Road, London, 187
buns, 187
  basic dough, 188
  Bath, 189
    discussed, 187
  black, Scottish, 360–61
  Chelsea, 188
    discussed, 187
  Chinese, steamed, 274
    discussed, 16, 50, 273
    filled with pork, 275
  hot cross, 346–47 and *illus.*
    discussed, 178, 344, 346
  kolache, 190
  lussekatter, 347–48
  see also rolls; sweet rolls
burst loaf, and solution, 50
butter, for bread dough, 33
buttermilk:
  biscuits, 244–45
    batter, for skillet scallion bread, 291
  in bran muffins, 230
  bread, 58
  in corn bread, 225
    Texas style, 295
  doughnuts, 253
  how to make, 59
  in macadamia nut and maple syrup
    bread, 218–19
  pancakes, 279 and *illus.*
    sunflower, 282
    wheat, 280–81
  in pumpkin corn meal muffins, 237
  in quince and black walnut bread, 220
  rolls, with honey, 161
buttermilk, winter, 59
butterscotch rolls, 186

campfire bread, discussed, 49
Canadian buttermilk honey rolls, 161
caramel:
  how to make, 35
  in Jewish rolled raisin bread, 119–20
  in pumpernickel bread, 113, 114

caramel (*cont.*)
  in rye beer bread, 112–13
caraway seed(s):
  in American black bread, 120
  black, and turmeric bread, 150
  on bread sticks, 327
  and mustard seed loaf, 222
  in rye beer bread, 112–13
  on rye twists (rolls), 173
Carolina Low Country, 96
carrot(s):
  -banana bread, 213
  and beet bread, dill-flavored, 136
  bread, 217–18
  -ginger bread, 129–30
  and tofu and soy milk muffins, 234–35
casings of bread:
  calzone Alicia, 336–37
  chicken *boereg,* 340–41
  ham (whole) in bread cozy, 334
  Italian pork bread, 130–32, *illus.*
    131–32
  pâté in brioche, 338–39 and *illus.*
  pollo in pane, 331–33
  sausage in brioche, 339
Caspian Pond Sunday corn bread, 86–87
casserole of yeast bread with corn
    "milk," 135
castagnaccio, discussed, 141
Caucasus Mountains, 58
cauliflower, in paratha filling, 293
celeriac-potato rolls (or bread), 163
challah, 358–59 and *illus.*
chapatis, discussed, 292
chauquehue, discussed, 282
Cheddar cheese:
  bread, 134
    as flowerpot bread, 321
  in corn bread with sesame seeds,
    294–95
  in meal-in-a-muffin (with apples,
    nuts), 233
  popovers, 243
cheese:
  bread, 134
    as flowerpot bread, 321
    with triticale and honey, 145
  in calzone Alicia, 336–37
  corn bread with sesame seeds, skillet-
    baked, 294–95
  cushions (*khachapuri*), 174–75 and
    illus.
  filling for Danish pastry, 206
  and ham whole wheat bread, 148
  in meal-in-a-muffin (with apples,
    nuts), 233
  in pita filling, 303

cheese (*cont.*)
  on pizza, 305, 335
  popovers, 243
Chelsea buns, 188
  discussed, 187
chernyi klib (rye bread), discussed, 17
chestnut(s), with chestnut flour bread, 141–42
chestnut flour:
  bread (or rolls) with chestnuts, 141–42
  in *pisticcini*, 207
chicken:
  boereg, 340–41
  pollo in pane, 331–33
chicken livers:
  in pâté in brioche, 338–39
  in *pollo in pane*, 331–33
chickpea flour, in socca, 307
Child, Julia and Paul, 60
Chinese breads:
  fried scallion bread, 262–63 and *illus.*
  steamed buns (*man-t'ou*), 274
    discussed, 16, 50, 273
    filled with pork, 275
Chinese parsley (cilantro), and curry and scallion bread, 151
chive(s):
  in biscuit-muffins, 238–39
  in calzone Alicia, 336–37
  in herb wheat bread, 78–79
choereg, 352
Christmas breads:
  Minnesota Swedish twists, 356
  pannetone, 357–58 and *illus.*
    discussed, 344, 357
  stollen, 349–50
    discussed, 344
  wreath, 353–54 and *illus.*
cider, in applesauce and hazelnut bread, 127–28
cilantro (Chinese parsley), and curry and scallion bread, 151
Cloche, La, 46, 47–48 and n., 365
  for Coburg loaf, 80
  for curry, cilantro, and scallion bread, 151
  for fig bread, with lemon zest, 149
  for olive bread with mint, onions, 144
  for rosemary and black walnut loaf, 140
  for Welsh planc bread, 284
  for whole wheat bread with cheese and ham, 148
Coburg loaf, 80–81 and *illus.*
  discussed, 16, 43, 45
coconut milk, in hoppers, 297

coffee cakes:
  Danish pastries, 199–206 and *illus.*
  Mennonite Streuselkuchen, 181
  ring, 182–83 and *illus.*
cookbooks:
  Beard, James: *American Cookery,* 236
  Brown, Helen Evans: *West Coast Cookbook,* 261
  Bugialli, Giuliano: *Fine Art of Italian Cooking, The,* 331
  Cook's Own Book, The, 221
  Hazan, Marcella: *More Classic Italian Cooking,* 331
  Jaffrey, Madhur: *World-of-the-East Vegetarian Cooking,* 234 n., 272
  King, Louise Tate, and Jean Stewart Wexler: *Martha's Vineyard Cookbook, The,* 280
  Lang, George: *Cuisine of Hungary, The,* 17, 178
  Lewis, Edna: *Taste of Country Cooking, The,* 241
  Manning, James: *Nature of Bread, The,* 9
  May, Robert: *Accomplisht Cook, The,* 112
  Roden, Claudia: *Book of Middle Eastern Food, A,* 301
  of Rundell, Mrs., 360
  World of Cheese, The, 134, 243
corn bread:
  Caspian Pond Sunday type, 86–87
  discussed, 17
  with oatmeal, 87–88
  Portuguese (*broa*), 88–89
  skillet-baked, with sesame seeds, cheese, 294–95
  with sour cream or buttermilk, 225
  Texas style, soft-as-pie, 295
  Walden wheat type (cooked in skillet), 89
corn meal:
  in Anadama bread, 85–86
  bread, *see* corn bread
  in hush puppies, 260
    discussed, 49
  in mixed grains bread, 84–85
  pancakes (as for blue corn), 282–83
  in Philpy (rice bread), 94–95
  in pumpernickel bread, 114
  -pumpkin muffins, 237
  in ryaninjun bread, 118
  sticks, *see* corn sticks
  in togus bread, 272
  varieties, 31, 86

corn "milk" (i.e. scraped), and yeast
    bread casserole, 135
corn sticks:
  corn meal and corn kernel, 240
  crackling bread type, 241
  peanut butter, 239
Corsican bread:
  pisticcini, 207
    discussed, 141
cottage cheese:
  pancakes, 281
  and zucchini graham bread, 146
cottage loaf:
  discussed, 16, 45
  oatmeal, 82–83 and *illus.*
cracked wheat, 32, 90
  and honey bread, 90
crackling(s):
  biscuits (*tepertös pogácsa*), 246
  bread sticks, 241
  how to make, 241
cranberry rolls, spiced, 167
cream of wheat *idlis,* 272–73
crempoq, 296
crêpes breton, discussed, 283
croissants, 195–98 and *illus.*
  discussed, 33–34, 191, 194–95
crumpets, 296
curry:
  and cilantro and scallion bread, 151
  in paratha filling, 293
Cypriot bread:
  olive, with mint and onions, 144
Cyprus, 144
Czechoslovakian breads:
  houskove knedlicky (bread dump-
    lings), 269–70
  kolache, 190

Danish bread:
  wheat-rye, with wheat kernels, 121
  see also Scandinavian breads
Danish pastries, 199–206
  braid, 203
  cockscombs, 201 and *illus.*
  coffee ring, 203
  dough, 199–200
  fillings for, 204–206
  icing for, 206
  lattice-work strip, 204 and *illus.*
  packages, 202
  pinwheels, 202 and *illus.*
  snails, 200 and *illus.*
dark (or black) bread:
  American, 120
  darkening agents for, 120

dark (or black) bread (*cont.*)
  discussed, 16, 110
  see also pumpernickel bread
date(s):
  -nut muffins, 236
  in wheat honey loaf, 211
Dauglish, John, 24
David, Elizabeth, 16
DeBole, Anthony, 105
DeGouy, Louis P., 228
dill:
  in beet and carrot bread, 136
  in biscuit-muffins, 238–39
  casserole bread, 128–29
dinner rolls:
  basic, 156–57 and *illus.*
  Parker House, 158 and *illus.*
  variant shapes, 158–59 and *illus.*
double loaf, 44 and *illus.*
dough:
  freezing, 50
  hurrying, 51
  kneading:
    in electric mixer, 38
    in food processor, 38–39
    by hand, 39–41, *illus.* 40
  mixing, 36–37
    in electric mixer, 38
    in food processor, 38–39
  rising, 41–43, 46, 51
  sponge method, 41, 57
doughnuts:
  brown sugar, 253
  buttermilk, 253
  discussed, 250, 251
  plain, 252
  raised, 254
    jelly, 255
Dull, Mrs. S. R., 334
dumplings, 269
  discussed, 266, 269
  made with bread, 269, 70

Earl Grey tea rolls, 171
ear-of-wheat shaped loaf, 64 and *illus.*
Easter bread:
  Greek (*lambrópsomo*) 350–51
  Russian (*choereg*), 352
Egyptian bread, ancient, 15, 16
elderberry muffins, 231–32
eliopsomo (olive bread with mint and
    onions), 144
English breads:
  Bath and Chelsea buns, 187–89
  Coburg loaf, 16, 80–81

English breads: cottage loaf (*cont.*)
 discussed, 16
 oatmeal, 82–83
crumpets, 296
hot cross buns, 346–47 and *illus.*
 discussed, 178, 344, 346
saffron, 71
see also Irish soda bread; Scottish
 breads; Welsh breads
English muffins, 288–89 and *illus.*
equipment, 363–66
 appliances, electric, 365–66
 crumpet rings, 296
 electric mixer, 38
 food processor, 38–9
 Magic Mill II, 28
 mail order sources (list), 367
 for mixing, kneading, shaping, 363–65
 muffin tins, 228
 Retsel home grinder, 28
 stovepipe, 60
 tortilla press (*comal*), 287, 364
 wok, 296
 see also *Cloche, La*

Falzone, Gaetano, 316
Fastnachts, 255–56
fats for bread dough, 32–33
fennel seeds:
 in American black bread, 120
 on bread sticks, 327
 in *vorterkaker* (Norwegian rye flat
  bread), 310
fig bread, with lemon zest, 149
Filippos, Ivan, 351–52
Finnish bread:
 hapanleipa (flat sour rye), 308–309
  and *illus.*
 see also Scandinavian breads
FitzGibbon, Theodora, 187
flat breads:
 flatbröd (Scandinavian), 310–11
 hapanleipa (Finnish sour rye), 308–
  309 and *illus.*
 pita, 301–302
 pizza, 304–305
 socca, 307
 vorterkaker (Norwegian rye), 309–10
 zata (or pideh), 306
Florence, Italy, 331
flour:
 mail order sources (list), 367
 milling of, 18, 26–28
  home processing, machines for, 28
  stone-ground, 27–28
 purity/contamination of, 16, 124

flour (*cont.*)
 types, description of, 28–32
 see also specific flours, e.g. rye flour
flowerpot breads, 320 and *illus.*, 321
 sunflower meal bread as, 138
fly-away rolls, Helen Brown's, 261–62
focaccia, discussed, 15
food processor, 38–39
 see also individual recipes
fogli di musica, discussed, 15
free-form sculptured bread, 322–23 and
 illus.
freezing:
 bread, 50
 bread crumbs, 55
 dough, 50
 French bread, 63
French bread, 60–66, *illus.* 61–62
 baguettes, 60–64, *illus.* 61–62
 ear-of-wheat shaped, 64 and *illus.*
 pans (plaques) for, 363
  homemade, 60 and *illus.*
 freezing, 63
 round loaves, 65–66
French breads:
 breakfast, 191
 brioches, 192–94
 croissants, 194–98
 crêpes breton, discussed, 283
 pain d'épice, 355
  discussed, 211
 socca, 307
fried breads:
 Chinese scallion, 262–63
 discussed, 49, 250
 doughnuts, 252–54
 Fastnachts, 255–56
 fly-away rolls, Helen Brown's, 261–62
 hush puppies, 260
 Navajo type, 256–57
 puris, 258–59
 sopaipillas, 257–58
 wild rice beignets, or fritters, 260–61
 see also skillet breads
fritters, wild rice, 260–61
Froissart, Jean, 278
fruit, *see* apple(s); applesauce; apricot;
 banana; blueberry/ies; cranberry;
 date(s); fig; elderberry; orange;
 pear; prune; raisin(s); rhubarb;
 strawberry

Gericke, Søren, 117
German breads:
 Christmas stollen, 349–50
 Fastnachts, 255–56

German breads (*cont.*)
Streuselkuchen, 181
ginger:
-carrot bread, 129–30
in cranberry rolls, 167
grating (method), 166 n.
in green tomato bread, 216
in *pain d'épice*, 355
sweet potato rolls, 166
gingerbread, Grandma McLeod's, 221
glaze for bread, 46
gluten flour, 31
Goldberg, Molly, 267
Good Friday, 178, 346
Graham, Sylvester, 10, 29
graham (flour):
bran rolls, 162
discussed, 29
in English muffins, 288–89
and soy bread, with alfalfa sprouts,
137
in sprouted wheatberry bread, 93–94
and zucchini and cottage cheese
bread, 146
grain mills, 28
mail order sources (list), 367
grains, ancient, 14, 15, 76
Grandma McLeod's gingerbread, 221
Greek breads:
for Easter (*lambrópsomo*), 350–51
fig, with lemon zest, 149
see also eliopsomo, 144
Green Mountain green tomato bread,
216
Gregory, Hanson, 251
griddle cakes (pancakes):
blueberry, 280
blue corn, 282–83
buckwheat (thin), 283–84
buttermilk, 279 and *illus.*
cottage cheese, 281
Scottish, discussed, 278
sunflower, 282
wheat, 280–81
Grigson, Jane, 189 n.
grissini (crisp bread sticks), 326–27

Hahn, Inger, 199
haidd (Welsh barley bread), 101–102
ham:
in bran muffins, 230
in bread cozy, 334
in calzone Alicia, 336–37
and cheese whole wheat bread, 148
in pâté in brioche, 338–39
in pita filling, 303

ham (*cont.*)
in pizza filling, 305
see also prosciutto ham
hamburger rolls, honeyed wheat, 164
hapanleipa (flat Finnish sour rye bread),
308–309 and *illus.*
hard rolls, 155
hard wheat flour, 29
Hartley, Dorothy, 124
Hazan, Marcella: *More Classic Italian
Cooking*, 331
hazelnut(s):
and applesauce bread, 127–28
filling for Danish pastry, 205
herbs:
in tomato bread, 132–33
see also basil; dill; mint; oregano;
rosemary; tarragon; thyme
herb wheat bread, 78–79
Hill, Nancy and Lewis, 231–32
history of bread, 14–18
hoe cakes, 294
holiday breads, 344
challah, 358–59 and *illus.*
for Christmas:
Minnesota Swedish twists, 356
pannetone, 357–58 and *illus.*; discussed, 344, 357
stollen, 349–50; discussed, 344
wreath, 353–54 and *illus.*
for Easter:
Greek (*lambrópsomo*), 350–51
Russian (*choereg*), 352
hot cross buns, 346–47
discussed, 178, 344, 346
King's Day ring, 345
lussekatter (St. Lucia's buns), 347–48
pain d'épice, 355
discussed, 211
homage/worship:
for bread, 17
for grain, 76
hominy grits muffins, 235
honey:
buttermilk rolls, 161
and toasted cracked wheat bread, 90
and triticale and cheese bread, 145
wheat loaf, with pecans, 211
honeyed wheat hamburger rolls, 164
Hong Kong, 345
hoppers, 297
hot cross buns, 346–47 and *illus.*
discussed, 178, 344, 346
hot dog rolls (as for hamburger buns),
164
Hourigan, Kathy, 222

housove knedlicky (bread dumplings), 269–70
Hubert, Karen, 238
Hungarian bread:
    tepertös pogácsa (crackling biscuits), 246
hush puppies, 260
    discussed, 49

icebox rolls, 160–61
idlis, cream of wheat, 272–73
Incas, and avocados, 172
Indian (Asian) breads:
    hoppers, 297
    cream of wheat *idlis,* 272–73
    naans, 290–91
    parathas, stuffed, 292–93
    puri, 258–59
        discussed, 250
Indian(s) (native American):
    and acorn meal, 207
    and blue corn, 282–83
    Chippewas, 97
    fried bread, 256–57
    Hopi, 138, 282
    Pueblo, 282
    steamed bread, 272
    and sunflower seeds, 138
    and wild rice, 97, 260
Iranian breads, discussed, 15
Irish soda bread, 222–23 and *illus.*
    discussed, 49
Italian breads:
    calzone Alicia, 336–37
    grissini (bread sticks), 326–27
    pannetone, 357–58
        discussed, 344, 357
    pollo in pane, 331–33
    pork loaf, 130–32, *illus.* 131–32
    round loaf, 65
        focaccia, discussed, 15

Jaffrey, Madhur, 297
    World-of-the-East Vegetarian Cooking, 234 n., 272
jelly doughnuts, 255
Jerusalem artichoke(s):
    bread with sunflower seeds, 139
    flour:
        bread, 105
        and raisin muffins, 232
    puréed (method), 139 n.
Jewish breads:
    bagels, 267–68
    challah, 358–59 and *illus.*
    matzoh, discussed, 18
    rolled raisin, 119–20

johnnycake, discussed, 17
Johnson, Maria, 15 n.

Karen's biscuit muffins, 238–39
kasha, *see* buckwheat
Kentucky, 224
Kerr, Sophie, 272
khachapuri (Georgian cheese cushions), 174–75 and *illus.*
khobaz, discussed, 99, 300
kielbasa, in *bubbat* (baked in bread dough), 337
King, Louise Tate: *Martha's Vineyard Cookbook, The,* 280
King's Day ring, 345
klenater (Minnesota Swedish Christmas twists), 356
kneading dough:
    in electric mixer, 38
    in food processor, 38–39
    by hand, 39–41, *illus.* 40
        testing, 40–41, *illus.* 41
knife for slicing bread, 51, 365
Knopf, Mildred, 326
kolache, 190
korovai (Ukrainian wedding bread), discussed, 3
krampoch, 296
Kuo, Irene, 273

lambrópsomo (Greek Easter bread), 350–51
Lang, George: *Cuisine of Hungary, The,* 17, 178
leavening process:
    early development of, 15
    see also baking powder; baking soda; pearlash; salt-rising bread; yeast
lemon peel/rind:
    in fig bread, 149
    in King's Day ring, 345
    in lemon tea rolls, 171
    in pannetone, 357
    in parsnip rolls, 165
Lewis, Edna, 150
    Taste of Country Cooking, The, 241
limpa (Swedish rye bread), 116
    discussed, 17
liquids for bread dough, 32
loaf breads, as rolls, 154
Lumberjack Mush bread, 106–107
lussekatter (St. Lucia's buns), 347–48

Macadam, John, 180
macadamia nut(s), 180
    and maple syrup bread, 218
    in Portuguese sweet bread, 180

Magic Mill II, 28
mahleb:
 in Greek Easter bread (*lampróp-somo*), 350–51
 in Russian Easter bread (*choereg*), 352
mail order sources (list), 367
malt, *see* barley malt, homemade; wheat malt, homemade
malt syrup, in barley bread, 101
Manning, James: *Nature of Bread, The,* 9
man-t'ou (Chinese steamed buns), 274
 discussed, 16, 50, 273
 filled with pork, 275
maple syrup:
 in bran muffins, 230
 in brown rice bread, 96–97
 grading, 83
 in green tomato bread, 216
 and macadamia nut bread, 218–19
 and oat flour bread, 103
 as sweetener, 35, 83–84
 in togus bread, 272
 and wheat flake whole wheat bread, 84
Martha's Vineyard, 88, 280
masa harina, for tortillas, 287
matzoh, discussed, 18
May, Robert: *Accomplisht Cook, The,* 112
Mayhew, Henry: *London Labour and the London Poor,* 228
McLeod, Grandfather, 360
 Grandma's gingerbread, 221
meal-in-a-muffin, 233
meat baked in bread, 330
 calzone Alicia, 336–37
 chicken *boereg,* 340–41
 ham (whole) in bread cozy, 334
 Italian porkbread, 130–32, *illus.* 131–32
 pâté in brioche, 338–39 and *illus.*
 pollo in pane, 331–33
 sausage in brioche, 339
meat loaf, in brioche (as for pâté), 338–39
Mennonite breads:
 bubbat, 337
 Streuselkuchen, 181
Mexican breads:
 King's Day ring, 345
 tortillas, 286–87
Middle Eastern breads:
 pita, 301–302
 zata (or pideh), 306

millet, 32
 bread, 98
Minnesota:
 Hiawatha Valley, 213
 Kolaches, 190
 limpa, 116
 Swedish twists, 256
mint:
 in chicken *boereg,* 340–41
 in olive bread, 144
mixed grains bread, 84–85
mixing dough, 36–37
 in electric mixer, 38
 in food processor, 38–39
 see also kneading dough
monkey bread, 318–19 and *illus.*
 as flowerpot bread, 320
Monterey Jack cheese:
 cushions (*khachapuri*), 174–75 and *illus.*
 and triticale and honey bread, 145
Morash, Marian, 336
Moroccan bread, 99–100
Moscow, 351
mozzarella cheese:
 in calzone Alicia, 336–37
 and ham whole wheat bread, 148
 on pizza, 305, 335
"muffin man," 228
muffins, 228, 236
 apple, 231
 bacon and peanut butter, 237
 biscuit type, 238–39
 blueberry, 229
 bran, 230
 date-nut, 236
 elderberry, 231–32
 English, 288–89
 of hominy grits, 235
 Jerusalem artichoke flour and raisin, 232
 meal-in-a-muffin, 233
 pans for, 364–65
 pumpkin corn meal, 237
 rhubarb oatmeal flour, 238
 tins for, 228
 tofu:
  with carrot and soy milk, 234–35
  with spinach, 233–34
museums of bread, 34
mushroom(s):
 bread, 323–24
 in pita filling, 303
mustard seed(s):
 and caraway seed loaf, 222
 in cream of wheat *idlis,* 273

mustard seed(s) (*cont.*)
  with curry, cilantro, and scallion
    bread, 151

naans (or *nans*), 290–91
Napa Valley, California, 219
New Orleans, 250
Navajo fried bread, 256–57
no-knead batter bread, 73
Norwegian bread:
  vorterkaker, 309–10
  see also Scandinavian breads
nuts:
  in banana carrot bread, 213
  in buckwheat biscuits, 245
  flour made from, 207
  in meal-in-a-muffin (with apples,
    cheese), 233
  in pumpkin bread, 217
  see also almond(s); chestnut(s); hazel-
    nut(s); macadamia nut(s); pe-
    can(s); pine nut(s); walnut(s);
    walnut(s), black

oat(s)/oatmeal, 31
  and corn meal bread, 87–88
  cottage loaf, 82–83 and *illus.*
  flour:
    in apricot and almond bread, 214–
      15
    and maple syrup bread, 103
    and rhubard muffins, 238
    in meal-in-a-muffin, 233
    in mixed grains bread, 84–85
    scones, 286
    in winter buttermilk, 59
oils for bread dough, 33
Ojakangas, Beatrice, 110, 111, 308
olive(s):
  bread, with mint and onions, 144
  in pita filling, 303
  in pizza filling, 305, 335
Oliver, William, 187
Olsen, Magnus, 121
onion(s):
  in bagels, 268
  in *naans*, 290–91
  in olive bread, 144
  rolls, 168–69 and *illus.*
orange:
  -blueberry bread, 213–14
  rolls (or bread), with glaze, 184
  zucchini bread, 215
orange juice:
  in apricot and toasted almond bread,
    214–15

orange juice (*cont.*)
  in black walnut, prune, and spiced tea
    bread, 224
  in blueberry orange bread, 213–14
  in orange rolls (or bread), with glaze,
    184
  in soy and graham bread, 137
orange peel/rind:
  in black bun, 360–61
  in bran muffins, 230
  candied:
    in *bara brith* (Welsh raisin bread),
      147
    in Chelsea buns, 188–89
    in Christmas stollen, 349–50
  in *limpa* (Swedish rye bread), 116
  in *lussekatter* (St. Lucia's buns), 347–
    48
  in prune bread, 125
  in zucchini bread, 215
oregano:
  in herb wheat bread, 78–79
  in pizza filling, 305
Oxford Symposium, 15n
oven, baker's:
  ancient, 15 and n.
  for French bread, 64–65
  steam in, *see* steam
  tandoor (Indian clay oven), 290

pain d'épice, 355
  discussed, 211
Palermo (N.Y.) bakery, 130
palm oil, red:
  substitute for, 150
  in turmeric and black caraway seed
    bread, 150
pancakes:
  blueberry, 280
  blue corn, 282–83
  buckwheat (thin), 283–84
  buttermilk, 279 and *illus.*
  cottage cheese, 281
  sunflower, 282
  wheat, 280–81
pannetone, 357–58 and *illus.*
  discussed, 344, 357
pans for bread, 47, 364
  brioche tins, 192
  for French bread, 364
    homemade, 60 and *illus.*
  muffin tins, 228
  pullman, 45 and *illus.*
  sizes, 47
  see also *Cloche, La*
Papashvily, George, 174

papaya bread rolls, 170
Paradissis, Chrissa, 144
parathas, stuffed, 292–93
Paris bakeries, 54, 125
Parker House rolls, 158 and *illus.*
  discussed, 154
Parmentier, Antoine-Auguste, 70, 105
parsley, Chinese (cilantro), and curry
  and scallion bread, 151
parsnip rolls (or bread), 164–65
Paul, St., 18 n.
peanut butter:
  and bacon muffins, 237
  corn sticks, 239
pear bread, 126–27 and *illus.*
pearlash (leavening agent), 25
pecan(s):
  in banana bread, 212
  in bubble (or monkey) bread, 318–19
  rolls (sticky buns), 185
  in wheat honey loaf, 211
Penn, Mrs. William, 185
pepper(s), hot:
  in corn bread, Texas style, 295
  in paratha fillings, 293
persimmon bread, discussed, 224
Philadelphia cinnamon buns, sticky
  buns, or pecan rolls, 185
Philpy (rice bread), 94–95
pideh (or zata), 306
piki, discussed, 282
pine nut(s), on *pisticcini,* 207
pisticcini, 207
  discussed, 141
pita, 301–302
  filling for, 303
pizza, 303
  dough, 304–305 and *illus.*
  filling, 305
  luncheon roll, 335
planc bread, 284–85
Plat, Sir Hugh: *Delight for Ladies,*
  189 n.
ploughman's lunch, 233
Poilane, Lionel, 54
pollo in pane, 331–33
Pompeian bread, 15
pooris, 258–59
  discussed, 250
popovers, 242
  cheese type, 243
poppy seed(s):
  on bread sticks, 327
  on challah, 359
  filling for Danish pastry, 205
  ground, 205 n.

poppy seed(s) (*cont.*)
  on hard rolls, 155
  in onion rolls, 168
  twists, Pennsylvania Dutch, 315–16
pork:
  bread, Italian, 130–32, *illus.* 131–32
  cracklings (how to make), 241
    see also cracklings
  in filled meat buns, 275
  in pâté in brioche, 338–39
  see also bacon; ham; prosciutto; sausage
Portuguese breads:
  corn bread (*broa*), 88–89
  sweet, with macadamia nuts, 180
potato(es):
  bread, 70
  -celeriac rolls (or bread), 163
  in poppy seed twists, 315–16
  in winter buttermilk, 59
potato water, 308 n.
Prague, Oklahoma, 190
preservation:
  of bread, 50
    see also freezing
  of dough:
    freezing, 50
    for ice box rolls, 160
  of flours and meals, 32
primitive bread (ancient), 14
problems in bread baking (and remedies), 50–51
prosciutto ham:
  with bread sticks, 326
  in calzone Alicia, 336–37
  and cheese whole wheat bread, 148
  in *pollo in pane,* 331–33
prune:
  and black walnut tea bread, 224
  bread, 125
  filling for Danish pastry, 205
pull-apart bread, 318–19 and *illus.*
  as flowerpot bread, 320
pullman loaf, 45
  pan, 45 and *illus.*
pumpernickel bread, 115
  with sourdough starter, 113–14
pumpkin:
  bread, 217
  -corn meal muffins, 237
  rolls (or bread), 164–65
  as sweetener, 118
pure triticale bread, 104
puri, 258–59
  discussed, 250

quick breads, 210
  apricot and toasted almond, 214–15
  banana, 212
    and carrot, 213
  black walnut, prune, and spiced tea,
    224
  blueberry orange, 213–14
  carrot, 217–18
  gingerbread, 221
  green tomato, 216
  Irish soda, 222–23
  macadamia nut and maple syrup,
    218–19
  mustard and caraway seed, 222
  pumpkin, 217
  quince and black walnut, 220
  sour cream or buttermilk corn bread,
    225
  strawberry almond, 219
  wheat honey loaf, with pecans, 221
  zucchini, orange-flavored, 215
quince:
  bread, 126–27 and *illus.*
    with black walnuts, 220
  cooking (method), 220 n.
  puréeing (method), 126 n.

radish(es), in paratha filling, 293
raisin(s):
  in black bun, 360–61
  bread:
    Jewish, 119–20
    Welsh (*bara brith*), 147
  and Jerusalem artichoke flour muf-
    fins, 232
Randolph, Mary: *Virginia Housewife,
    The,* 9, 296
restaurants:
  Anatole's, Copenhagen, 117
  Armen Bali's, California, 340
  Hotel Anderson, Minnesota, 213
  Old Chelsea Bun House, London, 187
  Parker House, 154
  Wine Country Inn, California, 219
Retsel home grinder, 28
Rhode Island, 86
rhubarb:
  cooking (method), 238 n.
  -oatmeal flour muffins, 238
rice:
  bread (Philpy), 94–95
  flour, in hoppers, 297
rice, brown:
  bread, 96–97
  flour, in bread, 95–96
rice, wild, 97
  beignets, or fritters, 260–61

rice, wild (*cont.*)
  bread, 97
  making flour, 97
rings, 45
  Christmas wreath, 353–54 and *illus.*
  coffee cake, 182–83 and *illus.*
  Danish pastry, 203
  King's Day, 345
  pear or quince bread, 126–27 and
    illus.
rising of dough, 41–43
  final, 46
  time, for dense loaf, 51
Rockport, Massachusetts, 85
Roden, Claudia, 17
  Book of Middle Eastern Food, A, 301
rolls:
  avocado, 172
  beer, Brazilian, 169
  Canadian buttermilk honey, 161
  chestnut, 141–42
  cranberry, spiced, 167
  dinner:
    basic, 156–57 and *illus.*
    Parker House, 158 and *illus.*
    variant shapes, 158–59 and *illus.*
  Earl Grey tea, 171
  fly-away (fried), 261–62
  graham bran, 162
  for hamburgers, honeyed wheat type,
    164
  hard, 155
  icebox, 160–61
  improvising from bread dough, 154
  khachapuri (Georgian cheese cush-
    ions), 174–75 and *illus.*
  onion, 168–69 and *illus.*
  papaya, 170
  parsnip (or pumpkin or squash), 164–
    65
  potato-celeriac, 163
  rye and walnut (as for bread), 117
  rye twists, 173
  sweet-potato ginger, 166
  tomato, 132–33
  see also brioches; buns; croissants;
    rolls, sweet
rolls, sweet:
  butterscotch, 186
  orange, with glaze, 184
  Philadelphia sticky buns, 185
  see also brioches; buns; croissants;
    Danish pastries; sweet breads
Romertopf, 365
rosemary:
  and black walnut round loaf, 140
  in calzone Alicia, 336–37

rosemary (*cont.*)
  in pâté in brioche, 338–39
  on *pisticcini,* 207
round loaf, 15, 45
  American black bread, 120
  applesauce and hazelnut, 127–28
  Coburg loaf, 80–81 and *illus.*
    discussed, 16, 43, 45
  corn bread, 86–87
  cottage loaf:
    discussed, 16, 45
    oatmeal, 82–83 and *illus.*
  curry, cilantro, and scallion, 151
  dill casserole, 128–29
  fig, with lemon zest, 149
  French, 65–66
  Greek Easter bread (*lambrópsomo*),
    350–51
  Irish soda bread, 222–23
  Italian pork bread, 130–32, *illus.*
    131–32
  Moroccan or Tunisian, 99–100
  olive, with mint and onions, 144
  pisticcini, 207
  prune, 125
  pumpernickel, 113–15
  rosemary and black walnut, 140
  ryaninjun, 118–19
  rye:
    with beer, 112–13
    limpa, 116
    Scandinavian, 111–12
  sourdough, 68
  vorterkaker (Norwegian rye flat
    bread), 309–10
  whole wheat with cheese and ham,
    128
  yeast bread with corn "milk," 135
  zucchini and cottage cheese graham,
    146
  see also *Cloche, La*
Russian breads:
  bubbat (sausage in bread dough), 337
  choereg (for Easter), 352
  khachapuri (Georgian cheese cush-
    ions), 174–75 and *illus.*
  korovai (Ukrainian wedding bread),
    discussed, 314
rutabaga-potato rolls, or bread (as for
    celeriac-potato), 163
ryaninjun bread, 118–19 and *illus.*
rye breads, 17, 110–11
  American black, 120
  with beer, 112–13
  hapanleipa (Finnish), 308–309 and *il-
    lus.*
  Jewish rolled raisin, 119–20

rye breads (*cont.*)
  limpa (Swedish), 17, 116
  pumpernickel, discussed, 17
    with sourdough starter, 113–14
  ryaninjun, 118–19 and *illus.*
  Scandinavian, 111–12 and *illus.*
  twists (rolls), 173
  vorterkaker (Norwegian), 309–10
  with walnuts, 117
  with wheat, Danish, 121
rye flour, 30
  in bread cozy for whole ham, 334
  breads, *see* rye breads
  in *pain d'épice,* 355
  in rosemary and black walnut round
    loaf, 140
  working with (hints), 110

saffron:
  bread, 71
  in *lussekatter* (St. Lucia's buns),
    347–48
  sweet bread, 179
St. Lucia's buns (*lussekatter*), 347–48
salt, in bread dough, 34–35
salt-rising bread, 69
  discussed, 25
Sardinian bread:
  fogli di musica, discussed, 15
sausage, garlic:
  in brioche, 339
sausage, smoked:
  in *bubbat* (baked in bread dough), 337
scallion(s):
  bread, in skillet, 291
  in chicken *boereg,* 340–41
  and curry and cilantro bread, 151
  in dill casserole bread, 128–29
  in dumplings, 269, 270
  in filled meat buns, 275
  fried bread, Chinese, 262–63 and *illus.*
  in mushroom bread, 323–24
  in pâté in brioche, 338–39
  in pita filling, 303
  in rosemary and black walnut round
    loaf, 140
Scandinavian breads:
  flatbread, 310–11
    discussed, 300
  lussekatter (St. Lucia's buns), 347–48
  rye, 111–12 and *illus.*
  see also Danish bread; Finnish bread;
    Norwegian bread; Swedish breads
scones, oatmeal, 286
Scottish breads:
  baps, discussed, 154
  black bun, 360–61 and *illus.*

Scottish breads (*cont.*)
  scones, oatmeal, 286
sculptured bread, free-form, 322–23 and
    illus.
  see also shaped breads
self-rising flour, 26
semmelknoedel (bread dumplings),
    269–70
semolina, 30
  bread, 98–99
  in Moroccan or Tunisian bread,
    99–100
sesame seed(s):
  in bagels, 268
  on bread sticks, 327
  on *choereg* (Easter bread), 352
  corn bread with cheese, skillet-baked,
    294–95
  in Moroccan or Tunisian bread,
    99–100
  on Sicilian twist, 316–17
  with sweet potato:
    bread, 142–43
    rolls, 166
shaped breads, 314
  bubble (or monkey, or pull-apart),
    318–19 and *illus.*
  challah, 358–59 and *illus.*
  choereg, 351-52
  Christmas wreath, 353–54 and *illus.*
  dinner rolls, 157–59 and *illus.*
  flowerpot breads, 320 and *illus.*, 321
  free-form sculptured, 322–23 and
    illus.
  grissini (bread sticks), 326–27
  korovai (Ukrainian wedding bread),
    discussed, 314
  mushroom, 323–24
  poppy seed twists, 316–17 and *illus.*
  Sicilian twist, 316–17 and *illus.*
  wheat sheaf, 325–26 and *illus.*
  see also rings; round loaf
shaping loaves, 43–46 and *illus.*
Shaw, George Bernard: *Man and Super-
    man,* 236
shortening for bread dough, 32–33
shredded wheat:
  bread, 106
  in wheat sheaf bread, 325–26
Sicilian twist, 316–17 and *illus.*
skillet breads, 49, 278
  crumpets, 296
  English muffins, 288–89
  hoe cakes, 294
  hoppers, 297
  naans (or *nans*), 290–91
  pancakes, *see* pancakes
  parathas, stuffed, 292–93

skillet breads (*cont.*)
  scallion bread, 291
  scones, oatmeal, 286
  sesame seed cheese corn bread,
    294–95
  Texas corn bread, 295
  tortillas, 286–87
  Walden wheat corn bread, 89
  Welsh planc bread, 284–85
  see also friend breads; pancakes
slashing loaf (method), 46
slicing, 51
  knife for, 365
Smith, Ned and Marge, 219
smørrebrød, discussed, 121
socca, 307
soda bread, Irish, 222–23 and *illus.*
  discussed, 49
soft-as-pie Texas corn bread, 295
sopaipillas, 257–58
  discussed, 49, 250
sour cream:
  bread, 58
  in *choereg* (Easter bread), 352
  in coffee cake ring, 182–83
  in corn bread, 225
  pancakes (as for buttermilk), 279
sourdough, 66–67
  biscuits, 247
  bread, 68
    discussed, 24–25
  starter, 67–68
    discussed, 24–25
    for pumpernickel bread, 113–14
soy flour, 31
  and graham bread, with alfalfa
    sprouts, 137
soy milk:
  homemade, 234 n.
  and tofu and carrot muffins, 234–35
spiced cranberry rolls, 167
spinach and tofu muffins, 233–34
sponge, 41
  for white bread (method), 57
sprouts:
  alfalfa, in soy and graham bread, 137
  wheatberry, in bread, 93–94
  sprouted wheatberry bread, 93–94
squash:
  bread (as for pumpkin), 217
  rolls (or bread), 164–65
  see also zucchini
starch-free bread, of Jerusalem arti-
    choke flour, 105
steam:
  for baking:
    bread, 16, 48
    Chinese buns, 273

steam: for baking (*cont.*)
    French bread, 64–65
    hard rolls, 155
    homemade device, 365
    sticky buns, 185
stollen, Christmas, 349–50
    discussed, 344, 349
Stone Age breads and grains, 14
stone-ground flour, 27–28, 29
storage:
    of bread, 50
        see also freezing
    of dough:
        freezing, 50
        for icebox rolls, 160
    of flours and meals, 32
stovepipe, 60
Stowe, Harriet Beecher, 118
strawberry-almond breakfast bread, 219
Streuselkuchen, Mennonite, 181
Sumerian bread, 15
sun chokes, *see* Jerusalem artichoke(s)
sunflower breads:
    with seeds, 138
    with wheat, 92–93
sunflower meal, homemade, 92
    in breads, *see* sunflower breads
    pancakes, 282
sunflower seeds:
    in pumpkin bread, 217
    and sun choke bread, 139
    and sunflower meal bread, 138
Swedish breads:
    Christmas twists, 356
    limpa (rye), 116
        discussed, 17
    see also Scandinavian breads
sweet breads, 178
    coffee cake ring, 182–83 and *illus.*
    Mennonite Streuselkuchen, 181
    pisticcini, 207
        discussed, 141
    Portuguese, with macadamia nuts, 180
    saffron, 179
    see also Danish pastries; sweet rolls
sweeteners, 35
    pumpkin (stewed) as, 118
    see also caramel; honey; maple syrup
sweet potato(es):
    discussed, 142
    ginger rolls, 166
    -sesame bread, 142–43
sweet rolls:
    butterscotch, 186
    orange, with glaze, 184
    Philadelphia cinnamon buns, 185
    see also brioches; buns; croissants;
        Danish pastries; sweet breads

symbolism of bread, 17–18

tandoor (Indian clay oven), 290
tarragon, in mushroom bread, 323–24
tea (in bread):
    in *bara brith* (Welsh raisin bread),
        147
    with black walnuts and prunes, 224
    rolls:
        Earl Grey, 171
        lemon, 171
tea breads, *see* quick breads
tepertös pogácsa (crackling biscuits),
    246
Thoreau, Henry David: *Walden*, 89
thyme, in herb wheat bread, 78–79
toasted brown rice bread, 96–97
toasted soy and graham bread with al-
    falfa sprouts, 187
toasting:
    flour, 96, 137
    sesame seeds, 143
tofu:
    bread, 72
    and carrot and soy milk muffins, 234–
        35
    discussed, 34, 233
    and spinach muffins, 233–34
togus bread, 272
Toklas, Alice B., 125
tomato(es):
    bread (or rolls), 132–33
    green, in bread, Green Mountain
        style, 216
    in pizza fillings, 305, 335
tortillas, 286–87
triticale, 30–31, 104
    bread, 104
    with cheese and honey, 145
troubleshooting, 50–51
Tunisian bread, 99–100
turmeric and black caraway seed bread,
    150
twisted or braided loaf, 44 and *illus.*
twists:
    for Christmas, Minnesota Swedish,
        356
    poppy seed, Pennsylvania Dutch, 315–
        16
    Sicilian, 316–17 and *illus.*
Tyree, Mable Cabell: *Housekeeping in
    Old Virginia*, 69

Ukrainian wedding bread (*korovai*), dis-
    cussed, 314
unbleached flour, 29
Uvezian, Sonia, 174

vanilla cream filling for Danish pastry, 204
vegetables, *see* beet; carrot(s); cauli-flower; celeriac; onion(s); parsnip; potato(es); pumpkin; rasdish(es); rutabaga; spinach; squash; sweet potato(es); tomato(es); zucchini
Vermont:
    farmhouse in, 280
    Green Mountain bread, 216
    Montpelier, 271
    mushrooming in, 323
    Walden, 89
Vienna, 246
Virginia, 166, 221, 224
vorterkaker (Norwegian rye flat bread), 309–10
Vresa, Toula, 149

Walden wheat corn bread, 89
walnut(s):
    in carrot bread, 217–18
    in chicken *boereg,* 340–41
    -date muffins, 236
    in green tomato bread, 216
    in orange zucchini bread, 215
    and rye bread, 117
    on Streuselkuchen, 181
walnut(s), black, 224
    and prune and tea bread, 224
    and quince bread, 220
    and rosemary round loaf, 140
Waters, Alice, 336
Wechsberg, Joseph, 269
Welsh breads, 284
    barley, 101–102
    planc, 284–85
    raisin (*bara brith*), 147
Wexler, Jean Stewart: *Martha's Vine-yard Cookbook, The,* 280
wheatberries, 30
    sprouted, 32
    bread, 93–94
wheat flake(s), 83
    and maple whole wheat bread, 84
wheat germ, 31–32
wheat kernels, in Danish wheat-rye bread, 121
wheat malt, homemade, 36
    in Jewish rolled raisin bread, 119–20
    in *limpa* (Swedish rye bread), 116
wheat-rye bread, Danish, 121

wheat sheaf bread, 325–26 and *illus.*
wheat-soy grits, in mixed grains bread, 84–85
wheat sprout bread, 93–94
"whigs" (sticky buns), 185
white bread:
    aerated ("A.B.C. bread"), discussed, 24
    basic, 55–57
        sponge method, 57
    discussed, 16
whole wheat bread, 78
    with cheese and ham, 148
    with herbs, 78–79
    with white flour, 77
        as flowerpot bread, 321
whole wheat flour, 29
whole wheat griddle cakes, 280–81
Wienerbrød, see Danish pastries
wild rice, 97
    beignets, or fritters, 260–61
    bread, 97
Williams, Chuck, 48 n.
winter buttermilk (of oatmeal and pota-toes), 59
wok, for hoppers, 297
World of Cheese, The, 134, 243
wreath, Christmas, 353–54 and *illus.*

Yankee togus bread, 272
yeast, 22–24
    compressed cakes, 24
    dry form, 23, 24
    homemade (method), 23
    testing for freshness (method), 24
yogurt:
    in banana bread, 212
    biscuits (as for buttermilk), 244–45
    bread, 58
    in brown rice flour bread, 95–96
    in cream of wheat *idlis,* 273
    in mixed grains bread, 84–85
    pancakes (as for buttermilk), 279
    in pumpernickel bread, 115
    in rye twists (rolls), 173
    in zucchini and cottage cheese graham bread, 146

zata (or pideh), 306
zucchini:
    bread, orange-flavored, 215
    and cottage cheese graham bread, 146